Mayeux, Steven M.,
1950-
   Earthen walls,
iron men

OCT 3 1 2006

Earthen Walls,
Iron Men

Earthen Walls, Iron Men

Fort DeRussy, Louisiana, and the Defense of Red River

Steven M. Mayeux

With a Foreword by
Edwin C. Bearss

The University of Tennessee Press / Knoxville

Library of Congress Cataloging-in-Publication Data

Mayeux, Steven M., 1950-
   Earthen walls, iron men : Fort DeRussy, Louisiana, and the defense of Red
River / Steven M. Mayeux ; with a foreword by Edwin C. Bearss. – 1st ed.
      p. cm.
   Includes bibliographical references and index.
   ISBN-13: 978-1-57233-576-9 (hardcover : alk. paper)
   ISBN-10: 1-57233-576-9

   1. Fort De Russy (La.)–History–19th century.
   2. Red River Valley (Tex.-La.)–History, Military–19th century.
   3. Louisiana–History–CivilWar, 1861–1865–Campaigns.
   4. United States–History–Civil War, 1861–1865–Campaigns.
   5. United States–History–Civil War, 1861–1865–Riverine operations.
   I. Title.
   F379.F665M395 2007
   976.3'6–dc22   2006035356

Contents

Illustrations

Foreword

Until 1955, although introduced to the Civil War a score of years before by my father, I had never heard of Fort DeRussy. This was not strange, because until 1953 I was entranced by the war in the East. First, while recuperating from World War II wounds in the San Diego Naval Hospital, I carefully read and was captivated by Douglas Southall Freeman's *R. E. Lee*, followed by *Lee's Lieutenants*. Then, in the late 1940s and early 1950s, Bruce Catton's masterful trilogy highlighting the Army of the Potomac reinforced my eastern orientation.

When I matriculated at Indiana University, from which I received my master's degree in history, I came to realize that there had also been a war in America's heartland. I wrote my thesis on "Maj. Gen Patrick R. Cleburne: Stonewall Jackson of the West." But my interest still did not extend to the trans-Mississippi. This soon changed, however, at first because of necessity, when I reported for duty as park historian at the Vicksburg National Military Park on September 28, 1955.

The Vicksburg Campaign, as President Abraham Lincoln realized much better and more effectively than President Jefferson Davis, straddled the Mississippi River, and I recognized that if I were to discharge my mission as park historian, I must focus on both sides of the river, as well as on the "Father of Waters." It was then that I first learned of Fort DeRussy. The catalyst was H. Allen Gosnell's *Guns on the Western Waters: The Story of the River Gunboats in the Civil War,* published in 1949. Drawing heavily on primary sources on the activities of *Queen of the West* and her daring captain, nineteen-year-old Col. Charles Rivers Ellet, Gosnell introduced me to Fort DeRussy. By the early 1960s, I had become fascinated with Ellet and his February 1863 cruise on the *Queen,* when he took his vessel up Red River to his ill-fated date with destiny at Fort DeRussy. In the mid-1980s, I thought so much of the February 1863 naval operation on Red River and Fort DeRussy's significant role in that episode that I devoted several chapters in volume 1 and one in volume 3 of my *Campaign for Vicksburg* trilogy to them and their relation to, and effect on, that monumental campaign.

Even so, it would be October 1994 before I visited Fort DeRussy. I did so as tour leader for Jerry Russell's annual Civil War Round Table Associates meeting held in Alexandria. On one of our field trips we visited Fort DeRussy and other Avoyelles Parish sites associated with Maj. Gen. Nathaniel Banks's Red River Campaign, the study group's focus. The site, although undeveloped, was impressive. Of lasting memory to the Russell group was the hospitality and respect for the site shown by the community, as well as an incident in which one of the tour's forty-seven passenger buses became high-centered astride the access road, much to the dismay of Mrs. Irby Bordelon, the property owner whose driveway we blocked.

My next visit to Fort DeRussy came two months later, as historian-guide for HistoryAmerica, a theme-oriented travel company that features multiday tours of historic sites. This tour, like the earlier Russell expedition, put the Red River Campaign at center stage and originated in Baton Rouge on December 4. When I arrived late that evening, waiting for me in the hotel lobby was Steven Mayeux. Although I had been introduced to Steven eight weeks before in the hurly-burly of that occasion, I did not remember him. But what a difference a one-on-one meeting and several hours discussing subjects of mutual interest with a fellow Marine makes.

Our conversation focused on the theme of the HistoryAmerica tour. As Mayeux shared his thoughts about Fort DeRussy, its history, and its significance, I was captivated. His knowledge of the area's Civil War history and associated sites was encyclopedic. He also gave me to review several monographs he had prepared on Fort Humbug and other campaign sites.

At the invitation of Pete Brown, owner-operator of HistoryAmerica, Steve joined the group on the day we visited Fort DeRussy and other areas associated with Banks's campaign in Avoyelles and Rapides Parishes. These on-site visits and his interaction with tour participants and the locals increased my respect for his skills in addressing the desires and needs of those ever-increasing numbers who strive to walk in the footsteps of history, which has given birth to heritage tourism.

My introduction to Steve has been a mutually rewarding experience. In the last twelve years our trails frequently crossed. These were associated with my work as guide-interpreter on tours of the region aboard *Delta Queen*, centering on Banks's too-long-overlooked 1864 campaign, for HistoryAmerica, and in my work with the Blue & Gray Education Association. On all of these occasions I worked closely with

Steve. In the meantime, Mayeux played a key role working with the local community, the Police Jury, and the State of Louisiana to have the significance of Fort DeRussy recognized and to establish the Fort DeRussy State Historic Site.

Long remembered is one cruise by *Delta Queen* up the Red River. As the *Queen* rounded a bend near Dunn's Bayou, and President Lincoln, portrayed by Jim Getty, held a press conference on the spardeck, the popular and historic vessel was ambushed by a four-gun Louisiana battery. An air of Civil War reality was provided by commands given in French and window-rattling blank charges.

Through these years Steve, an avid researcher, continued to follow the paper trail that led him to relevant archives and libraries as he exhibited the sleuthing skills we associate with Sherlock Holmes. To keep me informed on his progress, he provided for my review and comment drafts of selected chapters he hoped would become the comprehensive history of Fort DeRussy. I was impressed by his research, analytical, and writing skills, and I urged him to persevere. In doing so, possessing a rapport because of his heritage with the people of the region, he broadened his horizons to include the fort's and the Civil War's effect on both the white and black communities. Illustrative of his interest in this aspect of history—too often ignored—was research that led to establishing the identity of a number of slaves who were impressed by Confederate authorities to help construct the fort. Having identified those blacks who died while engaged in this work, he took the lead in securing a monument at the fort in their memory.

In October 2005 Steve informed me that the University of Tennessee Press would publish his manuscript to be titled *Earthen Walls, Iron Men: Fort DeRussy, Louisiana, and the Defense of Red River.* He asked if I would read the manuscript and if I deemed it worthy to prepare the foreword. Although I had read drafts of a number of chapters, this was the first time I had seen the entire manuscript, and I was enthused. Not only does Mayeux provide his audience with an excellent military history of Fort DeRussy, but equally important, he integrates the story of the fort with that of the people, be they soldiers and sailors, or civilians white and black, to give us a feeling of time and place. In doing so, he reaches beyond the Civil War, and thus *Earthen Walls* will appeal to the broad constituency that also relishes cultural history and heritage tourism.

Edwin C. Bearss
Historian Emeritus
National Park Service

Acknowledgments

This book was researched and written over a period of eleven years, and over that time I have received moral and intellectual support from a lot of people. A few provided relatively large masses of information; many provided little tidbits here and there. This book would not have been possible without all of them. Up to this point, the history of Fort DeRussy was nothing but "little tidbits here and there." To those who helped compile this information, thank you. It has been a long time, and I do not remember all of you. But I do appreciate all of you.

Some of those who helped I do remember. My wife, Vickie, springs to mind, along with my daughter, Mallory, and my son, Caleb. The kids tolerated my obsession, and Vickie's encouragement, support, and advice kept me going. Toward the end, it kept me sane. My old high school friend, Bill Rome, chanced to have a conversation with me some eighteen years ago that inadvertently led to me becoming the local "expert" on Fort DeRussy and eventually resulted in this book. Art Bergeron provided me with lots of obscure sources that I never would have found on my own. Gary Joiner provided me with other obscure sources and contributed maps. Randy Decuir accompanied me on some of my first "research expeditions." Wayne Stark, may he rest in peace, gave me information about the fort's cannons that I could not have gotten anywhere else. Teri Hedgpeth at the National Archives was a great help locating gunboat deck logs, and Page Gebsen at Broadfoot Research tracked down many service records for me, some of which were hidden under some very creative spelling. Numerous librarians provided me with assistance—Sherrie Pugh at Jackson Barracks, Alan Aimone at West Point, Bill Meneray at Tulane, and Mary Linn Wernet at Northwestern State University in Natchitoches all stand out. And Ed Bearss—what can I say? A Civil War historian who actually has "groupies." What greater inspiration could anyone ask for?

Thanks to the DeRussy clan—Debbie DeRussy Caraway, Michelle DeRussy Dodenhoff, Edith DeRussy, Steve Sheppard, and all the rest. The material they provided on Lewis was superb.

Thanks to my Texans—Richard Lowe, Kevin Boldt, Jack Parker, Steve Skelton, M. Jane Johannson, Fred Morse, and others—for all of the sources you discovered and for helping me with the right names for all my Texas POWs.

To the descendants of the men who fought at the fort—Thomas Handy and family, Frank Spencer, Sally Moore, Barry Morgan, and others—thanks for the information and encouragement.

Last but not least, to all the men and women whose story I told: You are all long dead and can not read this, but thank you anyway—for being who you were and doing what you did. It was a heck of a story. I hope I told it right.

Introduction

"Fort DeRussy has fallen, like Lucifer, never to rise again." So said the *Natchitoches Union* back in 1864, and for 130 years it looked like the Yankee soldier who wrote that article was right.

That all changed in 1994. In that year, a movement began to recover the fort from its hiding place in a patch of woods near the Red River, and I was charged with putting together a short history of the fort. Writing that history took nearly three months, after which I commented that I was "burnt out on Fort DeRussy." Little did I know that eleven years later I would still be researching and writing (with no end yet in sight) and that the little paper would grow to a full-length book.

The quest for the real story of Fort DeRussy has been fascinating. I quickly learned that there are three basic types of history: history as it actually happened, history as we can best determine happened, and history as we wish it had happened.

History as it actually happened is, unfortunately, unknown and unknowable. The big picture may be obvious enough, but when you get down to the details, things are not always so clear. If you only have one eyewitness to an event, you may think you know exactly what happened. The second eyewitness account usually presents a problem or two, and if there are several witnesses involved, everything tends to fall apart. One man's left is another man's right, one man's three o'clock is another man's five-thirty, and so on and so forth.

History as we can best determine happened is what you will find in this book. A lot of people were involved at Fort DeRussy, and they did not always agree on what they saw and did. Vantage points and attitudes differ from person to person, and memories grow fuzzy over the years. Many times, when the men who made the history could not agree on what that history was, I had to act as referee. Compromise was necessary. And no doubt, my bias comes through on occasion. Yet I have tried to present history as it happened.

"Tourism history," or history as we wish it had happened, is the third type. Grandpa was a gallant gentleman and a valiant warrior, defender of all that was good and holy; grandma was a ravishing beauty, intelligent, kind, and wise. Nobody really wants to know that grandpa was a scoundrel and a coward and that grandma was a miserable, hateful woman with a face that would make a freight train take a dirt road. And do we really want to find out that grandpa's pension was not due to battle wounds but to disability from a severe case of hemorrhoids brought on by weeks of stacking cannonballs?

I have tried to avoid tourism history. To the extent that I was successful, some people may not like what they read in this book. This is not intended to be an exercise in revisionist history, but in the process of researching this book, I occasionally found that the accepted version of some stories contained inaccuracies. These have been corrected.

The Fort DeRussy story was relatively brief. It began in mid-1862 and ended in mid-1864, and for a considerable part of that period the fort lay abandoned. Nonetheless, an awful lot happened in those few months. Naval battles, land battles, and battles between gunboats and shore batteries were fought; freedoms were won and freedoms were lost; one baby was born and a lot of grown men died, some quickly and some slowly; and acts of extreme cleverness, incredible stupidity, admirable loyalty, loathsome betrayal, noble heroism, and base cowardice all played themselves out. All of these comedies and dramas would change the world. They would change us.

For the past 140 years, Fort DeRussy has been a footnote in history books. Now the fort has its own history, with its own footnotes. Here is that story.

Chapter 1

Barbin's Landing

A decade before the start of the Civil War, Gorton's Landing was a bustling little steamboat landing on a bend in the Red River just a few miles north of Marksville, Avoyelles Parish, Louisiana. There were numerous landings on those reaches of the Red, but Gorton's proximity to Marksville gave it an edge. Most goods going into or out of the Marksville area passed through Lewis Gorton's warehouses. This made Gorton a lot of money, and it left some people in his debt. Unfortunately, not everyone was prompt in paying off their debts. On January 11, 1847, Gorton threw a shotgun across the pommel of his saddle and rode into Marksville to repossess a carriage. After a meal at a friend's home, he strolled over to Thomas B. Tiller's store, tore down his fence, and drove away in the recovered buggy. Tiller arrived a short while later and, along with his brother-in-law, J. Monroe Phillips, took off in hot pursuit. They caught up with Gorton half a mile north of the courthouse, and in the ensuing confrontation, Phillips shot and killed Gorton. The shooting was the talk of the town for a while. Gorton had a lot of friends, so Phillips lost no time in heading for parts unknown, leaving Tiller to stand trial alone. He was acquitted, after which he, too, left town for greener pastures.[1]

James Barbin, François Barbin, and Fabius Ricord bought the landing from Gorton's estate in 1850, and the establishment continued to flourish. Ownership of the landing changed over the years, but there was always a Barbin involved. Ludger Barbin bought into the operation in 1858, and by the end of 1859 he was the sole owner of "Barbin's Landing." (Older residents of the area continued to refer to the place as Gorton's Landing.)[2] The landing was a busy place, and the arrival and departure of steamboats probably made it the most exciting place in all of Avoyelles Parish. The Civil War would not change that.

---

1. John P. Waddill diary, manuscript in private hands.
2. The landing is also seen referred to as Gordon's Landing, but that is simply a misspelling of the Gorton name.

Ludger and Virginie Goudeau Barbin were the owners of Barbin's Landing. Fort DeRussy was built on their property. Virginie gave birth to her daughter Angelica at the landing just three days before the fort was captured in 1864. (Photographs courtesy of Randy Decuir.)

The story of Fort DeRussy starts with the fall of New Orleans in April 1862. Until that time, the citizens of central Louisiana had been relatively isolated from the war. True, there had been some bickering between neighbors—occasionally to the point of bloodshed—about the pros and cons of secession; and a lot of boys had gone off to the war in Virginia, some of whom had already died. Until the fall of New Orleans, though, central Louisiana itself was not threatened. But once the Union fleet had broken past the barrier of Forts Jackson and St. Philip below New Orleans, Flag Officer David G. Farragut could move his fleet up the Mississippi River as far north as Vicksburg. It was apparent that it was only a matter of time before Northern naval forces would choose to come up the Red River into central and northwestern Louisiana, and from there into Texas.

The first scare was not long in coming. In July 1862, the state militia headquarters was warned that Union gunboats and transports moving down from Vicksburg might attempt to come up the Red River. Lt. Col. W. T. Cheney, commanding officer of the Avoyelles Regiment, was ordered to take his men and anyone he could find from the recently disbanded Johnson's Special Battalion and the conscripts of the area and disperse along the river to harass the ascending boats.[3] It was suggested to Cheney that one of the best locations for a company of sharpshooters would be at Barbin's Landing. Other units in the area, particularly Capt. James McWater's cavalry company, were also ordered to the landing "by the shortest possible route."[4]

As it turned out, it was not an ascending gunboat, but a descending steamer that would generate the first military action—albeit a bloodless one—at Barbin's Landing. Capt. Wellington W. Withenbury, an entrepreneurial individual who seems to have served both Union and

3. This was not the first time the Avoyelles soldiers had been called to arms. On April 9, 1862, 409 men from the parish had arrived in New Orleans aboard the steamer *Dr. Batey*, from Barbin's Landing, for the purpose of defending the city. Among the men were Capt. Ludger Barbin and his eighty-man company of "Marksville Guards." (Coincidentally, Ludger Barbin's uncle, François Barbin de Bellevue, had been the officer-in-charge of the U.S. Marine detachment at the Battle of New Orleans in 1814–15.) *New Orleans Commercial Bulletin* 31, no. 85 (Apr. 10, 1862), copied in *Historical Military Data on Louisiana Militia* 126 (Apr. 1–Dec. 31, 1862): 6.

4. *Letters from Adjutant General, La. Militia, 1862–1865* (Jackson Barracks Military Library, New Orleans, La.), 33–34. On January 14, 1863, Lieutenant Colonel McWaters, now with the 2nd Louisiana Cavalry, was killed in action assisting in the defense of the gunboat *J. A. Cotten* on Bayou Teche.

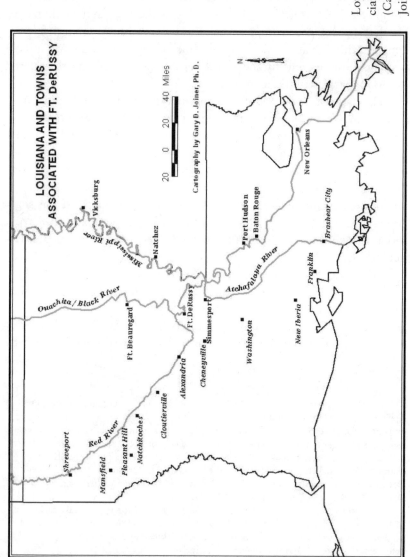

Louisiana and towns associated with Fort DeRussy. (Cartography by Gary Joiner.)

Confederate causes depending upon which best suited his current business condition, had recently switched allegiance to the Northern cause and was trying to escape to Union-occupied New Orleans with his steamboat. Local citizens attempted to stop the boat at most of the landings from Shreveport on downriver, but Withenbury successfully ran the gauntlet until his arrival at Barbin's Landing, where he found the "musket battery of forty men" contesting his passage. His escape attempt foiled, Withenbury was forced to return with his boat to Alexandria and further Confederate Service.[5]

The expected invasion did not materialize, but the concerns of the local population were awakened. On September 20, 1862, the Avoyelles Parish Police Jury (the parish's governing body), in conjunction with the other police juries along Red River, resolved to talk to the major general commanding and the governor of the state, requesting that they "contemplate erecting fortifications to defend Red River."[6]

The major general commanding was Richard Taylor, the only son of "Old Rough and Ready" Zachary Taylor, the twelfth president of the United States.[7] On November 1, Taylor reported to the Adjutant and Inspector General's Office in Richmond, Virginia, that in deference to the wishes of the citizens of Louisiana, he had made an inspection of the Red and Ouachita Rivers and had determined to erect defenses. However, finding no suitable location for defensive works below the mouth of Black River, each of these rivers would have to be defended separately.[8] Taylor also reported that as there were no engineer officers available in his district who were not otherwise engaged, he had appointed Col.

5. Richard B. Mills, "Alexandria, Louisiana: a 'Confederate' City at War with Itself," in *The Civil War in Louisiana*, Part B, *The Home Front*, ed. Arthur W. Bergeron (Lafayette, La.: Center for Louisiana Studies, 2004), 178.

6. Avoyelles Parish Police Jury minutes, Sept. 20, 1862, Avoyelles Parish Police Jury Records, 1861–1865, Avoyelles Parish Courthouse, Marksville, La. A parish is the political subdivision in the state of Louisiana, comparable to a county in other states. The governing bodies of these parishes are known as police juries.

7. General Taylor was also the grandson of Richard Taylor, a Revolutionary War army officer and the brother of Sarah Taylor, the wife of Jefferson Davis, future president of the Confederacy, until her untimely death from malaria in 1835. Taylor was the owner of Fashion plantation in St. Charles Parish, Louisiana, and made his living growing sugar cane before the war.

8. Secretary of War, *The War of the Rebellion: A Compilation of the Official Records of the Union and Confederate Armies*, 128 vols. (Washington, D.C.: GPO, 1880–1901), ser. 1, vol.15, p. 877 (hereafter cited as *ORA*; all references are to series 1 unless otherwise indicated). The fortifications for the Black and Ouachita Rivers were built at Harrisonburg, in Catahoula Parish, and were known as Fort Beauregard.

Lewis G. DeRussy, former commanding officer of the 2nd Louisiana Infantry, as superintendent of the work on the Red River. DeRussy was an engineer of known ability who had established a reputation as a civil engineer before the war and as an engineer on Maj. Gen. Leonidas Polk's staff at Fort Pillow and elsewhere after his departure from his infantry unit. Since he had been paid as a major of staff while working for General Polk, General Taylor recommended that he receive the same pay while working on the Red River defenses. Taylor also requested that he be sent eight 10- or 8-inch guns with which to defend the rivers.

General Taylor's report and requests were forwarded to Col. J. F. Gilmer,[9] chief of the Confederate Engineer Bureau. On November 14, Gilmer ordered Capt. W. H. James, a recently appointed officer in the Provisional Corps of Engineers, to report to Taylor for the duty of constructing defenses on the Red, Ouachita, and Atchafalaya Rivers, but James would not accept the orders. This being the case, Gilmer recommended that the appointment of Colonel DeRussy be accepted until another engineer officer could be sent to Taylor, and that at that time DeRussy be allowed to stay on as a civil assistant, should his services be deemed necessary.[10] As for the cannons requested, there were no 8- or 10-inch guns available. Col. Josiah Gorgas,[11] chief of ordnance, was able to locate two 24-pounders on siege carriages and two 32-pounders on barbette carriages at Charleston, South Carolina, and these guns, with ammunition and fixtures, were sent to Taylor on November 27. The guns were bound for the site from which Taylor and DeRussy had chosen to defend Red River—Barbin's Landing.

All of this action was too little, too late to the minds of the people of Avoyelles Parish. At the police jury meeting on November 24, with Colonel DeRussy present as an honored guest, the jury members argued that the fortifications at Barbin's Landing were not sufficient. A raft should be built across Red River, they decided, to block the river to

9. Jeremy F. Gilmer (1817–1883) was a North Carolina native and a West Point graduate, class of 1839.

10. Taylor was a step ahead of Gilmer in this matter. Taylor and DeRussy had made a tour of the lower Red on October 30 and had already picked a site for the defense of the river a good two weeks before Gilmer had made the James appointment. Maj. Gen. Richard Taylor to Gen. S. Cooper, Nov. 9, 1862, *ORA* 15:175.

11. Josiah Gorgas (1818–1883), a Pennsylvania native and an 1841 graduate of West Point, resigned his commission in the U.S. Army in April 1861 to serve in the Southern army. He was president of the University of Alabama in 1878 and the father of William C. Gorgas, who won fame for clearing the Panama Canal Zone of yellow fever, 1904–6. William Gorgas went on to become surgeon general of the U.S. Army during World War I.

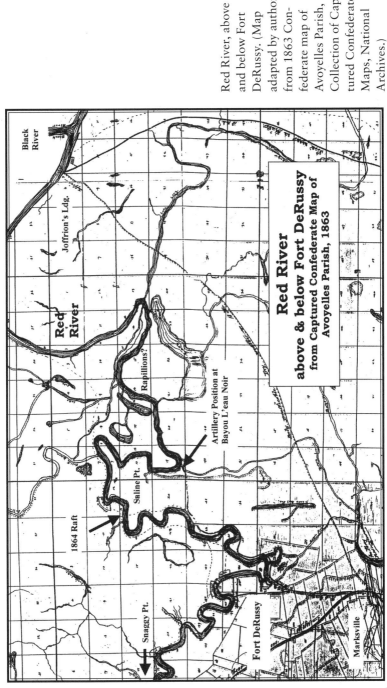

Red River, above and below Fort DeRussy. (Map adapted by author from 1863 Confederate map of Avoyelles Parish, Collection of Captured Confederate Maps, National Archives.)

Red River above & below Fort DeRussy
from Captured Confederate Map of
Avoyelles Parish, 1863

Black River

Joffrion's Ldg.

Red River

Rapillions?

Artillery Position at
Bayou L'eau Noir

Saline Pt.

1864 Raft

Snaggy Pt.

Fort DeRussy

Marksville

gunboats at a suitable point "not higher than the Rapillions."[12] In order to accomplish this task, one-fifth of the male slaves between the ages of eighteen and forty-five were to be called up to work on the obstruction. Owners were to be paid fifty cents per day per slave. In addition, ten thousand dollars was appropriated for supplies for this project. And since they were in a raft-building frame of mind, they decided they would also build a raft across Bayou des Glaises to defend it as well.[13] The raft-building plan hit an immediate snag, for on December 8 the police jury held another meeting and agreed at this time to request that the state of Louisiana repeal the law which prohibited the blocking of navigable streams as it pertained to Red River and Bayou des Glaises. The jury met again on December 20 and repealed the November 24 appropriations for ten thousand dollars, replacing them with parish notes for five thousand dollars for the obstruction of Bayou des Glaises and fifteen thousand dollars for the obstruction of the Red River.

The citizens of Avoyelles were not the only ones concerned with the fortifications at Barbin's Landing. On November 22, 1862, representatives from five northern Louisiana parishes and one Texas county met in Shreveport. The defense of the river was determined to be essential to the security of the area, and the individual parishes agreed to raise from forty-five hundred to twenty-five thousand dollars each to pay for the defensive works. On December 3, a Natchitoches Parish committee issued an appeal for slaves to work on the river defenses. Slave owners were assured that the slaves would be properly cared for, supervised, and not overworked. Slaves were to bring their own clothing, bedding, and tools, and the owners would be paid for their labor. By the end of the month, the state legislature had also weighed in on the matter, authorizing police juries to appropriate money and levy a tax for the river defenses and authorizing them to requisition slaves, tools, livestock, boats, wagons, and other materials necessary for work on

---

12. The location of the Rapillions, or "little rapids," is not known for certain, but a reference to "the head of the Rappions" in 1864 would indicate that they were probably a little below the lower end of Saline Point, between the mouth of Bayou L'eau Noir and the current-day location of U.S. Army Corps of Engineers Lock and Dam No. 1. Lt. Comdr. Seth Phelps to Adm. David D. Porter, in Frank Moore, *The Rebellion Record: A Diary of American Events* (New York: D. Van Nostrand, 1866), 8:519.

13. Avoyelles Parish Police Jury Minutes, Nov. 24, 1862. Bayou des Glaises is one of the larger bayous in Avoyelles Parish, and at the time of the war it was navigable by steamboat at certain times of the year. It runs somewhat parallel to Red River and empties into the Atchafalaya River at Simmesport.

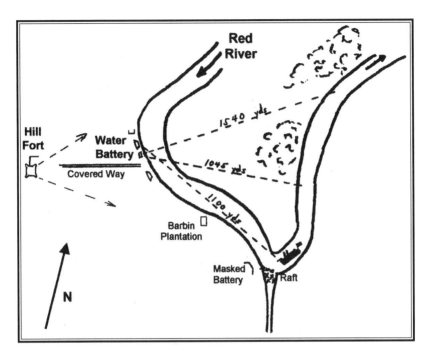

Fort DeRussy consisted of two parts, the Water Battery and the Hill Fort. Gunboats attempting to move up Red River had to navigate, for three-quarters of a mile, a narrow channel straight into the waiting guns of the Water Battery. The Hill Fort provided covering fire to protect the Water Battery from land attack. The Hill Fort's vulnerability to land attack was the fort's Achilles' heel. (Map by author.)

the defenses. The state would provide reasonable compensation for the impressed men and material.[14]

By December 12, 1862, slaves were at work on the fortifications at Barbin's Landing. At some unrecorded point in time, the fortifications began to be referred to as Fort Taylor. The fort's first armament consisted of two 32-pounder cannons. These could have been the two 32-pounders sent from Charleston, or they may have been two of the ten recovered 24- and 32-pounders which had been thrown into Barataria Bay and Berwick's Bay during the panic after the surrender of New Orleans.[15]

14. Jefferson Davis Bragg, *Louisiana in the Confederacy* (Baton Rouge: Louisiana State Univ. Press, 1941, 1969), 140–41.

15. Richard Taylor, *Destruction and Reconstruction: Personal Experiences of the Civil War* (New York: D. Appleton, 1879), 118–19.

From a tactical point of view, the location was excellent. The guns on the river bank, known as the "Water Battery," would be covered by a fort on the hill overlooking them. Located at the base of a sharp bend in the river, the Water Battery commanded the point at which an approaching gunboat was most vulnerable: the point at which the boat became a target but had not yet had time to lay her guns on the fort. A boat rounding the bend was funneled by the shallows on the north side of the bend into a very narrow channel, which the full firepower of the Water Battery was prepositioned to cover. After rounding the bend, an approaching vessel then had to move straight into the muzzles of the Water Battery for more than half a mile. In addition, the fort had a height advantage, looking down on the river. The approaching boat, on the other hand, had to fire up at the fort and could not lay its broadside guns on target until the bend had been rounded. The Red's narrow channel also forced attacking naval forces to assault the fort in single file. Another advantage lay in the twisting nature of the river, which allowed the smoke from an approaching steamer to be seen and the sound of the engines heard long before the boat arrived at the fort. An approaching boat passing the mouth of Bayou L'eau Noir, at the far end of Saline Point, would be almost fifteen miles from the fort by river but less than six miles by land. Sentinels there could get word back to the fort well in advance of the swiftest gunboat.

Yet the tactical situation at the fort had some shortcomings. At periods of low water, the water level in the river could be some fifteen to twenty feet below the river banks, leaving a boat passing in the river nearly hidden from view of the guns in the fort on the hill. This was compensated for by the location of the Water Battery on the immediate banks of the river, which could fire upon upcoming boats no matter what the water level. Also, while a drop in water level would give the guns on the hill less of a target, this same dropping water level would give the target, that is, an approaching gunboat, less maneuverability. Of possibly greater concern, during periods of extreme high water, the Water Battery on the riverbank would be inundated, and approaching gunboats would have a correspondingly extreme maneuverability.[16] An even more serious shortcoming was the fort's vulnerability to land attack. This was a well-known flaw, however, and it was accepted by all parties that the fort's mission was to prevent the movement of naval

16. This high-water situation did occur in early 1863 and again in 1865. For several reasons, it never had an effect on the outcome of any actions at the fort.

forces up the Red River, and that in the event of a land attack, the fort would fall. The land side was Fort Taylor's Achilles' heel.

Having a fort is fine, but it is not worth much if you do not have men to put in it. There is very little on record about the first troops to man the fort at Barbin's Landing. Capt. T. H. Hutton's Artillery (Company A, Crescent Artillery) was assigned to the fort on January 28, 1863. A two-gun section of the 3rd Maryland Artillery was sent to the fort from Vicksburg, Mississippi, aboard the steamer *Archer* in late January 1863. Companies C, H, and K of the 31st Tennessee Infantry were also sent from Vicksburg via Harrisonburg, Louisiana, about the same time. Upon the arrival of the Tennesseans at the fort, they found Capt. John Kelso in command. The Tennesseans arrived at the fort just in time to start a smallpox epidemic. One of their men, Joshua Boren of Hawkins County, Tennessee, had died of smallpox at Harrisonburg just prior to the departure for Barbin's Landing. The day after the Tennessee contingent arrived, eight to ten cases of smallpox broke out among them. The Barbin warehouse was turned into a hospital ward to care for the sick soldiers. They say that when it rains, it pours, and that was certainly true in this case. The skies opened, and the rain came down in torrents for two days and nights. The Red River overflowed its banks and inundated all of the flatlands around the Barbin place. The sick had to be removed from the flooding warehouse by boat and brought to the higher ground half a mile away. Years later, Lt. John Carson of Company H bemoaned the fact that the "movement cost many precious lives. . . . Many days were spent in caring for the sick and burying the dead. For a time it seemed that not a man would be left to tell the story of the ill-fated crew of Tennesseans."[17] The high water soon receded, and the soldiers—those who did not die of smallpox—recovered. By mid-February, the garrison at the fort was ready for action. It was not long in coming.

17. John M. Carson, "Capture of the Indianola," *Confederate Veteran* 32 (1924): 381.

Chapter 2

Her Majesty the *Queen*

The first assault by U.S. forces against the newly constructed Fort Taylor came in February 1863. Strangely enough, this attempt to capture the fort was made by neither the U.S. Army nor the U.S. Navy but by members of the Mississippi Marine Brigade, a peculiarly independent branch of the armed services that was not particularly answerable to any authority. The brigade's primary task was to act as a fast-reaction force against small Confederate units operating along the Mississippi River. The brigade had their own rams and transports, which were not under navy control, although they would act in conjunction with navy and army units when it suited them. They were notorious for their undisciplined behavior and excessive acts of looting and pillaging.[1] The Marine Brigade was not connected in any way with the U.S. Marine Corps.

In early February 1863, the brigade was assisting with Maj. Gen. Ulysses S. Grant's campaign to seize Vicksburg, Mississippi. Its ram, *Queen of the West,* under the command of nineteen-year-old Col. Charles Rivers Ellet,[2] had run under the Confederate batteries at Vicksburg and Warrenton, Mississippi, and had gotten into that section of the Mississippi River between Vicksburg and Port Hudson that was still held by the South. Of course, with *Queen of the West* now present, the South's claim to that part of the river was questionable.

Queen of the West was built in Cincinnati in 1854 as an ordinary Mississippi River side-wheel steamer of 406 tons carrying capacity, 181 feet long by 36 feet wide, drawing 6 feet of water.[3] She was acquired

---

1. In May 1864, there were complaints filed by officers of the U.S. Navy that members of the Mississippi Marine Brigade were even selling military equipment to Confederate soldiers. Lt. Cmdr. E. K. Owen to Porter, May 29, 1864, in Secretary of the Navy, *Official Records of the Union and Confederate Navies in the War of the Rebellion,* 30 vols. (Washington, D.C.: GPO, 1897–1927), ser. 1, vol. 26, p. 335 (hereafter cited as *ORN;* all references are to series 1 unless otherwise indicated).

2. Charles Rivers Ellet was born in Philadelphia on June 1, 1843.

3. Paul H. Silverstone, *Warships of the Civil War Navies* (Annapolis, Md.: Naval Institute Press, 1989), 161.

by the U.S. Army Quartermaster Department in May 1862, at which time Charles Ellet, the father of Charles Rivers Ellet, had converted her into a ram. To this end, her hull and deck had been strengthened and the bow had been filled solidly with heavy timbers to form the ram. The front thirty feet of her passenger deck had been converted into a gundeck. The pilothouse was protected from small-arms fire by timbers and iron plates. The machinery was protected by a bulwark of woodwork two feet thick and a double row of cotton bales ten or twelve feet high reaching a little above the floor of the gun deck and extending most of the way across the front of the boat and back along each side to within a few yards of the paddle wheels.

Although the *Queen* was a ram, she was also well armed, carrying a 20-pounder rifled Parrott gun along with three 12-pounder Porfield brass howitzers on her gundeck. The *Queen* was under orders to "burn, sink, and destroy"[4] Confederate shipping on the Mississippi, which she commenced doing at once. Between the mouth of Red River and Port Hudson, the Confederate steamers *A. W. Baker, Moro,* and *Berwick Bay* were quickly seized, along with large amounts of supplies for the Confederate garrison at Port Hudson. The *Queen* then returned to the Vicksburg area for more coal, and while there she added a 30-pounder rifled Parrott gun on the bow of her main deck and picked up another steamer, *DeSoto* (also armed with a 30-pounder Parrott), to assist in a second raid to Red River.

Queen of the West left Vicksburg again on Tuesday, February 10, along with *DeSoto* and a coal barge, the expedition reaching the mouth of Red River on the evening of the 11th. On the morning of Thursday, February 12, the little flotilla steamed down Old River to the mouth of the Atchafalaya, where *DeSoto* and the coal barge were left. The *Queen* proceeded down the Atchafalaya, capturing a train of twelve Confederate army wagons between the mouth of the river and Simmesport. At Simmesport, seventy barrels of Confederate beef were dumped into the river, and a few miles below Simmesport, another wagon train was attacked. The bulk of this train escaped into the swamps, but one wagon loaded with ammunition and officers' baggage was captured and burned. With nightfall approaching, the *Queen* turned about and headed back toward the mouth of the Atchafalaya, where *DeSoto* was waiting. As the ram reached the bend between Simmesport and Old River, where the twelve-wagon train had been captured earlier that day,

---

4. Porter to Secretary of the Navy Gideon Welles, Feb. 14, 1863, *ORN* 24:376.

a group of civilians fired into the boat from behind the levee. The captain of the *Queen*, First Master James D. Thompson, was struck in the leg by a musket ball, the slug breaking his shinbone and making its way upward, exiting through his knee. The *Queen* replied to this insult with fire from one of the brass deck guns, but the citizens escaped unharmed under cover of darkness. With Colonel Ellet muttering threats of vengeance, the *Queen* returned to the mouth of the river. But any celebrating done by the local heroes that evening was to be short-lived. They had, in the words of one Northern journalist, "allowed their patriotism . . . to outrun their discretion."[5]

Early the next morning, a local citizen came aboard the boat with the information Ellet was seeking. The firing had been done by residents of the plantations along the Atchafalaya between its mouth and Simmesport. Ellet cast off and steamed down the river to "pay them a visit." He rounded to near Simmesport, landing "at the plantation of one Graves—who almost acknowledged" firing at the boat. The planter was allowed to remove his family and furniture from his house, after which it, along with all the sheds and outbuildings, was burnt to the ground. The *Queen* then moved up to the next plantation and repeated the performance. The "dwelling house and negro quarters," along with a "magnificent sugar-mill," were burned.[6]

There were three newspapermen who had come along with *Queen of the West* on this expedition: Finley Anderson, with the *New York Herald;* A. H. Bodman, "Bod," from the *Chicago Tribune;* and Joseph McCullagh, "Mack," of the *Cincinnati Commercial*. Bodman gives this account of the drama that played itself out at the next plantation visited: "The third belonged to an old gentleman, who, with his son and two daughters, carried on the farm and worked the niggers. One of the young ladies admitted that the brother had fired upon the *Queen,* and only wished the one had been a dozen. She abused the Colonel and berated the Yankees. When she discovered that her abuse failed to move Col. Ellet, just as the flames began to curl around the housetop, like a brave and gallant girl, as she was, she sang, in a ringing, defiant

5. Bod [A. H. Bodman], "The Expedition of the Ram Queen of the West," *New-York Daily Tribune,* Mar. 6, 1863, 8. This was originally a *Chicago Tribune* article, dateline February 15, 1863, and can be found in both Moore, *Rebellion Record* 6:387, and H. Allen Gosnell, *Guns on the Western Waters: The Story of River Gunboats in the Civil War* (Baton Rouge: Louisiana State Univ. Press, 1949), 183 (hereafter cited as Bodman account).

6. Ibid.

tone, the 'Bonnie Blue Flag,' until forest and river echoed and reechoed with sweet melody."[7]

Colonel Ellet may have had his revenge, but the damage was already done. Captain Thompson's leg wound would be a determining factor in the outcome of the *Queen*'s raid and would play a significant role in the history of Fort DeRussy.

After burning the three plantations, Colonel Ellet set off up Red River and reached the mouth of Black River by nightfall. Ellet had earlier announced his intentions to go down the Mississippi and make contact with the Federal fleet below Port Hudson, but on learning of the existence of two fortifications (one up the Red, the other up the Black River), the impetuous Ellet determined to test the strength of at least one of these works, if not of both. Local Union sympathizers coming aboard his boat as he passed up the river assured him that the fort on the Red was very weakly garrisoned, with only two guns mounted. The fort was manned by conscripts, they said, who had no stomach for a fight and would break and run at the first sound of gunfire. Not only that, but the steamer *Louisville* had just passed up the river carrying a 32-pounder rifled cannon destined for the Confederate ram *William H. Webb* at Alexandria. With his recent successes fresh in mind, Ellet decided to go hunting. Early on the morning of the 14th, the *Queen* and *DeSoto* weighed anchors and continued up the Red. About 10 o'clock that morning, lookouts aboard the *Queen* reported a steamboat headed downstream toward the small Yankee armada. Shortly thereafter, *Era No. 5* steamed around a sharp bend in Saline Point, and her crew found themselves staring down the gun barrels of the Union gunboat.[8]

7. Ibid. According to family stories handed down over the generations, the man who shot Thompson was Charles Chalfant, the twenty-five-year-old son of plantation owners Nathaniel and Caroline Burrows Chalfant. Charles had been discharged from the 2nd Louisiana Infantry in 1861 for physical disability. In the Chalfant version, Charles's sisters Isabella (known as Belle and described as "cold, haughty and regal") and Emma had the Yankees drag their piano from the house, and one played while the other sang "The Bonnie Blue Flag" as the house burned. They also reported that in addition to burning the house, the Yankees burned the gin, the sugar house, the corn crib, and twenty-two slave cabins and stole the cattle and "cut the feet off of little calves." Family stories collected by Linda Ellen Perry, Chalfant descendant.

8. *Era No. 5* was a stern-wheel steamer of 115 tons, built in Pittsburgh, Pennsylvania, in 1860 for the "G. L. Kouns and Bros. Low Water Through Line, as High as Kiamichi," which was owned by the Kouns brothers of New Orleans. There were seven *Era* vessels operating in the Red River before the war, and they were numbered up to *Era No. 12* after the war. There were so many *Eras* operating in 1868 that two of them collided, the *No. 9* sinking the *No. 10* at the mouth of the Red River. William M. Lytle and Forrest Holdcamper, *Merchant Steam Vessels of the United States, 1807–1868:* "The

On the morning of February 12, *Era No. 5* had left Alexandria on her way to Black River with a cargo of forty-five hundred bushels of corn bound for Confederate forces in Arkansas. Upon arriving at the fortifications at Barbin's Landing, the *Era* was flagged down and informed that "a suspicious looking craft" had been seen at the mouth of Red River the night before. The *Era* tied up under the protection of the guns of the fort to await further word on this vessel. Four other vessels were stopped in a similar manner, all but the *Era* returning upstream after a short stop at the fort. At daylight on the 14th, no further word being heard of *Queen of the West*, the captain of the *Era* left the protection of the fort to make a run for the mouth of Black River. But before the *Era* found Black River, she found *Queen of the West*.[9]

Upon finding the *Queen* blocking passage of the river, the captain of the *Era* made a desperate attempt to turn about and run for the safety of the fort. With the *Era* half turned around, the *Queen* fired into the boat with her forward Parrott gun. The shell hit the *Era* in the stern, passing through the galley, demolishing a stove and wounding a Negro cook. With this one shot, the officers and passengers aboard the *Era* rushed the railings with sheets and white handkerchiefs, and *Era No. 5* quickly came under Union control. Upon boarding the *Era*, Colonel Ellet found among the passengers eighteen Confederate privates from the 14th Texas Cavalry and the 27th Louisiana Infantry, two Texas lieutenants,[10] and a German Jew named Elsasser, who had on his person thirty-two thousand dollars in Confederate money. Colonel Ellet strongly suspected this man of being a Confederate quartermaster. The privates were paroled and put ashore, along with the civilian passengers, and the officers and Elsasser were detained aboard the boat. George Woods, pilot of the *Era*, was ordered aboard the *Queen* to assist her pilot in directing the boat upstream to attack Fort Taylor.

Lytle-Holdcamper List" (Staten Island, N.Y.: Steamship Historical Society of America, 1975), 258; Silverstone, *Warships*, 246; J. Fair Hardin, *Northwestern Louisiana: A History of the Watershed of the Red River, 1714–1937* (Shreveport, La.: Historical Record Association, 1936), 326; Frederick Way Jr., *Way's Packet Directory, 1848–1983: Passenger Steamboats of the Mississippi River System Since the Advent of Photography in Mid-Continent America* (Athens: Ohio Univ. Press, 1983), 154.

9. Newspaper account published by the *Memphis Appeal*, quoted in J. Thomas Scharf, *History of the Confederate States Navy, from Its Organization to the Surrender of Its Last Vessel* (New York: Rogers & Sherwood, 1887), 354–55.

10. These men were identified as "Lieut. Daly of the Texas State troops and Lieut. Doyle of the 14th Texas" in the Bodman account. Lieutenant Doyle has been further identified as Lt. Christopher C. Doyle of the 14th Texas Cavalry.

That this was poor judgment on the part of Colonel Ellet would soon become obvious.

There is no question but that the shot fired at the *Era* was heard at the fortifications up the river. There could be no doubt in the minds of Captain Kelso and his men at the fort that *Era No. 5* had run afoul of the rumored Union gunboat. Any doubt that may have remained was erased when a courier arrived from the lookout post on the river at its junction with Bayou L'eau Noir. The cannons at the fort were prepared for action, and the Southerners waited.

Thirty miles away, at Simmesport, a steamboat carrying Gen. Richard Taylor was being flagged ashore. Several days earlier, Taylor had left Alexandria and headed downriver on an inspection trip of his river defenses. After checking on the works at Barbin's Landing, he had moved on to the fortifications at Butte a la Rose on the lower Atchafalaya. The sixty-man garrison there, armed with two 24-pounders, had recently repelled Federal gunboats attempting to pass up the river from Berwick's Bay. After complimenting the troops on their success and warning them of the presence of *Queen of the West* on the lower Mississippi, Taylor had headed back for Alexandria. But at Simmesport, he learned that the *Queen* had entered the Red and was now ahead of him on the way upriver. Disembarking, Taylor and his trusted aide, Maj. William M. Levy, set off across country for the fort to warn the garrison that the *Queen* was headed in their direction. In truth, Taylor seemed to lack a real sense of urgency concerning this mission: the general and his aide were driving a herd of cows along the way.

The weather the day before had been warm and "June-like," with leaves budding out on the willows along the riverbank and the men aboard the Union gunboats "walking about the hurricane decks in their shirt sleeves." But by early afternoon this Saturday the weather had changed, and as is typical of February in central Louisiana, winter had returned in full force. It was a cold, rainy day with a fierce north wind blowing. As they left the Bayou des Glaises Swamp and came up onto the Avoyelles Prairie below Mansura, the rain turned to sleet and hail, and the wind blew so hard that the cattle refused to face into it. At a plodding pace, they moved toward Marksville.[11]

It was 5:00 P.M. and almost dark when *Queen of the West* finally arrived at the fort, having made her way with considerable difficulty

---

11. Gosnell, *Guns on the Western Waters,* 184; Taylor, *Destruction and Reconstruction,* 122.

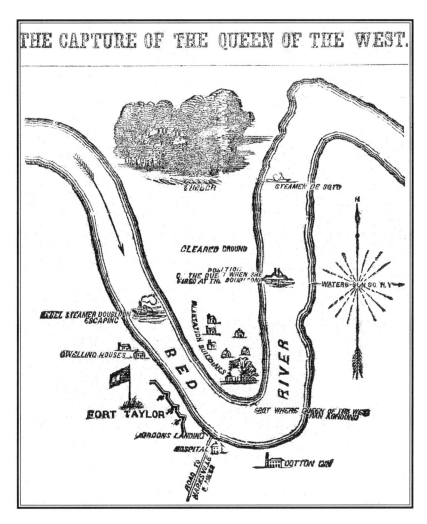

The *New York Herald* correspondent was captured with the *Queen of the West* and did not return to file his story until a year after the event. Given the short time that the correspondents who did escape were at the fort, this map is surprisingly accurate, even showing the location of the fort's hospital. (*New York Herald*, courtesy of Fort DeRussy State Historic Site library.)

through the many bends of the Red River. The *Era* had been left about fifteen miles downriver, near the point of her capture, with a coal barge and a guard of three or four men on board. *DeSoto* trailed a short distance behind the *Queen*. As the *Queen* approached the last bend before the fort, the lookouts spotted a line of dense black smoke, indicating a departing steamer. It was *Doubloon*,[12] loaded with corn, which had been turned around by warnings from the fort and sent back toward Alexandria. The *Queen*'s bow gun sent two percussion shells in the general direction of the smoke. These exploded in the vicinity of *Doubloon*, but did no damage to her. The shelling of *Doubloon* did have two effects. It caused many of the slaves detailed to work at the fort to rush out from their cabins along the river, waving white rags and handkerchiefs. It also ensured that the gunners in the fort knew that the steamboat about to come around their bend was not making a social call.

Five miles away, on the Avoyelles Prairie between Mansura and Marksville, General Taylor and his aide heard the cannon fire. Their sense of urgency finally inspired, they spurred their unwilling horses through the storm, toward the fort.

Queen of the West approached the bend in front of Fort Taylor at "slow bell" but with a full head of steam in her boilers. The sun was just setting as the *Queen* slowly pushed into view. The four 32-pounders in the Water Battery immediately opened fire on the ram, and even before the fourth shot had left the barrel, Colonel Ellet ordered the *Queen* backed out.[13]

It is a matter of debate as to who was piloting the *Queen* at this point. Scott Long of Indiana, the first pilot, guided the boat past the Confederate batteries at Vicksburg, but he was sick on this particular day. The second pilot of the *Queen* was Thomas W. Garvey of Pittsburgh, Pennsylvania. Despite his northern address, his loyalty to the Union was viewed with skepticism by some of his shipmates. By some accounts, Garvey was the pilot of the *Queen* as it rounded the bend.[14] Other accounts have the wheel under the control of George Woods, the Southern pilot of *Era No. 5*, who had been put at the wheel at bayonet point.[15] Yet another account places George Woods in the pilothouse,

12. *Doubloon* was a side-wheel steamer of 293 tons, 171.8 feet by 33.6 feet with a 6.5-foot draft, built in 1859 in Cincinnati. She was scuttled in the Red River in May 1864 but was later raised and repaired, then burned at New Orleans on June 24, 1867. Lytle and Holdcamper, *Merchant Steam Vessels*, 256; Silverstone, *Warships*, 246; Way, *Way's Packet Directory*, 132.

13. Col. Charles Rivers Ellet to Porter, Feb. 21, 1863, *ORN* 24:384.

14. Official report of Colonel Charles Rivers Ellet to Admiral David Porter, *ORN* 24:384–85; Warren D. Crandall and Isaac Newall, *History of the Ram Fleet and the Mississippi Marine Brigade in the War for the Union on the Mississippi and Its Tributaries* (St. Louis: Society of Survivors, 1907), 171.

15. Scharf, *History of the Confederate States Navy*, 354–55. Also see Finley Anderson, "A Year in the Confederacy: Account of the Special Correspondent of the Herald," *New*

forced "to assist at the wheel," supposedly assisting Garvey.[16] To further confuse the issue, on February 24, Adm. David D. Porter recommended a court-martial for "James Montgomery, pilot of the *Queen,* who, without doubt, treacherously ran her on shore when she was lost and proclaimed himself a secessionist."[17]

Whoever was at the wheel had to know that at this sharp curve in the river, the deepest part of the channel was on the outside of the bend, and the inside of the bend had a very shallow sandbar extending some twenty feet into the river. The *Queen* moved into the bend on the inside.

What happened next is generally agreed on in all accounts of the action. The *Queen's* pilot, whether Garvey or Woods, turned sharply to the right, and the *Queen* was quickly hard aground in the shallow area with a broken rudder. Sixty yards farther downstream she would have been out of sight of the Confederate guns. As it was, she was grounded broadside to the batteries of the fort, one thousand yards away. The guns aboard the *Queen* were facing forward and could not be brought to bear on the fort. The pilots tried, with what degree of enthusiasm we do not know, to back off the vessel, but their efforts were in vain. As cannon fire crashed into the boat, thunder rumbled above, a cold rain came down, and darkness settled in. George Wood made his escape in the confusion, leaping overboard and swimming for shore, leaving Garvey to handle the boat alone.

The Southerners in the Water Battery were firing enthusiastically at the stationary target, but the fading light was making it difficult to see the effects of their firing. The men on *Queen of the West* could have

---

York Herald, Mar. 6, 1864, p. 8 (hereafter cited as Anderson account). Anderson's article was published a little over a year after the incident, after his release from a Confederate prison. George Woods was arrested in April 1864 for his role in the *Queen of the West* incident. *ORN* 26:237.

16. This account, from the article "Second Cruise of the Queen of the West Below Vicksburg," is found without a byline in the March 6, 1863, *New York Herald,* and is attributed to Finley Anderson, the *Herald* correspondent, in Scharf, *History of the Confederate States Navy,* 355. Although that would be the logical assumption since Anderson was the *Herald* correspondent, Anderson could not possibly have written the article as he stayed aboard *Queen of the West* and remained in Southern prisons for the following year. Most likely, the account is by *Cincinnati Commercial* correspondent Joseph "Mack" McCullagh, (and is hereafter cited as McCullagh account). The McCullagh and Bodman accounts are similar, leading one to believe that they collaborated on their stories, but there are enough differences to indicate different authors.

17. Porter to Welles, Feb. 24, 1863, *ORN* 24:433.

The *Harper's Weekly* coverage of the capture of *Queen of the West* included this engraving. The yawl is seen headed downriver, along with men floating on cotton bales. Although this picture shows two yawls, there was only one involved in the escape.

told them that the effects were all too dreadful. A. H. Bodman, "Bod" of the *Chicago Tribune,* described the situation in detail:

> Shot were flying, shell were bursting, and worse than all, we could not reply. The enemy had our exact range, and every explosion told with fearful effect. Your correspondent sought the pilot-house, and thus became an unwilling witness of the terrible affair. Three huge thirty-two pounder shells exploded on the deck, and between the smoke-stacks, not twenty feet from our heads.
>
> The air was filled with fragments and exploding shells, which flew before, behind, and all about us. Soon we heard a crash among the machinery below. Word was passed up that the lever which regulates the engines was shot away. Another crash, and we learned the escape-pipe was gone. Still another, and the steam-chest was fractured. The whole boat shook with the rush of the escaping steam, which penetrated every nook and cranny. The engine-room was crowded with engineers, firemen, negroes, and prisoners, who had sought that place under the impression that it was the safest. All this time, while we supposed we were blown up, and looked every moment to be launched into eternity, the batteries played upon the unfortunate vessel, and pierced her through and through.

"Mack" McCullagh painted a similar picture in his account.[18] Both men described a scene of panic and pandemonium. As the "solid shot crashed through her cabins as if they were made of paper," steam from the shattered pipes in the engine room filled every cabin of the grounded boat, risking suffocation of the crew and scalding some individuals. As the shelling continued, the crew crowded to the rear of the vessel. Out on deck, one man guarded the yawl, threatening to shoot anyone who boarded it, as others commenced tumbling cotton bales into the river to use as makeshift rafts. Men leaped into the frigid water to take their chances floating downstream on the cotton-bale lifeboats. This was not a decision to be made lightly, and as Mack pondered the advisability of making the leap, the cotton bale he was studying drifted out of reach and was hit by a shell, blowing it "into a thousand fragments." Undeterred, Mack jumped into the river, found another bale, and floated down to *DeSoto.*[19]

18. While both accounts differ somewhat in detail, it is obvious that the two correspondents collaborated. Both men worked details of the other's experience into their stories.

19. McCullagh account.

This sketch of the *Queen*'s capture appeared in Crandall's *History of the Ram Fleet.* A mirror-image of this sketch more accurately depicts the true positions of the boat and fort and bears a striking resemblance to the *Harper's Weekly* illustration.

Meanwhile, Bod and several of the other men not comfortable with the idea of diving into the water convinced themselves that they could best help out by taking the yawl down to *DeSoto* and encouraging it to come closer. They pulled away in the small boat, leaving Master's Mate Thompson behind. As the yawl moved downriver, it passed several men making their retreat on floating cotton bales—among them Colonel Ellet.

While all three of the correspondents aboard the *Queen* were thoroughly awed by the "crash of the shell and roar of the guns" and "the shot hissing and screaming in dangerous proximity to their heads," Finley Anderson of the *New York Herald* was more poetic in his description of the scene: "The showers of rain fell on the deck as gentle dew compared with the showers of grape and canister; the flashes of the lightning and the flashes of the guns were sometimes simultaneous, the sound of the cannon and the noise of the thunder could scarcely be distinguished. The situation was fearful, but the sight magnificent."[20]

20. First quotes from McCullagh account. Anderson account.

The men aboard *Queen of the West* were undergoing one of the more horrifying aspects of Civil War combat. Thomas Knox, who was also a Union war correspondent, was a passenger on *Henry Von Phul,* a Mississippi River steamboat that was shelled by Confederate batteries near Morganza in late 1863. He described the feeling:

> I can hardly imagine a situation of greater helplessness, than a place on board a Western passenger-steamer under the guns of a hostile battery. A battle-field is no comparison. On solid earth the principal danger is from projectiles. You can fight, or, under some circumstances, can run away. On a Mississippi transport, you are equally in danger of being shot. Added to this, you may be struck by splinters, scalded by steam, burned by fire, or drowned in the water. You cannot fight, you cannot run away, and you cannot find shelter. With no power for resistance or escape, the sense of danger and helplessness cannot be set aside.[21]

Colonel Ellet was aware that he was in serious trouble as soon as the *Queen* grounded. In his official report to Admiral Porter, he stated that the "position at once became a very hot one."

Ellet determined to make it even hotter. Realizing that his boat would soon be captured, and no doubt recalling that one of his primary objectives had been to "get your vessel back safe,"[22] Ellet prepared to burn the *Queen* to keep her from falling into Confederate hands. To this end, he gave orders to lower the ram's yawl to evacuate the wounded Captain Thompson, but the yawl had already been taken. Even had the yawl been available, Colonel Ellet determined that "it was impossible to remove him; all the passages had been blocked up with cotton, the interior of the boat was intensely dark, full of steam, and strewed with shattered furniture."[23] With Thompson trapped aboard the boat, Ellet had to abandon his plan to burn the *Queen.* The boat's surgeon, David S. Booth, elected to stay aboard the ram to tend the wounded. Several other members of the boat's crew also chose to stay aboard and take their chances as prisoners of war rather than attempt to float to safety down the frigid river. Ellet was not among this group.

21. Thomas W. Knox, *Camp-Fire and Cotton-Field: Southern Adventure in Time of War* (Philadelphia: Jones Bros., 1865), 477.
22. Porter to Ellet, Feb. 8, 1863, *ORN* 24:374.
23. Ellet to Porter, Feb. 21, 1863, *ORN* 24:385.

Col. Charles Rivers Ellet,
commander of the *Queen of
the West* expedition, owed his
position to a textbook case of
nepotism. (Courtesy of Naval
Historical Center.)

He went over the side, found a cotton bale, and drifted down toward
the waiting *DeSoto.*

About this time, General Taylor and Major Levy arrived. They
were too late to warn the men at the fort but just in time to congratulate
them. As they pulled their exhausted horses to a halt, they saw *Queen
of the West* lying against the far shore, enveloped in steam.

Several conditions had come together by the time *Queen of the
West* rounded the bend in front of Fort Taylor to seal the fate of the vessel: The boat was under the command of a hotheaded, arrogant teen-
ager. Everything that had happened on the *Queen*'s expeditions so far
had confirmed Ellet's belief that he was a military genius who could do
no wrong. Every enemy force that he had met had quickly capitulated
to his superior firepower. Ellet's high opinion of himself was shared
by Admiral Porter, who wrote to Ellet's uncle, Brig. Gen. Alfred W.
Ellet, four days after the *Queen* was lost but before Porter had learned
of the loss, "I admire bravery whenever it is connected with judgment;
that is the reason I shove your nephew into all kinds of scrapes. He
is having a very good time below and playing the mischief with rebel
property."[24]

24. Porter to Alfred Ellet, Feb 18, 1863, *ORN* 24:424.

The boat's captain, the senior naval man on board, the man who knew the *Queen*'s abilities and weaknesses and how to best use the boat in a critical situation, was seriously wounded and incapable of assisting in the upcoming fight. Even more significantly, although *DeSoto* and *Era No. 5* were both standing by out of harm's way, Captain Thompson had not been transferred to either one of these boats. He was still aboard the *Queen*.

The fort had been warned of the approach of the *Queen* a good seven hours before she arrived, giving the fort plenty of time to prepare a warm reception. As if that had not been enough, the *Queen* gave another warning just minutes before coming into range of the fort's guns.

Fort Taylor had certain inherent advantages in fighting a gunboat coming up Red River. These have already been discussed, but in this case they were accentuated by the fact that the attack was coming at dusk. The gunners in the fort were familiar with the only possible approach the boat could take. The gunners aboard the *Queen*, on the other hand, were unfamiliar with the layout of the fort. On a dark, rainy evening, this would give additional advantage to the men in the Water Battery.

The *Queen*'s regular pilot, Scott Long, was sick and incapacitated at the time of the engagement. George Wood, a good Confederate river pilot, was in the pilothouse of *Queen of the West,* forced against his will to help the boat's substitute pilot, Thomas Garvey. Garvey, depending on which story you choose to believe, was either a Southern sympathizer or an incompetent pilot. And then there is always Admiral Porter's theory that the pilot was James Montgomery. Either way, the stage was set for Col. Charles Rivers Ellet to get his comeuppance.

All the *Queen's* Men Make Their Retreat

Colonel Ellet was now "getting his comeuppance" in no uncertain terms. He had abandoned his boat and left it in the hands of an enemy who would no doubt soon be using it against him. He was soaking wet, floating down the river on a cotton bale on a cold and stormy night. Floating along with the teenaged colonel were the bodies of men who had died because of his mistakes.

DeSoto had moved as close as possible to pick up survivors, but she could not come around the bend without coming under fire from the fort, as the glow from her furnaces would have given the cannons an easy target. After Ellet was taken aboard, 2nd Lt. John L. Tuthill and

Third Master Henry Duncan "bravely volunteered" to bring *DeSoto*'s
yawl to the *Queen* to assist in taking off men.[25] Tuthill and Duncan
made it back to the *Queen,* where they found that Ellet's assessment of
Master James D. Thompson's predicament was somewhat too severe. A
crew of men made their way to Thompson's cabin and was in the process of moving him up to the yawl when word came that the *Queen* was
being boarded. Finley Anderson describes the scene: "While we were
moving Mr. Thompson an excited soldier came rushing from the gun
deck into the cabin, shouting, 'I saw three boats full of rebels coming to
board us on the bow.' The poor wounded man was dropped, like a hot
potato, on the cabin floor; the word flew through the ship like wildfire
that the rebels were boarding us; the little boat which had been brought
up for the wounded officer was instantly cut loose, and was soon at
the *DeSoto* with the news that we were boarded." Tuthill managed to
escape with a boatload of passengers, but Master Duncan was not as
quick and was left behind. Once again, the *Queen* was left boatless and
with a wounded man aboard. Anderson continues: "I went out on the
gundeck to receive the rebels; but not a rebel was there to receive. The
abnormal imagination of the excited soldier must have created boats
and human beings out of the shadows on the water of overhanging
bushes on the shore. It was too late to get the wounded off, for the little
boat had gone."[26] As Confederate soldiers began to line the bank, calling for *DeSoto*'s surrender, she dropped downstream, drifting with the
current away from the fort, picking up survivors as she went.

The Confederates from the fort may not have been actually boarding the *Queen,* but they were losing little time in following up their
advantage. Darkness had settled, and the *Queen* was only barely visible on the far bank. There was no return fire coming from the boat,
and the guns in the fort had ceased firing. The only noise to be heard
now was the shouting of men and the rumble of thunder. The battle
seemed to be over, but one can never be too sure about these things.
To ensure that the Yankees on the far shore were not up to some sort
of mischief over there in the dark, one of the soldiers from the battery,
Lt. James Delahunty, ran down to the old warehouse at the landing
straight across the river from the stranded *Queen* and set fire to the
building. As the flames rose, they lit up the entire area and revealed a

---

25. Lieutenant Tuthill and Sgt. James H. Campbell were recommended for promotions for bravery for their actions in the engagement at Fort Taylor. *ORN* 24:386.
26. Anderson account.

white flag flying from the boat. The men remaining aboard the *Queen*, meanwhile, watched apprehensively as the crowd of men around the burning building grew. About an hour later, a boatload of soldiers from the fort, led by Capt. T. H. Hutton of the Crescent Artillery and 2nd Junior Lieutenant Delahunty (the warehouse burner), called for the surrender of the *Queen*.[27] Finley Anderson once again went up on deck to meet the Rebels, but Captain Hutton insisted that the boat had to be surrendered by the senior officer on board. Surgeon David Booth was the senior man on board, and he formally surrendered the vessel. Guards were immediately stationed throughout the boat, and an inventory was taken. The men from the fort found only thirteen officers and men remaining aboard, the others having escaped downstream. While the number of prisoners may have been disappointing, the quantity of armament and supplies taken was inspiring. The inventory listed one 32-pounder rifled Parrott gun, one 24-pounder rifled Parrott gun, four 12-pounder Porfield brass guns (one slightly damaged), along with "a tremendous supply of ordnance stores, a large supply of quinine, one fine case amputating instruments, one equally fine dental instrument, and other very superior cases of surgical instruments, clothing, bacon, flour, beef, pork, hard bread, and other stores in proportion."[28] This inventory did not include anything in the boat's magazine. The key to the *Queen*'s magazine was turned over to one of the Rebel officers, along with the warning that Colonel Ellet had been seen at the door just prior to his leaving and in all probability the magazine had been arranged to blow up when the door was opened. The officer, considering discretion the better part of valor, left the magazine locked. Further examination of the boat showed that of thirty-one shots fired from the batteries, a total of thirteen had hit the boat. Captain Kelso felt that this showed "precision and accuracy" on the part of his gunners.[29]

As *DeSoto* dropped downstream, a dense fog came up, making accurate navigation impossible, and less than three miles from the fort, *DeSoto* ran aground, unshipping one rudder. Dislodged, the boat

27. On July 10, 1863, Lieutenant Delahunty committed suicide by jumping in the river, probably somewhere near Alexandria. Arthur W. Hyatt diary, quoted in Napier Bartlett, *Military Record of Louisiana* (1875; reprint, Baton Rouge: Louisiana State Univ. Press, 1992), 10.

28. Report of Capt. John Kelso, CSA, commanding Fort Taylor, La., *ORA* 24, pt.1, 348. The designations of the Parrott guns in the inventory are incorrect and would be properly referred to as 30- and 20-pounders, rather than 32- and 24-pounders.

29. Ibid.

continued her turtle-like flight. For some three hours the steamer continued on, steering only by the alternate use of her side wheels. She moved with the current, sometimes head on, sometimes stern first, still picking up floaters from the cotton bales. Ten miles downstream, the *Queen*'s yawl finally overtook *DeSoto*. At 11:00 P.M., about fifteen miles below the fort, *Era No. 5* was reached.[30] As *DeSoto* pulled alongside, her second rudder became unshipped, making the steamer even less manageable than it had been before. Colonel Ellet, now in a panic over the pursuit he was sure must be just behind him, moved everyone onto *Era No. 5*. The coal barge, already in a sinking condition, was scuttled without even taking time to transfer a supply of coal to the *Era*. One man stayed aboard *DeSoto,* knocking out her water pipes and placing a keg of powder under the boilers. A trail of powder was laid to the keg, and a slow match laid on the trail. As the sailor jumped aboard the *Era,* she pulled off and was barely a quarter-mile away when *DeSoto* erupted in a tremendous explosion. Her 30-pounder Parrott gun went to the bottom with her.[31]

Joseph "Mack" McCullagh of the *Cincinnati Commercial* described the *Era*'s flight in an article for his readers:

> It was nearly twelve o'clock Saturday night before the *Era* was
> well under way again. Col. Ellet knew that the gunboat *Webb* was
> at Alexandria, sixty miles above Gordon's Landing, and he was certain she would attempt to pursue him. All hands were set to work
> to throw overboard the corn with which she was laden, and in the
> fog, thunder, lightning and rain she worried her way out of the Red
> River into the Mississippi. They cursed the fog then; they blessed it
> afterwards.
>
> Sunday morning the *Era* had reached the mouth of Old River.
> All day long, with no fuel but the corn with which she was laden,
> and a few cords of water-soaked cypress, which she found on the

---

30. This was probably in the Saline Point area. This part of the river was cut off by the Corps of Engineers in the 1930s, but large portions of the old river bed are still visible as either lakes or low areas. However, it may have been below Saline Point, as some Confederate records report the site as being "near Black River." Joseph Brent Letter Book 2 (hereafter cited as Brent Letter Book 2), Joseph L. Brent Papers, Louisiana Historical Association Collection, Howard-Tilton Memorial Library, Tulane Univ., New Orleans (hereafter cited as Brent Papers–Tulane).

31. Lest any relic hunters become too excited, the gun was recovered by the Confederates and was in Alexandria by June 18, spiked and with a burnt carriage but in repairable condition. Over fifteen hundred pounds of coal was also recovered from the coal barge. Brent to Whitt, June 18, 1863, Brent Letter Book 2.

bank of the Mississippi, and with which she found it impossible
to make steam enough to give her headway, the fleeing steamer
attempted to get up the river. Forty miles in twenty-four hours is
poor sailing under the most unfavorable circumstances; yet the
Era made scarcely that. At Union Point she was run aground. This
delayed her three hours. How this delay affected the fugitives may
easily be imagined. They knew that the *Webb* was at Alexandria,
sixty miles above Gordon's Landing, and they felt assured she would
start in pursuit when she heard of their repulse at Fort Taylor. At the
best, even if she laid over for the fog—a thing hardly likely under
the circumstances—she could be but a short distance behind. Those
on board, anticipating their capture, were discussing the probabili-
ties of escape by skiffs and yawls to Port Hudson.

The carpenter had managed to construct a spar from the forest
near where the *Era* was aground, and after three hours' hard work
the steamer was afloat again.[32] Colonel Ellet's first duty afterward
was to place the pilot under arrest.[33]

Whether pilot Garvey's grounding of the boat was due to treachery or incompetence is still a matter for debate. Ellet was convinced it
was treachery. At any rate, the treachery concept gave him an excellent
scapegoat for the loss of the *Queen* in front of the batteries. Ellet gave
his version of the grounding at Ellis Cliffs, below Natchez, Mississippi,
in his official report of the loss of his vessel:

Opposite Ellis Cliffs, Mr. Garvey ran the *Era,* a boat drawing less
than 2 feet of water, hard aground, actually permitting her wheels to
make several revolutions after she had struck. It was with the utmost
difficulty that she could be gotten off. The disloyal sentiments openly

---

32. "Sparring" was a standard, although somewhat tedious, process used to get
steamboats off of sandbars and other shallow spots. Hardin, in *Northwestern Louisiana,* 326, describes the process: "All boats carried heavy timbers called spars, one placed
on either side of the boat, and set at an angle, with the foot of the spar bearing on the
river bottom. A cable was carried over the spar, connected to a winch, and as the cable
pulled, the boat was lifted upward and forward. Repeated over and over, the boat labori-
ously 'walked' over the obstruction to deep water beyond."

33. "Bod," the other journalist aboard the *Era,* gives a similar but not identical account, although his description of the "thunder, lightning, rain and fog" on the trip down
Red River leads one to believe that there may have been some collaboration between the
two newspapermen. Bod has the *Era* leaving at 10:00 P.M., not midnight. Bod has the *Era*
picking up wet cypress at Union Point, and the grounding occurring at Ellis Cliffs, which
concurs with the statement of Colonel Ellet. Bod also has the *Era* being aground for four
hours, instead of Mack's three. And Bod adds an additional misfortune: the starboard
wheel was "dropping to pieces." Bodman and McCullagh accounts.

expressed by Mr. Garvey a few hours previous to this occurrence rendered it necessary for me to place him under arrest, and forced upon me the unwilling conviction that the loss of the *Queen* was due to the deliberate treachery of her pilot. It is to be regretted that the unfortunate illness of Mr. Scott Long, who piloted the *Queen* past Vicksburg, rendered it necessary for me to trust the *Queen* to the management of Mr. Garvey.[34]

Garvey's "disloyal sentiments" have not been preserved. This is unfortunate, as it would have been interesting to hear what Colonel Ellet considered disloyal. Disloyal to whom, or to what? Surely, if Garvey said, "I hope the Rebels catch us and sink us and every other Union boat on the Mississippi" that would qualify as disloyal. But would the statement "I hope I never get sent up the river again on a boat commanded by a bone-headed, runny-nosed general's kid" qualify? If it would, there were quite possibly a lot of "disloyal sentiments" to be heard on the decks of *Era No. 5* that day.[35]

Mack's description of the flight of the *Era* continues:

They had just passed Ellis' Cliffs, when, through the fog, the look-out discovered the black chimney of some passing steamer. At that distance, and because the hull of the steamer was still enveloped in dense vapor, it was impossible to make her out. That she burned coal, as was evident from the black smoke pouring from her chimneys, was enough to satisfy the crew of her character. It was the Federal steamer *Indianola*. No more fear of the *Webb*.

34. Colonel Ellet to Porter, Feb. 21, 1863, *ORN* 24:385. Porter forwarded this report to Secretary of the Navy Gideon Welles on February 23, and on February 24 he recommended that "James Montgomery, pilot of the *Queen*," be court-martialed because, in addition to grounding the boat at Fort Taylor, he "ran the *New Era No. 5* on shore under what he supposed to be a battery." Porter to Welles, *ORN* 24:433. Nothing seems to have come of these charges, as on June 3, 1863, James Montgomery was piloting the ram *Switzerland* and was commended for "coolness and courage" under "a very heavy fire of musketry directed at him" in an engagement with Confederate troops at Simmesport, Louisiana. Ellet to Capt. Henry Walke, *ORN* 25:156.
35. At Pilot Garvey's general court-martial for his actions in the grounding of *Queen of the West*, the convening authority found that "it has no right to take cognizance of the matter—the prisoner being in its opinion neither officer, non-commissioned officer, nor private, and therefore not subject to the consequences of a violation of the articles of war, and that it has no authority over offenses against Navy Regulations." Garvey was held for a second court-martial, but "though long held in arrest . . . no evidence was ever adduced to sustain the charge, and it was finally allowed to drop, and the accused officer went free." Crandall and Newall, *History of the Ram Fleet,* 238, 240–41.

The *Era* was laid alongside the *Indianola* and coaled. The crew
had eaten nothing for thirty-six hours,[36] and were nearly famished.
The *Indianola* fed them. They were coatless and bootless, some of
them, and the *Indianola* clothed them. They had lost their arms
and ammunition in the *Queen,* and these were supplied by the
Indianola.[37]

USS *Indianola* was a godsend for the fleeing Union men. Its presence raised them "from the depths of despair . . . to the heights of
exaltation."[38] And with good reason. *Indianola* was a behemoth. The
Queen and *Indianola* were both side-wheel steamboats of about the
same length, but there the similarities ended. In addition to her paddlewheels, *Indianola* was also powered by two screw propellers. The
Queen's armament consisted of five cannons mounted about the decks.
The largest of these was a 30-pounder Parrott gun, which had a bore
diameter of 4.2 inches and fired a shell propelled by a charge of three
and a quarter pounds of powder. *Indianola,* although armed with only
four cannons, had two 11-inch guns mounted in its forward casemate.
These guns' shells were propelled by charges of fifteen pounds of powder. The sides of the casemate were sloped at an angle of thirty degrees
from the perpendicular and the entire casemate was plated with iron
from two to three inches thick, the heaviest plating being on the front.
The casemate had gunports which could be closed with 3-inch iron
shutters and rolled open on tracks for firing. Another two cannons,
these 9-inch, were in the casemate on the aft end of the boat. The 9-
inch guns' shells were propelled by thirteen-pound charges of powder.
These guns were protected by two-inch iron plating aft and one-inch
plating on the sides. Along the sides of the boat were iron bulwarks,
one-half-inch thick and pierced with loopholes for small arms, which
could be lowered onto the deck when desired. The decks were also
armored, although more lightly than the casemates. Also, nozzles had
been arranged in such a manner that should boarders manage to get on
deck, live steam from the boat's boilers could sweep the decks.[39]

36. Bod has the men going hungry for forty-eight hours, instead of Mack's thirty-
six, except for "a little stale and sour corn-meal, found in the bottom of a barrel."
37. McCullagh account.
38. Bodman account.
39. A. T. Mahan, *The Navy in the Civil War,* vol. 3, *The Gulf and Inland Waters*
(New York: Charles Scribner's Sons, 1883), 111–12. Scharf, *History of the Confederate
States Navy,* 362.

Like *Queen of the West,* the *Indianola* also had run the batteries at Vicksburg, under orders to join up with and protect the *Queen* and *DeSoto.* Although too late to protect the *Queen,* the *Indianola* did succeed in protecting the *Queen*'s crew. When the refugees from *Era No. 5* had been fed and clothed, *Indianola* and the *Era* turned around and headed downstream, the *Era* in advance. They were hunting now, instead of being hunted. They had been moving just over half an hour when smoke was seen in the distance. The *Era* went ahead to reconnoiter while *Indianola*'s decks were cleared for action. With the agreed-upon signal, one long whistle blast, the *Era* announced the identity of the approaching steamer. The *Webb* had arrived.

On Wednesday, February 4, Lt. Col. William S. Lovell, CSA,[40] had been ordered to proceed with all possible dispatch to Trinity, Louisiana,[41] to take command of the Confederate ram *William H. Webb.*[42] He finally found the boat at Alexandria on the evening of Tuesday, February 10, and was disappointed by what he saw. With the exception of a little caulking on the outside, no preparations had been made to prepare the *Webb* for service. The other two boats which were to be fitted out, *Grand Duke*[43] and *Louis d'Or,*[44] had not even been shown that small amount of attention. Colonel Lovell took command of the *Webb* the next morning and began to prepare the small fleet for combat. He immediately ran into difficulties. No carpenters wanted to work on the

40. William Lovell was the brother of Confederate general Mansfield Lovell, the former New York City streets commissioner who was commanding officer in charge of the defense of New Orleans when it fell to Union naval forces in April 1862.

41. Trinity, at the junction of the Ouachita, Black, and Little Rivers, is now known as Jonesville.

42. *William H. Webb* was a side-wheel ocean liner of 655 tons, built at New York City in 1856, and was about two hundred feet long. She was originally used as an ice-breaker in the East and was sold to New Orleans merchants in 1861. She was commissioned as a Confederate privateer and seized three vessels before being sent up the Red River after the capture of New Orleans. At the end of the war, she made a historic dash for freedom from the Red River down the Mississippi but was confronted by the USS *Richmond* below New Orleans on April 24, 1865, and was beached and burned to prevent her capture. Way, *Way's Packet Directory,* 488.

43. *Grand Duke* was a side-wheel packet, 205 feet long by 35 wide, built in Jeffersonville, Indiana, in 1859. She was commanded by Capt. J. M. White (1823–1880) of Cloverport, Kentucky, a steamboatman of legendary fame in his own time. *Grand Duke* accidentally burned at Shreveport on September 25, 1863. Way, *Way's Packet Directory,* 196.

44. *Louis d'Or* was a side-wheel packet of 343 tons, 181 feet long by 32.6 feet wide, built in Cincinnati, Ohio, in 1860. Way, *Way's Packet Directory,* 294.

boats, nor could the colonel find laborers to work for him. The local committee in charge of the defense of Red River agreed to lend him fifty slaves, with the understanding that they were not to go aboard *Grand Duke,* which had had a case of smallpox on board a few days earlier. It was not until Friday, February 13, that Lovell got the number of carpenters and laborers he needed. But he would not be able to dwell on his good fortune for long. At 1:30 Sunday morning, word reached Alexandria of the attack on Fort Taylor. The outcome of the attack was not yet known, so Lovell prepared to go down and assist the fort with his boats. The *Webb* had steam up at 7:00 A.M., and by 9:00 A.M. a detachment of one hundred soldiers were aboard, and the *Webb, Grand Duke,* and *Louis d'Or* headed downriver for Barbin's Landing. Upon arriving there, they found *Queen of the West* already in Confederate hands.

They did not dawdle at the fort. Lovell stopped just long enough to go aboard the *Queen* and have a short conversation with Finley Anderson. Anderson gave this version of the meeting: "Lieut. Colonel Lovell asked me if the Union gunboat *Indianola* was at the mouth of Red River. I answered, 'I do not know, sir.' He insisted as politely as possible that I should give him positive information. I then replied, 'I have already stated that I do not know; and if I did know her precise position I should certainly not tell you.' 'Well,' he said, 'that's right. So far as you yourself are concerned you shall be treated well; but if I catch Colonel Ellet I'll put him down below,' pointing to the hold of his vessel. We then exchanged parting complements, and he stepped aboard the *Webb,* which went cutting down the river." The three boats continued their pursuit of the fleeing Yankees, just as Colonel Ellet had known they would. The *Webb* passed the burnt hulk of *DeSoto* and continued down, stopping occasionally to pick up escapees from the *Queen.* One of these men, Second Mate Cyrus Addison, confirmed that Ellet was expecting to meet *Indianola* at the mouth of the river and advised them to keep a "bright lookout" for the ironclad. Addison realized that he was in the same boat as his captors, both literally and figuratively, and had no wish to be a part of the small flotilla should it confront *Indianola.* The boats arrived at the Mississippi River at nine o'clock that evening. By that time, the fog had become so thick that the *Webb* had to tie up to the bank. It was now impossible to keep a "bright lookout" for anything. From nine o'clock Sunday night to nine o'clock the next morning, the *Webb* managed to creep only a few miles. The fog the fleeing Yankees had cursed was now protecting them. It lingered, never breaking for the entire day. The *Webb* continued to make her way slowly up the Mississippi, and as the boat approached Ellis Cliffs at 5:15 in the evening, a pair of chimneys were spotted sticking up through the fog. Confident that he had at last found *Era No. 5,* Colonel Lovell pushed on. Then another pair of chimneys were spotted. The *Webb* paused. The second boat seemed to be riding mighty low in the water—too low for an ordinary steamer. More like an ironclad. The *Webb* had found the *Era,* and along with her, *Indianola.* The ironclad was, by various estimates, one and a half to two and a half miles away. Lovell did not intend for her to get any closer. It was time to abandon the chase.

With the long whistle blast of *Era No. 5* ringing out behind her, the *Webb* headed downstream as fast as the fog would allow. *Indianola* fired two shots with her 11-inch bow guns at maximum elevation. Both rounds fell short, although one came within 150 feet of the rapidly moving boat. The *Webb* attempted to return the fire as she ran into the fog, but faulty friction primers failed to fire. The *Webb* soon disappeared in the thickening fog, and *Indianola* and *Era No. 5* were forced to anchor for the night at Glasscock Island. The *Webb* could not afford that luxury and continued downstream, managing to find *Grand Duke* and *Louis d'Or* and get them turned around and headed back up the Red. The pursuit of the crew of *Queen of the West* had come to an end.

Chapter 3

The *Indianola* Affair

The Preparation

When the *Webb* arrived back at Fort Taylor on Wednesday morning, February 18, Lt. Col. William S. Lovell was put in charge of the forces at the fort, replacing Capt. John Kelso. There were no assurances that *Indianola* would not attempt to force her way past the fort, just as *Queen of the West* had. The men remained at a high state of alert.

Fort Taylor had been a busy place during the few days since the *Queen* had attacked. Capt. T. H. Hutton stayed aboard the *Queen* throughout the night of the capture and saw to it that the prisoners were well treated—"with great respect and courtesy," as Finley Anderson put it. Captain Hutton had been a regular army officer before the war and had been a prisoner of war after the capture of New Orleans, so he was sympathetic to the plight of his captives. On the morning following the attack, Captain Kelso toured the boat. Anderson, upon being introduced to Kelso, shook his hand and said, "I'm very sorry to meet you under the present circumstances." Kelso looked Anderson in the eye and replied, "I'm damned glad to meet you under the present circumstances." Before leaving the boat, Kelso had the wounded removed and cared for. On Monday morning the boat was towed a short way up the river to the fort, and there she was visited by many of the curious citizens from the surrounding area. One visitor in particular caught the attention of the prisoners: an old spinster with "weapons of war bristling on the belt around her waist."[1]

Captain Kelso was justifiably proud of his captured ram, but the first order of business was to determine how badly the ram was damaged and how much work would be needed to put her back in service. To this end, Maj. Joseph L. Brent, chief of ordnance and senior artillery

---

1. All quotes in this paragraph are from the Anderson account.

officer in the Army of Western Louisiana, arrived from Alexandria to examine the boat. He was under orders to repair her there, if practicable; if not, she would be towed to Alexandria for repairs. Upon boarding the boat, Major Brent found an officer and squad of men guarding the captured crew members. The officer in charge of the prisoners took Brent aside and told him that one of the prisoners had turned over the key to the boat's magazine, along with a warning that Colonel Ellet had been seen at the magazine just before he abandoned ship. In all probability, the prisoner hinted, the magazine was rigged to blow up when the door was opened. Given this information, the officer had decided to allow Brent the honor of opening the magazine. Major Brent, finding himself with a damaged engine and possibly a booby-trapped boat, decided to move the boat to Alexandria for repairs.

Upon arrival at Alexandria, Major Brent prepared to open the magazine. There was no point repairing the engine if the whole boat was going to blow up. As soon as the boat had docked, the Confederate crewmen were all sent ashore. Brent and the Union prisoners remained on the boat. The major was aware of an event that had occurred in Virginia earlier in the war, in which Confederate prisoners and civilians had been forced to march down a road in front of Union troops because the Federals feared that the area had been mined. With this as a precedent, Brent felt it was only reasonable that the *Queen*'s crewmen should share his fate. He went to the prisoners and explained the situation: Colonel Ellet had been seen at the magazine shortly before leaving the boat; one of their fellow prisoners supposed that the door was booby-trapped; Major Brent was now going to open the door, and the prisoners would be with him when he did it; and if anyone had anything to say, this was the time to say it. Brent was amazed, and relieved, when one of the prisoners hopped up and said that there was nothing to worry about. When Ellet left the boat, the prisoner opined, he was so nervous and upset that he did not have the composure to booby-trap a door and was only concerned with getting off the boat. If he was seen in the magazine, the prisoner continued, it was only to get out some valuable, but the prisoner doubted seriously that he had been in the magazine at all. Major Brent and that prisoner then proceeded to the magazine and unlocked the door without incident.

Surgeon David Booth and most of the other prisoners were shortly transferred to the Confederate steamer *General Quitman* and sent down the river as part of a prisoner exchange that was already in the works, resulting in their release much earlier than would normally have been the case. Some of the prisoners were not as lucky. First Master James D. Thompson, who was shot near Simmesport several days earlier and whose condition was the reason for the *Queen* not being burned, had been getting progressively sicker as infection set in his wound. Master Thompson had written a letter to General Ellet (Colonel Ellet's uncle) just before the expedition left Vicksburg, stating that should he be killed, he wanted the pay due him to go to his fiancée in Illinois. The request proved prophetic. When the *Queen* arrived in Alexandria, Thompson was removed to a private house to be cared for but died in agony on February 26. He was buried in a local cemetery, but after the war his body was disinterred and now rests in the Alexandria National Cemetery in Pineville, Louisiana. His final pay was sent to his fiancée, as requested.[2] David Taylor, the scalded engineer, was more fortunate and slowly recovered from his wounds. Nathan A. J. Smith, a local man who had been picked up by the *Queen* as she approached the fort, was accused of giving information to Colonel Ellet. He was sentenced to be hanged but died of pneumonia in the Rapides Parish jail two weeks after his imprisonment. Finley Anderson, the newspaperman, was put in the local jail and later sent to Camp Ford prison camp in Tyler, Texas. He remained in prison for eleven months due to his supposed attempts, or encouragements, to burn the *Queen* after she grounded. After his release, he wrote a two-part story for his newspaper detailing his capture and life in Southern prisons. Anderson's account of the capture of *Queen of the West* differs substantially from the official reports.

With the prisoners now off the boat, Major Brent pressed forward with the repairs. Rapides Parish was scoured for the needed pipes and fittings for the engine repairs. Capt. Josiah Chambers stripped his cotton gin on Bayou Roberts of a steam gauge and other necessary fittings. The cotton bales armoring the boat had become loose and displaced, and the service of skilled stevedores was required to repack them. There was no bracing behind the bales, so they had to be properly packed to give them the necessary solidity. Huge fires were built on the riverbank at night and work proceeded around the clock. Large crowds gathered on the levee to watch and offer assistance. While the work was underway, the *Webb* returned to Barbin's Landing from her run up the Mississippi, sending up word to Alexandria that *Indianola* was in the Mississippi River between Vicksburg and Port Hudson. This situation

2. Anderson account; Crandall and Newall, *History of the Ram Fleet*, 165, 176; Burial Records, Alexandria National Cemetery.

was not acceptable to General Taylor. A Union gunboat in that portion of the river could cut off the large amounts of cattle and other supplies that were crossing the Mississippi to supply the Confederate armies east of the river. After several days of nonstop work, Brent reported to General Taylor that the *Queen* would be able to make her way down-river to Fort Taylor that night if the mechanics were allowed to continue work on the vessel as she made the trip.

This was the news for which Taylor had been waiting. Brent was ordered to take command of the *Queen of the West* and the *Webb*. He was to proceed immediately to Fort Taylor, where he was to finish repairs on the *Queen* and provide his boats with the crews, arms, and supplies necessary for an expedition into the Mississippi to capture or sink *Indianola*. Maj. William Levy, now commanding at the fort, was to provide assistance "to fit out the expedition in the shortest possible space of time."[3]

Joseph Brent was stunned by the order. He was prepared to outfit the expedition, but he had not expected to be assigned to lead her into action. "I was absolutely amazed at the order," he recalled years later, "as I had no idea or anticipation that I would be assigned to such a duty. I had absolutely no experience with Mississippi boats, or naval affairs, and my experience in life had furnished me with nothing that would aid me in the enterprise." In fact, Brent had been a lawyer in civilian life. He went on to explain his pride in being chosen for the job; in spite of the fact that he realized he was leading a suicide mission, he also understood the absolute necessity of removing *Indianola* from the river and was honored because he knew his assignment meant that Taylor thought that he could do the job. Nevertheless, Brent felt that Taylor's faith was somewhat misplaced.

Brent directed his body servant, a free man of color named George Kelso, to bring to the boat a few of Brent's personal belongings, primarily some clothes. To Brent's surprise, Kelso insisted that he be allowed to accompany the expedition. In spite of Brent's protestations concerning the extreme hazards of the mission, and the great likelihood that failure and death would be the outcome, Kelso pushed the issue. He had a lot of experience aboard riverboats, he pointed out, and he could be very useful should Brent be wounded. Brent reluctantly gave in,

---

3. Special Order No. 49, from Headquarters, District of Western Louisiana, quoted in Joseph L. Brent, *Capture of the Ironclad "Indianola"* (New Orleans: Searcy & Pfaff, 1926), 13.

and George Kelso became the first volunteer on the *Indianola* expedition. He was not the last. As word spread through Alexandria that the *Queen* was going after *Indianola,* the riverbank soon became crowded with volunteers offering their services. Brent first picked his engineers and pilots. John R. Allabaugh was selected as chief engineer, with Elias Wood, John Crawford, F. Montross, and O. W. Daniel as assistants. The pilots were L. Milligan, W. Melloy, W. Dunbar, and Frank Littrell. Capt. C. H. White of Alexandria was assigned as ordnance officer, and Capt. T. Tonk and Lieutenants C. Stanmeyer, Charles Hunter, and Fisk were put in charge of the boat's guns.[4] Lt. K. B. Hyams, son of Lt. Gov. Henry Hyams, was assigned as quartermaster and commissary officer of the *Queen.* Capt. James Mangum, a Texas officer in town on leave, also volunteered and was put to work as Brent's adjutant. A Mr. Prather also came along and ended up serving as an acting lieutenant in charge of two light guns. There were plenty of volunteers for all positions, with one exception. No one wanted to serve as a stoker. The job of coal heaver—feeding the furnace in the hot, enclosed engine room of a river steamboat—was unpleasant in the best of circumstances. In this situation, one would experience all of the hazards of a deckhand or soldier, as well as the hazards inherent to working in proximity to a steam engine, but have a much more physically demanding job, without even the slightest possibility of any of the glory that might come to the men in the fight. And should the boat be sunk, the chance of escaping from the engine room was virtually nil. This was a job with no future and no applicants.

There was another problem, possibly more severe, aboard *Grand Duke.* This boat had been picked to go along with the expedition as a tender, but there had been a case of smallpox aboard the steamer some days previous. *Grand Duke* was supposed to carry carpenters and laborers down to Fort DeRussy to assist in fitting out the expedition, but the dread of contracting smallpox made it impossible to get anyone to go aboard the steamer. The problem was only resolved by replacing *Grand Duke* with another steamer, *Grand Era.*

---

4. Lieutenant Fisk was probably Lt. H. L. Fisk of the Beauregard Battalion, Louisiana State Militia, who was captured aboard *Queen of the West* in April 1863. Most of the other men in this list can not be identified from Booth's list of Louisiana Confederate soldiers, and it is likely that either names are misspelled or these men were members of local militia units. Andrew B. Booth, comp., *Records of Louisiana Confederate Soldiers and Louisiana Commands* (New Orleans: Office of the Commissioner, Louisiana Military Records, 1920).

The stoker shortage was finally solved by hiring a crew of temporary stokers to go with the boat only as far as Fort Taylor. The boat left Alexandria at ten o'clock at night, taking with her a full crew of mechanics who worked on the engines all the way down to the fort. The mechanics were accompanied on the trip by a crew of stevedores still repacking cotton bales. The boat arrived at the fort at daylight on Saturday, February 21, and shortly thereafter the mechanics and stevedores reported their jobs finished.[5] They were paid, along with the temporary stokers, and the boats were left with their small crews of pilots, engineers, and staff.

When Major Brent realized how few men he had left aboard *Queen of the West,* he appealed to Captain James McCloskey, then in command of the *Webb,* for any spare crewmen that the *Webb* might have. He learned that the *Webb* was as short of crew as the *Queen* but that she had an excess of men in another department. The night before, Captain McCloskey had ordered ashore a company of Texas infantrymen from Burnett's 1st Texas Sharpshooters Battalion who had been quartered on the boat, so that he might clean up and organize his vessel. Unbelievably, the Texans' company commander had refused to leave, saying his men were much more comfortable on the boat than they would be ashore. Brent was incredulous. While Texas troops were known for their lack of military discipline, this was going too far. Brent ordered McCloskey to return to the *Webb* and bring the boat up alongside the *Queen.* He then had breakfast, after which he went up to the fort to visit the commanding officer there, his old friend Maj. William Mallory Levy.[6]

Levy had only recently taken command of Fort Taylor. Lieutenant Colonel Lovell was put in command by order of General Taylor on February 18. When Taylor arrived at the fort shortly after that date, he had released Lovell from the duty and appointed Levy, his assistant inspec-

---

5. In *Destruction and Reconstruction,* 123, Richard Taylor says that the *Queen* left Alexandria on the nineteenth, which would have it arriving at the fort on the twentieth. In disagreements of this sort, the author defers to Brent on the grounds that Brent's *Capture* is a firsthand account and is much more detailed (seventy-three pages), as opposed to the two-page, secondhand account given by Taylor.

6. Levy was born in Isle of Wight, Virginia, on October 31, 1827. He died in Saratoga, New York, on August 14, 1882 (age fifty-four) and was buried in the American Cemetery in Natchitoches, Louisiana, on December 11 of that year. Hardin, *Northwestern Louisiana,* 381–82. William Levy Funeral Card, Cammie G. Henry Research Center, Watson Memorial Library, Northwestern State Univ., Natchitoches, La. (hereafter cited as Henry Research Center).

tor general and close friend, as post commander. This all happened rather quickly, as by sunrise on the twenty-first, Levy was in charge.

Levy was an imposing figure, both mentally and physically. In 1875, some twelve years after his tenure as commander of Fort Taylor, he was described as a person of "extraordinary physical appearance. . . . He was a six-foot individual, with a magnificent head and handsome face set upon a pair of giant shoulders, a finely-molded body, and the leg of an Apollo Belvidere. He exposed a cranium which for ponderousness rivals, if it does not excel, that of Daniel Webster, mounting up in rugged ledges, as it were, until it formed such an intellectual dome as bespoke the mental giant. His chin was exceedingly massive, his mouth just a little sensuous, and a pair of effulgent gold spectacles added brilliancy to two already bright eyes, bulging in a manner quite fanciful, but denoting great power of speech. He was just such a man as would be taken for a chief among ten thousand."[7] Levy had been a lawyer of some repute in Natchitoches before the war and had also been editor of the *Natchitoches Chronicle*. It was said that "he had, as a lawyer, amassed a large fortune. His pretensions have always been of an aristocratic character. In his poorest days he managed to live in a fine mansion, drove blooded horses, and kept an establishment worthy of one who enjoyed a stated income. His eloquence was of the most brilliant and persuasive character, carrying juries by storm, and swaying multitudes by its invisible power."[8] He served as a lieutenant in Company F, 1st Regiment, Virginia Volunteers in the Mexican War, and in April 1861 he organized the Lecompte Guards (Company A, 2nd Louisiana Infantry) from the men of Natchitoches Parish and served as their captain. He was promoted to colonel of the 2nd Louisiana in July 1861, when Col. Lewis DeRussy resigned from that post. It was while serving in this position near Yorktown, Virginia, in April 1862 that Levy and Brent first became acquainted. On the last day of that month, however, Levy's persuasive power of speech failed him. Elections were held on that date for regimental officers and Levy was defeated. Brent felt that this was because Levy's "rigorous ideas of discipline rendered him unpopular."[9]

7. "Some Interesting Ante-War Reminiscences of Sherman," by A. B. C., in a Cincinnati newspaper dated June 7, 1875, J. T. Walker Collection, Henry Research Center.

8. Ibid.

9. Brent, *Capture,* 21. While Levy may have been unpopular with his troops, in later years he was always well received by the card-playing crowd. Levy was a wealthy man and a bad poker player, a combination that endeared him to his table mates. A. B. C.

He resigned from the service and returned to Louisiana, where he took a job as a staff officer to General Taylor.

When Brent returned from his visit with Major Levy, he found the *Webb* tied up alongside the *Queen,* her Texas "guests" still aboard. Captain Mangum was sent to the *Webb* with orders for the Texans' company commander to form his company on deck for the colonel's inspection, and that order was immediately carried out. Major Brent described the situation:

> Upon my adjutant reporting the company as duly paraded, I went on board dressed in full uniform, and found the men drawn up in very irregular and defective order, with, however, the officers in proper position.
>
> After saluting, I informed the men that, by General Taylor's order, I was placed in command of the "Queen" and the "Webb" gunboats, and that I thereby assumed and entered upon my command.
>
> I then said that Captain McCloskey had reported to me that, upon the previous day, he had ordered the captain to take his company ashore, and to my amazement, Captain McCloskey said that his order was disobeyed, and I then ordered the captain forthwith to march his company ashore. He answered that he had no comfortable quarters ashore, and thought it would be better to remain aboard.
>
> I ordered the lieutenant, the next ranking officer of the company to step forward, and I told him that the Captain had not obeyed my order, and was placed under arrest, and thereupon I ordered Adjutant Mangum to advance and take his sword from the captain and put him in arrest, which the adjutant promptly did.
>
> I then said that further disobedience to my orders would be summarily punished, and ordered the lieutenant to march his company ashore. The lieutenant and the men seemed quite dazed at this order; and the captain declared he was ready to obey my orders; but I said to the lieutenant that he was in command of the company, and I ordered him forthwith to march his men ashore. The lieutenant immediately gave the proper order and the men marched ashore, and I ordered the captain to be confined in a stateroom and the affair terminated. Subsequently, the captain made statements that satisfied me that his comprehension of what he had done was as hazy as his experience, and I followed the affair no further.[10]

10. Brent, *Capture,* 21–23.

In retrospect, the event is laughable—a company of Texas soldiers would choose to go on a suicide mission rather than trade their comfortable quarters on a steamboat for camping out. They were either incredibly brave or incredibly stupid. Perhaps both. But this incident seemed to set the tone for the rest of the expedition. This same lack of awareness that there are some things that just "aren't done" would serve the Confederates well in the upcoming days.

No doubt word quickly spread through the fort that Major Brent was not a man to be trifled with. Brent may not have had any particular naval abilities, but he was a capable and qualified leader. General Taylor had chosen well, despite Brent's misgivings.

With this crisis out of the way, Brent began to get his boats ready. He still had to provision, arm, and organize both boats, and he needed to obtain crews for both fighting and navigating. There was also the pressing question of who would feed the furnaces.

Supplies of provisions and ammunition were readily obtained from the fort. Getting men who were willing to fight was also no problem. Indeed, there were more volunteers, both officers and men, than were needed. Brent was given the small detachment of the 3rd Maryland Field Artillery that was serving at the fort. These men were under the command of Sgt. E. H. "Ned" Langley, and they were eager to go aboard the boats. The detachment from the 31st Tennessee was also given to Brent, along with Captain Carnes, Lt. H. A. Rice, and Lt. John M. Carson. Brent also received Company A of the Crescent Artillery. Brent was still short twenty-five men, however, and Major Levy suggested that he take them from Burnett's Sharpshooters.

Although he had only been in command of the fort for a couple of days, Major Levy had obviously caught on quickly that the Texans were trouble, and the more of them that he could send down the river, the better off he would be. But Major Brent was also aware of the Texans' lack of domestication and agreed to take them on the condition that he would take only volunteers and no officer above the rank of second lieutenant.

The soldiers were all on the boats by noon and were put to work "squaring away" the vessels. This was working, not fighting, and the men began to complain almost immediately. Brent described the situation:

> One of the many incidents showing the difficulties to be encountered, was illustrated by an infantry officer, who happened to be the senior in rank upon the "Webb." I told him to take command of all

the detachments and put them to work cleaning up, putting away the stores and generally getting ready. After he had been at work for some time, I discovered that the progress of the work was slow, and upon investigation it appeared that this ranking officer had no control over the men; and that, when they openly neglected to do what he ordered, he only begged "the gentlemen," as he styled them, to help him, and his orders and beggings were equally disregarded.

I immediately selected Lieutenant Handy, a junior officer in whom I had confidence, and put him in command of the troops upon the "Webb," in place of the incompetent senior, and the work then advanced more rapidly, as I had placed the right man in control, in disregard of rank.[11]

In spite of the undisciplined nature of Brent's band of warriors, he did have the number of men he needed to fight his vessels. But he still did not have stokers, and without men to feed the furnaces, Brent's fleet was not going anywhere. The problem of where to find stokers seemed to have an easy solution. Brent lamented that "there were no white men suitable for that work" around the fort, but he could not help but notice that there were a large number of black laborers working on the fort and the log raft in the river in front of the fort. Given the emergency nature of the situation, there was one very obvious and simple answer: draft the necessary slaves to stoke the furnaces. But as Brent was quickly learning, nothing was going to be that easy on this expedition.[12]

The slaves working at the fort had been sent there in response to the call put out by General Taylor to planters upriver from the fort. These planters, realizing that they would be the ones benefiting from the defense of the river, responded appropriately. The slaves were sent to work at the fort, but with certain provisos. The slave owners knew that if they sent slaves to the fort to be worked by men with no investment involved, in all likelihood their slaves would be worked to death, or at least worked until they were worthless. Therefore, the slaves were to be worked only under the supervision of a planters committee. Major Levy, close friend of a large number of Natchitoches Parish planters who had slaves working at the fort, was well aware of this.

11. Ibid., 24–25. Lt. Thomas H. Handy, the replacement commander, was twenty-three years old and had been a clerk and a liquor salesman in New Orleans before the war. He normally served as second in command of Hutton's Artillery (Company A, Crescent Artillery). Handy family scrapbook. Copy in possession of author.

12. Brent, *Capture*, 25.

Brent, still under the impression that he had found an obvious source of stokers, went to Major Levy and asked that stokers be furnished from the workers at the fort. Levy positively refused, pointing out that the slaves were under control of the planters and that he had no right to give them to Brent. Brent knew that Levy was from Natchitoches and offered to take Levy off the hook with his friends by coming into the fort with his own crews and seizing the number of slaves necessary. But, he pointed out, he was the naval commander and did not have the right to enter the fort and make seizures there; to do so could possibly lead to a conflict between the naval expedition and Levy's troops in the fort. So unless Levy would agree beforehand not to interfere with Brent's overstepping his jurisdiction, Brent could not take the slaves. Levy refused to agree to this, and "there ensued frequent and warm discussions" between the two.[13]

Brent was dumfounded. The "discussions" continued on and off all day, until nearly sunset. Brent had used every argument, he was ready to "proceed and attack the enemy in obedience to General Taylor's orders," he was crippled only by the lack of stokers, every moment lost gave the enemy added advantage (as if they needed it) and increased the possibility that other gunboats might get by Vicksburg to reinforce the lone *Indianola,* and Levy was under orders to assist Brent in every possible way. But Levy was adamant. What Brent asked for was "not in his power" to give.[14]

Between confrontations with Levy, Brent consulted with his boat captains on other possible sources of stokers. They concluded that, even considering the "exorbitant" wages Brent was offering to pay, slaves were the only source. The engineers and boat captains were practical men. Even if Brent could get white stokers to volunteer, they pointed out, "they would be unwilling to go out with such a crew."[15]

The showdown between *Queen of the West* and the Water Battery had occurred just at sundown on the 14th. Now, at sundown on the 21st, another showdown was going to take place. Brent made one last visit to Levy's quarters and told him that the expedition was ready to sail if Levy would provide them with stokers. As expected, Levy gave the same reply he had given all day. And then Brent lowered the boom:

13. Ibid., 27.
14. Ibid., 28.
15. Ibid.

I then sat down at his table and wrote him, that my expedition was ready to enter the Mississippi river and engage the enemy as ordered by General Taylor, as soon as I had stokers, that there were large numbers of negroes suitable for this work in his Fort, and I asked him:

First. To deliver me a suitable number of stokers; Second. Failing this, to authorize me to seize and impress them with my own men.

I further wrote that if he failed to comply with my request, and to execute his orders from General Taylor, to furnish me every aid, I would suspend all my movements, and send a courier to General Taylor, informing him that the expedition was ready to sail but was arrested for want of stokers, that Major Levy had them, but refused either to deliver to me, or to authorize me to seize them, and that my movements are paralyzed by his actions, and that I would await further orders. I handed Levy this letter, and said that I regretted that he imposed so disagreeable a duty upon me.[16]

Levy read the letter slowly. He realized that he was between the proverbial rock and a hard place. He had his loyalty to his friends in Natchitoches on the one hand, and General Taylor on the other. He could not be held responsible for the success of the operation, but he could definitely be held responsible for its failure. Levy hesitated and then, reluctantly, gave in. He would interpose no objection to Brent's exercising, within Levy's jurisdiction, the force necessary to equip the expedition, but he "disclaimed all responsibility therefor and would continue to do so." Brent said that was fine with him and that Levy was welcome to tell his planter friends that Brent was solely responsible for the impressments.

Major Brent quickly made his way down to the boats and ordered Captain McCloskey to take some men and gather up the necessary number of laborers, just now coming in for the evening. McCloskey was to select only the healthiest and most able-bodied and to give preference to volunteers. And he was to take enough men so as to make the labor light for them. For all the uproar it had generated, the actual impressment went without incident. McCloskey returned shortly to the boats with his stokers in tow. He reported to Brent that he had the required number of men and that they were not only willing but actually anxious to go, "as it diversified the routine of their lives."[17] This incident caused Richard Taylor to remark in his memoirs, "It was a curious fea-

16. Ibid., 29.
17. Ibid., 30.

The cotton-clad ram *Queen of the West.* (Courtesy of Naval Historical Center.)

ture of the war that the Southern people would cheerfully send their sons to battle, but kept their slaves out of danger." He also noted that a "famous din was made by the planters, and continued until their negroes were safely returned."[18]

Brent now had everything he needed and was ready to go. But the sun was going down, and with the new crewmen just coming aboard, he determined that it would be better to leave in the morning. The night was spent in organizing the boats.

The sun rose on the morning of February 22 to find Brent's flotilla anxiously awaiting departure. The two gunboats, *Queen of the West* and *Webb,* were tied to the bank, touching one another. *Grand Era,* under Captain Kouns, was tied nearby.[19] In the chilly morning air, the 135 soldiers from the *Webb* and *Queen of the West* were formed up on the deck of the *Webb* for inspection. The engineers, crew, and stokers were present as spectators, perched on cotton bales, hanging on the woodwork, observing the spectacle from every possible vantage point. No doubt there were spectators on the riverbank as well, watching the historic event. Day had fully dawned when Major Brent came aboard to inspect the troops.

18. Taylor, *Destruction and Reconstruction,* 124.
19. The *Grand Era* was a side-wheel packet of 323 tons, 171 feet by 33 feet by 6.1 feet, built in Louisville, Kentucky, in 1853. She was originally named the *R. W. McRea.* She was dismantled in 1864, and her machinery went into the CS ironclad *Missouri.* Silverstone, *Warships,* 247; Way, *Way's Packet Directory,* 196, 386. Her captain was either John H. or G. L. Kouns, both from a large steamboating family whose members served as steamboat captains on both sides of the conflict.

The inspection was brief, as was the speech that followed. Captain Mangum, the adjutant, first read aloud General Taylor's order assigning Major Brent to "Supreme command of the expedition." Then the major addressed his men:

> The commands and men were entire strangers to me, and I to them. The skeleton organizations represented four States, Tennessee, Texas, Louisiana and Maryland. They had been hastily gathered from the garrison of the fort, on board the so-called gunboats the previous day, and were strange to their commanding officers and the guns they were to fight, and the boats they were to man. They combined men from the cities and the farms, and many of them from the remote interior of Texas, where navigable rivers and steamboats were unusual objects.
>
> I told the men that I was a stranger to them, as they were strangers to me, but they must give me a certain degree of confidence, because I had been selected by our military commander as a suitable person to lead the expedition, and that I preferred to make no promise beyond assuring them that I would carry them where the enemy was, and then attack him, and therefore if there were any present who did not have stomach for the certain fight into which I would lead them, they had better then express the disinclination to go, as after we left, they would be required beyond peradventure to share the perils and the dangers of our enterprise.
>
> While I was speaking, the sun rose above the horizon, and its first rays fell upon me and the listening ranks—my adjutant, Captain Mangum, whispered to me "It is the sun of Washington's birthday."
>
> I concluded by saying that the sun just risen seemed to bring us a good omen, as it ushered in the 22nd of February, the birthday of George Washington, the Father of our Country, and that the freedom and liberty for which we were now battling were just the same as he battled for in the Revolutionary days; and I prayed that God might bless our efforts as his had been blessed.
>
> My brief address seemed to have been well received; and in a few minutes we were under way, steaming towards the enemy as fast as possible.[20]

20. Brent, *Capture*, 31–33.

The Chase

Years later, when recalling the departure of the expedition against *Indianola,* Joseph Brent would say: "I doubt whether any commander ever had an expedition of poorer promise against as formidable and well equipped an enemy."[21] It was a masterpiece of understatement.

As Brent's flotilla sailed off down the river, the realization of how poorly prepared he was to lead the group hit him. "I, myself, the commander of the expedition, was not as well equipped as these poor boats," he reminisced years later. "I had absolutely no experience in river navigation, or naval armament or affairs, and my theoretical knowledge was such as might be expected of a lawyer, who previous to the war was active in his profession, and was without any military or naval experience, or even the study thereof, whatsoever."[22]

And just how well equipped were "these poor boats"? Let us first consider the *Webb*'s main gun. Major Brent describes it: "Upon her deck was mounted a thirty-two pound navy gun, banded and rifled upon the Brooke system, a formidable gun for that day, shooting an elongated projectile weighing eighty pounds. The gun was mounted upon an old barbette carriage fastened by a pintle in the deck, which had been strengthened by a few braces to support the gun carriage. The gun traveled upon a flat rail, but the weight of the gun and carriage, and the inexact work, made it very difficult to traverse, while the height of the heavy gun was so great that its gravity was uncertain and threatening."[23] The fact that the gun had *never been fired* was a cause of serious concern to the gun's crew. The officer in charge of the gun reported that he did not think that the gun *could* be safely fired. The recoil of the first shot, he felt, would surely bring the gun and carriage tumbling to, and possibly through, the deck. The *Webb* had two other light field pieces on her upper deck, but this was small comfort to the men manning the main gun.

The instability of the *Webb*'s big gun was not Major Brent's only cause for concern about his artillery. There was no question about the courage of the men recruited from Fort Taylor to work the guns. There was, however, a question about their ability to work the guns. The bow gun of *Queen of the West* was put under the command of Sergeant

21. Ibid., 33.
22. Ibid., 35.
23. Ibid., 34.

Langley and his detachment of the 3rd Maryland Artillery. They were good field artillerists, but they had never before fired a gun of this caliber and were "utterly unacquainted" with the ammunition the gun used. And that was the good news. None of the other guns even had crews. Crews were formed as the boats moved downriver, and with the help of the officers and men of the Crescent Artillery and 3rd Maryland, who had "some theoretical, and a little practical knowledge of guns," the crews were instructed and practiced in loading and firing the guns. Practice continued until nightfall.

Artillery problems did not end there. An ammunition service had to be organized and practiced in supplying the guns, almost all of which were of different calibers and requiring different ammunition. And in keeping with the general tone of the expedition, the magazines were all located some distance from the guns.

The main problem of the infantrymen was a general lack of military discipline. Major Brent had been required, of necessity, to take along twenty-five volunteers from Burnett's Texans. When accurate rosters were made on the second morning out, Brent found an additional ten Texans aboard. Apparently, these men found the accommodations aboard the *Webb* completely irresistible. Perhaps Brent's problem was not so much a lack of military discipline as the extreme degree to which his 1st Texas Sharpshooters carried this lack.

The boats themselves were poorly equipped by design; that is, they were never built to be used in combat. The *Queen, Webb,* and *Grand Era* were river packets, not gunboats. While the *Queen* and *Webb* had been modified for use as rams, they were still basically packet boats. Their armor consisted of loosely packed bales of cotton, sufficient to protect against small-arms fire, but the impact of artillery was likely to send bales tumbling onto the decks, a dangerous situation in itself. The cotton-bale armor presented another problem, which Major Brent would soon discover through firsthand experience.

About twenty miles down the river, the fleet from Fort Taylor met *Dr. Batey.* The *Batey* was coming up the Red from Port Hudson, and she, too, was searching for *Indianola.* If Brent's expedition was ill prepared to take on *Indianola,* then what could possibly be said about *Dr. Batey?* Like Brent's boats, she was armored with cotton bales and armed with a 20-pounder rifled Parrott gun, two lighter guns,[24] and

---

24. These guns were either 12-pounder brass howitzers or 6-pounders, belonging to Boone's Artillery (Second Louisiana Light Artillery).

250 men with rifles. But the *Batey* was not powerful enough to do any damage as a ram, so the plan, if it could be called such, was for the *Batey* to somehow come alongside *Indianola*, then for the men to swarm aboard and capture the boat. The plan was one of desperation, edged with lunacy, and had to have been contrived by a man with an utter disregard for reality and either a serious death wish or a sincere faith in God. The boat was commanded by Lt. Col. Frederick B. Brand—the son of a preacher, appropriately enough—of Miles's Legion, and was manned by volunteers from the Port Hudson garrison. Capt. Richard M. Boone was chief artillery officer, and Lt. Samuel M. Thomas commanded the twenty-four men manning the two light guns of Boone's Artillery.[25] The men on the *Batey* had been unaware of the expedition from Fort Taylor, but were no doubt glad to find Major Brent instead of *Indianola*.

Major Brent may have been happy at first to find an additional vessel to add to his fleet,[26] but after inspecting the *Batey* and learning of Brand's "plan," he began to regret the encounter. He felt sure the *Batey* would be useless in an engagement with *Indianola* but did not have the heart to send such determined men back to Port Hudson. And who could say? Maybe there would be a use for them somewhere up the river. Brent reluctantly added *Dr. Batey* to his flotilla.

The first day on the river was spent in on-the-job training. While the artillerymen and ammo haulers practiced their jobs, the sharpshooters had positions picked for them and duties assigned. Signals were arranged for calling men to general quarters as well as for communicating between boats. The standard method of signaling with flags could not be used, as the only flag aboard was the Confederate flag. So a code was devised using lanterns of different colors and steam whistles, and certain men aboard each boat were instructed in the code.

The most exciting moment of the day came when it was determined to fire the *Webb*'s main gun to see if it would indeed fall off the boat.

---

25. Lieutenant Colonel Brand served in the U.S. Navy before the war and had held a commission as a lieutenant in the Confederate navy earlier in the war. Captain Boone was commanding officer of Boone's Artillery. He was raised near Jackson, Louisiana, and owned a plantation below Simmesport, at what is now Odenburg. He was killed during the siege of Port Hudson. Lieutenant Thomas was second in command of Boone's Artillery. Arthur W. Bergeron Jr. and Lawrence Hewitt, *Boone's Louisiana Battery: A History and Roster* (Baton Rouge: Elliot's Bookshop Press, 1986), 10.

26. Major Brent was appointed by General Taylor as "Supreme Commander" of the attempt to sink *Indianola* and therefore would remain in command of the expedition in spite of the fact that Lieutenant Colonel Brand outranked him.

The gun was loaded with a solid shot and fired. To the amazement of some and the delight of all, the gun, carriage, and boat all stayed in one piece, "though the barbette carriage did not seem as stable as it ought to have been."[27] The morale of the gun crew was greatly improved.

The fleet passed the mouth of the Black River that evening. There had been some speculation that *Indianola* might be waiting for them there, but the river was empty. Major Brent was anxious to see what the day's work had accomplished, though, and decided upon a drill. With no prior warning to the men, the signal was given to all the boats to prepare for action and go to quarters. In less than five minutes every man was in place and every gun was served and ready to fire. Brent was "pleased to see the fruits realized by the untiring efforts of the officers, to organize and instruct, in less than a single day, the men under them, so that in a few hours after we were brought together, we had learned how to place ourselves in position to fight our boats as organized men, and not as an incoherent mass." He boasted that the "ill-assorted detachments of men, which in the morning were without any experience in the peculiar service in which they were employed, were thoroughly organized and welded together into an obedient mass, ready in theory to give instant battle, and if their skill and acquirements were very moderate, their spirit was good, and the fixed routine established gave a certain degree of confidence."[28]

The expedition continued down the Red, and upon reaching the mouth of the Atchafalaya, two properly equipped signal service men were found and added to the retinue. These men were a welcome addition and helped considerably with the fleet's communication problems.

The fleet entered the Mississippi after dark, and it was here that Major Brent fully expected to find *Indianola*. But once again, the ironclad was not to be found. A decision now had to be made: Had she gone upriver or down? Brent landed on the east bank of the Mississippi, at Acklen's plantation, in search of information.[29] Yes, *Indianola* had been here, said Joseph Acklen. But she had left two days earlier.

27. Brent, *Capture,* 38.
28. Ibid., 36–38.
29. Acklen's plantation was across the Mississippi from the mouth of the Red. The plantation is now the site of the Louisiana State Penitentiary's Angola Prison Farm. Joseph Alexander Smith Acklen, a wealthy Tennessean, was born in 1816 and was a veteran of the Texas Revolution. He was a fervent Southerner and had left Nashville and moved to one of his several Louisiana plantations after Nashville was occupied by the Union army. He died suddenly in September 1863, from either malaria, pneumonia, or a carriage accident. The record is unclear.

Indianola had chased the *Webb* away from *Era No. 5* on February 16, a
Monday, and had tied up to shore in a heavy fog shortly after that. She
had moved down to the mouth of Red River on Tuesday morning, along
with *Era No. 5*, which remained with her until noon on Wednesday and
had then left for Vicksburg. Unable to procure any Red River pilots,
Capt. George Brown and *Indianola* maintained a blockade at the mouth
of the Red until the following Saturday, February 21. At that time his
intelligence network reported that *Queen of the West, Webb,* and four
cotton-clad steamboats with boarding parties were fitting out to attack
Indianola. Captain Brown decided then to leave Red River and go up
the Mississippi to gather cotton bales "to fill up the space between the
casemates and wheelhouses, so as to be better able to repel the boarding parties."[30] Brown makes no mention of how valuable those bales
would be when he returned with them to Union-held territory, nor does
he mention what his share of the prize money for those bales would
have been, but one would have to be very naïve to think that he was not
aware of these things. Certainly *Indianola* did not need any additional
armor. By Sunday afternoon, Brown "had procured as much cotton as
I required, and concluded to keep on up the river, thinking that I would
certainly meet another boat." It is a safe bet that "as much cotton as
I required" could be read as "as much cotton as I could find." At any
rate, Brown explains in his report that he felt that Admiral Porter might
be somehow concerned for the welfare of *Indianola*, so he continued
upriver in order to allay any fears the admiral might have.[31] *Indianola*
still had two coal barges in tow, one lashed to either side. With a good
supply of coal and a good supply of cotton, *Indianola* abandoned her
blockade of the Red River and headed back upriver toward Vicksburg.
Now, not only were the dogs on the chase, but the rabbit was running as
well. But this rabbit was quite capable of tearing these dogs to shreds.

   That point was made quite clear to Major Brent when he landed
at Acklen's plantation. Joseph Acklen, "an intelligent and observant
man," met privately with Brent. Acklen had seen nearly all of the Union
boats on the river, he told Brent, and *Indianola* was "the most formidable of all." She alone could destroy all of Admiral Farragut's fleet,
he said. When told that Brent intended to pursue her, he strongly urged
Brent "to abandon the enterprise, declaring it simply an act of folly, in

   30. Capt. George Brown to Welles, May 28, 1863, *ORN* 24:380.
   31. "I then concluded to communicate with the squadron as soon as possible, thinking that . . . Admiral Porter would expect me to return when I found that no other boat
was sent below." Ibid.

This painting of *Indianola* was done by L. A. Schirmer, one of Brand's Desperados, in 1864. The original can be found at Port Hudson State Historic Site. Note the cotton bales stacked ahead of the wheelhouse. (Permission to publish from Louisiana Office of State Parks, Department of Culture, Recreation and Tourism.)

view of the weak boats we had, and would result simply in the loss of my boats and men, without any possibility of success."[32]

Brent now knew which way *Indianola* had gone, and after obtaining information from Acklen on the location of the nearest woodyard, he set out again. The night was brightly moonlit, and the boats easily found the woodyard a few miles upriver. Brent described the situation: "When we landed at the woodyard, quite a number of negroes came eagerly to us, believing that we were Union boats. Our men failed to reveal their true character, and the negroes were profuse in their tenders of service to the Union people, as they believed us to be. We immediately set them to work, loading us with wood as long as the supply continued."[33] Loading completed, the boats continued upstream. Throughout the night the boats were hailed by contrabands (runaway slaves) on the bank, "begging to be taken on board, as they believed us to be the Union gunboats, and often in the distance we could distinguish bands of them, rushing along in eager pursuit of our boats." Brent was struck

32. Brent, *Capture*, 39.
33. Ibid., 40.

by one fact: "What an enormous advantage the friendship of the blacks gave the Union forces, was very apparent, and could not have been bought with money."[34]

The boats continued upriver, burning wood now to conserve their remaining coal for combat. In the open stretches of the Mississippi, Major Brent was able to take stock of his fleet. The *Webb* was by far the fastest of the boats, rated as "very swift." *Grand Era,* lightly loaded as she was, also did well in the big river, having "good speed." But *Queen of the West* was "slow," making barely five miles an hour against the current, and the poor old *Batey* could not even keep up with the *Queen.* Speed was of the essence, as Brent had to catch *Indianola* before she got to the protection of the Union forces below Vicksburg, but at the same time, he did not want to abandon the brave men on the *Batey.* As foolhardy and reckless as they were, they might come in handy when the bullets started flying. There was only one thing to do. *Grand Era* was sent back to offer the *Batey* a tow. Colonel Brand gladly accepted, and lines were attached. Onward they continued, the *Webb* scouting ahead, the *Queen* chugging along as best she could, and *Grand Era* and *Dr. Batey* huffing and puffing in the rear. Somewhere up ahead lay the fearsome *Indianola*—also fighting against the current with a coal barge attached on either side. The barges provided her with a constant supply of coal but destroyed her maneuverability and speed. Captain Brown, sure that he would meet with reinforcements at any minute, refused to abandon the barges. Major Brent was counting on the barges to give him the edge he needed, and when he landed at Natchez early on the morning of February 23, he was given good news. While *Indianola* had been forty-eight hours ahead of him at Acklen's plantation, she was only twenty-five hours ahead when he landed at Natchez.

The *Webb* arrived first at Natchez, and by the time the other boats made the landing, large crowds had gathered on the bluffs.[35] The men of the expedition were given a heroes welcome: The "whole city gathered along the banks of the river and hailed us with loud hurrahs." And there was more good news waiting for them as well. A gas plant in the city had gone out of business and had a good supply of coal still on the

---

34. Ibid., 42.

35. Brent's account of his visit at Natchez is confusing in that several times he specifically refers to the visit as occurring on a Sunday. In 1863, February 23 was a Monday. Brent also refers to February 24 as a Monday, while it was (of course) a Tuesday. Brent's account was written in 1900, thirty-seven years after the event, which may be the reason for the confusion. Ibid.

USS *Indianola*, by Oscar Parkes. (Courtesy of Naval Historical Center.)

USS *Indianola* as depicted in *Harper's Weekly,* 1863 (Courtesy of Naval Historical Center.)

grounds. Captain McCloskey spoke to the mayor of Natchez about the expedition's need for coal and inquired about the possibility of obtaining a few tons for the boats. The mayor immediately went to see Major Brent, declaring to him that anything in the city was at the disposal of Brent's fleet, free of charge. Brent accepted graciously but stressed the need for speed. The mayor departed, and soon carts loaded with coal began arriving at the landing. Natchez Under-the-Hill rapidly took on a holiday atmosphere. The black cart drivers were shouting and laughing, racing their carts back up the bluff for more coal, which was some distance from the river. Crowds continued to line the banks, bursting into occasional spontaneous cheers. Yet not all of the behavior was morale building. Individual citizens—planters, businessmen, and clerks—were constantly slipping away from the crowd, taking Major Brent and his men aside and pointing out the futility of these boats trying to take *Indianola*. They had seen *Indianola*, they said, and this was folly. But the soldiers were determined to see this through to the finish.

The coal hauling was taking more time than Brent could afford, and after five hours he thanked the mayor and citizens but said his flotilla could not wait any longer. With some coal yet undelivered, the boats slipped their mooring ropes. The men on the banks cheered and the ladies waved handkerchiefs as the boats steamed upstream. No doubt the men on the boats returned the cheers, but as the boats moved out of sight of the landing, their thoughts returned to the mission. They were aware now that their chance of success was slight, but they kept any misgivings to themselves. Brent increased the frequency of drills, both to prepare the men and to keep their minds off the stories they had heard at Natchez.

Once again, the fleet traveled all night, and at every landing Brent inquired of *Indianola*'s passing. Although thirty hours behind when he left Natchez, Brent found that he was rapidly gaining on *Indianola*. She was making barely two miles an hour, while Brent was making nearly five. By Tuesday afternoon, February 24, the *Webb* and *Queen* were in striking distance, while *Grand Era*, which continued towing the *Batey*, was far behind and out of sight. But Brent had no intention of attacking *Indianola* in broad daylight, and he trailed behind. He had made calculations to strike between 9:00 and 10:00 P.M., and with time to kill, he waited with his rams at Berry's Landing, eight miles above Rodney, Mississippi.

Brent was concerned about going into combat without his tender, *Grand Era*. He knew the chances were that at least one of his boats would be crippled in the upcoming attack, and he knew that her assistance would probably be necessary—if not to save a boat, then at least to save the lives of men aboard the boats. The lack of *Dr. Batey* and Colonel Brand's "Desperadoes" was not considered too serious, but *Grand Era* was sure to be needed. A letter was left at Rodney, to be delivered to the trailing boats as they passed, telling Colonel Brand that Brent would wait at the position above Rodney until 3:00 P.M., and that at that time they would have to leave in order to catch *Indianola* before she reached the safety of the U.S. forces below Vicksburg. If the two boats were unable to make that rendezvous, *Grand Era* was to cut loose from the *Batey* and join Brent with all possible speed. Brent left Rodney at noon, and just before the 3 o'clock deadline, *Grand Era* and *Dr. Batey* hove into view. With the whole fleet together again, final preparations were made.

Major Brent recalled: "The men were brought to quarters again, the magazines opened, and the appropriate ammunition for each gun was brought out. Every man's position and movements were indicated, the magazine and approaches examined, and men instructed in the entire routine of work and even contingencies, arising from the effects of hostile fire, were sought to be guarded against."[36] The sharpshooters were also placed in positions and instructed to fire on the enemy whenever within range, even if no one was visible on *Indianola*. The men on the *Batey*, still intending to board the ironclad, were instructed to loop their blankets over their shoulders. When boarding, they were to hold their blankets in front of themselves as shields against the steam and boiling water they expected to be sprayed with from *Indianola*'s boilers.[37] Brand's Desperadoes were living up to their nickname.

With preparations completed, the men were inspected and dismissed, and the sharpshooters on the *Queen* were instructed to fire off all their rifles. The rifles had been loaded the day before, and the major wished all the men to have fresh charges in their weapons. The rifles were fired in volleys. As the men stepped back after discharging their weapons, they found to their amazement that they had set the boat afire.

The cotton-bale armor on the *Queen* was old. The bagging on the bales had been ripped and torn, and tufts of cotton poked up everywhere among the bales. The discharge of the firearms had ignited hundreds of these tufts, and the cry of "Fire!" rose up throughout the vessel. Buckets, pumps, and hoses were put to work, and the fires were contained before spreading. It was obvious that more planning was needed. It would be difficult enough to sink *Indianola* without the rams going into action as blazing balls of fire.

The fleet got underway as soon as the fires were extinguished. Fire brigades were formed aboard the boats, and men were assigned to wet

36. Ibid., 47.
37. Linn Tanner, "The Capture of the Indianola," Oct. 6, 1902, manuscript letter in private hands.

down the cotton before the boats went into action. Buckets were filled with water, hoses were left screwed to pump discharge outlets, and tarpaulins were spread under the guns and over especially hazardous spots. One more problem encountered and solved. Now all they had to do was sink *Indianola*.

At Grand Gulf, Brent learned that *Indianola* was four hours ahead, or nine miles at the most. Brent's calculations were right on target. At nine o'clock, Brent had the *Queen* switch her fuel from wood to coal to increase his steam pressure. All lights were blacked out. A faint haze of smoke was detected on the horizon. Was it from *Indianola?*

The *Indianola* had finished loading cotton on February 22 and was pushing her way slowly northward. On February 23, the smoke of pursuing boats was seen in the distance. Captain Brown put half of each watch on deck as lookouts but refused to cut away from his coal barges. He was sure that at any moment another boat would come to his assistance, and he wanted to have fuel for his colleagues when they arrived to help him fend off his pursuers. He continued moving upriver, and a day and a half later, at 9:30 P.M. on February 24, he was just above the head of Palmyra Island. Another fifteen miles would find him safe in Union-held territory.

The increased vibrations from the engines told Major Brent that the coal was indeed increasing his steam pressure. The safety valve on the *Queen* was set at her extreme limit. The river rushed beneath the boat's hull, and a layer of clouds obscured the moon.

Major Brent went to his cabin, buckled on his revolver and artillery saber, then "knelt in prayer to the God of Battles."[38] As he rose, his hand rested on his sword, and the realization hit him that, in all probability, he would be swimming in the Mississippi River before the night was over. He unbelted his sword and left it in the cabin.

As Brent returned to the pilothouse, the *Queen* came around the bend at the lower end of Davis Island.[39] Barely discernible, a dark shape lay off in the distance. Engine bells rang full speed ahead. The chase was over. The attack had begun.

---

38. Brent, *Capture,* 50.

39. At the time of the attack, Davis Island was not quite an island, but was connected to the bulk of the State of Mississippi by a very narrow neck of land. The island belonged to Joseph Davis, brother of Confederate president Jefferson Davis.

The Attack

Four miles up the river, *Indianola* watched as her pursuers rounded the bend. She cleared her decks for action and turned her head downstream to meet them.

The darkened *Queen of the West* led the assault, with the *Webb*, the faster of the two boats, five hundred yards to the rear and well off to one side. Two miles or more to the rear were *Grand Era* and *Dr. Batey*, with lights brightly burning so as, hopefully, to confuse *Indianola*.

In keeping with the tone of the expedition, there was no complicated plan of attack. Brent summed it up: "My plan of battle was simply to ram the enemy, and to continue ramming him as long as our boats held together and floated. I did not have enough men to think of boarding, as we knew he carried a numerous crew, and hence our only resource was to undergo his fire and ram, and ram, until the contest was decided."[40]

Fortunately for Major Brent, *Indianola*'s crew was not nearly as numerous as he thought. Captain Brown did not have enough men to man both his forward and stern batteries. The 11-inch guns in the forward casemate were manned and waiting as the dark shapes moved rapidly over the water toward them.

Aboard the *Queen*, Captain McCloskey was now stationed on an elevated platform overlooking the bow and the guns, and Major Brent was positioned outside of the pilothouse, "which towered like a pinnacle above the deck," where he could communicate with the pilots through the openings in the armored pilothouse. The thrill of the attack surged through Brent's body. The throb of the racing engine, the splash and spray as the boat pushed through the water, the slapping of the paddlewheels, the palpable excitement in the cold night air—everything came together to block out the fact that men would very shortly die. No doubt some on the boats felt fear, perhaps even terror, but for most of the young men aboard, this was the high adventure that they had come for.

The *Queen* charged forward. The *Webb*, a quarter of a mile behind and off to the left, was a dark formless blot. Away in the distance the fires of *Grand Era* and the *Batey* glowed brightly, the boats still lashed together. The dark mass of *Indianola* gradually began to take shape, the coal barges on her sides now visible, extending beyond the bow.

40. Brent, *Capture*, 51.

At one thousand yards, Captain McCloskey called to Brent, asking permission to open fire. Permission was refused. Brent did not want to waken the sleeping giant until the last moment. And sleeping she seemed to be. The *Queen* was now close enough to see that the coal barges only extended back to the wheelhouse, and she now steered to ram *Indianola* just behind the coal barge and the port wheel. And still *Indianola* slept. No man on deck, no roaring cannon, no sound of any engine or turning wheel.

The lack of action aboard *Indianola* was frightening to Brent. Was he flying into a trap? Was *Indianola* protected by some unseen device? At 150 yards distance, Brent could stand it no longer. McCloskey was directed to open fire with the artillery, two Parrott guns and one brass 12-pounder, and the sharpshooters were instructed to fire and to continue firing without pause. The ball had opened. The smoke of the first volleys had not cleared when the *Queen* was upon her prey. But moments before the collision, *Indianola*'s engines sprang to life, backing the boat rapidly. Instead of plunging into the unprotected hull of *Indianola*'s stern, the *Queen* crashed into the center of the coal barge. With a smashing, grinding roar, the *Queen* penetrated into the mass of barge and coal, cutting entirely through until she slammed into the hull of *Indianola,* still with force enough to break and displace iron plates and damage the machinery that drove the side wheels, causing *Indianola* to depend on her propellers alone for maneuvering through the rest of the engagement.

The *Queen*'s pilot had been previously instructed to back off as soon as the blow was delivered, and Brent was amazed to find that the *Queen* remained against *Indianola*'s side. Ordering the pilot to back off, Brent was remonstrated by the pilot, who informed Brent that he was backing, and at full power, and that the boat was not moving. As if to add emphasis to his words, the safety valve blew with a shrill scream, and still the *Queen* remained embedded.

The sharpshooters continued to fire amid the shrieking whistle of the safety valve, the throbbing of the engine, the churning of the wheels, the Rebel yells of the men, and the frustrated shouts of the officers. Surely the "volunteer" stokers in the engine room, picking themselves up from the deck where they had tumbled, must have wished that they were back hauling dirt at Fort Taylor. The *Queen*'s rifled Parrott, exposed on the bow and extending over the deck of *Indianola,* was reloaded and fired again by Acting Lieutenant Langley and his 3rd Marylanders, her 30-pound ball bouncing off the armor of *Indianola* and whistling off into the distance, leaving hardly a scratch to mark its impact. Through all of this, the guns of *Indianola* remained silent.

Embedded as he was in the side of his foe, Brent's thoughts naturally turned to boarding. With only thirty-five sharpshooters to form a boarding party, the chance of success was slim, to be sure, but there seemed to be no other options. On the verge of calling for the men to board *Indianola,* Brent saw one portion of the coal barge start to slide off with the current. She had floated only a few yards when the *Queen* backed with a jerk, free finally from the friction of the coal which had held her to *Indianola.* Backing away, the *Queen* was passed by the charging *Webb,* "running like a railway express," making her first dash against *Indianola.*

The men on the *Queen* and *Webb* exchanged cheers as the *Webb* flew by. At one hundred yards, the *Webb*'s main gun—the source of so much conjecture a few days earlier—let fly with an eighty-pound bolt. The projectile ricocheted into the heavens. The heaviest gun in Brent's fleet had just made a direct hit on *Indianola,* at a hundred yards range, resulting in "a slight superficial scaling and an indentation [in *Indianola*'s armor plating] of less than ⅛ inch."[41] But on the bright side, the gun remained fastened to the deck.

After being rammed once, and fired into twice by artillery, *Indianola* finally decided to participate in the action. The two 11-inch guns in the forward casemate fired at the *Webb* as she passed broadside in front of *Indianola* at such close range that the smoke from the blast enveloped the bow of the *Webb.* Amazingly enough, one round was a clean miss, while the other merely took off the *Webb*'s bow railing.

The first pass of the *Webb* was nearly a miss. *Indianola* was backing, and the *Webb* passed in front of *Indianola,* barely hitting her bow but hitting at an angle the second coal barge, which extended forward on the starboard (right-hand) side of *Indianola.* The momentum of the *Webb* pushed it down the length of the barge, between the barge and the ironclad, popping the lines which held the barge to the gunboat, until the *Webb* impacted into the starboard wheelhouse. The coal barge floated away from *Indianola,* while the *Webb* drew away without receiving further fire.

The *Queen* wheeled quickly around and came at *Indianola* again. Captain Pierce, in the *Webb,* felt that his lighter boat needed more speed, so he headed upstream before charging back, this time with the

41. Ibid., 57.

current aiding him. The *Queen*'s second charge received fire from both of *Indianola*'s forward guns, both clean misses. The blow was a glancing one on the curve of *Indianola*'s bow. As she bounced off and ran alongside *Indianola,* the artillery and sharpshooters aboard the *Queen* poured a constant fire into their opponent, while riflemen aboard *Indianola* responded in kind. The boats were so close at one point that pistols were used. In this or another pass, shots from one of the rams entered a gunport and mortally wounded one of the Union sailors, which "greatly demoralized the gun detachments."[42] The *Queen* again made a rapid turn and came at *Indianola* for a third ram.

As the *Queen* came charging back, *Indianola* fired again, and again missed clean. The *Queen* had finally lined up exactly where she wanted and headed for *Indianola* at a point midway between the starboard wheel and stern. *Indianola,* now stripped of her coal-barge armor, lay motionless as the *Queen* rammed hard and squarely into her, tearing away her rudder and smashing a hole in her hull. The impact threw everyone on both boats to the decks. The cheers of the men on the *Queen* rose above the sound of the rifles and artillery.

As the *Queen* backed off, *Indianola* swung around, and the *Queen* found herself in the unenviable position of being directly in front of the 9-inch guns of *Indianola*'s stern battery. Both guns fired on the *Queen* at so close a range that the heat and shock from the blasts was felt by the men aboard the *Queen*. Incredibly, one of the shells again flew wide. Then the *Queen*'s luck ran out. The second shell's passage is described best by Major Brent:

> The other struck us traversely, entering on our left side, just in front of and above our boilers, traversing and crossing the gun deck where were all of our artillery, except the thirty pound Parrott, disabling four guns, killing two men outright, wounding four men, and bespattering our deck and even the pilot-house with blood and pieces of human flesh.
>
> Continuing its progress, the shot passed across our decks at an angle, and left us after striking the bales of cotton upon the extreme edge of our starboard side. Many bales were displaced, tumbling into the water, and others—fifteen or twenty bales—were driven out by the tremendous force of the projectile and went floating and whirling through the air, like leaves blown about by a strong gust of wind.

42. Ibid., 59.

Owing to the displacement of a weight, exceeding probably ten tons, from the extreme edge of one side, the *Queen* suddenly careened to the left, as if she was about to turn over; the engineer shut off steam, the cries of the wounded arose, mingling with the loud commands of Captain McCloskey, as he put a strong force to break out and throw overboard from the left an equivalent weight of bales, to restore the equilibrium of the boat, which was rapidly effected, whereupon we started again our wheels.[43]

The fight had now been going on for about an hour, and while it might seem like the men of *Indianola* had been doing nothing, such was not the case. Surgeon H. M. Mixer, in his account of the combat, felt that Lieutenant Commander Brown was fighting his boat like a veritable whirling Dervish:

The construction of her [*Indianola*'s] pilothouse was such that in the night her pilots could see nothing, and the management of the vessel was therefore devolved entirely on Lieutenant-Commander Brown, who knew that everything depended upon protecting her vulnerable part from the rams.

To accomplish this he exposed himself everywhere. He stood upon the hurricane deck, swept by volleys of musketry, grape, and canister shot, looking out for the rams, giving orders to his pilots, and with his revolver firing upon the pilots of the enemy. He stood on his knees on the grating on the main deck to see to it that the engineer correctly understood the orders from the pilots. He went to the casemate repeatedly and ordered the fire to be reserved until the rams were close upon us then fire low. He aimed and discharged one of our guns himself, but the working of our guns was of necessity left largely to his subordinate officers.[44]

Captain Brown concurred with Mixer's description of the pilot-house. "The peepholes in the pilothouse were so small," he said, "that it would have been a difficult matter to have worked the vessel from that place in daylight, so that during the whole engagement the pilots were

43. Ibid., 60–61. In his official report the day after the event, Brent credited all the damage on the *Queen* to two shells, one hitting the guns and the other hitting the cotton, and these fired into the *Queen* immediately after the second ramming. The account quoted here was written in 1900, long after the event, but seems to be more thought out and is more detailed than the after-action report. I lean toward the lengthier report as more accurate.

44. Surgeon H. M. Mixer to Welles, Apr. 26, 1863, *ORN* 24:394.

unable to aid me by their knowledge of the river, as they were unable to see anything."[45] The descriptions of Brown and Mixer tend to give one the impression that Brown was the only even remotely competent naval man aboard the vessel, and Brown's competence has been seriously questioned in most accounts of the engagement. The vessel certainly seems to have been manned—or more accurately, undermanned—by a particularly inexperienced crew.

With the *Queen* temporarily out of action, *Indianola* tried to make her escape, or at least gain a position of better advantage. A quick examination of the *Queen* showed that the 20-pounder Parrott[46] and three other small guns were disabled, leaving the *Queen* with only her bow Parrott and one light howitzer. And the loss of the cotton bales left the *Queen* in an unbalanced situation, with her bow up and stern "unduly depressed" in the water. The three impacts with the ironclad had also jarred her engine out of position, particularly the tumbler block that held her main shaft. The chief engineer reported to the bridge that another ram "would dislodge the block and cause the main shaft to fall down, producing wreckage of the machinery, if not of the boat itself." One more ram, and the *Queen* would be dead in the water.[47]

As the crew of the *Queen* tried to right the steamer, the *Webb* charged by. Having made a wide turn upstream, then, apparently, spending some time getting into position for another ram, the *Webb* rushed by the *Queen* with a full head of steam, to the cheers of the men of the *Queen*. The *Webb* hurled herself into *Indianola*, striking her in the exact spot the *Queen* had just ruptured. According to Brent, the "sharp bow of the *Webb* penetrated as if it were going to pass entirely through the ship." The *Webb* rose up from the water from the force of the collision, and water poured into *Indianola*'s broken hull. The outboard bearing of *Indianola*'s wheelshaft was carried away, and the starboard wheel dropped, leaving the vessel unmanageable. *Indianola* took the impact without response from her batteries. The *Webb* backed off and came around for a third attack. Her bow had been smashed in from the impact of the second ramming, and unknown to her captain at the time,

45. Brown to Welles, May 28, 1863, *ORN* 24:380–381. Lieutenant Commander Brown is referred to as Captain Brown on occasion because although his rank was lieutenant commander in the navy, he was captain of *Indianola*.

46. The 20-pounder Parrott had been disabled on its second shot, during the initial charge on *Indianola*, with a blown vent piece. Brent to Maj. E. Surget, Feb. 25, 1863, *ORN* 24:403.

47. Brent, *Capture*, 62, 65.

a hole eighteen inches long and two to eight inches wide had opened just a foot above her water line. The *Webb* had one more ram left in her, and then she was going down. *Indianola*, meanwhile, was sinking. Captain Brown threw his signal books overboard and attempted to use his screw engines to run *Indianola*'s bow into the Louisiana shore to allow his crew to escape. His attempts were futile, and although three sailors made it to shore with a line, the current pulled *Indianola* back into the river and she drifted helplessly downstream.[48]

As the *Webb* closed in for her third ram, "she was greeted by a voice, announcing the surrender of the *Indianola*, coupled with the request that she be taken in tow as her machinery was out of order and she was rapidly making water and would soon sink." A hawser was tied to the crippled prize, but it snapped under the weight of the ironclad when the *Webb* began to pull.[49]

While all of the ramming was going on, *Dr. Batey* had cast off from *Grand Era* and stood off a short distance from the combat, all the while sending volleys of rifle and artillery fire into *Indianola*. Some time after the *Webb*'s second ram, Major Brent hailed the *Batey* that *Indianola* was sinking, and Colonel Brand made his move. Charging up (as best he could in *Dr. Batey*) alongside *Indianola*, Brand gave the order, "Prepare to Board." Captain Brown called out that he was sinking. "Do you surrender?" inquired Colonel Brand, unaware the Brown had already surrendered to the *Webb*. "I surrender," responded Brown, again. Brand stood down his boarders and went aboard *Indianola* to receive Brown's sword. The battle, which had lasted one hour and twenty-seven minutes, ended at 11:07 p.m.[50] The impossible had been accomplished. As Gen. Richard Taylor said, "No more gallant feat has illustrated the war."[51]

Indianola had failed in her attempt to ground on the western bank, where she would have soon been under Union army control, and was slowly drifting downriver with the *Webb* and *Dr. Batey* when the *Queen* was finally able to pull alongside. The *Queen* tied to *Indianola*, with her

48. Ibid., 61–65; Brent to Surget, Feb. 25, 1863, *ORN* 24:404; Brown to Welles, May 28, 1863, *ORN* 24:381.

49. Brent, *Capture*, 63.

50. Brent to Surget, Feb. 25, 1863, *ORN* 24:405; Mixer to Welles, Apr. 26, 1863, *ORN* 24:394.

51. Endorsement of Maj. Gen. Richard Taylor to report of Major J. L. Brent, Mar. 1, 1863, *ORN* 24:408.

bow touching the bow of the *Webb*. Major Brent climbed down from his perch next to the pilot and leaped onto the wall of cotton bales that had protected his boat, from where he intended to jump down to the main deck of the *Queen* and proceed to *Indianola* to examine his prize.

The battle was over, but the slapstick aspect of the expedition continued. As Brent landed on the cotton bale wall, some twelve feet above the *Queen*'s deck, he found that the repeated rammings and artillery fire had loosened the bales. The bale he landed on had shifted forward and stuck out somewhat over the bales below it. Brent described his situation:

> The impulse of the jump caused me to land with great force upon the outer edge of the overhanging bale of cotton, which readily yielding to my weight, tilted, and dropped me twelve feet to the deck. Fortunately I fell nearly in a sitting position, my legs hanging over the water just outside of the deck and my body resting upon the round timber or plate forming the edge of the deck. Very much jarred by the fall, I was striving, with the assistance of my arms, to raise myself up, when the displaced bale, weighing over four hundred pounds, following me in my fall, struck me fairly in the lower portion of my back and shot me below the surface of the water, and I struggled to the surface with great difficulty, scarcely able to use my left leg. I had fallen into the water just as I stood, in heavy uniform and shoes, with my revolver and field glasses attached to me, and both were lost.[52]

The "Supreme Commander" of the expedition that had just wrested control of the Mississippi River from the United States of America was now splashing helplessly in the river between two boats that floated back and forth in the current, threatening to crush him unless he drowned first. Then there was always the chance that he would be sucked under the *Queen*'s paddlewheel, which slowly revolved, first forward, then backward, maintaining the vessel's position. Brent's cries for help went unnoticed by the celebrating men above. *Indianola*'s officers had opened her steam release valves, and steam was pouring out with a continuous roar. The four Southern boats were exuberantly blowing their whistles, and the men were shouting and cheering. Brent's situation was getting critical when one of the black stokers aboard the *Webb* happened to

---

52. Brent, *Capture*, 66. Had Brent not removed his heavy sword and belt just prior to the battle, he almost surely would have drowned.

notice him and inquired "what was the matter." This stoker had obviously been recruited for his brawn and willingness to work, not for his intellectual prowess.

After some discussion and delay, the stoker returned with a rope, which he threw to Brent, and the major was pulled to safety. Brent then proceeded, barely able to use his left leg and sorely bruised all over his body, to the upper deck of *Indianola,* where he located Lieutenant Colonel Brand in conversation with Lieutenant Commander Brown. Brent did not receive the courtesy from Brown that a conqueror usually receives from a vanquished foe:

> I immediately addressed an enquiry to Lieutenant Brown, which he answered in an indifferent manner, which indicated that, in his opinion, I had but little right to address him, and, turning, he resumed conversation with Colonel Brand. This was not wonderful, as I presented a most undignified and woeful appearance. I was without hat or cap, my uniform was sodden and dripping with water, and I limped and stooped and no doubt excited in his mind the impression that I was drunk and guilty of an impropriety in speaking to him. I then said, "Colonel Brand, you had better explain to Lieutenant Brown by what right I speak to him."[53]

This misunderstanding was quickly cleared up, and Brent then examined his prize. He appointed Lt. Thomas Handy as prize master and got to work trying to bring order back to the boats, as they had gone completely wild during his short absence. Brand's crew of Port Hudson Desperadoes were again living up to their name. They "were engaged in loot and plunder, and there was absolutely no effort made to protect the ship or establish order."[54] Brent had Captain McCloskey assemble an armed guard from the *Webb* to come aboard *Indianola* and restore order. The Southerners, after some coaxing and some threatening, were soon back aboard their respective crafts. The captured crew was mustered on deck, and small details of these men were allowed to go below and gather blankets and personal articles. Unfortunately for the Union sailors, Brand's men had been rather thorough in their pillaging, and many a Yankee tar slept without a blanket that night.

Brent retired to his cabin to change into some dry clothes while his captains examined *Indianola* to ascertain her condition. They found

53. Ibid., 72.
54. Ibid., 73.

rising water in the holds, unserviceable paddle wheels, and boilers drained of steam and water. They reported to Brent's cabin, where they found him only half-clothed; even with the aid of George Kelso, Brent was bruised to the point where he could hardly dress. The men conferred, and Captain McCloskey suggested they try to pull *Indianola* across the channel to the east bank, where she would be safe from recapture by Union cavalry. The worst that could happen was that the boat would sink in midstream, but that was preferable to allowing her to return to Union control.

The prisoners were put aboard *Grand Era,* and all the ropes and hawsers that could be found were gathered. Lines were passed under *Indianola* and tied to the *Queen* and *Grand Era,* one on either side of the prize. The *Webb* steamed in advance, *Indianola* in tow, while *Dr. Batey* helped by keeping out of the way. All the boats then headed for the eastern shore as rapidly as possible, men with axes standing by the lines should *Indianola* start to pull the towboats under. The boats crept across the river, *Indianola* slowly filling with water and pulling down the other boats, until just seventy yards from shore. The *Queen* was by then listing dangerously, and she and *Grand Era* were forced to cut away. Still the *Webb* pulled, until *Indianola* struck hard aground on a sandbar, her lower decks submerged. *Indianola* was now secure in Confederate territory.

On a scale of human endeavor, the accomplishments of the men of Brent's expedition can not be overrated. Their goal was impossible. Had it not been for the unbelievable incompetence of the crew of *Indianola,* every one of the Southern boats would now rest on the bottom of the Mississippi River. This truth is acknowledged by even the most egregious Union apologists. Boynton, in his *History of the Navy during the Rebellion,* seems quite frustrated when he says, "Much allowance must be made for the unmanageable condition of the *Indianola,* the darkness of the night, and the attack of four vessels at once. Still, with no evidence of lack of courage, the battle seems to have been conducted in a confused and helpless way; and if there was seamanship or skill, it does not appear in the accounts which have been given."[55] Admiral Porter, a man who never missed an opportunity to belittle his Southern opponents, also expressed his consternation: "I had every reason, on this expedition, to demand the most perfect success." He continued,

55. Charles B. Boynton, *The History of the Navy during the Rebellion* (New York: D. Appleton, 1869), 2:383.

"There is no use to conceal the fact, but this has, in my opinion, been the most humiliating affair that has occurred during this rebellion." And he bemoaned the fact that his officers did not "have the wisdom and patriotism to destroy their vessels, even if they had to go with them."[56]

Lieutenant Commander Brown, on the other hand, tried to look on the positive side. In his report of the incident, he pointed out that he had surrendered a sinking vessel to an overwhelming force of four boats mounting ten guns and manned by over one thousand men. He had killed two officers and thirty-three men, and no telling how many had been wounded. And he had heard that all four of the guns on *Indianola* were destroyed before they could be removed. In fact, the boat was not sinking when the battle started; only two of the boats actually attacked him; the guns aboard them were totally ineffective against his armor; all four of the boats were manned by a total of less than five hundred men, including stokers; his attackers' loss was two men killed and five wounded; and guns were salvaged from the *Indianola,* despite early rumors to the contrary.

It would be nice to say that the courage and determination of the men of Brent's expedition played a significant part in the outcome of the war, but that, too, would be dishonest. In fact, the aftermath of the capture was as comical as the rest of the affair.

Wednesday morning, February 25, found *Indianola* hard aground near the east bank of the river. After the burial of the wounded Yankee sailor who had died during the night, the Confederate boats set off downstream, leaving Lt. Thomas Handy and his prize crew aboard *Indianola* with orders to raise the vessel, if possible. The men, "having no Elisha with us who could make iron swim," determined that their time could be put to better use, and "with improvised grab hooks, fished out of the sutler's store of the *Indianola* many useful articles which were badly needed."[57] And what were these men's priorities concerning "badly needed" articles? That question is probably answered in a later report, which stated that "with the exception of the wine and liquor stores . . . nothing was saved."[58] The prize crew was also joined by about one hundred men from shore, armed with two 6-pounder field pieces and fifteen muskets.

56. Porter to Welles, Feb. 27, 1863, ORN 24:390.
57. Carson, "Capture of the Indianola," 382.
58. Col. Wirt Adams to Maj. J. J. Reeve, Mar. 1, 1863, ORN 24:411.

The prize crew aboard *Indianola* may have been celebrating, but nobody else was. Admiral Porter and the Union navy were very concerned over the whereabouts of one of the few ironclads then present in the Vicksburg fleet—and should she come up the river flying the wrong flag, there was no comparable boat to send against her. Colonel Brent's flotilla, meanwhile, was in a disabled condition and would be unable to defend itself or *Indianola* should the Union navy send another ironclad below the Vicksburg batteries; Colonel Brent did not know how few ironclads Admiral Porter then had available.

And then one of those strange coincidences of war occurred, most fortuitous for the Yankees but with dire consequences to the reputation of the men who had so valiantly fought and captured *Indianola*. The Union forces surrounding Vicksburg were having trouble locating all of the Confederate batteries in the city. To get the Southern batteries to show their locations, it was decided to send a fake gunboat down the river, to draw the fire of the Southern cannon. A dummy ironclad was made from an old barge upriver from Vicksburg. It was lengthened with log rafts, a pilothouse and wheelhouses were constructed, and smokestacks were made from pork barrels. During the night of February 25, with Admiral Porter unaware that *Indianola* was in Confederate hands—in fact, unaware that the gunboat was even in danger—smudge fires were set at the bases of the "smokestacks," and the realistic-looking (from a distance) "ironclad" was pushed off from the riverbank. The barge took the current and sailed majestically past the batteries at Vicksburg. Like Uncle Remus's tarbaby, it did not even bother to reply to the fierce shelling it received as it passed.

Word soon reached the Southern fleet downriver: A huge and formidable ironclad had made her way past Vicksburg and was heading toward *Indianola*. *Queen of the West* got a look at the oncoming ironclad off in the distance and set off downstream spreading the warning. Neither *Queen of the West* nor *William H. Webb* were capable of any further ramming (the *Webb*'s bow was stuffed with mattresses to keep her from sinking), and the guns aboard both of these boats had proven themselves ineffective against ironclads. The Confederate fleet began what Lieutenant Colonel Brand politely described as a "stampede."[59] Guns were thrown overboard, and *Indianola* was blown up and abandoned with her superstructure burning. The little Confederate fleet

59. Lt. Col. Fredk. B. Brand to Maj. Gen. Gardner, Feb. 26, 1863, *ORN* 24:409.

This *Harper's Weekly* version of the destruction of *Indianola* shows considerable artistic license. *Harper's* seems to have had a policy of putting a floating log in every picture of a gunboat on the Mississippi.

scooted down the river to safety, the swift *Queen* running into *Grand Era* in the process.

While the valiant men of Major Brent's command were able to overcome the overwhelming odds against them on the river, they were helpless when it came to fighting the juggernaut of the Union propaganda machine. The tale of the *Indianola* affair was rewritten by Admiral Porter and his willing accomplices in the Northern press. David Porter was a prodigious liar, capable of and willing to exaggerate an acorn into an oak tree at any opportunity.[60] By the time Porter and the writers of *Harper's Weekly* were through with the story, the men who had attacked and captured *Indianola* were made out to be a cowardly bunch of buffoons who raced for their lives at the very shadow of a Union ironclad. As recently as 1996, the respected *Civil War Times Illustrated* magazine published an article parroting Porter's spin on the incident.[61] Even the Southern newspapers of the day mocked the men of Brent's expedition. The belief that "one Southerner could whip a dozen Yankees" was so strongly entrenched in the South that it was simply accepted that the expedition should capture *Indianola,* patch up whatever damage had been done, and then take the boat either up or down the river and destroy whichever Union fleet they should encounter. That *Indianola* should merely be destroyed was simply not enough. Newspapers in Vicksburg and Richmond were scandalized by the cowardly behavior of the men who fled from the mock ironclad. One can only assume the soldiers would have received the same treatment had they been paddling canoes and armed with bows and arrows. They were Southern men, after all, and the superhuman was expected of them. Surprisingly, the attitude among the men of the expedition was

60. Adm. David Porter's memoirs, *Incidents and Anecdotes of the Civil War* (New York: D. Appleton, 1885) and *The Naval History of the Civil War* (1886; reprint, Mineola, N.Y.: Dover, 1998) are rife with examples, as are the *Official Records of the Union and Confederate Navies*. For instance, when Porter ran past a Confederate battery of four guns while aboard *Cricket* on the Red River in 1864, he told of the boat being struck by nineteen shells in the first volley. And while *Cricket*'s deck log says the artillery firing was supported by three hundred riflemen, Porter numbers the accompanying riflemen at three thousand. In another incident in April 1864, Porter received a report that one of his officers had been killed by "a cowardly scamp" firing from the bank. Three days later, when Porter passed the report on to his superiors, the "cowardly scamp" was magnified into "a large body of cavalry."

61. James M. Powles, "The Ironclad that Never Was," *Civil War Times Illustrated* 35, no. 6 (Dec. 1996): 66–70. For an even more recent example, see "Admiral Porter's Ironclad Hoax," by Donald L. Barnhart Jr., in the September 2003 issue of *America's Civil War* magazine.

basically the same as that expressed by the Southern papers, except for the fact that they only held the few men left aboard *Indianola* to blame for losing their prize.

A closer examination of the facts reveals that not all of the panic was on the Confederate side. William Tecumseh Sherman, the legendary Union general, was so concerned by the Confederate fleet below Vicksburg that he had the recently captured *Era No. 5,* which was also in the river below Vicksburg, dismantled and sunk in deep water to prevent her recapture by the Rebel boats he felt certain would soon be on her.[62] And while Porter claimed afterward that the dummy ironclad was a cleverly contrived plan to cause the Confederates to abandon *Indianola,* contemporary accounts by Porter himself indicate that the mock boat was sent downriver for the purpose of discovering the locations of Confederate batteries in Vicksburg and causing them to expend ammunition. In a letter published in the March 25 *New York Times,* Porter states clearly that when the barge was launched, he was not aware that *Indianola* was even in jeopardy, much less captured.[63] As for the tale that *Indianola* was "blown to atoms" by the fleeing Confederates and that "not a gun was saved," it simply was not so. One 11-inch and both 9-inch guns were recovered by the Confederates, who were back in possession of *Indianola* by March 4 and attempting to raise her. Some time after that, the Union naval forces would take possession of *Indianola,* but she would never see service again. She was not floated again for more than a year and a half and was then sold for scrap.

The Confederate "stampede" made it successfully back to Fort Taylor. All of the "volunteer" stokers from the fort's labor force were returned none the worse for wear, which was a great relief to all of the Natchitoches planters and, no doubt, to Major Levy. Within days, bickering would start in the Alexandria and Port Hudson newspapers over whether the rams or *Dr. Batey* had captured *Indianola.* This argument would continue on in the pages of the *Confederate Veteran* well into the next century.[64] By March 9, the damage to the Southern rams had been repaired at the Alexandria boatyards. And along the lower reaches of Red River that March 1863, the occasional drowned Yan-

62. This was much to the dismay of Charles Rivers Ellet, the young colonel who had gone up Red River with *Queen of the West* and *DeSoto* and had nothing to show for his troubles but *Era No. 5.* W. T. Sherman to Col. Charles R. Woods, Feb. 27, 1863, *ORN* 24:396; Charles Rivers Ellet to A. W. Ellet, Mar. 1, 1863, *ORN* 24:387–388.

63. "Bache's Quaker," *Harper's Weekly,* Mar. 28, 1863. "Admiral Porter's Dummy," *Harper's Weekly,* Apr. 11, 1863.

Adm. David Porter's own sketch of the destruction of *Indianola* in the presence
of the unimaginatively named USS *Wooden Dummy.* The sketch is labeled the
"recapture" of *Indianola.* Porter refused to engage in historical accuracy even
when given the opportunity. (Courtesy of Naval Historical Center.)

kee would be pulled from the backwaters, a reminder of *Queen of the
West*'s visit to the fortifications at Barbin's Landing and a good excuse
for the Marksville newspaper editor to remind everyone what would
happen to anyone who had the temerity to invade Avoyelles Parish.[65]

The propagandized version of the dummy gunboat story has taken
on a life of its own and to this day refuses to die. There were two fake
gunboats launched from the Vicksburg area. When it was discovered
that the first dummy had caused the destruction of *Indianola,* a second
and much-refined dummy was launched on the night of March 9 and
was so authentic that it fooled Union gunboats sent down to salvage

64. "The Indianola Again," *Southern Sentinel* (Alexandria, La.) 1, no. 1 (Mar. 21,
1863): 1. "Heroes of the Confederate Navy," *Confederate Veteran,* Sept. 1896, 313.
"Capture of the Indianola," *Confederate Veteran,* Dec. 1898, 573. "A. P. Richards,"
Confederate Veteran, May 1914, 226. "Capture of the Indianola," *Confederate Veteran,*
1924, 380–83.

65. A soldier pulled from a raft of logs in Lake St. Agnes on March 6 was described as
"a huge Yankee. . . a man of very large dimensions and seemingly of great physical prowess." His personal belongings included a navy pistol "of superior quality" and a pipe with
the name Adams Butler carved on it. "The Fate of the Invader," *Pelican* (Marksville, La.),
Mar. 21, 1863, p. 1. There was no one named Adams Butler in the list of missing from
Queen of the West, and given the Mississippi Marine Brigade's penchant for thievery, it is
quite possible that this soldier was carrying someone else's pipe at the time of his death.

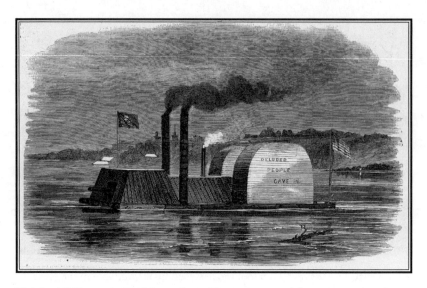

This is the *Harper's Weekly* version of Porter's *second* dummy. Modern historians have combined the two vessels into one.

Indianola in April. This impostor also caused a considerable waste of powder and shot by the Confederate guns at Vicksburg, but nothing more. *Harper's Weekly* published sketches of both dummies (two weeks apart, and with the second sketch clearly labeled "Admiral Porter's Second Dummy"), but over the years the two have become conflated into one, the first published occurrence of this being Porter's own memoirs, *Incidents and Anecdotes of the Civil War,* published in 1885. One 1962 volume went so far as to label one of the sketches as "another artist's less correct conception of the same dummy ram," and the 1996 magazine article repeated the error. To this day, it is accepted as historical fact in numerous books and articles that the "Black Terror" was a clever ruse by Porter to cause the destruction of *Indianola.*[66] It simply was not so. Nonetheless, Admiral Porter's embarrassing loss has been immortalized as an example of his incredible resourcefulness.

66. Edward Mooney diary, Mar. 9–10, 1863, transcript, Gray and Blue Naval Museum, Vicksburg, Miss. (hereafter cited as Mooney diary); Admiral Farragut to Welles, June 13, 1863, *ORN* 20:294; "Bache's Quaker"; "Admiral Porter's Dummy." The list of writers taken in by Porter's hoax is lengthy. A partial list would include Gosnell, *Guns on the Western Waters;* Philip Van Doren Stern, *The Confederate Navy: A Pictorial History* (Garden City, N.Y.: Doubleday, 1962); John D. Winters, *The Civil War in Louisiana* (Baton Rouge: Louisiana State Univ. Press, 1963); John D. Milligan, ed., *From the Fresh-Water Navy, 1861–1864: The Letters of Acting Master's Mate Henry R. Browne and*

Not all of the exaggeration was on the Union side. A most interesting version of the capture of *Indianola* is presented in a 1917 *Confederate Veteran* article, in which Commodore Joseph Edward Montgomery, CSN, saw *Indianola* run the Vicksburg batteries. He then quickly made his way to Alexandria, took the *Webb* and a crew of twenty-eight men into the Mississippi, found *Indianola,* and rammed and sank her. In addition to this small accomplishment, Commodore Montgomery—so the story continued—was a trusted advisor to Jefferson Davis, raised the *Merrimac,* captured General Grant's horse (and returned it to him the next day), was put in supreme command of the defense of the Mississippi River by the Confederate Congress, in one of his many battles had thirty-six bullet holes perforate his clothing without wounding him, and had many other equally amazing experiences. The commodore also "taught Samuel Clemens the art of steam-boat piloting and gave the great humorist his pen name of Mark Twain." In fact, the commodore was one of the riverboat pilots who taught Mark Twain, and from the commodore's account of the capture of *Indianola,* we may also surmise that he taught the young pilot a thing or two about telling tall tales.[67]

Acting Ensign Symmes E. Browne (Annapolis, Md.: U.S. Naval Institute, 1970); John D. Milligan, *Gunboats Down the Mississippi* (New York: Arno Press, 1980); Jerry Korn, *War on the Mississippi: Grant's Vicksburg Campaign* (Alexandria, Va.: Time-Life Books, 1985); Bergeron and Hewitt, *Boone's Louisiana Battery;* A. A. Hoehling, *Damn the Torpedoes: Naval Incidents of the Civil War* (New York: Gramercy Books, 1989); Powles, "Ironclad that Never Was"; Chester G. Hearn, *Admiral David Dixon Porter: The Civil War Years* (Annapolis, Md.: Naval Institute Press, 1996); *Ellet's Brigade: The Strangest Outfit of All* (Baton Rouge: Louisiana State Univ. Press 2000); and *Naval Battles of the Civil War* (San Diego, Calif.: Thunder Bay Press, 2000); Clint Johnson, *Civil War Blunders* (Winston-Salem, N.C.: John F. Blair, 1997); Marshall Scott Legan, "The Confederate Career of a Union Ram," *Louisiana History* 41, no. 3 (Summer 2000): 277–300; and Barnhart, "Admiral Porter's Ironclad Hoax." Mahan, on the other hand, in volume 3 of *The Navy in the Civil War,* did note that Porter was unaware of *Indianola*'s situation when the dummy was launched, but that book was published in 1883, before Porter's *Incidents and Anecdotes.* E. Cort Williams, an eyewitness to the event, also acknowledged in an 1888 Military Order of the Loyal Legion of the United States sketch, "The Cruise of 'The Black Terror,'" that Porter was unaware of *Indianola*'s situation when the dummy was launched. Concerning the nom de guerre "Black Terror," in the only recorded instance of Porter referring to the dummy by name, he unimaginatively called the boat "USS *Wooden Dummy.*"

67. But he apparently had nothing to do with giving Mark Twain his name. Commodore Montgomery, a well-known riverboat captain, was in charge of Confederate naval forces at the Battles of Plum Point and Memphis. (He really was.) Eloise Tyler Jacobs, "Commodore Montgomery: A Confederate Naval Hero, and His Adventures," *Confederate Veteran* 25 (Jan. 1917): 26–27; Mark Twain, *Life on the Mississippi* (Hartford, Conn.: American Publishing, 1883), chaps. 28 and 49.

Chapter 4

Dueling Gunboats

At some undetermined time between mid-February and mid-March 1863, the name Fort Taylor dropped from common usage and the fortifications at Red River began to be referred to as Fort DeRussy.

Also by mid-March 1863, Major Levy had departed and command of Fort DeRussy was turned over to Lt. Col. Aristide Gérard of New Orleans, with Maj. Paul E. Theard as his artillery officer. The Marksville newspaper boldly endorsed the new commander, stating that a "more able, energetic and gallant officer cannot be found in the Confederacy. . . . In the full vigor of manhood . . . his martial air betrays the French trained soldier." Gérard soon returned the favor, loaning the short-handed editor of the *Pelican* two former pressmen from Hutton's Artillery to assist in publishing the paper.[1]

Other changes were also being made in the fort's personnel. On March 6, the hard-fighting but hard-to-control 1st Texas Sharpshooters boarded the steamer *Nina Simmes* and departed for Port Hudson.[2] Perhaps the chance at another steamboat ride was just too much for them to resist? The detachment of 3rd Maryland Artillery was also gone, now permanently attached to *Queen of the West*. The 11th Louisiana Infantry Battalion arrived at the fort in March and was enlisting members there in early April.[3]

Work continued on the fortifications. On March 13, Lieutenant Colonel Gérard published General Order No. 4, announcing an expected Federal attack on Port Hudson and stating that the "probability is that some federal gun boats will pass the batteries and that an attempt will be made to avenge the defeat of the Queen of the West, so victoriously

1. *Pelican* (Marksville, La.), Mar. 21, 1863, p. 1; and Apr. 18, 1863, p. 1.
2. "Record of Events for First Battalion, Texas Sharpshooters, May 1862–October 1863," Janet B. Hewett, ed, *Supplement to the Official Records of the Union and Confederate Armies*, 100 vols. (Wilmington, N. C.: Broadfoot, 1994–2001), vol. 68, pt. 2, pp. 527–36 (hereafter cited as *ORA Supplement*).
3. Booth, *Record of Louisiana Confederate Soldiers*.

captured by you at this very Fort." A call was made for volunteers to "share the glory and dangers of the defenders of Fort DeRussy."[4]

By the next day, a part of Gérard's prediction had come to pass. Admiral Farragut had passed the Port Hudson batteries with *Hartford* and *Albatross,* and once again the mouth of Red River was accessible to the U.S. Navy. DeRussy's defenders knew that it would be only a matter of time before the fort would be tried again. On March 17, Gérard requested more ammunition for the guns at the fort. By his calculations, he could only defend the fort for six hours and twenty minutes if he were to fire each of his big guns (one rifled 32-pounder, three smoothbore 32-pounders, and two smoothbore 24-pounders) once every five minutes. His shells outnumbered his powder charges, and Gérard requested that he be sent enough powder to match his projectiles, which would allow him to fight for ten and a half hours. He also asked for two more big guns, 9- and 11-inch Dahlgrens, should they be available. His field pieces included 6-pounders and a 3-inch rifled Parrott gun.[5]

In addition, Gérard suggested "erecting a masked battery of light pieces at the bend of the river below the fort. That battery would open its fire only when the enemy would have passed the point. That cross fire (fire de revers) would be very effective against the gunboats, whose stern is generally the most vulnerable point."[6] Gérard was getting ready to fight.

The March 21 issue of the *Pelican* published Gérard's call for volunteers, with commentary on a nine-man unit, the "Volunteers of Mansura," who had already pledged themselves to the defense of the fort. There was also an account of the "1st Day's Fight at Port Hudson" and the running of the batteries there. But the expected movement up Red River did not come, so the work continued on the earthworks and water batteries, including the colonel's masked battery. Work was also progressing on a raft of logs in the river immediately below the fort. It was described on March 2 as a kind of water gate, being able to "swing across the river to stop boats from passing."[7] Now it was being made

    4. *Pelican* (Marksville, La.), Mar. 26, 1863, p. 1.
    5. Lt. Col. Gérard to Major E. Surget, Hd Qrs. Fort De Russy, Mar. 17, 1863. Joseph Lancaster Brent Papers, Jackson Barracks Military Library, New Orleans (hereafter cited as Brent Papers–Jackson Barracks).
    6. Ibid.
    7. William L. Ritter, "Sketch of Third Battery of Maryland Artillery: Paper No. 3," *Southern Historical Society Papers (SHSP)* 10 (Oct.–Nov. 1882): 467.

into a more permanent fixture. Timbers were sunk in the river bottom, braced and reinforced with bolts and chains and tied to trees on the bank. The raft would stop the approach of any Union gunboats and could be covered by the guns of the fort.

When the April 18 issue of the *Pelican* was issued, Lieutenant Colonel Gérard was no longer asking for volunteers but was instead notifying all Avoyelles Parish planters of Special Order No. 110, "inviting" all owners of more than five slaves to send one-fifth of their male work force to Fort DeRussy, each equipped with a blanket and an ax or spade. Anyone not accepting this invitation within ten days would be "made to furnish double the number." Planters were assured that their slaves would be returned shortly and that "only a few days will be necessary to finish the works."[8] But before the ten days would expire, the need for laborers at the fort would be over.

By April 24, the situation had changed drastically from a week earlier. The battery at Butte a la Rose had fallen to the Yankees, opening the Atchafalaya to the Union navy. Admiral Porter had run eight gunboats (seven of them ironclads) past the Vicksburg gauntlet on the night of April 16. Admiral Farragut's *Hartford* and *Albatross* were still in the Mississippi above Port Hudson. And the gallant *Queen of the West* had been sunk by Union gunboats in the lower Atchafalaya basin, with great loss of life, including several of the men of the 3rd Maryland Artillery who had helped capture it two months earlier.[9] Fort DeRussy had been strengthened by the arrival of Capt. Edward T. King's Battery (the St. Martin Rangers) aboard the steamboat *J. A. Cotten II* (formerly *Mary T*),[10] which had been chased up from the lower Atchafalaya by the advancing Yankees, but in spite of that, the situation was bleak.

It was obvious to everyone that it was only a matter of time before Union gunboats were once again at Fort DeRussy. But the real problem was not so much the Union navy as it was the Union army. Marching up from the Bayou Teche region, General Banks's troops were already

---

8. *Pelican* (Marksville, La.), Apr. 18, 1863, p. 1.

9. Sergeant Edward H. Langley, one of the heroes of the *Indianola* affair, "and all but four of his men remained upon the *Queen*, and were lost in the general destruction of the vessel." William L. Ritter, "Reminiscences of the Confederate States Navy: Letter from Captain William L. Ritter," *SHSP* 1 (May 1876): 362–63.

10. After the destruction of the Confederate gunboat *J. A. Cotten* in Bayou Teche, the steamer *Mary T.* was renamed *J. A. Cotten II*. It was often referred to as *Cotton*, or sometimes *J. A. Cotton*, as was the original *J. A. Cotten*. To add to the confusion, it was also frequently called *Mary T.*

Lt. William Hervey, Hutton's
Artillery. Hervey, a New
Orleans native, was present at
all three battles at the fort and
at the capture of *Indianola*.
(Courtesy of Frank Spencer.)

at Opelousas and steadily moving overland toward Alexandria. It was
a well-accepted fact that the "battery at Fort DeRussy cannot stand a
land attack."[11] With the Union army less than fifty miles away, Gérard
issued Special Order No. 201, ordering Lt. William Hervey to "remain
until the fort and public property will be as completely destroyed as
possible."[12] He was to be assisted by Lieutenant Curry and his command of pickets, and as the fort was abandoned, a long whistle blast
from *Grand Duke* signaled Hervey, Curry, and their men to begin the
destruction.

They did their work well, but apparently somewhere along the
chain of command there had been a misunderstanding. According to
the charges at Gérard's court-martial in July, Gérard had been ordered
by Major General Taylor to "evacuate Fort De Russy, and, if possible,
to save all the guns and stores." Gérard, the charges further stated, "did

---

11. E. K. Smith to Cooper, Apr. 23, 1863, *ORA* 15:387.
12. Special Order No. 201, Headquarters, Fort DeRussy, Apr. 24, 1863. Original in
possession of Frank Spencer, Houston, Texas, great-great-grandson of William Hervey.
The original orders have a small sketch of the fort scribbled on the back.

not use proper diligence and obedience to said orders but did destroy a considerable quantity of Government property and stores which it was possible to save, and threw into the river two 32-pounder guns, and endeavored to destroy one other 32-pounder gun by subjecting it to a great heat." Gérard was acquitted at the court-martial.[13] But the 32-pounders lying on the bottom of Red River would set the stage for the second battle at Fort DeRussy.

While the Confederates had been working diligently on improving Fort DeRussy, the Union navy had been doing their best to come up and see how the work was progressing. The gunboats *Arizona*[14] and *Estrella*[15] had come up the Atchafalaya and had joined *Hartford* and *Albatross*[16] at the mouth of Red River. Admiral Farragut, aboard *Hartford*, had heard rumors of the abandonment of Fort DeRussy and on May 3 issued orders to Lt. Cmdr. John Hart, captain of *Albatross*, to make a reconnaissance up the Red with *Estrella* and *Arizona* assisting him. In particular, they were to ascertain—by inquiry and also by observation—whether or not Fort DeRussy really was abandoned.

The three gunboats entered Red River at 9:45 on the morning of May 3, 1863. The first leg of the journey was uneventful. It was quickly found that *Estrella* was by far the slowest of the three boats, and this was going to cause the expedition to take longer than expected. Good progress was made nonetheless, and at noon a skiff was intercepted crossing the river and three prisoners were taken.[17] Near the mouth of Black River, boats were sent ashore to visit the houses at Joffrion's Landing, and Lieutenant Commander Hart was pleased to learn that neither steamboats nor troops had passed that way for some time. By sunset the flotilla had reached Saline Point, a dozen or so miles below Fort DeRussy, and there they tied to trees for the night. Acting Vol. Lt.

---

13. General Orders No. 30, Hdqrs. Trans-Mississippi Department, Shreveport, La., July 18, 1863, *ORA* 22:933–34.

14. *Arizona* was an iron-hulled side-wheel steamer of 950 tons, two hundred feet long by thirty-four feet wide with an eight-foot draft. She was built in 1858–59 at Wilmington, Delaware, by Harlan and Hollingsworth and before the war operated out of New Orleans carrying passengers and cargo along the Gulf and Atlantic Coasts. Silverstone, *Warships*, 69.

15. *Estrella* was a single-screw steamer of 438 tons, 178 feet long by 26 feet wide, with a 6-foot draft. Ibid., 90.

16. *Albatross* was a wooden-hulled, three-masted, single-screw steamer of 378 tons, 158 feet long by 30 feet wide, with a 13-foot draft. Ibid., 87.

17. The prisoners were William Mills, ferry master; James Bunch, Confederate soldier; and James Kayes, farmer. Lt. Cmdr. John Hart to Farragut, May 6, 1863, *ORN* 20:79.

U.S. Gun Boat Albatross. Off Mobile. September 25ᵗ 1863

USS *Albatross*, sketched several months after the Gunboat Fight at Fort DeRussy. (Courtesy of Naval Historical Center.)

Daniel P. Upton, captain of *Arizona,* took the initiative of sending a boat with muffled oars upriver after dark, and two Frenchmen were taken from the first house found and returned to the gunboats. Through an interpreter, the two men freely gave the sailors all the information they had, which was that the fort was being abandoned, the guns were being taken to Alexandria, and no boats had recently passed their houses.

At 5:00 A.M., the fleet got underway once again, *Albatross* leading, followed by *Estrella,* with *Arizona* bringing up the rear. The two Frenchmen were put ashore at their homes, and the fleet continued working its way through the sharp bends in the river. The bottom had changed from soft mud to sand, increasing the chances of grounding on the shallow points and bars. It was nearly 7:00 A.M. when Captain Hart rounded a bend and spotted the first Confederate picket station. But to his surprise, there was no picket manning the post. A pile of pine knots, meant to be lit and send up clouds of black smoke to warn of an approaching danger, stood alone on the river bank. And when a lone figure did appear a short distance away, it turned out to be not a Rebel sentry, but a local man declaring strong Union sentiments and offering assistance. He was taken aboard and put to work assisting the pilot. As the boats continued upstream, the lookout in *Albatross*'s crow's nest reported the smoke of steamboats in the distance, which the recently embarked Union man declared to be the smoke of steamers loading the fort's ironwork for removal, along with the 11-inch gun from *Indianola*. This was an error on the part of the local turncoat that was repeated not only in Captain Hart's official report of the incident but also in nearly every tale of this event that has been published since that time. There was an 11-inch gun at the fort earlier, and it may have been from *Indianola,* but that gun had been ordered to a position upriver in late April. The gun in question was one of the 32-pounders that had been tossed in the river by the overenthusiastic Colonel Gérard.[18]

Captain Hart took this opportunity to prepare for what he hoped would be a quick capture of the steamers at the fort. His men were given breakfast, and the decks were then cleared for action. The crew enthusiastically prepared for the upcoming fight. Hart's orders called for him to "throw a few shells" from a point below the fort to ensure that it was abandoned.[19] But since Hart knew that the fort was not abandoned, he determined that a surprise attack on the steamboats there would be his best option.

At 8:20, *Albatross* passed another abandoned picket station, the pile of pine knots lying solitary on the bank. Once again, no alarm went up. At 8:40, the bend before the fort came into view. The 30-pounder Parrott gun at the bow was carefully aimed, and the broadside guns were made ready to fire as soon as the bend was cleared.

John Kelso, commanding officer of the old Fort Taylor when *Queen of the West* was captured, had come back to the fort on the night of May 1. He had been sent down from Alexandria aboard *Grand Duke* to recover the guns and other salvageable material that had been thrown in the river during the panicked "skedaddle" of late April. Early on the morning of May 4, the work was being completed. One of the submerged 32-pounders was just being loaded onto a barge with the rest of the recovered material when pickets under the command of Lt. H. A. Frederic reported the approach of Union gunboats. Apparently the picket stations had not been as abandoned as Captain Hart had thought. Kelso immediately ordered *Countess,*[20] Capt.

18. Hart to Farragut, May 6, 1863, *ORN* 20:80; Capt. John Kelso to Surget, May 13, 1863, *ORN* 20:91; E. K. Smith to Cooper, Apr. 23, 1863, *ORA* 15:387.
19. Farragut to Hart, May 3, 1863, *ORN* 20:74.
20. *Countess* was a side-wheel packet boat of 198 tons built in Cincinnati in 1860, 150 feet long by 30 feet wide, with a draft of 4 feet 8 inches. She was incorrectly reported as burned to prevent capture by the Union navy on the falls at Alexandria in March 1864. Silverstone, *Warships,* 246; Way, *Way's Packet Directory,* 113; Phelps to Porter, Mar. 16, 1864, *ORN* 26:30–31.

George Hite commanding, to take the barge in tow and move it up to Alexandria. *Grand Duke,* with the Crescent Artillery aboard, and *Cotton* (the recently renamed *Mary T*), with the St. Martin Rangers under Capt. Edward T. King aboard, prepared for the approaching gunboats. Captain Kelso had successfully defended this site in February and was more than ready to do it again. Captain King was a cantankerous individual who did not know the meaning of the word "quit" and possessed more than his share of combat experience.[21] Both the Crescent Artillery and St. Martin Rangers were combat veterans. Captain Hart, far from making a surprise attack on unsuspecting and undefended Confederate steamboats, was about to get a surprise himself. *Grand Duke* and *Cotton* were no simple transports. They were gunboats in their own right, well armed and manned by determined men. The second Battle of Fort DeRussy was about to begin.

As *Albatross* rounded the bend, Captain Hart took in the situation at a glance. The two Confederate steamers were moored to the earthworks, their hulls below the high bank. Both vessels were pointed downstream, facing directly into the broadside of *Albatross,* at a distance of only five hundred yards. The raft of logs, anchored to trees on both banks, separated the Rebel boats from Hart's fleet. And the Southerners were waiting for them.

On the south bank of the river, thirty to forty Confederate cavalrymen opened fire with carbines from behind the levee. Two shells were fired from the Southern gunboats before *Albatross* responded. Her starboard beam to the Rebels, *Albatross* let go with a five-gun salvo—the 30-pounder Parrott on the forecastle, three 32-pounder broadside guns, and the rifled 12-pounder Dahlgren howitzer on the quarter. The Confederate boats replied in kind. The area erupted in fire and smoke as the three gunboats slugged it out. As Captain Hart described the situation, "It [the firing] was kept up on both sides vigorously until a dense cloud of smoke gathered between us; when it cleared away we went at it again. The enemy . . . sent their shot and grape thick and fast; another cloud of smoke obscured us, and we took advantage of the occasion to turn our

21. Capt. Edward T. King had served aboard the first *Cotton* (*J. A. Cotten*) in severe fighting on Bayou Teche in late 1862 and early 1863. King's niece, Grace King, would be a prominent figure in Southern literary circles in later years. Grace's Uncle Edward was an influential figure in her life. (I will never forget the look of horror that crossed the face of a Louisiana State University English professor when it was suggested that Grace King's main claim to fame is that a girls' dormitory at LSU is named after her.)

This unsigned sketch of the Gunboat Fight of May 4, 1863, was done by someone who was obviously on the scene. The details on the boats are too accurate to be happenstance. Note the long, straight stretch of river that gunboats would have to traverse into the guns of the Water Battery. The artist was probably Helmuth Holtz, a sailor aboard *Estrella* who had sent earlier drawings to *Harper's Weekly*. The original pencil sketch now hangs in the Spring Street Historical Museum in Shreveport. (Permission to publish from Spring Street Historical Museum, Shreveport, Louisiana.)

steamer so as to present the port battery to the enemy."[22] As *Albatross* was turning, a 32-pounder ball crashed through her wheelhouse, carrying away the wheel and killing Seaman John Brown and Pilot Isaac B. Hamilton, a Red River pilot from New Orleans who was on loan to *Albatross* from *Hartford*.[23] Archibald Merritt, *Albatross*'s regular pilot, was thrown across the room by the same shot and had both hands ripped by splinters from the shattered wheel. Although urged repeatedly to report to the ship's surgeon, Merritt remained at his post, giving directions and advice through the remainder of the action. The crew of the *Albatross* now needed all the expert advice they could get, as the vessel was in a critical situation; she could not be steered from the wheelhouse and would soon drift into the bank of the narrow river unless she could be steered manually by block and tackles set up on the exposed deck. Captain Hart described the situation:

> Scarcely a moment was to be lost. The relieving tackles were manned and the executive officer, Mr. DuBois, was ready for the emergency. There was no pausing or wavering on his part: had there been it might have resulted in precisely such a catastrophe as happened to the *Queen of the West* at this same place.
>
> The current of the river and the eddies were working at cross purposes, and it seemed that the steamer for awhile could not be managed. Our bows were aground and then our stern, as we went ahead or backed, and it required the nicest management and undivided attention. No one but a cool man could have been able to accomplish what was desired, and Mr. Dubois did all that was required: he received prompt attention both from those in charge of the engine and those in charge of the helm.
>
> The cavalry on shore was making efforts to pick off our men at the relieving tackles, and the solid shot and grape began to tell seriously upon our hull.[24]

Quartermaster James Brown "stood on the gun platform of the quarterdeck, exposing himself to a close fire of musketry from the

---

22. Hart to Farragut, May 6, 1863, *ORN* 20:81.

23. Admiral Farragut much regretted the death of Hamilton, who had just become a pilot and was the sole support of his sisters and widowed mother in New Orleans. Farragut to Welles, May 6, 1863, *ORN* 20:78. Hamilton was buried at Acklen's plantation, across the Mississippi from the mouth of Red River. After the war his body was moved to the Natchez, Mississippi, National Cemetery (section 5, plot 81).

24. Hart to Farragut, May 6, 1863, *ORN* 20:81.

shore, and rendered invaluable assistance by his expert management of the relieving tackles in extricating the vessel from a perilous position." For his actions that day, the thirty-seven-year-old New Yorker would be awarded a Medal of Honor.[25]

Captain Hart was having serious problems with his own boat, not to mention the two Confederate boats to his front, but he was perhaps even more infuriated with the actions of *Estrella* and *Arizona*. They were within hailing distance, and Hart repeatedly called them to come forward to his aid. They did not. Fearing that his voice could not be heard, he had Mr. DuBois hail them with his speaking trumpet (essentially a megaphone) until the trumpet was knocked from his hands by a Minié ball, after which DuBois continued to call for them to come up. But the two boats never approached, seemingly satisfied to lay back and throw an occasional shell over the narrow neck of land between them and the two Rebel gunboats.

What Hart did not realize (as he was preoccupied at the time) was that his first maneuvering had involved a backing of his wheels, which had in turn caused *Estrella* to also begin backing. *Estrella,* in addition to being slow, had a bent rudder and bad steering chains and was very difficult to steer. In backing, she was caught by the current and ended up very nearly across the channel. This in turn caused *Arizona* to have to back off. By the time *Arizona* was able to get past *Estrella,* and *Estrella* was able to get straightened out, the battle was over. At their courts-martial in July, in which Lt. Cmdr. Augustus P. Cooke and Acting Lt. Daniel P. Upton, captains of *Estrella* and *Arizona*, respectively, were charged with keeping out of danger and failure to engage the enemy, both men argued that with *Albatross* bouncing from bank to bank, as she admittedly was, there was no way that they could come forward without ramming their own flagship. The argument was effective, as both men were acquitted of all charges and returned to the command of their boats.[26]

While *Albatross*'s steering and engine crews were busy trying to extract her from her precarious position, her gun crews were also busy fighting a battle. Twenty minutes into the fight, a shot from *Albatross*'s bow Parrott gun (aimed by Acting Master George Mundy) severed *Cotton*'s steam pipe, disabling her engines and scalding the face and

25. Medal of Honor citation, Quartermaster James Brown, USN.
26. General court-martial transcripts of Lt. Cmdr. Augustus Cooke and Daniel P. Upton, GCM 3288 and 3289, Microfilm Roll 110, Vol. 101, RG125, NA.

neck of engineer Emile Dugas. *Cotton's* pilot, William Turner, was wounded in his shoulder and arm. Shortly after that, *Grand Duke* had all her steering apparatus shot away, and she was soon shot up to the point that "all the mechanical contrivances by which communication is conveyed from one part of the boat to another, bell ropes, speaking tubes, etc., were shot to pieces. Captain [J. M.] White reported . . . that he thought his boat unmanageable. The fight continued, however, with unabated energy."[27] With *Grand Duke* lying helpless in the river, a suggestion was twice made by "one having authority" that the boat run up the white flag. Lt. Thomas Handy, one of the heroes of the *Indianola* affair, was infuriated. "Not while there is a man to pull a lanyard," he angrily replied.[28] *Grand Duke* fought on.

A shell exploding on the deck of *Cotton* threw Pvt. Thomas Burns and Pvt. John O'Quinn overboard, drowning them. Aboard *Grand Duke,* a tragic "friendly fire" accident was responsible for most of the casualties. The gun crew of the 32-pounder aboard that boat was blown up when the private hauling cartridges to the gun[29] brought two cartridges in one load, handed one cartridge to the gunner and dropped the other underneath the burning fuse which was being used to fire the cannon. The results of that explosion, said Cpl. John Muller, was that "everyone of that gun's crew was badly blown up [and] wounded for life." Pvt. James Wallace, one of that crew, was badly burned, lost the use of his hands for a long period, and lost his left eye.[30]

Albatross was giving the Confederate boats a severe drubbing, but she was receiving one as well. Captain Hart's after-action report describes the situation aboard:

> We were hit repeatedly, a second shot [the first hitting the wheel-
> house] passing under the wheelhouse, tearing the decks; a shot passed

27. Hart to Farragut, May 6, 1863, *ORN* 20:82; "Fort De Russy, May 4, 1863, Consolidated Report," Confederate States Army Casualties: Lists and Narrative Reports, 1862–1865, War Department Collection of Confederate Records, Microfilm 836, Reel 2, RG 109, NA; Kelso to Surget, May 13, 1863, *ORN* 20:91.

28. "Eloquent Tribute of Rev. Dr. Markham," obituary of Col. Thos. H. Handy, unknown (New Orleans?) newspaper, July 26, 1893, in Handy family scrapbook.

29. Pvt. Charles W. Heno, Crescent Artillery.

30. Thomas Burns, Microfilm Reel 1, Claim 67, Act 116; John O'Quinn, Microfilm Reel 1, Claim 44, Act 116; James Wallace, Microfilm Reel 1, Claim 426, Act 96; and John Muller, Microfilm Reel 2, Claim 720, Act 116, Confederate Proofs and Land Warrants, Louisiana State Archives, Baton Rouge. Thomas Burns's widow claimed that he was killed in the fight with "the Yankee Gun Boat *Albert Ross.*"

through the hull near the water line; another passed clean through both sides and just grazed the steam drum; another one went through the smokestack. The mainmast was cut half in two close to the deck; the foremast was hit about 15 feet from the deck; another shot cut the foreyard in two, which was lashed to the rail; the same shot in its flight tore up the deck and scattered splinters in every direction. We were hulled eleven times, and serious damage was done to our rigging and spars. We were forty minutes in action, fighting at a distance of not over 500 yards, and during that time we fired fourteen broadsides that were well directed, and while turning our head around so as to head downstream we used our muskets and rifles.[31]

In the midst of all the smoke and fury of battle, Captain Kelso was astonished, as well as outraged, to see an unexpected "reinforcement" coming downriver to his aid. The barge with the salvaged 32-pounder had broken loose (or been cut loose) from *Countess* and was floating into battle on the current. It lodged against the raft, a tempting prize for whoever would win the fight.[32]

The battle lasted for about forty minutes, by which time all parties were feeling used up. By the time *Albatross* managed to get turned around, her captain was more than ready to break off contact with the two Southern gunboats:

The *Albatross* went into the action all alone; two steamers were before her guns with a greater number of guns than she carried; on the upper decks of those steamers were sharpshooters, ensconced behind large square timbers and cotton bales, and, besides, there was a force of cavalry on shore that was constantly firing upon the steamer.

I could not require my brave crew to do any more than they had done, and I withdrew from my precarious position as deliberately as I had entered it, firing as I went, having done all that lay in my power to disable the enemy; but they were behind earthworks, cotton, and heavy pieces of timber, and I was in a thin, frail steamer, whose sides a Minié ball could easily penetrate.[33]

31. Hart to Farragut, May 6, 1863, *ORN* 20:81.
32. Lieutenant Commander Hart said that the barge with the gun was tied to one of the two steamboats he saw when he rounded the bend. Captain Kelso said that he had sent *Countess* and the barge on their way ten minutes before the shooting started. As Hart never mentions seeing *Countess* or any other third boat, I think that Kelso's statement is the more accurate of the two, and that Hart saw the barge and gun when it returned.
33. Hart to Farragut, May 6, 1863, *ORN* 20:82.

As *Albatross* steamed downstream, *Arizona* hailed her, requesting permission to go into action against the Rebel boats. Hart, infuriated at their apparent cowardice a short while earlier, ordered both *Arizona* and *Estrella* to follow him downstream.

Back at the fort, the victors were not doing well. *Albatross* had gotten off forty-two shots in the course of the battle, and many of them had found targets. Both *Cotton* and *Grand Duke* were crippled. *Cotton* was without steam and in an unrepairable condition. *Grand Duke* was unsteerable, having been shot to pieces and set on fire five times during the engagement. Kelso had seen *Albatross* withdraw "apparently uninjured" and was sure that the Union boats were just dropping down a short way to gain a better position to fire on his unprotected flank. A quick examination of *Grand Duke* showed that by passing the word from man to man, she could be "handled exclusively through the engines." Feeling that if they remained at their present position "our destruction would be probable," Kelso moved *Grand Duke* up the river a short distance and made hasty repairs. He then returned to the fort. Taking *Cotton* and the barge in tow, *Grand Duke* and company limped slowly upriver. A short way above the fort they met *Countess,* which relieved them of the errant barge. Fort DeRussy was now truly abandoned.[34]

In the second Battle of Fort DeRussy, the Union navy suffered two men killed, one man (Seaman George Fife) seriously wounded in the thigh by a cannon shot, three men slightly wounded, and one gunboat badly torn up. Confederate forces lost two men killed, had one officer and sixteen men wounded to varying degrees, and had two gunboats badly torn up. Thomas Burns and John O'Quinn became the first Confederate soldiers to die in action at Fort DeRussy. The battle ended in a victory for the Confederates, although at the time, both sides thought they had been whipped.

There is no doubt but that Lieutenant Commander Hart was seething as he headed *Albatross* back down the river. He had not wanted to abandon the fight, but he feared that he would be deserted by his two consorts had *Albatross* become disabled.[35] The sting of defeat is painful, but to add to that the feeling of betrayal by his fellow naval officers must have been bitter indeed. Cooke and Upton, tailing along in *Estrella* and *Arizona,* must have been equally angry. They knew by

34. Kelso to Surget, May 13, 1863, *ORN* 20:91.
35. Theodore DuBois testimony, general court-martial transcript, Augustus P. Cooke.

now that Hart thought them to be cowards, and they were equally sure that they had been denied the opportunity to engage the enemy and made to look like cowards because of poor prior planning and clumsy maneuvering on the part of Hart, the expedition leader. Hart felt that his mission had failed because of the cowardice and/or ineptitude of Cooke and Upton. Cooke and Upton felt, on the other hand, that they were going to be used as scapegoats to cover Hart's self-induced failure. The situation was not conducive to good morale.

A short-term solution to the problem presented itself later that same evening. As the three boats steamed down toward the mouth of the Red, they met reinforcements in the form of a portion of the fleet of Adm. David Porter, with Porter himself in command. The fleet consisted of three ironclads, *Benton, Lafayette,* and *Pittsburg;* the river gunboat *General Price;* the ram *Switzerland;* and the tug *Ivy* on their way up the river to cooperate with General Banks in the capture of Alexandria. After a brief consultation, Admiral Porter decided that *Estrella* and *Arizona* would continue upriver with him and *Albatross* would return to the mouth of the river and rejoin Admiral Farragut. This decision was based on the fact that *Arizona* and *Estrella* were still in fighting trim and could therefore be of use to Porter, while *Albatross* had wounded aboard and was in need of repair. *Albatross* also had a deeper draft than any of the other vessels and would be more likely to run aground on the upper reaches of the Red. Whatever the reasons, the departure of *Albatross* was probably satisfactory to all three of the captains involved. *Albatross* continued downstream. John Hart would shortly forget about Fort DeRussy altogether, as on the night of June 11, while "suffering from an attack of temporary mental aberration caused by remittent fever," he put a pistol to his head and blew his brains out.[36]

---

36. *Albatross* was involved in the siege of Port Hudson at the time. Hart was buried at Grace Episcopal Church, St. Francisville, Louisiana. David C. Edmonds, ed., *The Guns of Port Hudson: The Investment, Siege, and Reduction* (Lafayette, La.: Acadiana Press, 1984), 2:178, 183. Hart's Masonic funeral, attended by both Union and Confederate officers, is celebrated to this day in St. Francisville in an annual "The Day the War Stopped" commemoration. Some historians believe that this celebration is a good example of "Tourism History."

Chapter 5

All Good Things Must End

The eight boats with Admiral Porter continued on their way up the Red River. On the evening of May 5, they arrived at Fort DeRussy prepared for a fight, but this time the fort was deserted. The raft across the river was rammed several times on one end by *General Price*, creating a hole that allowed passage of the other boats. Seamen from *Benton* were put to work dismantling the raft, but finding that they could not do any significant damage to it, they returned to the boat. The fleet spent the night moored to the bank at the fort. Fort DeRussy, now in Union hands, was closely examined that night by Porter, who determined that it would take too much time to destroy it. Early on the morning of May 6, the Union fleet set off up the river, but not before *Benton* put in some bow gun target practice on the Water Battery casemates. Otherwise, the fort was left undamaged.[1]

The fort would not remain undamaged for long. Porter's fleet arrived at Alexandria on the morning of May 7 and took possession of the city. When General Banks arrived with his army the following morning, Porter turned the city over to Banks, and on May 9, Porter was back at Fort DeRussy with his flagship *Benton*. Porter had been in a hurry to get to Alexandria on his way upriver, but now he had time. Immediately upon *Benton*'s arrival at the landing, working parties were sent out to demolish whatever could be destroyed in the fort. While marines guarded them, one party set fire to one of the casemates on the riverbank, while another party under Gunner Willets was engaged in blowing up the raft. The work continued on the next day. By then Master's Mate O'Grady had managed to round up a crew of contrabands from the neighborhood, and they were helping with the destruction of the fort. Gunner Willets and a crew of four men had the task of blowing up the 32-pounder that remained at the fort, in all probability the gun that Gérard had tried to

---

1. Porter to Welles, May 7, 1863, *ORN* 24:645; deck log, USS *Benton*, RG 24, NA.

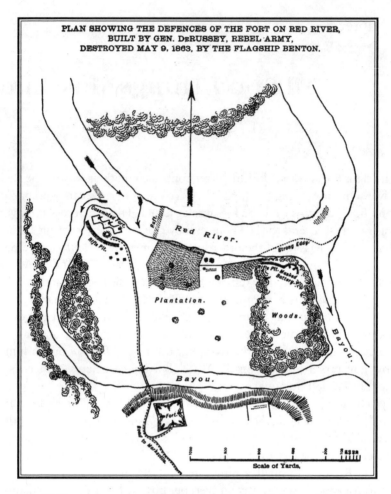

This 1863 map from the *Official Records of the Union and Confeder-ate Navies* (vol. 24) has the Hill Fort seriously out of position. It was west, not south, of the Water Battery.

destroy "by subjecting it to great heat." Willets was more successful. Master's Mate Zimmerman was in charge of a cutter throwing railroad iron (from the fort's armor plating) into the river, and Master's Mate Dumont's six-man crew was recovering chain from the raft.[2]

The destruction of the raft allowed Porter the opportunity to invent one of his frequent self-aggrandizements. The raft, he said in a report to

2. Deck log, USS *Benton* (also abstracted in *ORN* 24:684–85).

Secretary of the Navy Gideon Welles, he had "blown up, sawed in two, and presented to the poor of the neighborhood." What a charitable man, to present "the poor" with a river full of logs! But the truth is even more outrageous. Porter had actually given the raft to "a party, who were to have it on the condition that they sawed it in two and towed it below Black River." In short, Porter did not "give" anybody anything. He had hired men to clean up the river, saving his men from having to do the job themselves. And he had paid them with firewood, which they would no doubt either sell back to the U.S. Navy, or—should the U.S. Navy leave the river—to the Confederates. On May 17, Porter sent a letter from north of Vicksburg to Capt. Henry Walke of *Lafayette,* who had been left in charge of the naval forces in Red River. Walke was to make sure that the raft had been moved.[3] It is more than a little ironic that on that same date, in General Order No. 52, Admiral Porter ordered that "that class of persons who are in the habit of stating exaggerated accounts of anything should be excluded from the vessels of the squadron."[4]

Benton, with the philanthropic Porter aboard, left DeRussy on May 11. The Water Battery casemates were a shambles, totally demolished. The abandoned 32-pounder had been burst, gun carriages and casemates were burnt, and all other removable items of use to the Rebels had been hauled off, destroyed, or thrown in the river. Even Colonel Gérard's masked battery six hundred yards down the river was destroyed. The main fort on the hill, however, had not been touched. It would take two to three weeks to pull it to pieces, Porter determined, and he did not have the powder to spare to blow it up. But he was sure that his remaining vessels in the river would "work at it occasionally" and it would "soon be destroyed."[5]

But Fort DeRussy would not soon be destroyed. General Banks's northward movement stalled in Alexandria, and he was soon on his way south and east to besiege Port Hudson. The departure of the army from central Louisiana also resulted in the departure of the navy. By May 20, the Red River at Barbin's Landing had been vacated. Union gunboats would continue to come up the lower Red in June and July and would

---

3. Porter to Welles, May 13, 1863, *ORN* 24:646; Porter to Walke, May 17, 1863, *ORN* 24:652.

4. General Order No. 52, May 17, 1863, *ORN* 24:678. Ironically, this was just one day after Porter had written a friend that "had I been general and admiral at the same time I could have entered Vicksburg three months ago." Porter to Foote, *ORN* 24:678.

5. Porter to Welles, May 13, 1863, *ORN* 24:646.

Although Adm. David
Dixon Porter was an
interesting writer, his
tales frequently wan-
dered from the facts.
Histories based on
Porter's documentation
should be viewed with
skepticism. (Courtesy
Fort DeRussy State
Historic Site.)

even ascend up the Black. But gunboats would not approach Fort
DeRussy again in 1863. As the Union army moved from Alexandria
to Simmesport, on its way to Port Hudson, the Confederates followed
closely behind. By the end of May, Fort DeRussy was once again in Confederate hands.

We cannot leave the 1863 destruction of Fort DeRussy without one
last look at the raft. It seems that "the poor of the neighborhood" never
did get their firewood, nor did the entrepreneurial party who would have
hauled it below Black River. On the morning of May 20, *General Price*
arrived at the Atchafalaya River with the raft in tow, to enable "the
troops [Banks's men, now at Simmesport] to cross their artillery and
baggage trains." Banks's army did cross the Atchafalaya at Simmesport
during that period on a pontoon bridge made from nine steamboats with
their gangplanks in line, as well as on other steamers acting as ferries.
There is no account of anyone crossing either artillery or baggage wag-

ons on a raft of logs. And with the departure of the army for Port Hudson, the Fort DeRussy Raft of 1863 disappears from recorded history.[6]

For all his bluster, Porter can be an entertaining fellow, provided one is careful to sort through his tales for the occasional kernel of truth. In his postwar reminiscences, we get another sample typical of the admiral's sea stories:

> Farragut had cautioned me against a ram said to be building up Red River. After finishing with Fort De Russy I began to inquire about the ram, for I did not desire to suddenly encounter such an enemy while turning a bend in the river, and perhaps lose one or more of my vessels.
>
> I entered into conversation with a man whom we met near Fort De Russy, and said to him, "Well, stranger, I hear you have a Confederate ram up here somewhere. Whereabouts is she?"
>
> "Lemme think," said the native, scratching his head while going through the thinking process. "Yes, thar is a ram 'bout eight miles above hyar."
>
> "Is it a powerful one?" I inquired.
>
> "Wall, I reckon you'd think so ef you seen it; it's the allfiredest strong thing ever I seen, an' I guess at buttin' it ud knock them ar bows of yourn into smithereens."
>
> "How large is it?" I asked.
>
> "Wall, it's 'bout the biggest thing I ever seen."
>
> "Tell me all about it," I said, for I was beginning to get interested.
>
> "Wall, Gin'ral," said the man, "that's easier said than done. It's an allfired buster, an' kin beat all creation at buttin'. That's all I knows about it. I seen it on Mr. Whitler's place, as I tole yer, eight miles above hyar; an' one day, w'en I was up thar, whar thar war a bull weighin' twenty-eight hunder, an' as soon as the bull seen the ram he 'gan to paw the airth an' throwed up his tail, an' the ram put down his head an' the bull bellered, an' they went slap dash at each other, an' ef that ram didn't knock daylights out o' that bull, and knock his tail out by the roots, and his horns off, and lay him out as flat as a pancake, I'm a liar!"
>
> "But," said I, "I am asking you about a Confederate ram—a vessel covered with iron."
>
> "Wall, Gin'ral," said the man, "I don't know nothin' 'bout any Confed'rit ram, but I'm sure the one I seen could knock the bows of

6. Selim E. Woodworth to Porter, May 22, 1863, *ORN* 25:126; Richard B. Irwin, *History of the Nineteenth Army Corps* (1892; reprint, Baton Rouge, La.: Elliott's Book Shop Press, 1985), 153, 346–47.

them ar turtles ov yourn afore you could wink, an' I reckon he mus'
be a Confed'rit ram, seein' he war born in these parts."

Any apprehensions I might have had in regard to a Confederate
ram were put at rest, and I made no more inquiries.

I was afterward informed that this simple native whom I had
questioned was a Confederate officer in disguise, who regaled
his friends with the story of how he had beguiled the Yankees.
However, he was entirely welcome to his little joke.[7]

7. Porter, *Incidents and Anecdotes*, 187–88.

Chapter 6

Rebuilding Gibraltar

A blank exists in the history of Fort DeRussy from early summer to fall 1863. There is a logical explanation for this—nothing happened. While it would seem like the Confederates would have started repairs and improvements during this period, they did not. The Union navy was prohibited from approaching the fort during the summer due to low water, but the Union army was active in the area throughout the summer and into the fall. Fort Beauregard, on the Black River at Harrisonburg just forty-two miles north of DeRussy, was temporarily occupied by Union soldiers in early September. From the south, Union forces approached as close as the Opelousas-Washington area, forty-five miles away, and remained there through most of October. The people were disheartened and General Taylor encouraged the planters to move their slaves from the threatened regions, many going to Texas.

Taylor kept up a correspondence with the planter committees of the area and asked that one thousand slaves be held in readiness for whenever they were called. The planters were agreeable to this arrangement but pointed out that it would be difficult. After the Confederate victory at the Battle of Bourbeau on November 3, Taylor decided that it was safe to start work on the Red River defenses again. He called for his work crews but was only able to get half of his expected laborers, and that after serious delay and with an even more serious lack of tools. When Lt. E. H. Wells made a scouting trip through Avoyelles Parish in mid-October 1863, he described Fort DeRussy as "now a ruin."[1]

Had Brig. Gen. William R. Boggs, chief of staff to E. Kirby Smith, had his way, Fort DeRussy would have remained a ruins. Boggs strongly supported defending the lower Red by building a fort at the mouth of

1. Taylor to Brig. Gen. William R. Boggs, Jan. 19, 1864, *ORA* 34, pt. 2, 890–92; E. H. Wells to Major General Walker, Oct. 16, 1863, John G. Walker Papers, Southern Historical Collection, Manuscripts Department, Wilson Library, Univ. of North Carolina, Chapel Hill (hereafter cited as Walker Papers).

Black River. If one only examines a map, this proposal appears to be a good idea. One fort could defend both the Red and Black Rivers, and steamboats could travel freely from one river into the other. But this option had been considered by Taylor and DeRussy in late 1862, and their opinion at that time was that a fort at that site was impractical and the Red and Black Rivers would have to be defended separately.[2] The land at the mouth of Black River was kitchen-table flat and was inundated in high-water years. Boggs apparently refused to see these limitations and pushed for the construction of "an inclosed work of a diamond shape (conforming to the locality), with four bastions; the parapet should be at least 40 feet thick and 12 feet high, with a wide, deep ditch all around. Four or five chains of railroad iron under the guns of the work would be of great advantage. I do not think that there is any other point on the river that can be so easily fortified after a foothold is made, that can be as easily defended, or offers so many advantages."[3]

Confederate troops were back in the Avoyelles Parish area in numbers in late September, October, and November 1863 but were usually on the move. Soldiers were in constant motion, bouncing from Evergreen in central Avoyelles Parish to Big Cane in northern St. Landry Parish, to Morgan's Ferry on the Atchafalaya (near present-day Melville), back to Evergreen, then Simmesport, then back to Evergreen again. But by late November, the Union forces in Louisiana had settled down for the winter, and the Southern forces, no longer having to respond to Union threats, did the same.

By early December 1863, General Boggs's recommendations had been overruled and Fort DeRussy was once again an active Confederate fort. The fort was garrisoned by members of Maj. Gen. John G. Walker's Texas Division. Walker's "Greyhounds" were campaign- and battle-hardened veterans who had spent the summer and fall of 1863 marching all over northern and central Louisiana.[4] The division was divided into three brigades. First Brigade, under the command of Brig. Gen. James M. Hawes, consisted of the 13th Texas Dismounted Cavalry, the 12th, 18th, and 22nd Texas Infantry Regiments, and Haldeman's Battery of light

2. Taylor to Cooper, Nov. 1, 1862, *ORA* 15:877.
3. Boggs to Taylor, Oct. 15, 1863, *ORA* 26, pt. 2, 322–323; Boggs to Taylor, Oct. 19, 1863, *ORA* 26, pt. 2, 338; Smith to Taylor, Oct. 20, 1863, *ORA* 26, pt. 2, 341–342; S. S. Anderson to Maj. Henry T. Douglas, Oct. 31, 1863, *ORA* 26, pt. 2, 375.
4. Although Capt. Elijah Petty wrote to his daughter that "Walker's Division has travelled more and fought less than any troops in the Confederacy." Norman D. Brown, *Journey to Pleasant Hill: The Civil War Letters of Captain Elijah Petty, Walker's Texas Division, CSA* (San Antonio: Univ. of Texas Institute of Texan Cultures, 1982), 290.

artillery. Second Brigade, under Col. Horace Randal and consisting of the 28th Texas Dismounted Cavalry, the 11th and 14th Texas Infantry, Gould's Battalion, and Daniel's Battery of light artillery, was spread out in campsites throughout the Marksville–Fort DeRussy area. Third Brigade, under the command of Brig. Gen. William R. "Dirty Shirt" Scurry and consisting of the 16th Texas Dismounted Cavalry, the 16th, 17th, and 19th Texas Infantry, and Edgar's Battery of light artillery, would winter near Simmesport and keep an eye on the Atchafalaya River.[5]

Wintering at Fort DeRussy was a welcome respite after the marching and fighting of 1863. Walker's Division began a policy of issuing furloughs, beginning with married men, some of whom had not seen their families since the start of the war. In at least one case, the furlough recipient found an unpleasant surprise waiting for him upon his return. Col. Edward Clark, former governor of Texas and commander of the 14th Texas, was one of the first to leave on furlough. While Clark was gone, his regiment was picked to garrison the fort, and Lt. Col. William Byrd—second in command of the 14th Texas and acting commander in Clark's absence—was placed in command of Fort DeRussy. On his return, Clark resumed command of his regiment, but Byrd kept his position as post commander. This put Colonel Clark in the unnatural and totally unacceptable position of serving under his own junior officer. Of course, Clark refused to submit to Byrd's orders, and in order to settle the situation, the 14th Texas was relieved as the garrison unit and one company was assigned from each regiment of the division to serve at the fort. This consolidated regiment was the core of the fort's garrison, along with a few additional Louisiana units later on.[6]

The lottery system of determining furloughs was probably the only fair way to operate such a program, although some of the bachelors in the division no doubt felt cheated. Even the married men were not completely thrilled. As Pvt. John Simmons, 22nd Texas Infantry, wrote his wife, "If they keep up this system of furlough, the married men will all get home by the last of September."[7] With furloughs so desirable, and no immediate action by the Yankees expected, General Walker devised

5. The command of Hawes's brigade would be turned over to Brig. Gen. Thomas N. Waul in late February 1864.

6. John C. Porter, "Life of John C. Porter and Sketch of His Experiences in the Civil War," Eighteenth Texas Infantry File, Confederate Research Center, Hill College, Hillsboro, Tex., 26–27 (hereafter cited as John Porter memoir).

7. Simmons to Dear Nancy and children, Jan. 22, 1864, in Jon Harrison, ed., "The Confederate Letters of John Simmons," *Chronicles of Smith County, Texas* 14, no. 1 (Summer 1975): 25–40, 38–39 (hereafter cited as Simmons Letters).

another method by which a soldier could get a furlough. In mid-January it was announced that any soldier who could procure a new enlistee for the division would get a sixty-day leave. Many a letter soon arrived in Texas pointing out that various nephews and neighbors would soon be eligible for conscription[8] and encouraging them to make their way over to Marksville and enlist before that happened. Typical is the plaintive request of Private Simmons: "Nancy, if your brother Willie has to go in the army, I wish he would come here to me, for I don't think he can go to a better place in the army—and by his coming here I could get a furlough of sixty days as soon as he comes. Nancy, if you can get anyone to come here and join our company, I can get a furlough of sixty days. I would be willing to pay them something."[9] Whether or not it was a letter of this type that brought young Andrew Green to Fort DeRussy to enlist in Company H of the 18th Texas, we will never know. But he did join that unit in late February 1864, while that company was serving as part of the garrison regiment at the fort.

Some of the men at the fort were a little too anxious for their furloughs. There were some desertions during that winter, both by men just picking up and leaving and by men who obtained furloughs and refused to return until brought back under guard. In a January 21 letter to his wife, Jonathan Knight informed her that "one of them will be shot as soon as he is court marshell[.] One of Randle's Brigade will be shot tomorrow for the same crime."[10]

A wintering army has several basic needs. Food and water are essential, of course, but those things are essential throughout the year. One thing that the Walker's Greyhounds had not needed—or at least had not had—that they now considered necessary was decent shelter. Tents were in short supply, and in the rain, snow, and ice of the coldest winter in forty-two years, tents, in any case, were not acceptable. Scurry's Brigade, down on the Atchafalaya, moved into the abandoned slave quarters on the Norwood and Smith plantations.[11] The two brigades

    8. The soldiers were not always in favor of conscription. After hearing a rumor that everyone between the ages of sixteen and sixty would be conscripted, Jonathan Knight wrote to his family on January 11 to "tell Lafayett I say for him to stay under 16 as long as he can." However, in the same letter he encouraged Ben "to come" and join up so that Jonathan could get his furlough. Knight to Dear Wife and Child, Jan. 11, 1864, Jonathan T. Knight Letters, Gary Canada Collection, Keller, Tex. (hereafter cited as Knight Letters).
    9. Simmons to My dear Nancy, Feb. 25, 1864, Simmons Letters.
    10. Knight to Dear Wife and Child, Jan. 21, 1864, Knight Letters.
    11. Most of the original inhabitants of these dwellings had left when the Union army passed through these plantations in May on the way from Alexandria to Port Hudson.

wintering near the fort were not as fortunate. They had to build their own shanties, which was not too difficult as there was plenty of wood available. These homemade buildings were probably not as winter-proof · as the slave quarters, but given the nature of slave quarters, they were probably not much worse, either. In a letter to his wife on January 8, 1864, Capt. Theophilus Perry complained that the ground had been frozen since Christmas and that "we are making little board huts and shelters to live in." On January 29 he gave her a more complete description of his new home, "a little shanty made of slabs and a great big chimney filling up one end of it. The regiment [28th Texas Dismounted Cavalry] has built good houses . . . about two miles from Marksville and two from Fort DeRussy." Hutton's Artillery returned to Fort DeRussy on Tuesday, January 26, and began building shelters the next day, and on Sunday Sgt. John Murray announced to his diary that his "clapboards" had all been "rived" and that he was now the proud owner of a log shanty ten feet wide by twenty feet long by twelve feet high.[12]

The soldiers of the consolidated garrison regiment had the dubious honor of having to build two sets of winter quarters. The Clark-Byrd showdown did not take place until late January, and the various companies chosen to garrison the fort to replace the 14th Texas had already built shelters with their respective regiments. They were not happy about having to move and rebuild, being taken "out of our winter quarters, after a stay of not more than two weeks, in the dead of winter, on account of the contrariness of one or two individuals." Be it ever so humble, there's no place like home. Tom Fullilove, an overseer of slaves at the fort, also had to make a move when his job moved him from the fort to the raft that was being built downriver. Like the Texans, he was not happy at having to leave "a domicile which he said was comparatively comfortable—viz, a platform of rough boards, 7 ft. x 4 ft. on 2 ft. blocks which kept him off the wet ground—over this floor a roof was made of 3 poles on each side stuck in the mud, & meeting on top. A blanket on either side made the sides of the tent & into this hut he & another overseer, Capt. Lacy—crawled side by side thankful for shelter."[13]

12. Theophilus Perry Letters, Presley Carter Persons Papers, Duke Univ. Library, Durham, N.C. (hereafter cited as Perry Letters) (also in M. Jane Johansson, *Widows by the Thousand: The Civil War Letters of Theophilus and Harriet Perry, 1862–1864* [Fayetteville: Univ. of Arkansas Press, 2000]); John C. Murray diary, Collection 524, No. 52, Howard-Tilton Memorial Library, Tulane Univ., New Orleans (hereafter cited as Murray diary).

13. John Porter memoir, 26; Mrs. Thomas Pope Fullilove Journal, typescript by Jane Fullilove Mason from the original manuscript, 1982.

The health of the troops at Fort DeRussy that winter was surprisingly good. During the winter of 1862–63, Walker's Division was quartered at Camp Nelson, Arkansas, and the fatality rate from disease that season had been horrendous. But in spite of the extreme weather, the most prevalent sickness among the soldiers during the winter of 1863–64, other than the normal diet-related stomach problems, seems to have been the common cold, sore throats, and other relatively minor cold-weather ills. This could be attributed to the fact that only the stronger men had survived the previous winter. It certainly could not be attributed to a high degree of medical care. The treatment of choice for coughs seems to have been an eggnog spiked with whiskey or brandy, with rum used if these were not available. Captain Perry strongly recommended the eggnog treatment. "I drank one this morning, and found it did my cough much good. It makes one expectorate freely & easily. I advise you by all means to drink one every morning," he wrote to his wife. The following morning, he notified her, "I took an egg nog early this morning, one before dinner and shall take another just before going to bed. This is strong treatment, I think; but I shall stop when I recover from my cough."[14] Capt. Elijah Petty of the 17th Texas was another strong advocate of the eggnog treatment, although he seemed to use it more as a preventative than as a cure. Capt. Harvey Wallace of the 19th Texas used the eggnog treatment (with rum), along with "dogwood and Cherry Bitters," as an aid in recovering from malaria and the effects of the quinine treatment.[15]

Unfortunately, not all of the illnesses were of such a nature that they could be treated with eggnog and rum. Pvt. William A. "Colonel" Tarleton was in "a most pitiable condition" in late February. "He is altogether out of his mind. The doctors call it Insanity. I fear that he will not recover," Perry informed his wife. Perry had an old schoolmate living in Marksville, Alfred Irion, who had earlier offered to care for Perry in his home should he become sick. Perry accepted the offer on behalf of Tarleton, but on February 23, Tarleton died of typhoid fever.[16] There was also smallpox in the vicinity of the Yellow Bayou fortifica-

14. Perry to Dear Harriet, Feb. 21, 1864, Perry Letters.
15. Wallace to Dear Achsah, Feb. 24, 1864, in Stephen R. Skelton, ed., *Through the Valley of the Shadow of Death: The Civil War Manuscript Collection of Captain Harvey Alexander Wallace* (Westminster, Md.: Willow Bend Books, 2004), 260.
16. Perry to Dear Harriet, Feb. 21, 1864, Perry Letters; M. Jane Johansson, *Peculiar Honor: A History of the 28th Texas Cavalry, 1862–1865* (Fayetteville: Univ. of Arkansas Press, 1998), 86.

tions in late January, but a quickly established quarantine kept it from spreading.[17]

There was another need that the soldiers had been unable to tend to during their marching that they now had time to address, and this was a need of a much less physical nature. The men were far from home and loved ones, they were engaged in a most dangerous occupation, and Christmas was rapidly approaching. All of these things came together to give many of the men a powerful desire for spiritual nourishment. There had been a strong spirit of revivalism among Walker's Texans in the fall of 1863, and the approach of Christmas did nothing to diminish it. Brush arbors were built and preachers held well-attended revivals on a nightly basis. For those more earthly of the troops, other arbors were made for more earthly entertainment. Christmas Eve found both of the structures full. Inside one "were seated a couple of fiddlers, making elegant music on their fiddles. Around the fire, groups were dancing jigs, reels, and doubles. Even the officers' colored servants had collected in a group by themselves, and, while some timed the music by slapping their hands on their knees, others were capering and whirling around in the most grotesque manner, showing their white teeth as they grinned their delight, or 'yah, yah'ed, at the boisterous fun." On the other end of camp, the other arbor

was beautifully lighted up with burning pine-knots. Gathered under the arbor were a number of soldiers, quietly and attentively listening to the words which fell from the lips of the preacher standing in their midst—the preacher with his gray locks and wrinkled brow showing the foot-prints of time. Amongst the groups of eager listeners were men just entering the threshold of life, yet whose vocations placed their feet upon the verge of the grave. The rows of tents, the black groupings of adjacent shelters, all made an impressive scene. Occasionally, mingling with the preacher's words, came laughter from some group assembled round a camp-fire near by, or a shout of some unthinking, free-hearted stroller about camp. Words rich with eloquent meaning rolled from that aged preacher's lips, like rippling waves of ocean, successively, rapidly, breaking upon a sandy shore; the light of hidden power burned in his eyes, as he pleaded—warned his hearers of the life to come, and the consequences of an unprepared condition for its hidden realities. The exhortation finished, a closing hymn was sung, rolling its waves of fine melody out upon

17. Petty to My Dear Wife, Jan. 24, 1864, in Brown, *Journey to Pleasant Hill*, 316.

the night's still air, over the adjacent prairies. The benediction pro-
nounced, the audience dispersed.[18]

And thus passed Fort DeRussy's second Christmas.

The day after Christmas was pay day. Walker's Texans "received
four months pay, in Confederate money, a species of money not very useful to the soldier," according to Pvt. Joseph Blessington of the 16th Infantry. Captain Perry, of the 28th Dismounted Cavalry, agreed, telling
his wife on December 23 that "provisions are not so scarce, but Confederate money is about worthless." (To emphasize the matter, Perry
also asked his wife to sell some of their property, but added, "I do not
want any Confederate money except to pay debts with.") So much for
pay day.

Even though the money was "about worthless," the soldiers found
ways to spend it. A little went for clothing and some was sent home, but
most of the money was spent on food. The Commissary Department did
what it could but generally provided rather poor provisions. Most of the
soldiers' money was spent buying meat and vegetables from local citizens.
The poor beef provided by the army received additions of pork, bacon,
goose, honey, molasses, flour, potatoes, and whatever else could be procured by the soldiers. Pens were built outside of the shanties for geese and
shoats. Prices were high, but the soldiers were hungry. A chief complaint
about the cold weather was not only that it made living uncomfortable
but also that it had damaged the local potato crop. The soldiers' food-
stocks were also supplemented by the ever-welcome packages from home.
Canned peaches and "Mother's Pound Cake" were equally rejoiced over.
The government-issued food was avoided if possible. In mid-February the
issued beef had gotten so bad that some of the men in Scurry's Brigade
decided to have a little fun with the matter by holding a funeral and
burying their rations. They "set out with the beef with horns, bells, pans
and etc all beating & ringing & created quite a general excitement. Col.
[George W.] Jones got mad and ordered all under arrest." Around fifty
men were arrested, at which time tempers began to flare and the matter
became serious. When it was explained to Colonel Jones that no disre-
spect had been intended to him, he calmed down and released the men,
but the incident stirred up discontent among the troops.[19]

18. Joseph P. Blessington, *The Campaigns of Walker's Texas Division* (New York:
Lange, Little, 1875), 159–60.

19. Petty to My Dear Wife, Feb. 16, 1864, in Brown, *Journey to Pleasant Hill*, 324–25.

Not all of the troops' time was spent in keeping warm and finding food. Everyone was aware that winter would be over all too soon, and to that end construction and improvement projects were ongoing. In October, Lieutenant Wells had described the fort as "a ruin." Of course, the fort could not be defended in its ruined condition. It was accepted as a fact that when spring arrived, so would the Yankees. Everyone from Lt. Gen. E. Kirby Smith, the department commander in Shreveport, down to the lowliest field hand knew that when the spring rise came on Red River, Union gunboats would be coming up to test the strength of Fort DeRussy. And to make sure that DeRussy would be up to the challenge, General Taylor assigned Capt. David French Boyd, chief of engineers on his staff, to the job of overseeing the repairs at the fort. Before the war, Boyd had been a professor at the Louisiana State Seminary of Learning just up the river in Pineville and had made a good impression on the institution's president, William Tecumseh Sherman. He had made an equally good impression in the early days of the war on Taylor, when Boyd had served under him in Virginia. Boyd was the right man for the task, a serious, no-nonsense, self-motivating sort of fellow. He replaced a man who had definitely *not* been the right man for the job. Capt. Edward Gotthiel had been relieved from duty by Taylor because of "his entire incompetency as an engineer."[20]

The Labor Situation

Boyd found his work cut out for him. He would work through one of the most severe winters in memory on a job that would find him short of both skilled and unskilled laborers, equipment and material. As early as January 2, General Taylor was pressing his superiors in Shreveport for labor and tools for the works at DeRussy, but he and Boyd would find the Confederate bureaucracy as difficult to deal with as any Yankee gunboat.

While Fort DeRussy was built primarily with slave labor, Boyd could not get enough slaves to finish the works in the time allotted. That being the case, he was required from time to time to call upon the nearby troops to aid in construction projects. On January 13, Taylor had General Walker provide Captain Boyd with as many carpenters as he could find in his division. And by January 20, Taylor reported, "I have now some 2000 soldiers in addition to the negroes at work on the Red River defences."

20. Taylor to Boggs, Jan. 19, 1864, *ORA* 34, pt. 2, 891.

The winter period may have been a welcome respite for the soldiers protecting Fort DeRussy, but for the slaves working on the fort it was a different story. The winter of 1863–64 was the coldest winter in central Louisiana since 1822. There were frequent rains, occasional snows, and from late December through mid-January the weather was intensely cold, causing "the formation of ice, to an extent previously unknown in this latitude."[21] As early as December 7, 1863, Tom Fullilove wrote to his wife, "The negroes are beginning to complain already of short rations but Capt. May says they shall be well fed. I think the commissary here is cheating in weights but I hope it will be corrected." As the winter wore on, the situation got worse. In late January, Fullilove again wrote to his wife, this time from the raft site downstream from the fort: "A negro was drowned the day before yesterday at the piling about 50 ft. above our log way, the body could not be found, however no effort was made until today. We are hard run down here I assure you. Yesterday we worked about half the day in the rain and ½ of the negroes are nearly naked and nearly all of them with shoes not fit to wear. Often the mud is so deep & so stiff that their shoes get pulled in pieces."[22]

The slaves working under these conditions were being pushed to finish the fortifications before the weather moderated and the Yankees came. In late December there were 500 slaves working on the DeRussy defenses, 280 laboring on the raft and the other 220 working at the fort itself.[23] But by January 31, disease and desertion had reduced the number of slaves at the raft to less than half that number. "A good many, some 25 or 30 are sick and coming in every day, and mud and water everywhere it rains and only 110 hands at work," Fullilove reported to his wife. On January 28, a cavalry company was sent out for "gathering up in the parishes of Rapides, Natchitoches, and Sabine negroes that have run away from Fort DeRussy and whose owners reside in said parishes."[24] The conditions at the fort were so unacceptable to the slaves that they were running away *to* home.

---

21. Taylor to Boggs, Jan. 20, 1864, *ORA* 34, pt. 2, 898.

22. Jane Fullilove Mason, "Dear Lizzie: Letters of a Confederate Cavalryman," 22, 29, unpublished manuscript, 1982. Copy in possession of author.

23. Perry to Dear Harriet, Dec. 29, 1863, Perry Letters. The figure of "500" is interpreted as "270" by Johansson in *Widows by the Thousand*, 190. This would have only 90 slaves working at the fort. The original figure is smudged and hard to read, but I argue that both the figure and the context point toward the figure being "500."

24. Mason, "Dear Lizzie," 29; Captain May to Captain Boyd, Jan. 28, 1864, Letters Sent, District of West Louisiana, 133–34, vol. 76, RG 109, NA

As the month of January slipped away, General Taylor realized that he needed more workers if he was going to have the fort ready to greet the Yankees in early March. On January 20, perhaps in an effort to relieve the two thousand soldiers he had working, Taylor put out a call for "one fourth of all the able bodied male slaves between the ages of 18 and 45 belonging to Sugar planters in Rapides Parish, La., who were exempted from furnishing negroes" because they had been needed for the sugar harvest. With the harvest now finished, the planters were to send their slaves to Fort DeRussy equipped with "necessary cooking utensils for the number of slaves sent; and . . . an axe and a spade, or shovel."[25] When one planter complained of the conditions his slaves would be subjected to, Taylor pointed out that the defense of the river was the defense of the planters along the river, so planters should be eager to cooperate. Taylor again reassured the planter that "every arrangement has been made at the works below to secure the comfort and well being of negroes, that can be made. Temporary huts have been erected for their shelter; bountiful rations are issued to them, and a skillful Surgeon has been sent there, provided with medicines to attend them if taken sick. Last year the rations allowed to negroes at Fort DeRussy were larger than the rations allowed to soldiers, and this winter there has been an increase in the rations to negroes at Fort DeRussy etc over the allowance of last year."[26] Taylor's assurances can readily be called into question. Capt. Harvey Wallace of the 19th Texas wrote to his wife on February 10 concerning the situation with the slaves at the fort: "Oh How I pity these poor negroes here. They work them from daybreak until dark and about half feed them. They look so bad I never would let them have one of mine to treat this way. I would feed them in the woods first." At least sixty-nine slaves died while working on the Fort DeRussy defenses. Nearly all died of diseases contracted while working there, although at least one drowned.[27]

25. May to W. L. Sandford, Jan. 19, 1864, Letters Sent, District of West Louisiana, 50, vol. 75, RG 109, NA.

26. May to G. Mason Graham, Feb. 2, 1864, Letters Sent, District of West Louisiana, 167–70, vol. 76, RG 109, NA.

27. Your Harvey [Wallace] to My Dear Achsah, Feb. 10, 1864, in Skelton, *Through the Valley*, 258–59; Louisiana State Auditor's Records, 1862–1865, Louisiana State Archives, Baton Rouge; "Deaths in 1863," Marshall Ledger Book, Marshall-Furman Papers, Louisiana and Lower Mississippi Valley Collection, Hill Memorial Library, Louisiana State Univ., Baton Rouge. A granite monument dedicated to the memory of these slaves now stands on the grounds of Fort DeRussy.

In 1999, this monument was dedicated to the slaves who died during the construction of Fort DeRussy. It may be the only monument in the country that honors the contributions made by slaves to the Confederate war effort. (Photograph by author.)

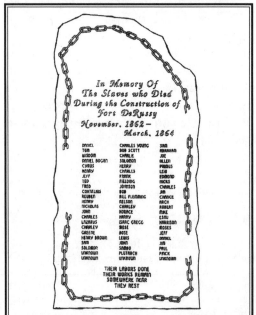

In Memory Of
The Slaves who Died
During the Construction of
Fort DeRussy
November, 1862 –
March, 1864

DANIEL	CHARLES YOUNG	SAM
TOM	BOB SCOTT	ABRAHAM
WISDOM	CHARLIE	JOE
DANIEL BOGAN	SOLOMON	ALLEN
CYRUS	HENRY	PRIMUS
HENRY	CHARLES	LEW
JEFF	FRANK	EDMOND
TED	FIELDING	HICKS
FRED	JOHNSON	CHARLES
CORNELIUS	BOB	JIM
REUBEN	BILL FLEMMING	CHANCE
HENRY	NELSON	ARCH
NICHOLAS	CHARLEY	ROBERT
JOHN	HORACE	MIKE
CHARLES	HARRY	ESAU
LAZARUS	ISAAC GREGG	HARRISON
CHARLEY	MOSES	MOSES
GREENE	BOSE	JEFF
HENRY BROWN	LEWIS	DANIEL
SAM	JOHN	JIM
SOLOMON	SAMBO	PAUL
UNKNOWN	PLUTARCH	PRICK
UNKNOWN	UNKNOWN	UNKNOWN

THEIR LABORS DONE
THEIR WORKS REMAIN
SOMEWHERE NEAR
THEY REST

Sketch of monument dedicated to the slaves who died during the construction of Fort DeRussy. (Author's personal collection.)

Slave owners were compensated for the loss of slaves working on state projects, whether the loss was from death or absconding, the average compensation being between eighteen hundred and twenty-two hundred dollars per slave. This compensation was apparently more of a temptation than one slave owner could resist. His slave, Daniel Bogan, was serving as a bugler with a Confederate unit, the St. Mary's Cannoneers, in early 1863 when he was ambushed and shot by Union soldiers. The slave/soldier was brought to Fort DeRussy, where he succumbed to his wounds. His owner filed for compensation for a slave who died at Fort DeRussy and was reimbursed for the loss. As a general rule, slaves serving with the army were the owner's responsibility and would not be paid for, but this plantation owner had other slaves who were working at the fort and apparently was able to slip in the appropriate paperwork. The ruse went undetected until 1998, by which time the statute of limitations (as well as the lifespan of all parties involved) had long since expired.[28]

The labor shortage was compounded in mid-January by an uncalled-for display of immaturity by Maj. Henry Douglas, chief engineer of the Trans-Mississippi Department. Douglas served under Lt. Gen. E. Kirby Smith, the department head. General Taylor also served under Smith, as district head. David Boyd was Taylor's chief engineer and thereby served under Taylor. Taylor was responsible for the defense of Fort DeRussy, but Douglas was responsible for the construction of Fort DeRussy. Boyd was also answerable to Taylor as concerned the defenses of the fort and was answerable to Douglas as concerned the construction of the fort. As if this bureaucratic tangle were not enough, Richard Taylor had little regard for Douglas's ability as an engineer, and Taylor was not the kind of man who hid his feelings on matters of this sort. There was little love lost between Taylor and Douglas, and Boyd was caught in the middle.

The situation came to a head in mid-January. Major Douglas, as chief engineer of the department, was stationed in Shreveport. Captain Boyd was on site at the fort, and at some time in early January, Colonel DeRussy, the fort's first chief engineer, had come down from Natchitoches to visit. While inspecting the fort with Captain Boyd, the subject of the labor shortage was discussed, along with possible ways to alleviate it. As they viewed the bombproofs then under construction, one of

---

28. Out of respect for the descendants of the guilty party, the source of this incident will not be revealed. But it did happen. The irony, of course, is that the owner was paid in Confederate money.

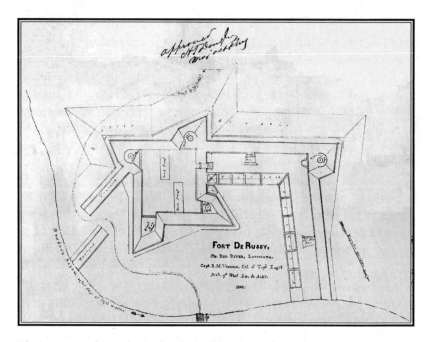

This map was drawn by Richard Venable, chief of topographical engineers of
the District of Western Louisiana. It shows the fort as it was supposed to be
built, varying slightly from how the completed fort looked. Most of the main
features can still be found. (From Jeremy Gilmer Papers, Southern Historical
Collection; permission to publish from Wilson Library, University of North
Carolina–Chapel Hill.)

the engineers pointed out that by using some of the fort's railroad iron to
cover the bombproofs, instead of covering them with earth as originally
planned, they could save a good deal of time and labor. Major Douglas
had intended to use the iron to defilade the north and east fronts of the
fort, but both Boyd and DeRussy decided that the same objective could
be obtained by raising the south and east fronts about three feet. In fact,
that method accomplished the objective better than would have been
done using the iron in its originally intended way, which the two engineers determined would only provide partial protection to the north and
east fronts. Boyd discussed the situation with Taylor, who approved the
change. Time was of the essence, and neither Boyd nor Taylor felt the
need to get permission to make the change. As a result, Douglas was not
consulted.

When Major Douglas found out about the change, he was furious.
He immediately notified Boyd: "Unless my plans are carried out I shall

not send more force to Fort DeRussy, except by orders from Lieutenant-General Smith." To add emphasis to his words, Douglas recalled the two hundred desperately needed slaves who were on their way to DeRussy from Shreveport. If Boyd was going to build the fort the easy way, he obviously did not need any more workers. Douglas then presented his case to Kirby Smith, who sent a letter to Taylor telling him that Douglas, "as chief engineer, will be held responsible for the character of the works erected."

Taylor immediately fired back. "Utter confusion must necessarily follow this condition of affairs," he wrote. "When I applied for an engineer officer, I did not for a moment suppose that I surrendered my volition and all control of my district. I wished the benefit of the best engineering advice that could be obtained, reserving the right to make such modifications in proposed plans as might appear best for the service."[29] Taylor was right, of course. A commanding officer must have the authority to use his various occupational specialties as he sees fit, taking or refusing the advice as the situation warrants; otherwise chaos reigns, as in this case. For a major of engineers to overrule the commanding general of a district is absurd. Nonetheless, that was the situation Taylor was dealing with, and his commander was backing the major. This was undoubtedly one of the reasons that Taylor later said that the "commander of the 'Trans-Mississippi Department' displayed much ardor in the establishment of bureaux, and on a scale proportioned rather to the extent of his territory than to the smallness of his force. His staff surpassed in numbers that of Von Moltke during the war with France; . . . Hydrocephalus at Shreveport produced atrophy elsewhere."[30] As department commander, Smith was no stranger to complaints. "I have been accused of frivolity throughout the department for riding out with my wife before office hours for three hours to pick blackberries," he once remarked.[31] Smith was well aware that it was impossible to make everybody happy all the time, but in this case he was severely hamstringing Taylor.

Taylor was left with no choice but to appease Douglas. The engineer was invited down to the fort, and he and General Smith made an inspection there along with General Taylor sometime after January

29. Boyd to Taylor, Jan. 17, 1864, *ORA* 34, pt. 2, 893; Taylor to Boggs, Jan. 19, 1864, *ORA* 34, pt. 2, 891–92.
30. Taylor, *Destruction and Reconstruction,* 153.
31. Smith to Brig. Gen. Henry McCulloch, Sept. 13, 1863, *ORA* 26, pt. 2, 223.

20.[32] By that time Taylor had also received a few engineering sugges-
tions from General Walker. Walker was never a big fan of the fort, not
liking to "fort up" his men. Nevertheless, his men were there and he felt
that the fort should be defended as best it could. To this end, he suggested that the 9-inch Dahlgren and the rifled 32-pounder Seacoast Gun
that were mounted in the fort on the hill be moved down to the Water
Battery. These were the two best guns in the defenses, and the hilltop
positions would not allow them to be used to their greatest effective-
ness. Based on his experiences "at Evansport and Aquia Creek, on the
Potomac, and Drewry's Bluff, on James River," Walker pointed out:

> The fire from guns of whatever caliber at vessels in motion is
> extremely uncertain at distances greater than 200 or 300 yards,
> especially with inexperienced gunners. The most effective guns
> should therefore, I think, be placed in the water battery. Where they
> now are not more than 1 shot out of 10 would be accurately aimed;
> even if the gunners could see the enemy's vessel, which they cannot
> do until the river has risen from 12 to 15 feet above its present stage,
> whereas, with a rise of 3 or 4 feet, the enemy's most formidable
> ironclads can ascend the river to Alexandria.
>
> Until the water in the river has reached almost its maximum
> height the only really effective guns for the defense of the river cannot
> be used at all. I therefore recommend that the 9-inch and 32-pounder
> (rifled) be removed as soon as possible to the water battery.[33]

Walker also pointed out that "in rear of the fort there is a range of
hills of superior elevation, say, from 8 to 10 feet, which in the possession of the enemy renders the whole position untenable; in other words,
it is its key point. These elevations should at once be crowned by earthworks for infantry and light artillery." And while he was dispensing
advice, Walker also suggested that Boyd be "furnished with 400 or
500 additional negroes and 40 or 50 more ox teams, the latter being
indispensable."[34]

Major Douglas left the fort on January 25, after agreeing to allow
Boyd to make some of the suggested changes. The big guns were moved

32. Taylor to Boggs, Jan. 20, 1864, ORA 34, pt. 2, 897; May to Walker, Jan. 23,
1864, Letters Sent, District of West Louisiana, vol. 76, RG 109, NA.
33. Walker to Surget, Jan. 17, 1864, *ORA* 34, pt. 2, 894.
34. Ibid.

down to the Water Battery.[35] But the additional slaves and oxen did not arrive, and, possibly as a result, the earthworks on the high ground west of the fort were never built. It would not be until March 3 that Capt. W. R. Devoe, the engineering officer from Trinity (now Jonesville), would be ordered "to proceed to Fort DeRussy with his negroes and tools and assist in the completion of that work."[36] By then it would be too late.

The Equipment Situation

It was not only labor that was in short supply at the fort. Equipment was also scarce. The first work force to arrive at the fort after the November callback were "very destitute of tools." On January 2, General Taylor continued to bemoan "the scarcity of tools."[37] Captain Boyd found that tar was unavailable on January 15, and on January 17 he complained that the lack of proper rope to run the piledriver at the raft had the operation there "hobbling along painfully slow."[38] The lack of equipment led to a certain amount of borrowing, which was not always appreciated. At one point General Taylor had to remind Major Byrd that "the oxen belonging to the Siege Battery at Fort DeRussy will not be used under any circumstances for purposes other than the use of the Battery."[39] But borrowing, with or without permission, was often necessary. Lt. W. L. S. Bringhurst, the fort's ordnance officer, had to borrow wagons from the Engineers, and his stores could not be moved from the boat landing until the Engineers had an available wagon. This led to frequent exposure of ammunition and other equipment to inclement weather, an undesirable situation. Lt. James Fuller, chief of artillery, was in a similar situation when he wrote to the district's chief of artillery to point out that the heavy battery at the fort did not have a lantern. Working in a dark magazine without a lantern

35. Oddly enough, a range map of the fort dated March 4, 1864, shows both the 9-inch gun and the 32-pounder positions in the hill fort. However, the guns were in the water battery when the fort was attacked on March 14. F. G. Burbank, "Plan of Ft. DeRussy and environs, with table of distances. March 4, 1864," Louisiana Historical Association Collection, Howard-Tilton Memorial Library, Tulane Univ., New Orleans.

36. Taylor to Boggs, Mar. 3, 1864, *ORA* 34, pt. 2, 1015.

37. Taylor to Boggs, Jan. 19, 2, 1864, *ORA* 34, pt. 2, 892, 815–16.

38. Boyd to Taylor, Jan. 17, 1864, *ORA* 34, pt. 2, 893.

39. May to Byrd, Jan. 13, 1864, Letters Sent, District of West Louisiana, vol. 76, RG 109, NA.

was "impossible," he explained, and he needed at least four. His task was also crippled by lack of a wagon. The gun carriages could not be put in proper shape because no wheelwright was available, and when a wheelwright was finally located in Marksville in late January, there was no wagon available to bring the wheels to him. Once again, artillery had to wait on the acquiescence of the engineers.[40] And as spring approached, construction staggered on.

The Armament Situation

The first order of business upon reestablishing Fort DeRussy was to rearm it. Or so it would seem. In fact, the process of getting suitable weapons to the fort was a drawn out process that went on for far too long.

The first heavy guns to arrive at DeRussy did not show up until January 8, but they were mounted by January 11. These four siege guns—three 24-pounders and one 30-pounder Parrott, on siege carriages—were meant to be in place only temporarily, "until the permanent guns were in position." The three 24s had been captured at Brashear City (now Morgan City, Louisiana) and were not highly regarded. General Taylor felt that it would "be no great loss if they fall into the enemy's hands" and planned to send them up Black River to Trinity when he no longer needed them at DeRussy.[41] By January 15, Taylor had one 9-inch Dahlgren and one rifled 32-pounder in positions at the fort on the hill.

The 9-inch Dahlgren was capable of throwing a seventy-two-pound shell nearly two miles. The Dahlgren design had a good safety record; it fired a large shell relative to its weight, with an economical powder charge, and it required a smaller gun crew than other models of similar size. This particular gun was cast in 1856 or 1857 at the Tredegar Iron Works in Richmond, Virginia, and for some unexplained reason was not accepted by naval inspectors at that time. The 32-pounder, a Model of 1829 Seacoast Gun cast in 1834, was originally a smoothbore but had been banded and rifled by the Confederates. While not as powerful as the Dahlgren, it was also a formidable weapon. But once again the fort's supply problem reared its ugly head. Only fifty rounds of ammunition had accompanied these two guns. Also, the excellent 32-pounder gun had to be mounted on a slightly too small 24-pounder carriage. With no proper carriage-making facilities at either DeRussy or Alexan-

40. Fuller to Brent, Jan. 27, 1864, Brent Papers–Tulane.
41. Taylor to Boggs, Jan. 8, 11, 1864, *ORA* 34, pt. 2, 842, 852; Perry to Harriet, Jan. 12, 1864, Perry Letters.

dria, the Engineers and ordnance workers once again had to make do. Taylor requested more ammunition be sent at once, along with another 9-inch gun.[42]

Taylor was also counting on *Missouri,* a Confederate ironclad built at Shreveport, to arrive at the fort and aid in the defense of the river. The water level in the river never allowed *Missouri,* with a draft in excess of ten feet, to make the voyage down to DeRussy.[43]

January 20 found Fort DeRussy hotly embroiled in the Boyd-versus-Douglas, earth-versus-iron debate. It also found the fort in possession of two 32-pounder "carronades." These two consecutively serial numbered naval guns were cast in 1847, but no record exists of their ever having served on any ship. It is likely that they were among the 1,198 heavy guns captured by the Confederates at Gosport Navy Yard in April 1861. These guns arrived at the fort without carriages, and General Taylor was anxiously awaiting the arrival of the carriages and his second 9-inch Dahlgren. He was also waiting for Major Douglas's "permission" to move his good guns down to the Water Battery, and no doubt his jaws were tightly clinched at the thought of that.

Taylor's jaws must have been even more tightly clinched on January 27 when he learned that department headquarters in Shreveport had decided that they would keep the other 9-inch Dahlgren that had been promised the fort. Taylor fired off an angry letter to headquarters pointing out that Fort DeRussy had been designed for two 9-inch guns and that even Major Douglas had assured him that the second gun would be arriving at any time. Taylor's intelligence operatives were keeping him well informed on Union activities in New Orleans, and he knew that preparations were already under way for a push up the Red. He had also been recently informed of the fact that *Missouri* would not be coming down to help with his river defense.[44] The fort needed

42. Taylor to Smith, Jan. 8, 1864, Taylor to Boggs, Jan. 15, 1864, Boyd to Taylor, Jan. 17, 1864, *ORA* 34, pt. 2, 843, 872, 892–93. Edwin Olmstead, Wayne E. Stark, and Spencer C. Tucker, *The Big Guns: Civil War Siege, Seacoast, and Naval Cannon* (Alexandria Bay, N.Y.: Museum Restoration Service, 1997), 87, 99. Stark to author, personal correspondence, Nov. 30, 1998. The histories of these guns are for the most part informed speculations on Stark's part.

43. Smith to Taylor, Jan. 4, 1864, Taylor to Boggs, Jan. 15, 1864, *ORA* 34, pt. 2, 819, 872. In June 1998, after millions of dollars had been spent on the locks and dams of the Red River Navigation Project, the pilots of the steamboat *Delta Queen* still refused to attempt passage of the Alexandria-Shreveport segment of Red River during low water. *Delta Queen* draws nine feet—fifteen inches less than *Missouri.*

44. Taylor to Boggs, Jan. 27, 1864, *ORA* 34, pt. 2, 918–19.

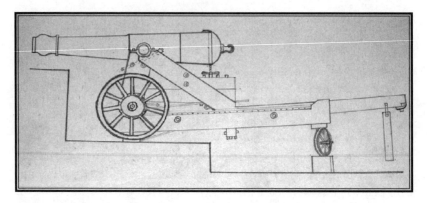

David Boyd's sketchbook included this drawing of a 24-pounder on a barbette carriage. Guns like this were mounted at Fort DeRussy while Boyd was
chief engineer at the fort. (From David Boyd Papers; permission to publish
from Hill Memorial Library, Louisiana State University, Baton Rouge.)

weapons, it needed them mounted, and it needed them *now*. Taylor
would get his second 9-inch gun, but it would be over a month before
it arrived at the fort.

Ordnance crews mounted the big guns as they trickled in to the
fort, and the artillerymen were kept busy with gun drills, learning how
to maintain and fire their pieces. Two 24-pounders were moved from
the water batteries to the hill fort. Distances were measured, a range
map was prepared, and the artillery was practiced. A quantity of burnt
32-pounder shot was collected, cleaned up, and tested to make sure
that all seventy-nine fit the bores of the cannons that would be firing
them. By the end of the day on March 2, the casemate battery, covered
with a double layer of railroad iron, was ready to receive its guns. The
second 9-inch Dahlgren was expected shortly.[45]

On March 10, Maj. Joseph Brent (hero of the *Indianola* expedition), now district chief of artillery and ordnance, made an inspection
visit to Fort DeRussy. On his inspection of the Water Battery, Brent
found one of the 9-inch Dahlgrens and one smoothbore 32-pounder
in the iron-covered casemate. While the 9-inch gun was a fine piece,
the 32-pounder was an old Naval Gradual Increase gun cast in 1827.
It had been in Gosport Navy Yard in 1849 and was obsolete then.[46] In

45. Walker to Surget, Mar. 2, 1864, *ORA* 34, pt. 2, 1016.
46. Stark to author, Nov. 30, 1998, personal correspondence.

the "new" barbette battery just downriver, the two 32-pounder carronades were mounted, and preparations were being made to mount the rifled 32-pounder and the second, newly arrived, 9-inch Dahlgren. But Brent was chagrined to find that the engineers were planning to put all of their eggs in one basket—or at least all of their best guns in one casemated battery. As soon as a new 9-inch Marsilly carriage arrived from Shreveport, Brent reported to General Taylor, the second 9-inch gun was to be mounted in the iron casemate alongside the other 9-inch gun. Major Douglas was now staying at the fort, so this plan had been approved, if not suggested, by him. From his report to Taylor, it is obvious that Brent did not think any more of Douglas's tactical abilities than did Taylor:

> I would respectfully report to you, that in my opinion it is extremely hazardous, to place so much dependence upon the iron casemate. This casemate would then contain the two IX in guns and 32 pdr and in case of any accident to it, the main defense of the river would be involved in it. In order to allow the two guns already mounted to be traversed to the right and left, it has become necessary to cut almost entirely away from both sides of the port holes, the heavy braces, which the Engineers placed there, considering I suppose, that they were needed to make secure and solid the iron casing and its backing. This cutting away leaves the impression on the mind of a weakness in the casemate, and it seems to me, that the impact of a heavy solid shot near the port-hole at 1500 yds range would crush it in. In this, not being an Engineer, I may be mistaken, and speak with diffidence of their work, but such is certainly the impression produced on one.
>
> If then this heavy armament were placed in the Battery, and an accident to the casemate were to ensue arising either from the fact referred to, or from any other cause, we would find, that one shot of the Enemy might disable these three guns, upon which necessarily a concentrated fire would be brought, from the fact of their being so close together.
>
> If this IX in gun were retained in its present position, and its carriage placed in the iron casemate, it could then be mounted there, after experience had shown, that the casemate was perfectly safe and reliable; and in the mean time its greater field of fire in the Barbette Battery, would enable the movements of the enemy to be more entirely brought under effective fire.[47]

47. Brent to Taylor, Mar. 11, 1864, Brent Papers–Tulane.

The iron casemate was built to inspire confidence. The iron plating was made of two layers of railroad iron, "the upper tier reversed and laid into the interstices of the lower." This plating was backed by twenty inches of solid oak timber.[48] It looked impregnable. But as Brent was aware, looks can be deceiving.

The second Marsilly carriage never arrived. When the Union army and navy arrived at Fort DeRussy on March 14, 1864, the two 9-inch guns were still spread out in separate batteries. In the four-hour battle that ensued, neither gun fired a shot.

In numerous Union reports concerning the armament of Fort DeRussy, in both 1863 and 1864, reference is made to the captured 9- and 11-inch guns of the USS *Indianola* being present. They were not. Of the four big guns aboard *Indianola* at the time of her capture, one was destroyed and three were removed (two 9-inch and one 11-inch). All of these guns apparently went to Shreveport, as two of them were aboard CSS *Missouri* when she was surrendered to the Union navy at the end of the war.[49] Although they obviously had to pass by the fort on their way up the Red in 1863, none of these guns were ever mounted at Fort DeRussy.

---

48. Moore, *Rebellion Record* 8:430.

49. One 9-inch (F.P. 572) and one 11-inch (F.P. 115). Edward Lull, Robert Tate, and Jno. Swaney to Foster, June 14, 1865, *ORN* 27:242.

Chapter 7

Outlying Defenses

Fort DeRussy did not stand alone in its defense of the lower Red River. The Confederates believed in defense in depth. The fort defended the river, and just as the redoubt on the hill defended the Water Battery, outlying defenses defended the fort. There were four positions defending Fort DeRussy, at varying distances and directions from the fort, giving varying types and degrees of protection.

Fort Humbug

Fort Humbug, a descriptively if not inspiringly named fortification, was a complex of forts and earthworks constructed at the junction of Yellow Bayou and Bayou des Glaises, two miles up Bayou des Glaises from its confluence with the Atchafalaya River at the village of Simmesport. Humbug was designed to protect the overland route leading to Fort DeRussy from the Atchafalaya River. There appears to have been no official name for Fort Humbug. The soldiers who built the fort referred to it as Fort Humbug, but the Union troops who observed it referred to it (or its component parts) variously as Fort Humbug, Fort Scurry, Fort Taylor, Fort Lafayette, Fort Morgan, and Fort Carroll.[1]

The first recorded mention of the construction of the fort was by Capt. Elijah Petty, 17th Texas, in a letter to his wife dated December 15, 1863: "I expect we will remain near this place some time as we have commenced fortifying at Yellow Bayou about one or two miles further

---

1. Cloyd Bryner, *Bugle Echoes: The Story of Illinois 47th* (Springfield, Ill.: Phillips Bros., 1905), 99; T. B. Marshall, *History of the Eighty-Third Ohio Volunteer Infantry: The Greyhound Regiment* (Cincinnati, The 83rd Ohio Volunteer Infantry Association, 1912), 13, 144; Homer B. Sprague, *History of the 13th Infantry Regiment of Connecticut Volunteers during the Great Rebellion* (Hartford, Conn.: Case, Lockwood, 1867), 213; *ORA* 34, pt.1, 337; Arthur D. McCullough diary, 1862–65, May 18, 1864, Illinois State Historical Library, Springfield (hereafter cited as McCullogh diary); Stephen E. Ambrose, ed., *A Wisconsin Boy in Dixie: Selected Letters of James K. Newton* (Madison: Univ. of Wisconsin Press, 1961), 109.

up Bayou De Glaze than our present camp."[2] The fortifications at Fort Humbug, on the west bank of Yellow Bayou and on both banks of Bayou des Glaises, consisted of "extensive works extending for near two miles in length" and included "forts, glacis, rifle pits etc etc."[3] Pvt. Jonathan T. Knight of the 19th Texas described the earthworks as "a great work we are diging a ditch one and a half miles long 9 feet deep and twenty feet wide and cuting the timber a mile at each end of the ditch."[4] There were two main forts involved in the project, Fort No. 1 being on the west bank of Yellow Bayou where it entered Bayou des Glaises, and Fort No. 2 being half a mile farther south, also on the west bank of Yellow Bayou. The additional earthworks connected these two forts.[5]

The four regiments of Scurry's Brigade were camped in abandoned slave quarters from one to three miles farther up Bayou des Glaises and worked on the fortifications on a rotating schedule, one regiment working every fourth day, seven days a week. It was noticed, however, that "the boys don't work well on Sunday. They don't have the vim that they would on another day."[6] Working by reliefs, the individual soldiers would work for one hour and rest one hour. The cold weather and frequent rains (including at least one snowfall) made for miserable working conditions.[7] The soldiers had plenty of corn bread and poor beef, as well as sugar and molasses, with occasional pork, potatoes, and flour. Like their colleagues at Fort DeRussy, they supplemented their rations with purchases from the locals and, when the opportunity presented itself, poaching. Free-roaming pigs abounded in the neighborhood and were a particularly appealing target. Captain Petty was also impressed with the number of bee trees that the men were able to find, which provided as much as 160 pounds of honey per tree.[8]

2. Brown, *Journey to Pleasant Hill*, 292–93.

3. Ibid., 304.

4. Knight to Dear Wife and Child, Dec. 28, 1863, Knight Letters.

5. Local legend has it that there was a third fort on the north side of Bayou des Glaises known as Fort Gum due to its having been built from the logs of gum trees.

6. Brown, *Journey to Pleasant Hill*, 301, 305.

7. Jan. 4, 1864. "We have been to the fortifications to work to day and it had been raining on us nearly the whole time. It was mud and slosh all the time which made it hard & disagreeable work." Ibid., 301.

Jan. 7, 1864. "It has been quite cold and wet for over a week. Some little snow fell the other night. It rains at least once a week and frequently two a week. It is a miserably wet time and mud mud mud is all the go." Ibid., 301–2.

Jan. 11, 1864. "Last night it rained and we have slosh and mud to day. It is a safe rule to say that it will rain a least once a week here." Ibid., 303.

8. Ibid., 293.

The name Fort Humbug stemmed from the average soldier's belief that the fort was, in fact, useless. In a letter to his wife dated December 20, writing from "Camp on Bayou Des Glaise," six miles from Simmesport, Dr. Edward Cade stated, "Our command is engaged in throwing up quite an extensive line of earth works, though I think it labor thrown away as they are perfectly useless."[9] Captain Petty explained the situation in a letter home to his wife in mid-January:

> This is one of the routes by which Ft. DeRussy can be flanked. But there are 3 other routes by which it can be flanked either of which is as good or better than this and why this alone is defended is more than I can tell. The other routes that I refer to are First By the way of Berwicks Bay, New Iberia etc the way that Genl Banks approached Alexandra last spring, Second By the way of Morgan's ferry up Bayou Rouge by Cheneyville etc, and Third and best route is up Red River, up Black river, up Little River through Catahoula lake and by water to within 18 miles of Alexandra. If we had a force and works to guard all these routes I could see some practicability in the work that we are doing here. Otherwise it appears nonsensical.[10]

Captain Petty need not have worried. When the Yankees did come, they would come up the predicted path.

Another problem that existed with the defense of Fort Humbug was the fact that its southern flank was defended solely by a usually impassable swamp, which would be dry and quite passable in March 1864, leaving the fort susceptible to encirclement. Construction continued on the Fort Humbug fortifications until March 3, 1864, and the Confederate's "Grand Skedaddle" began at this fort on March 12.[11]

Life for Scurry's Brigade at Fort Humbug was similar to life up at Fort DeRussy. The men worked and drilled during the day, foraged for food when they could, and partied when the opportunity presented itself. On Monday, January 18, Samuel Farrow wrote to his wife, "Some

---

9. John Q. Anderson, *A Texas Surgeon in the C.S.A.* (Tuscaloosa, Ala.: Confederate Publishing, 1957), 85.

10. Brown, *Journey to Pleasant Hill*, 304.

11. Petty gives the date for the end of construction as March 3, while Blessington says work continued until March 5. Union sources say that the fort was abandoned on March 13, because on that date they ran off several Confederate wagons that had returned for tents and kitchen utensils that had been left the day before. Brown, *Journey to Pleasant Hill*, 374; Blessington, *Campaigns of Walker's Texas Division*, 166; Bryner, *Bugle Echoes*, 99; *ORA* 34, pt. 1, 304–5.

of the boys has life enough to have a dance tonight amongst themselves. I hear the fiddle and hear them dancing. They are in a gin house with their frolic." On February 26, David Ray wrote to his sister, "Several ladies have just left camp who had come in to hear the bands play, and another deputation from Bayou Choupique is expected in this evening." The ladies of the neighborhood were apparently fascinated by the presence of so many dashing young Texans. Ray also wrote to his mother about a review on March 2, which took place on a cold, windy, rainy day: "But nevertheless the presence of a fair number of ladies lent a charm and animation to the whole scene and everything passed off nicely." Elijah Petty spent so much time writing to his wife about the ladies of the Simmesport area that it is almost embarrassing to read his letters. On February 29 he wrote, "You say that you will send me two shirts to work in on the fortifications and one to visit the ladies in. Why did'nt you not the reverse the number and send me one for fortifications and two for ladies as I had rather visit the ladies twice than to work on the fortifications once."[12]

Union forces had been made aware of the construction of Fort Humbug by early January 1864. On January 7, Charles C. Dwight, commanding officer of the 160th New York Volunteers, reported receiving word from Lt. Comdr. Frank M. Ramsay, commander of the gunboat squadron at the mouth of Red River, that "the enemy is fortifying at the junction of Bayou Yellow and Bayou DeGlaize, about 1 mile west of the Atchafalaya."[13] In a report dated January 8, Lieutenant Commander Ramsay officially reported learning from a refugee that a "small fortification has been built back of Simmesport at the junction of Yellow Bayou with Bayou des Glaises, and there is a breastwork, with a couple of fieldpieces, about half a mile below Simmesport, on the Atchafalaya."[14]

By January 12, Ramsay had picked up "several deserters and refugees" and noted that "they also confirm the report about the fortifica-

12. Farrow to Dearest Josephine, S. W. Farrow Letters, Samuel W. Farrow Papers, Barker History Center, Univ. of Texas, Austin (hereafter cited as Farrow Letters); Ray to Dear Sister; Ray to Very Dear Mother, Mar. 6, 1864, David M. Ray Letters, Barker History Center, Univ. of Texas, Austin (hereafter cited as Ray Letters); Brown, *Journey to Pleasant Hill*, 332. Ray also mentioned that the women visitors were "mostly French and speak the French language. Two of them were educated at Bardstown, Kentucky, and can speak English." A surprisingly large number of the wealthier French citizens of Avoyelles Parish sent their children to Bardstown for their higher education.
13. Dwight to Stone, Jan. 7, 1864, *ORA* 34, pt. 2, 36.
14. Ramsay to Porter, *ORN* 25:680.

tion at the junction of Yellow Bayou and Bayou des Glaises. Scurry's Brigade is stationed there. He has only field guns."[15] More confirmations followed. On January 23, Brig. Gen. George L. Andrews (commanding, Port Hudson), reported "two negroes just in from Grosstete report 600 of Walker's command were at that place on Wednesday last conscripting colored men, mules, and oxen, to be used on fortifications at Simsport, which place the rebels are reported to be fortifying."[16] On January 28, Brig. Gen. Daniel Ullman, also at Port Hudson, reported that four deserters, one refugee, and one prisoner had been brought in and had provided information that "General Walker has erected a large and strong work at the junction of Yellow Bayou and Bayou De Glaize."[17]

Remnants of Fort Humbug's Fort No. 2 can be seen along Louisiana Highway 1, just west of the town of Simmesport. It is listed in the National Register of Historic Places. The other earthworks no longer exist.

The Raft

The raft below Fort DeRussy, designed to provide a passive defense against any approaching Union gunboats, was not a new idea. Red River had historically had trouble with naturally occurring rafts and logjams, and the raft placed in the river below the fort in 1863 had played a significant role in the Confederate naval victory on May 4. But unlike the raft of 1863, which was only four hundred yards below the Water Battery of the fort and well within range of the fort's guns, the 1864 raft was built nearly eight miles downriver from the fort. The 1864 raft was also unlike the earlier model in that this raft was huge. Had everything gone according to plan, the raft would have created an impenetrable logjam several miles long.

A cardinal rule when building barrier-type defenses of the nature of the raft is that the barrier must *always* be covered by fire. Otherwise, it is only a matter of time before the approaching enemy's engineers remove the barrier. This rule was followed in 1863, and the raft worked wonderfully. But it was ignored in 1864, and so the Confederate raft served only to add proof to the old adage that "there is nothing so completely worthless that it can't, at the very least, be used as a bad example."

15. Ibid., 685.
16. *ORA* 34, pt. 2, 135.
17. Ibid., 172.

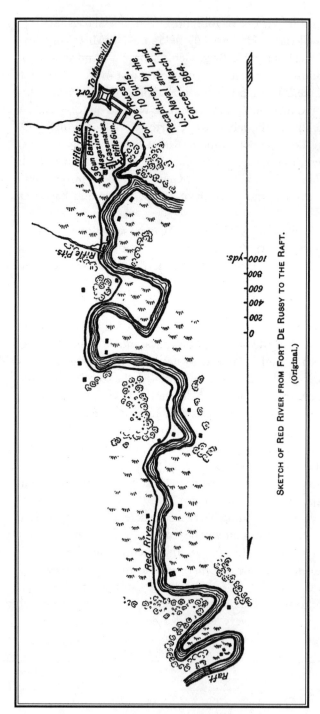

SKETCH OF RED RIVER FROM FORT DE RUSSY TO THE RAFT.

(Original.)

The 1864 raft across Red River was well out of sight and range of the fort's guns. This dismissal of a basic military axiom doomed the raft to failure. (From *Official Records of the Union and Confederate Navies*, vol. 26.)

The raft was not thought to be worthless to the people who were building it. Both Captain Boyd and General Walker felt that it was of prime importance to the river defenses. Although Boyd was discouraged by the lack of men available to work on the raft, he had high hopes for the obstruction, stating that "if successful, it would be worth all the forts and columbiads [large cannons] in the Trans-Mississippi Department."[18] Walker had similar feelings. "I place more reliance on the raft," he said, "than upon the guns of Fort DeRussy." He acknowledged that its location was not the best but felt that that could be overcome:

> It was a serious mistake, I think, in putting the raft beyond the reach of the guns of Fort De Russy, which would, to a very great extent, have protected it against the enemy's working parties for its removal. However, if the piling now placed proves sufficiently strong to sustain the weight of the accumulating timber, and the inhabitants along the banks of the river be instructed and required to use all their hands and teams in throwing trees into the river, the entire space from the piling to Fort De Russy can be filled up with a solid mass of timber impenetrable to gun-boats of any description and defying all efforts for its removal. To effect this, however, infinitely larger means must without delay be placed at the disposal of the engineer in charge of the work.[19]

Walker's caveat nullified the whole proposal. Boyd's labor supply was not even adequate, much less infinite. Walker felt that five hundred more slaves and fifty more ox teams, "the latter being indispensable," would allow the raft to be finished properly. But Boyd had to make do with what he had on hand.[20]

The first pilings for the raft were driven on Christmas Day 1863, and five days later there were 280 slaves at work on the project. Union intelligence operatives were reporting on the raft and its new location as early as January 7, 1864. By January 15, the raft was closed and river traffic was cut off. Work continued on the raft pilings, though sometimes at a snail's pace due to lack of proper rope for the pile driver. By February 16, the raft was completed.

The raft was a complex affair. A large mass of heavy timber was sunk in the river, above which a series of pilings were driven ten to twelve feet

18. Boyd to Taylor, Jan. 17, 1864, *ORA* 34, pt. 2, 893.
19. Walker to Surget, Jan. 17, 1864, *ORA* 34, pt. 2, 894.
20. Ibid.

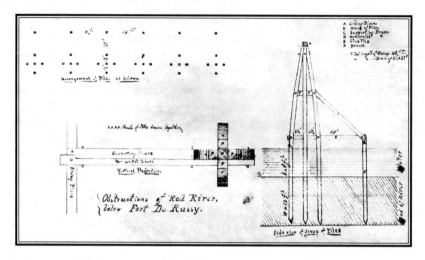

The 1864 raft below Fort DeRussy was no haphazard affair. Although beset with problems due to Mother Nature and a lack of tools, the obstruction was carefully engineered. In the end, good engineering and slave labor were no match for steam power and rising water. (From Jeremy Francis Gilmer Papers, Southern Historical Society Collection; permission to publish from Wilson Library, University of North Carolina–Chapel Hill.)

into the river bottom in T-shaped clusters sixteen feet apart, and these supported by a second row of shorter pilings, both rows of pilings being tied together by braces, chains, and heavy iron plates. Behind the pilings was a huge tangle of trees and brush.

    The pilings were started on each side of the river and by the end of January extended out into the river 175 feet on one side and 75 feet on the other. But with the river dammed to that extent, the current in the open part of the channel made work on the raft both difficult and dangerous. Each night the river would take away most of the days work, and men working on the raft began to question whether the two sides would ever meet in the middle. To add to the difficulties, the current and the natural buoyancy of the pilings caused many of them to pull up from the river bottom. "One whole cluster came up at one time after being fastened together," a discouraged overseer reported to his wife.[21] But finally the raft was completed.

    Even after the completion, improvements to the raft continued. Four regiments of Texans were kept busy throwing trees into the river

---

21. Fullilove to wife, Jan. 31, 1864, in Mason, "Dear Lizzie."

behind the raft for over a week.[22] When the men of the 28th Dismounted Cavalry returned to camp after their duty there, there were differing views on the strength of the raft. And well there might have been.

The raft's designers failed to take into consideration a basic law of physics: When an irresistible force comes up against an immovable object, something has got to give. Many of the soldiers throwing trees into the river were of the opinion that, in this case, the pilings were what was going to give. They were right. Volney Ellis, 12th Texas, wrote his wife on March 4 that the "raft which we have been so long constructing below Fort DeRussy has been swept away by the first freshet, and no obstruction now interposes between the fort and the mouth of the river." Theophilus Perry passed the same information on to his wife on March 9, telling her that after a heavy rain, the "raft across the river has washed away. It commenced giving away and then all floated off in one great mass."[23] Both men's letters exaggerated the situation, but the raft had given way. The current had eaten into the north bank of the river, and a large chunk of the raft had wedged its way through the growing crevasse. Portions of the rifle pits dug on the bank also tumbled into the river. But most of the raft remained and would prove a distinct obstacle to the Union fleet when it did move on Fort DeRussy.

Although the "Confederate Dam" was marked on topographical maps as recently as 1945, there are no remnants of it today. The raft was located on the Saline Point reach of Red River, and a cut-off in 1938 cut the bend off from the river channel. The site of the raft silted up heavily after the cut-off was made, and while the old channel at that point is still recognizable, the raft site is now in a cotton field about a mile north of Red River. Tractors now plow where ironclads once paddled.

It is ironic that the Confederate dam at Saline Point quickly faded into obscurity. A similar project—this time accomplished by the Union army—took place just upriver at Alexandria a few months later, when Col. Joseph Bailey dammed Red River in order to raise the river level and save the Union fleet. That dam was built by several army regiments, which included many trained lumberjacks as well as several black

22. Perry to Harriet, Dec. 29, 1863, Feb. 21, 1864, Perry Letters. Dwight to Stone, Jan. 7, 1864, Surget to Mouton, Jan. 15, 1864, Taylor to Boggs, Feb. 16, 1864, *ORA* 34, pt. 2, 36, 873, 971.

23. Thomas W. Cutrer, ed., "'An Experience in Soldier's Life': The Civil War Letters of Volney Ellis, Adjutant, Twelfth Texas Infantry, Walker's Texas Division, C.S.A," *Military History of the Southwest* 22 (Fall 1992): 109–72, 149; Perry to Dear Wife, Mar. 9, 1864, Perry Letters.

engineer regiments, from a potential work pool of more than thirty thousand men. The material for Bailey's Dam consisted of an unlimited supply of building material from the homes, barns, warehouses, and cotton gins of Alexandria and the tree-lined banks of the north side of the river, along with premade barges that could be floated out and sunk in position. The damming process was assisted by dozens of steamboats in the river complete with machine shops and blacksmithing capabilities. It took Bailey two weeks in the balmy days of May to complete his project, and it was hailed then—and to this day—as an engineering masterpiece and a technological marvel.

The Confederate dam, on the other hand, was built by several hundred malnourished and poorly clothed slaves—simple field hands. The building material for the dam had to be cut from the surrounding woods. Hand tools were in short supply, and even rope for the piledrivers was hard to find. And yet the river was closed off in three weeks, with the dam completed four weeks after that, during the dead of the coldest winter in recent memory. But the most obvious difference between the two dams is that almost nobody has ever heard of the Confederate dam at Saline Point. As was the case with the *Indianola* affair, the Rebels at Fort DeRussy were no match for the Yankee propaganda machine.

A much smaller raft, which was used as a movable gate in the river, was located about half a mile below the fort's water batteries. This water gate could alternately close off either the river channel or the mouth of Bayou Rouge. At periods of high water, shallow-draft vessels could have used a Bayou Rouge–Spring Bayou–Old River route to bypass the large raft downstream. This route could explain how the legendary "Lost Cannon of Old River" got to its supposed site.[24]

Artillery Position at Bayou L'eau Noir

Sometime prior to January 15, Captain Boyd notified General Taylor of a site near the mouth of Bayou L'eau Noir, "a fine position for masking light artillery immediately on the bank of the river." The position was less than two overland miles from the raft, although it was seven river

24. In the 1950s, fisherman Joseph Kelone snagged a net in Old River. On diving down to untangle it, he found that it was caught on a cannon barrel. Attempts by Kelone to recover the cannon were unsuccessful. Local legends now place the gun at several different sites in the river, all of them places where a cannon would not be likely to have been. As far as I have been able to determine, no one presently alive has seen the gun. Each alleged site, however, has die-hard enthusiasts who insist that their position is the correct one.

miles downstream. The position was also only six land miles from the fort, though nearly fifteen by river. General Walker examined the site personally on January 16 and immediately ordered Maj. J. J. Canon to have his battalion of sharpshooters, stationed two miles below that point, to construct rifle pits and artillery cover at the bayou.[25] The works were constructed, but apparently no artillery was ever put in position there. When the Union fleet came up Red River in mid-March 1864, the abandoned battery position was noted,[26] and the name Battery Bend was used for that section of the river throughout the Red River Campaign. The earthworks seem to have been something of a headache to the Union gunboats patrolling the area. On May 5, Acting Vol. Lt. John V. Johnston, captain of USS *Forest Rose*, wrote to the commanding officer of USS *Tallahatchie*, "There is four embrazures in battery bend and will be in your beat if you can with safety to your men blow them up you had better do so. You can do it by digging a hole and put in a jug of powder with slow matches. I do not give you this as an order but a suggestion."[27] On the morning of May 12, the gunboats *Argosy* and *Nymph* landed men at the site and destroyed the earthworks.[28]

Battery Bend, like the raft site, was cut off from Red River by the Saline Point Cut-off. Battery Bend, however, ended up on the south side of the new river channel. Like the raft site, this section of the old channel is also now a cultivated field. As an indication of the severity of the silting that has occurred here since the cut-off, two Indian mounds that stood on the bank of the river at Bayou L'eau Noir have been silted over, as has another mound about a half mile from the raft site.

Artillery Cover at Long Bridge

The light works, or artillery cover, at Long Bridge were not built in conjunction with the Fort DeRussy construction, but they did participate in a

25. Surget to Boyd, Jan. 15, 1864, Surget to Walker, Jan. 15, 1864, Boyd to Taylor, Jan. 17, 1864, Walker to Surget, Jan. 17, 1864, *ORA* 34, pt. 2, 872, 873, 893–94.

26. "At 1.30 PM during the day we passed a deserted masked battery with 12 embrasures in it for four field pieces." Mooney diary, Mar. 13, 1864. Deck logs, USS *Carondelet*, Mar. 14, 1864, RG 24, NA, and USS *Benton*, Mar. 14, 1864.

27. Johnston to Comdg. Officer, Gunboat No. 46, May 5, 1864, Gregory A. Coco Collection, Bendersville, Pa. *Tallahatchie* had a rather colorful postwar career. Renamed *Coosa*, it towed a traveling circus for a while then settled on the Ohio River near Cincinnati, where "she quickly won a debatable reputation for running disreputable moonlight excursions. Several Sunday schools cancelled contracts for picnic parties." It burned (arson) in 1869. Way, *Way's Packet Directory*, 110.

28. Deck logs, USS *Nymph* and USS *Argosy*, May 12, 1864, RG 24, NA.

minor way in the defense of the fort. The trenches and low parapets were built by Louisiana troops earlier in the war. They were situated on the edge of the high ground of the prairie overlooking the long bridge across a swampy stretch of ground along Boutte de Bayou, between Bayou des Glaises and the Avoyelles Prairie.[29] The Long Bridge site was sometimes referred to as "Magnolia Hills" by Texas troops passing through the area. It is located about midway between Fort DeRussy and Fort Humbug. Unlike the artillery position at Bayou L'eau Noir, several hundred feet of the artillery cover at Long Bridge can still be seen, although portions of the works have crumbled down the hill over the years.

29. Blessington, *Campaigns of Walker's Texas Division*, 172.

Chapter 8

The Winter of Our Discontent

Fort DeRussy was a military camp, and there is an old unwritten military idiom that says that busy soldiers cause less trouble than bored soldiers. That rule was applied that cold winter of 1863–64. When the soldiers were not moving cannon or unloading steamboats or throwing trees into the river or scrounging for food, chances were they could be found participating in that time-honored tradition of parade-ground drilling. In late January a drill competition between the best regiments of Hawes's and Randal's brigades was announced. The prize was to be a "fine flag," but there was a rumor that a few furloughs would be thrown in to sweeten the pot.[1] Preliminary competitions were held, and on January 20 the finals took place between the 12th Infantry of Hawes's Brigade and the 11th Infantry of Randal's. It seemed to one soldier that "the entire army" was present, and the drill competition was held in a county-fair-like atmosphere. The 8th Regiment walked away with the honors, and the flag was awarded by General Walker "in a neat and appropriate speech."[2] Whether furloughs were handed out is not recorded.

While Texans made up the majority of the troops at Fort DeRussy, there were also some Louisianians present. Boone's Artillery, consisting primarily of residents of central Louisiana, was stationed at the fort for a short period in January. These men had been captured at Port Hudson in July 1863 and had been exchanged and reentered into active service in December. Boone's Battery was released from duty at the fort on January 26, when the steamer *General Beauregard* arrived at the fort with Hutton's Artillery aboard. Hutton's Artillery, Company A of the Crescent Artillery, was originally a New Orleans unit but now had members from throughout Louisiana. Hutton's men were regulars

1. Perry to Harriet, Jan. 29, 1864, Perry Letters.
2. John Porter memoir, 26–27; Blessington, *Campaigns of Walker's Texas Division*, 164.

at Fort DeRussy, having been present for the capture of *Queen of the West* and the pursuit of *Indianola* the past February and at the *Albatross* fight in May.

Among the men of Hutton's Artillery was the colorful, opinionated, and always outspoken Sgt. John Murray. Were Murray alive today, he would be the strongest of Libertarians. He possessed both an intense belief in personal freedom and a strong sense of duty. His feelings toward those whose sense of duty was not as strong were straightforward. Murray had no use for conscripts.

On February 7, several conscripts arrived in camp to fill vacancies in Captain Hutton's Battery. "The boys don't like conscripts, there will be trouble with these fellows," Murray warned. And sure enough, just two days later he notified his diary that he had been "promoted to Sergeantship this morning, reduced to the ranks this evening for refusing to mess with conscripts." Murray was outraged. "Because our mess got refractory and would not let our conscripts negro cook for them, our colonel must break myself and [Sgt. J.] Dodd, and for a thing that any volunteer would rebel against, for a lot of infernal conscripts who had to be guarded constantly, and who I knew would run at the first appearance of a Yank. For our company officers as well as our colonel could not see those things, and so we had to submit in silence to the decree of '*superiors*' who seem to forget that war must cease sometime and that many soldiers are in for better circumstances than themselves, and sacrificed everything to enlist their names upon their country's scroll of fame."[3] Murray would have felt vindicated had he known that in 1881, Aristide Dauzat, one of the conscripts who joined the unit on February 3, testified in court that he left the unit as soon as the Yankees arrived and only rejoined it when the Union army had left the area. His punishment for deserting in the face of the enemy? Captain Hutton "cursed me a little and sent me to my company."[4]

Murray went into a deep depression after his demotion. He felt that Lieutenant Colonel Byrd, a Texan, was unfairly persecuting the Louisiana units. When Captain Hutton's men refused to build living quarters for the colonel, the whole company was made to march around the fort carrying 32-pound cannonballs. Murray complained that "several other instances of *tyranny* were displayed by our 'magnificent' colonel,

---

3. Murray diary.
4. Aristide Dauzat testimony, *Oden Deucatte v. United States,* French-American Claims Commission Files, NA.

and always upon the Louisianians." When the artillerymen killed a hog, they had their heads shaved and "were made to work on fortifications with the Negroes. One day our whole mess had killed a calf in order to get something to eat. For so doing, we were fined five dollars apiece, and had twenty days extra guard allotted to us. With such an officer in command, it cannot be wondered at that we came, as it were, 'demoralized.'" Murray felt that Byrd, "though a brave man, knew not how to respect the rights of a soldier serving his country through patriotism alone, and who done everything to make us miserable, though he was unconscious of it. He, as commander of the post, imposed on us duties that any volunteer would rebel against, and then we would be treated as disobedient soldiers for disobeying his commands."[5] It seems that General Taylor was not the only one having problems with his commanding officer.

Capt. Edward T. King's Battery, the St. Martin Rangers, was another Louisiana unit stationed at DeRussy. Like Hutton's men, King and his company had also been engaged in the fight with *Albatross* the previous May. King's men were now designated as the fort's "Siege Battery."

In early February, Captain Boyd, the post engineer, once again ran into serious trouble. This time, however, it was not due to Major Douglas or a lack of laborers and supplies. About four o'clock on the afternoon of Wednesday, February 3, while bringing the fort's payroll from Alexandria, Boyd was ambushed on the north side of the river by a band of fifteen Jayhawkers. Unaware that he was carrying five thousand dollars in Confederate money stashed about his person, the men took him prisoner and carried him to Natchez, Mississippi, where he was "sold" to Union authorities there for one hundred dollars. As the Jayhawkers were moving their captive across the Black River at Mrs. Beard's, below Trinity, the boat they were in capsized, and in the confusion Boyd was able to push the payroll into the mud of the riverbank. The Jayhawkers never realized their prisoner was rich. Neither did they give any consideration to the fact that he was literate, and that at the first opportunity he would make a list of all their names and send it to the Confederate authorities in the area. But in spite of the fact that their names were known and there was a shoot-on-sight order out on all Jayhawkers, at least some of these men lived to procreate, because their descendants still survive in significant numbers throughout central Louisiana.[6]

5. Murray diary.
6. See Appendix F in this book for a list of the men who captured David Boyd.

Back at the fort, no one knew quite what had happened to Captain
Boyd. Rumors abounded that he had been ambushed by Jayhawkers, but
it was not until the following Monday that General Taylor learned that
Boyd was still alive and in Natchez. On Tuesday, Boyd's personal effects
were inventoried, including a horse, saddle, and saddle blanket that were
on loan to Ludger Barbin. Barbin's wife was eight months pregnant at
the time, so perhaps Boyd felt that Barbin had need of a good horse.

Not everyone was doing such mundane chores as inventorying.
North of the river, Maj. R. E. Wyche's Battalion of Louisiana State
Troops was ordered to comb the area for Jayhawkers. The order was
not ambivalent: "Such outrages must be punished with a strong hand,
and you are therefore directed to scour this portion of the country thoroughly, and every man found with arms in his hands, against whom reasonable suspicion exists of a determination to resist the laws, will be shot
by you on the spot. Such men must not be arrested."[7] Before the month
was out, Walker's Texans would also be involved in sweeps against the
Jayhawkers, and slave-tracking dogs would also be put on their trails.

The Confederates never were able to clean up the Jayhawkers in
lower Catahoula and Concordia Parishes or the surrounding areas. It
is interesting to note that in early 1865, when Union forces controlled
some of these same areas, the Yankees had just as much trouble with
these individuals as the Confederate authorities did.[8] To the present day,
some residents of these areas will argue that the descendants of these
Jayhawkers are just as bad as their grandpappies ever were.

As if the Jayhawkers and an expected invasion were not problem enough, the army at the fort was also beset by internal problems.
Morale was low, not only among the Louisiana troops but also among
the Texans, and not because of the weather or the lack of supplies.
These men were Confederate soldiers, and they could live and fight on
blue beef and bare feet all year long, if need be. As John Simmons wrote
to his wife, "We are getting enough to live on and no more, but if we
fare no worse we won't grumble."[9] But they had been severely aggravated for most of the winter by the cotton trading that they saw going
on between their senior officers and the Yankees. The trade had been
carried on most of the winter, and by late February and early March
the enlisted men were fed up. "There is quite a brisk trade carried on

7. Surget to Wyche, Feb. 4, 1864, *ORA* 34, pt. 2, 944.
8. Otis F. R. Waite, *New Hampshire in the Great Rebellion* (Claremont, N.H.:
Tracy, Chase, 1870), 390–91.

from this point with the Feds or citizens of New Orleans and smugglers who live along the river," David Ray wrote to his wife from Camp Glenwood, near Simmesport, in early March. "Government officers furnish these traders with cotton for which they give in return medicines, clothing, and articles of general merchandise, which is causing considerable dissatisfaction in the army. The men say they do not believe in fighting and trading with their enemies at the same time, and that they derive no benefit from it, and think the trade is carried on for the benefit of the high officials. A large quantity of goods, among which was a lot of coffee, passed here yesterday on the way to Division headquarters. I fear that there is too much truth in some of the complaints. . . . Someone has published a scurilous song expressing their contempt and dislike of the trade."[10] Samuel Farrow was of the same opinion: "They are letting the Yankees have cotton. I saw about 100 bales going to the river today. All the officers have paid up bills for articles, clothing and anything in the dry good line that they need. . . . My opinion is that if they are going to trade with and fight the Yankees both at the same time, that the poor men that are in the field had better go home."[11] William Tamplin of the 11th Texas Infantry wrote, "We Have a verry good camp. We are Station about one mile and a Half from Marksville. Our officers are trading with the Yankeys everry day."[12] Tamplin may not have been as educated as Ray and Farrow, but it did not take a lot of education to see that something fishy was going on. Joseph Blessington explained, "Many of the troops suspected there was foul play used in some manner or shape, and meetings were held among themselves, denouncing the cotton-buying scheme as an act of treason to the honest and patriotic people of the South. . . . Many of our men that were taken prisoners at Pleasant Hill, afterwards recognized some of the said cotton-buyers acting in the capacity of staff officers to General Banks, the Federal commander."[13]

The officers, of course, justified the trading. Captain Perry wrote to his wife on February 14 that she should have received some cloth from him and that "I will try to get you some calico soon. . . . Gen. Walker is

9. Simmons to My dear Nancy, Feb. 25, 1864, Simmons Letters.

10. Ray to Very Dear Mother, Mar. 6, 1864, Ray Letters.

11. Farrow to Dearest Josephine, Jan. 18, 1864, Farrow Letters.

12. Tamplin to Tincia, Feb. 20, 1864, William Tamplin Letters, Louisiana and Lower Mississippi Valley Collections, Hill Memorial Library, Louisiana State Univ., Baton Rouge.

13. Blessington, *Campaigns of Walker's Texas Division*, 162.

conniving at a little trade with the Yankees for necessary articles. Cotton exposed to their raids and which they will get if they advance into the country is carried down and sold to them or exchanged rather for these articles." This in spite of the fact that on February 3, General Taylor wrote to General Walker specifically forbidding the cotton trading that was going on: "No permission to trade can be given; it is against an act of Congress to send cotton and some other specified articles to the enemy. My desire to alleviate the distress of the people induced me to wink at the trade for a few bales for family supplies. Abuses of this forced me to execute the law rigorously."[14] Walker continued to "wink," however, and on February 11 one soldier near Simmesport wrote, "Government trains are still continually passing here loaded with cotton."[15] The troops got more and more resentful. "For the last two months the Government has been hauling cotton to the Yankees," Private Simmons wrote to his wife, "and what do you think they have gotten for it? Fine boots and calico for the officers and their wives! But there is not a thing for the privates who have borne the burden of the war, and who have always stood to their part. Let it come as it may, this thing of long-legged boots and calico is creating a great deal of dissatisfaction in this army."[16]

The situation finally came to a head on March 4, just one week after the above letter was written, with a mutiny by the dismounted cavalry units of Walker's Division. They were aggravated by the cotton trade, like all the other units were, but in addition to that, they had the additional grievance of being "dismounted." A dismounted cavalry unit is, as the name suggests, a unit of horsemen who have had their horses taken from them. There could be perhaps no greater offense to a mid-19th-century Texan than to have his horse taken away. To add injury to insult, being dismounted also meant a cut in pay, infantry pay being lower than cavalry pay. Rumors from back home indicated that cavalry units were being raised in Texas, while the units in Walker's Division remained dismounted. Dismounting, poor food, low pay, lack of furloughs, cotton trading with the Yankees—What's a fellow to do? The men of the 28th Texas Dismounted Cavalry were good Rebels, so they did just what you might expect. They rebelled.

    14. Taylor to Walker, Feb. 3, 1864, *ORA* 34, pt. 2, 939–40.
    15. Diary of William Quensell, Haldeman's Battery, in Edgar E. Lackner, "Diaries of Edwin F. Stanton, USA, and William Quensell, CSA," *East Texas Historical Journal* 18 (2): 25–59 (hereafter cited as Quensell diary).
    16. Simmons to My dear Nancy, Feb. 25, 1864, Simmons Letters.

Capt. Theophilus Perry, Company F, was caught between a rock and a hard place. He had been writing home, bragging to his wife about the good deals he could get on hard-to-find merchandise. And now his men were refusing to "do any duty whatever." Perry was aware of the fact that the cotton trade with the Federals was one of the causes of his men's dissatisfaction, but he did not seem to connect the mutiny to his own purchases. In the very letter in which he tells his wife of the mutiny at the fort, he bemoans the fact that "I do not know when I shall be able to make a fitting purchase for Mother." The mutiny spread, but after work stoppages on March 4 and 5 the revolt was subdued by the officers of the companies involved. With a few exceptions, the men seem to have quickly settled down after the initial disruptions. Perry arrested four men in his company, and others were arrested in Gould's Battalion and some other regiments. Four days after the affair, Perry felt that most of his men who were involved were "penitent, and will never enter into another affair of the kind," being "very much ashamed of their conduct" in "this disgraceful affair." But one of Perry's men, Jacob Beahm, "a bad case," was still under arrest at that time, and Perry thought that he would probably be shot after his court-martial, along with some of the other ringleaders. Also under arrest in the days after the mutiny were Perry and four of his fellow company commanders in the 28th Texas, as well as officers from other units at the fort. Perry's indignation knew no bounds at this outrage. "We are as innocent as children, and will so prove," he proclaimed in a letter home to his wife. He felt that Col. Eli Baxter was using his company officers as scapegoats in the affair to remove the stigma of mutiny from himself. Baxter seems to have regretted his hasty action in arresting his own officers, and was soon heard remarking that "he prays for a fight. Then all things will be dropped."[17] His prayers would soon be answered.

The mutinous units were moved to a camp on Lake Pearl, twelve miles from the fort. They left Fort DeRussy just days before the rest of the Confederate army.

While the Confederates at Fort DeRussy were preparing to defend the fort, the U.S. forces were preparing to take it. In the last days of February and the first days of March, a Union naval flotilla was gathering at the mouth of Red River. Red River Landing had been a permanent U.S. gunboat station since the summer of 1863, but the west

17. Theophilus Perry to Dear Wife, Perry to Dear Harriot; letters, Mar. 9, 13, 1864, Perry Letters.

bank of the Mississippi had generally been in Confederate possession. Paymaster E. D. Whitehouse of USS *Choctaw* had been at the landing since July 1863, and in all that time had "been on shore but 3 times on account of guerrillas."[18]

This situation changed in early March. By the tenth of the month there were twelve ironclads, four tinclads, and three wooden gunboats—"enough to eat Red River up," according to one Union seaman—staged at the landing.[19] Some of these gunboats had already made a tentative probe up the Red during the first days of March but had turned up Black River and attacked Fort Beauregard at Harrisonburg instead of proceeding up the Red to Fort DeRussy. The gunboats had been repulsed at Fort Beauregard and had returned to the mouth of the Red on March 5, some of them "completely riddled with shot and shell," to join the other gunboats accumulating there to await the arrival of army troops from Vicksburg.[20]

With the presence of a gunboat fleet manned by more than nine hundred sailors and marines, the crews of the boat were now free to go ashore with little fear of Confederate harassment. The monotony of shipboard life was now broken for small-arms practice, baseball games, foot races, and one inspection and dress parade for Admiral Porter. Officers would also take parties out to buy provisions from the local plantations. On the surface, the gunboat crews and the locals seemed to get along famously, now that the navy was present in force.[21] Capt. Frank Church, USMC, wrote in his diary of a visit by some of his new neighbors on March 3: "Several Secesh ladies from a plantation in the neighborhood came up on horseback to see the ship. Two of them were really beautiful and rode splendidly."[22] Church, of course, had no way of knowing that he was just a few miles from the spot where one of these "Secesh ladies," or at least one of their close friends, had sung "The Bonnie Blue Flag" while she watched the crew of *Queen of the West* burn down her home. One of the young ladies lost no time in

18. Diary of Capt. Frank Church, USMC, Mar. 2, 1864, in James P. Jones and Edward F. Keuchel, eds., *Civil War Marine: A Diary of the Red River Expedition, 1864* (Washington, D.C.: History and Museums Division, Headquarters, U.S. Marine Corps, 1975), 35 (hereafter cited as Church diary).

19. Mooney diary, Mar. 11, 1864. Edward Mooney, USN, served aboard USS *Lafayette* and kept a detailed diary of his time in the navy.

20. Church diary, Mar. 5, 1864.

21. Ibid., Mar. 1–10, 1864.

22. Ibid., Mar. 3, 1864.

riding the few miles to Simmesport and reporting to the Confederate troops at Fort Humbug on the Union armada that was growing at Red River Landing. In 1875, when the first history of Walker's Texas Division was printed, her exploits were recalled: "The heroism of this young lady, riding several miles through the woods, showed what Southern women would do for their country. It is to be regretted that her name was not jotted down to adorn the pages of this history. Yet she is not forgotten in the minds of Scurry's Brigade."[23] The cannonading at Fort Beauregard had been heard by the Confederate troops at Simmesport and Fort DeRussy and was an ominous sign of things to come. With the arrival of the messenger from Red River Landing, there was no longer any doubt whatever that the Yankees were coming.

23. Blessington, *Campaigns of Walker's Texas Division*, 167.

Chapter 9

The Grand Skedaddle

At 4:00 P.M. on March 10, 1864, the long anticipated Union movement against Fort DeRussy began. With the firing of a signal gun, twenty transport steamers packed with ten thousand men of the U.S. Army's 16th and 17th Corps and elements of the Mississippi Marine Brigade,[1] escorted by the ironclad USS *Benton,* set off down the Mississippi from Vicksburg for the mouth of the Red River. The 16th and 17th Corps were made up mostly of midwestern men and boys, from Missouri, Iowa, Wisconsin, Indiana, Illinois, Ohio, and Minnesota, with one regiment of New Yorkers thrown in. By all accounts, these battle-hardened veterans of Vicksburg and other campaigns lacked the refinement and sophistication of their eastern comrades in the 19th Corps, but as fighters they were second to none. The expedition was under the command of Brig. Gen. Andrew Jackson Smith, a no-nonsense regular army officer with combat experience against both southern Confederates and western Indians.[2] Smith's men were to advance up Red River, reduce Fort DeRussy, and link up with Maj. Gen. Nathaniel P. Banks and his 19th Corps, who would be marching overland from southern Louisiana. They were to meet in Alexandria on March 26, from whence they would continue up Red River to Shreveport and Texas, sweeping any Confederate resistance before them. Banks, the overall commander of the expedition, had a seriously lackluster military reputation.

By 11:00 A.M. on Friday, March 11, the boats from Vicksburg were arriving at Red River Landing, joining the nineteen U.S. Navy gunboats

---

1. It cannot be emphasized often enough that the Mississippi Marine Brigade was not connected in any way with the U.S. Marine Corps. There were, however, U.S. Marines aboard some of the navy gunboats on this expedition.

2. It was somewhat ironic that A. J. Smith would be commander of the troops assaulting Fort DeRussy. Smith was a graduate of the U.S. Military Academy, studying as a cadet there from July 1834 to July 1838. During this period, the superintendent of the academy was Maj. René Edward DeRussy, brother of the fort's eponym. If Smith did not know Lewis DeRussy personally, he certainly knew of his family.

already there. The transports had not been at the landing long before some of the soldiers made their way ashore to cook and forage—"They brought in many chickens and hogs"—and by nightfall one house ("a big fine house," according to Col. John Williams of the 8th Wisconsin) and a cotton gin were already on fire. "Just about dark, some one set fire to a large house; it illuminated the scene until late at night. There always seems to be some in every army who delight in the destruction of property," explained Capt. Edmund Newsome of the 81st Illinois.[3] Gen. A. J. Smith's soldiers were known for their predisposition to burning and looting—they were, after all, on loan from the command of Gen. William Tecumseh Sherman, who would gain infamy burning his way across Georgia later in the war—and the Mississippi Marine Brigade's reputation was even worse. The troops were called back aboard ship and Marine guards (real U.S. Marines) were sent ashore to guard the widow Torras's property.[4]

In fairness, it must be pointed out that not all of the Union troops agreed with the concept of indiscriminate destruction. Several writers remarked on the fires and were vehement in their condemnation of this behavior. Capt. William Stewart, of the 95th Illinois, commented,

> Strange with what ardor soldiers jump at the chance of burning and destroying something & grumble if they are not permitted. Their bump of destructiveness must be large or else grows active by use until it becomes morbid and a power.
>
> I can't bear it, and it requires the strongest kind of provocation to make me consent to it. It looks so wanton and outrageous. Gen[eral Smith] has issued strenuous orders against meddling or destroying any property on pain of death and hold the officers responsible.[5]

3. Edmund Newsome, *Experience in the War of the Great Rebellion* (1880; reprint, Murphrysboro, Ill: Jackson County Printing, 1984), 65. John M. Williams diary, Mar. 11, 1864, Wisconsin Historical Society, Madison.

4. Church diary, Mar. 11, 1864. E. H. Wells, "Sketch of the Country between Atchafalaya and Mississippi Occupied by Maj. Gen. Walker's Division during Part of November and December 1863," within a letter to Major General Walker, from Mountville, La., Oct. 16, 1863, Walker Papers.

5. Captain William R. Stewart diary, Mar. 14, 1864, Manuscript Division, Univ. of North Carolina Library, Chapel Hill (hereafter cited as Stewart diary). All of the Stewart diary entries are misdated, events being marked as one day after the actual day of occurrence.

A journalist covering the expedition had similar feelings about the event:

> I should not be a faithful historian if I omitted to mention that the conduct of the troops since the late raid of General Sherman [to Meridian, Mississippi], is becoming very prejudicial to our good name and to their efficiency. A spirit of destruction and wanton ferocity seems to have seized upon many of them, which is quite incredible. At Red River landing they robbed a house of several thousand dollars in specie, and then fired the house to conceal their crime. At Simmsport, a party of them stole out, and robbed and insulted a family two miles distant. In fact, unless checked by summary example, there is danger of our whole noble army degenerating into a band of cut-throats and robbers. I am glad to say that General Smith is disposed to punish all offenders severely.[6]

Both these men state that General Smith promised swift and severe punishment for any of his men caught pillaging. The conduct of Smith's men in the days to follow (after the Red River Campaign, the area of Louisiana visited by the expedition would be referred to as the "Burnt District"), and the fact that Smith himself was seen riding through downtown Alexandria just two months later, shouting to his men, "Hurrah, boys, this looks like war!" as they put the city to the torch, would seem to indicate that Smith was not as concerned about civilian property as he would have had people believe.[7]

At 8:30 the following morning, the armada hoisted anchors and moved out of the Mississippi into Old River, then turned south into the Atchafalaya. It made for an impressive display.[8] The gunboats, mounting more than two hundred guns, led the way and provided escort. There were the ironclads *Benton, Carondelet, Chillicothe, Choctaw, Eastport, Essex, Lafayette, Louisville, Mound City,* and *Pittsburg;* the monitors *Neosho, Osage,* and *Ozark;* the tinclads *Argosy, Black*

---

6. Moore, *Rebellion Record* 8:430. The information concerning looting of slave quarters and the burning of the house at Red River Landing is corroborated by Capt. George Burmeister, 35th Iowa. George C. Burmeister journal, 1864, transcript in possession of Ginny Torres, Tacoma, Wash. (hereafter cited as Burmeister journal).

7. David C. Edmonds, ed., *The Conduct of Federal Troops in Louisiana During the Invasions of 1863 and 1864* (Lafayette, La.: Acadiana Press, 1988), 152.

8. Although the lead boats left at 8:30 A.M., the fleet was so large that the transport carrying the 35th Iowa did not leave its anchorage until a little before noon. Burmeister journal.

Hawk, Cricket, Fort Hindman, Gazelle, Juliet, and *Little Rebel;* and
the timberclads *General Bragg, General Price,* and *Lexington.* Nestled
safely among the gunboats were the ordnance steamer *Judge Torrance;*
the ram *Samson,* now serving as a blacksmith boat and towing a carpenter shop; the tug *Dahlia;* the hospital boat *Woodford;* and the troop
transports *Adriatic, Autocrat, Baltic, Clarabell, Des Moines, Diadem,
Diana, Emerald, Hamilton, Hastings, Henry P. Chouteau, J. H. Lacy,
James Battle, John Raines, Liberty, Mars, Sioux City, South Wester,
Thomas E. Tutt,* and *W. J. Ewing.*[9]
     The sight of the flotilla inspired awe and no small amount of con-
fidence in the men aboard:

> As the fleet of gunboats and transports moved up the channel of
> the old river, about noon of the 12th, the scene as presented to the
> eye of the soldier from the hurricane deck of the *South Wester,*
> was truly grand. At times the fleet moved in groups or clusters,
> and in some bends the whole could be seen at one view, and as the
> transports were densely packed from boiler to hurricane deck, with
> soldiers in blue, together with the gaudy uniforms of the marines
> on the gunboats, and all with the stars and stripes floating in the
> breeze, was a scene not soon to be forgotten.[10]

The soldiers aboard the boats were aware that they were part of an
historic occasion:

> It was an exceeding fine country on either side of the river; and,
> as the boats, one by one, passed down the placid waters of the
> stream, and moved in toward the shore the sight was really charm-
> ing. Never before, in he history of the Nation have the waters of the
> Atchafalaya bore so magnificent a prize, or these shores witnessed
> so magnificent a scene. 1st the daring gun-boats, then the trans-
> ports, each clad in blue, and then the small, swift dispatch boats;
> all have found their way into the forests of Louisiana, upon these
> waters unknown to fame.[11]

     9. Deck log, USS *Benton;* Mooney diary; Capt. William Rion Hoel, "The Red
River Expedition of 1864" (excerpt from Capt. William Rion Hoel diary), *S&D Reflec-
tor* 10, no. 3 (Sept. 1973): 11–16.
     10. John Scott, *Story of the Thirty Second Iowa Infantry Volunteers* (Nevada,
Iowa, 1896), 130–31.
     11. Charles H. Lewis to Friend Rich, Mar. 17, 1864, in *History of Buchanan County,
Iowa 1842 to 1881,* ed. C. S. and Elizabeth Percival (Cleveland: Williams Brothers Pub-
lishers, 1881), 197.

Captain Stewart of the 95th Illinois seems to have been as impressed by the sound of the fleet as he was by the sight:

> They move majestically—slow—but onward. The Transports from the head belch out 3 bellowing whistles which is caught up by the next and next and sometimes 2 or 3 vie in an ufonious [euphonious] concert much resembling the bellowing of cattle at the smell of blood—Wonder if they too smell blood and therefore bellow—but we are under way and all safely over, ours [*John Raines*] fetching up the rear followed by the hospital boat.[12]

The scene as presented to the eye of the Confederate pickets on the banks of the Atchafalaya at Simmesport seems not to have been as impressive—at first. Most of the gunboats had left the column and moved up Red River instead of going down the Atchafalaya, leaving only *Benton, Carondelet, Chillicothe, Louisville, Mound City,* and *Pittsburg* escorting the transports. But more significantly, the boats had strung out as they moved down the river, and the first reports arriving at General Scurry's headquarters back at Fort Humbug indicated that three crowded troop transports and a two-gunboat escort had arrived at the town. Scurry estimated this to mean an attacking force of about two thousand men, and he immediately prepared his command, numbering fourteen hundred, to move to Simmesport and throw the invaders back into the river. But before Scurry's Brigade could leave Fort Humbug, two miles distant from the Atchafalaya, the reports began to change. By 3:30 P.M. there were five transports docked at Simmesport, and light skirmishing was taking place between mounted Confederate pickets and some of the first Union troops to debark. By 4:15 another fourteen transports had arrived. The pickets who had been watching the banks of the Atchafalaya soon arrived at Humbug, on the "double-quick" and out of breath. The odds, it seems, had changed. The riverbanks "were literally crowded with live Yankees," the sentries reported. "They informed us, furthermore, that they lost all their cooking utensils, and, if they had not been better runners than the Yankees, they would have had *them* with their cooking utensils."[13]

Scurry's estimate of "live Yankees" to his front quickly ballooned from two thousand to eighteen thousand (the actual count was probably

12. Stewart diary, Mar. 13, 1864. Three whistles was the signal for close order. Newsome, *Experience in the War,* 119 n.
13. Blessington, *Campaigns of Walker's Texas Division,* 167.

somewhere near eleven thousand, with perhaps an additional nine hundred naval personnel). To make matters worse, most of Scurry's small cavalry force—his army's eyes and ears—was cut off by the arriving Union forces. The Yankee army at Simmesport now had access to a road, just a few miles north of the town, that went to Moreauville and bypassed the fort. Should the Northerners take advantage of this road, Scurry would have no cavalry scouts to alert him and could soon find himself encircled. Add to this the fact that the swamp that was supposed to defend Fort Humbug's southern flank was dry and passable this year, and it all came out to one unsettling reality—the position at the fort was untenable. Scurry would have to fall back beyond Moreauville, so that any encircling Yankees would still be to his front. He would also be putting himself closer to the rest of Walker's Texas Division, just on the off chance that one Texan could not whip ten Yankees—or "a cowpen full," as one Mississippi soldier put it after the war. That soldier went on to explain, "I soon found that the Yankees could shoot as far and as accurately as I could, and from then until the end of the war I was fully of the opinion that the United States Army was totally prepared to give me all the fight I wanted."[14] Scurry's Brigade had been waiting all winter to fight the Yankees, but as Scurry's updated reports continued to arrive at General Walker's headquarters, it became apparent that the Union army landing at Simmesport was totally prepared to give Scurry's Brigade *more* than all the fight it wanted. Walker ordered Scurry to fall back to the Long Bridge beyond Moreauville, and at 10:00 P.M. on Saturday night, March 12, 1864, Fort Humbug was abandoned. Fort DeRussy's first line of defense had dissolved with hardly a shot being fired, and the Red River Campaign's Grand Skedaddle was on.

Over the years, much has been written about the reasons for the Red River Expedition. There have been many accusations that the campaign was in fact a "mercantile expedition," organized primarily for the purpose of capturing the large amounts of very valuable cotton that remained in the Red River Valley in 1864. This cotton would help the Union war effort and the Northern textile mills, but more important, according to the more cynical writers, it would enrich a number of cotton speculators with political connections. While the senior officers involved in the campaign denied that cotton was the reason behind the move up Red River, citing other reasons of a tactical and political

---

14. Mamie Yeary, ed., *Reminiscences of the Boys in Gray, 1861–1865* (Dallas: Smith & Lamar, 1912), 215.

nature, many of the Yankee enlisted men and junior officers seemed to believe that "cotton stealing" was the primary motivating factor that sent them into central Louisiana that spring.

Whether or not cotton stealing was the primary reason for the expedition, the U.S. Navy certainly lost no time in getting down to the business of hauling cotton. The gunboats of the fleet arrived at Simmesport around noon on March 12, and by 1:30 P.M., USS *Louisville* had already taken on board twenty-three bales of cotton. Navy prize laws made the capture of cotton a profitable enterprise for the sailors and officers involved, and at 3:00 P.M. *Benton* also sent men ashore looking for cotton. The hunt for cotton seems to have taken precedence over the security of the boats and landing site. The sailors from *Benton* were skirmishing with Confederate pickets within half an hour. No casualties were reported on either side, but the *Benton* deck log does mention that seven bales of cotton were brought aboard the following morning. Perhaps this was an early indication of the navy's priorities in the early part of the Red River Expedition.[15]

By early that Saturday evening, Simmesport was thronging with Northern soldiers who had come ashore to cook. They did not find much to visit in the town. In early 1864, Simmesport was "a name without a place. Although there were the ruins of several burned buildings, yet two small vacant dwellings comprised the town."[16] When the U.S. ram *Switzerland* reconnoitered the town in June 1863, the "frail wooden boat" was shelled severely by a Texas battery in a small fort next to the village and three sailors were seriously wounded. *Switzerland* returned the next day with the ironclads *Lafayette* and *Pittsburg,* much like a small boy bringing his big brothers back to handle the schoolyard bully. The Texans were run off and the town burned.[17] In March 1864, little remained of the town but the site.

And on this Saturday night in 1864, the Texans were run off again. Around 10:00 P.M., while the Yankees unloaded at Simmesport,

15. In the latter part of the Red River expedition, the navy's priority would be saving itself from destruction. But at this early stage, cotton was king. In addition to the cotton taken aboard *Louisville* and *Benton* that afternoon, *Carondelet* and *Pittsburg* each got an additional three bales. Deck logs, USS *Pittsburg* and USS *Louisville*, RG 24, NA, and USS *Carondelet* and USS *Benton*.

16. Harris H. Beecher, *Record of the 114th Regiment N.Y.S.V.: Where It Went, What It Saw, and What It Did* (Norwich, N.Y.: J. F. Hubbard Jr., 1866), 354. Elijah Petty only counted "one house standing here and many chimneys." Brown, *Journey to Pleasant Hill*, 283.

17. Walke to Porter, June 4, 1863, and Ellet to Walke, June 3, 1863, *ORN* 25:154–56.

Scurry's Brigade abandoned Fort Humbug and set off up the road for Moreauville, marching toward the crescent moon that shone high above them in the western sky. Breaking camp at night is not an easy task; items tend to get overlooked and left behind. This occasion was no different, and on arriving at Moreauville at two o'clock in the morning it was found that tents and cooking utensils, along with some other items, were missing. Men and wagons were sent back to the fort to recover the missing equipment, but on nearing the fort the Texans found several regiments of early-rising Yankees approaching it "in line of battle with fixed bayonets."[18] The recovery mission turned into a footrace as the Rebels tried to get their wagons turned around and headed back for Moreauville. The Yankees followed in hot pursuit, and after a chase of several miles they captured six wagons and about twenty men. Some of the other Texans managed to get away. The Union soldiers, who referred to the earthworks at Fort Humbug as "Fort Scurry," were under the impression that the wagons were the tail end of the general retreat from the fort, and one sarcastic fellow reported that the Rebels, "taking the name of their fort for their motto, 'skurried' away across the country to a place of safety, leaving the entire armament of the fort and a considerable quantity of stores for our particular benefit."[19] The Yankees were somewhat surprised, but no doubt pleased, to find "the camp broken up and the enemy gone; the bridge leading across the stream burning, and evidence of a fright. There were two extensive earthworks, still incomplete, and a prodigious raft being constructed across Bayou Glaize so as to prevent the gunboats ascending the little channel during high-water."[20] Charles Lewis of the 27th Iowa described the fort and surrounding area:

> Three miles back from the river, at Bayou Blaize [des Glaises], the
> enemy had constructed strong fortifications, which, if filled with
> guns and men, would have commanded the broad and level tract of
> country between them and the river. Large trees had been felled on
> either side of this broad clearing, which formed an excellent abat-

18. Maj. John C. Becht to Col. Oscar Malmross, May 25, 1864, *ORA* 34, pt. 1, 323.
19. John M. Williams, *"The Eagle Regiment," 8th Wis. Inf'ty Vols.* (Belleville, Wis.: Recorder Print, 1890). In his official report of the action, A. J. Smith said that Scurry's Brigade "abandoned their work and fled at his [General Mower's] approach. He [Mower] pursued them about 2 miles." Smith to Sherman, Sept. 26, 1865, *ORA* 34, pt. 1, 305. The earthworks were also referred to as Fort Taylor, but that name did not lend itself to clever witticisms. Burmeister journal.
20. Moore, *Rebellion Record* 8:430.

tis. On our way out to the fortifications we saw much of southern vegetation that was new to us. The tall, spreading evergreen, the large sycamore, and the oak, were all clad in drooping festoons of Spanish moss, which hangs in endless quantities from almost every tree, giving the grove a funereal aspect. A large bridge, which spanned a stream fifty feet in width, directly in front of the earthworks, had been burned.[21]

After an examination of the abandoned fort, the Union troops returned to Simmesport, arriving there around 6:00 P.M. There they were ordered to "draw five days rations of hardtack, coffee and salt, and an extra supply of ammunition, and be ready to start at any moment."[22] That moment was not long in coming. By early that night (8:00 to 9:00 P.M., by most accounts) the Union army at Simmesport was on the road to Fort DeRussy.

21. Lewis to Friend Rich, Mar. 17, 1864.
22. Scott, *Story of the Thirty Second Iowa,* 131. Charles Lewis, 27th Iowa, said that each man received eighty rounds of ammunition.

Chapter 10

Here They Come Again

Jobe Roberts of the 41st Illinois Infantry wrote a pleasant little description of the movement on and capture of Fort DeRussy: "Here [Simmesport] we disembarked and took up the march for Fort DeRussy on Red River and we have to march fifteen miles. And as we went along, we past through a number of French villages and there are pretty flowers in bloom and all nature putting on her new frock for summer, the birds singing and the people happy and glad to see us and we marched on to Fort DeRussy and get in the rear of the Fort at 5 p. m., and surrounded it and form a battle line and they ordered us to charge and away we went and in twenty minutes the fort is ours and the flag is US."[1]

Actually, there was a bit more to it than that. The lead elements of the march on Fort DeRussy stepped off around 8:00 P.M. on Sunday night, March 13, but it was nearly midnight before the end of the column left Simmesport. In spite of the difficulties in maintaining an orderly column during a night march, the first units in the line had covered nine miles by midnight, stopping then to camp near the Howard plantation, close to the present-day community of Hamburg. The men quickly made coffee and grabbed a meal, then lay down to sleep. Their comrades in the rear of the column were not having it so easy. At 5:00 P.M., the 95th Illinois was told to prepare to march by 6:00 P.M., but it was not until nearly 11:00 P.M. that they left Simmesport. The accordion effect that all foot soldiers are familiar with is particularly noticeable on a rough road on a dark night, and the last regiment in line did not get to bed down until 3:00 A.M. The lead elements were up and moving at 4:00 A.M., while the trailing units slept until sunrise. In spite of the necessary stopping and starting, the night was cool and the marching was not particularly unpleasant. The 117th Illinois left Simmesport at sundown then had to stack arms and wait for "teams

---

1. Jobe Roberts, *The Experience of a Private in the Civil War* (Sylvan Beach, N.Y.: published by author, 1904), 35.

& ambulances & artillery to get ready," and at 8:00 P.M., one soldier recorded in his diary, "we started on our moonlight march. The moon went down & we went on-on-on till a few minutes before two o'clock when we halted & rec'd orders that reveille would be at four. This left us only two hours to sleep & the quicker we got to bed the more sleep we would get. This was the longest night march we had made but we were fresh & the roads were good & dry, so we made it easy enough."[2]

By sunup the entire column was back on the road. The Confederate pickets near Moreauville heard them coming before they saw them. "The sound of numerous drums in the distance" kept getting louder, but there was no way to tell exactly how many troops were approaching, until 8:30 A.M. when the head of the Union column arrived in Moreauville, "a dusty and hog-afflicted little place, without a hotel, and with but few or no Anglo-American residents, and one or two small stores."[3] The column came up the Cut-Off Road from the Howard plantation, and after passing through the village filed left along Bayou des Glaises, moving toward the crossing at Lemoine's Ferry.[4] The Confederate pickets reported back to General Walker on the awe-inspiring sight they had seen—the Union column "extended for 2 ½ miles along the banks of the DeGlaize, through the village of Moreauville, and disappeared in the cut-off in the direction of the Atchafalaya."[5] Fifteen to seventeen thousand men, Walker estimated, and maybe thirty or forty pieces of light artillery, with some three hundred cavalry. The estimates were all high. There were about ten thousand men coming up the road, infantry and cavalry combined, and the light artillery consisted of two batteries, or twelve guns. Apparently, it looked like more.

Nonetheless, Walker's Texans attempted to stem the oncoming blue tide. The Yankees were not impressed: "They fell back as we advanced, attempting to burn bridges and retard our progress. We pressed them closely, and although several bridges were fired, little damage was done to affect our progress."[6] Sniping from the far bank of the bayou was

---

2. Benjamin R. Hieronymus diary, Mar. 13, 1864, Illinois State Historical Library, Springfield (hereafter cited as Hieronymus diary).

3. Walter Prichard, ed., "A Tourist's Description of Louisiana in 1860," *Louisiana Historical Quarterly* 21 (1938): 1146.

4. The site of Lemoine's Ferry is now officially known as Desselle's Crossing, but for years it has been known to the locals as the Cow Bridge.

5. Walker to Surget, Mar. 19, 1864, *ORA* 34, pt. 1, 598.

6. Col. William T. Shaw to Capt. J. B. Sample, Mar. 17, 1864, *ORA* 34, pt. 1, 352.

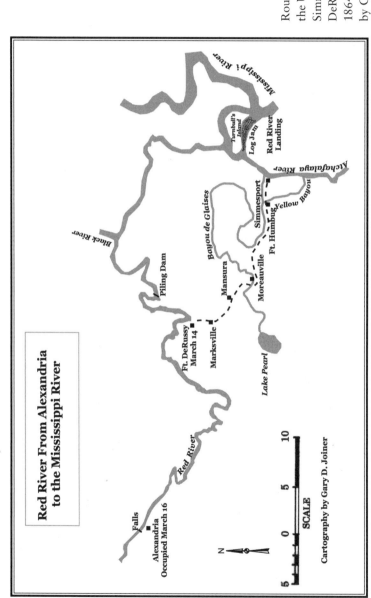

Route of march of the Union army from Simmesport to Fort DeRussy, March 14, 1864. (Cartography by Gary Joiner.)

Red River From Alexandria to the Mississippi River

Mississippi River

Turnbull's Island

Log Jam

Red River Landing

Atchafalaya River

Bayou de Glaises

Simmesport

Yellow Bayou

Ft. Humbug

Black River

Piling Dam

Mansura

Moreauville

Marksville

Ft. DeRussy March 14

Lake Pearl

Falls

Alexandria Occupied March 16

Red River

N

SCALE

5   0   5   10

Cartography by Gary D. Joiner

equally ineffective. A soldier in the 27th Iowa reported that "Bayou Blaize, though narrow, is quite deep even at this dry season, as I can attest after having tried to ford it in pursuit of rebels."[7]

Things had not been boring at Fort DeRussy since the Yankees landed at Simmesport. On Wednesday, March 9, General Walker reported that the preparations at Fort DeRussy would be completed in ten days. On that same day, Captain Devoe was calling for planters along the river to dump as much driftwood as could be found into the river. General Taylor nervously watched the race to complete the fort: "If I can complete De Russy, so as to get it off my hands, it will be a great relief."[8] But hours after he made that comment, on Saturday night, March 12, a courier arrived at Fort DeRussy notifying the post that time had run out. The Yankees were at Simmesport in force, and Fort Humbug was being evacuated.

Walker immediately began moving Hawes's and Randal's brigades from the Marksville–Fort DeRussy area to Long Bridge, just below Mansura, where they joined up with Scurry's Brigade as it fell back from Fort Humbug. By afternoon on March 13, Walker's Division was occupying the high ground and light artillery works at the head of the bridge. There they waited. Taylor, meanwhile, was sending a reassuring message to Walker. "The enemy," he was sure, "have not transportation enough to move more than 6,000 men at a time, and 4,000 of your men can whip any such force." But the confident tone did not run through the whole message: "We must risk a great deal to prevent the loss of our material at De Russy. . . . I repeat, the loss of our material at De Russy and the occupation of Alexandria by the Federals would be a great disaster, and, therefore, we must take more than ordinary hazards in fighting." About the time Walker was receiving that message from Taylor, Taylor was receiving a message from Walker. Taylor's heart must have sunk when he read it: "I feel most solicitous for the fate of Fort De Russy, as it must fall as soon almost as invested by the force now marching against it."[9]

At daybreak on March 13, Taylor sent word to Walker to pack up everything unnecessary at Fort DeRussy and send it to Alexandria. This Sunday was definitely not a day of rest. With Walker's Division moved

7. Lewis to Friend Rich, Mar. 17, 1864.

8. Taylor to Boggs, Mar. 12, 1864, *ORA* 34, pt. 1, 491.

9. Taylor to Walker, Mar. 13, 1864, *ORA* 34, pt. 1, 493; Walker to Taylor, Mar. 13, 1864, *ORA* 34, pt. 1, 492.

down to Long Bridge, the 380 men left at the fort were busy. A company of riflemen were sent a mile or two downriver under the command of Capt. Seth Mabry of the 17th Texas to keep an eye out for advancing Yankee gunboats. The steamboat *Frolic* was on her way down from Alexandria to help with the evacuation, while *Countess* and *Dixie* were already at the landing, loading up slaves, tools, and property. With the slaves gone, final preparations for the attack had to be completed by the "labor of the garrison."

Capt. Edward T. King's Battery was particularly busy. The battery had been ordered to evacuate its two 30-pounder Parrott guns from the fort, but after the guns had been loaded aboard one of the steamboats, orders came to send them overland to Alexandria. The guns were disembarked, but sending them cross country was easier said than done. The typical Civil War field piece tube was about six feet long and weighed between seven hundred and one thousand pounds. By contrast, the gun tube of a 30-pounder Parrott is ten feet long and weighs in at forty-two hundred pounds. Somehow, the guns were mounted on field carriages and sent on their way north, each gun lumbering slowly across the prairie pulled by teams of oxen. The guns "presented such a novel appearance that, when first seen by our troops, they created no little merriment. A witty soldier, incited by the comical idea of artillery drawn by oxen, exclaimed, at the top of his voice, 'here goes your *Bull* battery'; and by that appellation these pieces were afterwards known during the entire campaign."[10]

The Bull Battery were not the only refugees from the fort as the Yankees approached. On Friday, March 11, as the men in the fort made their preparations to deal out death, the miracle of life occurred at the

10. Edward T. King to Editor, *New Orleans Times Democrat,* June 27, 1910, p. 14, Edith Garland Dupré Library, Univ. of Louisiana, Lafayette (hereafter cited as King letter). King was eighty-eight years old when the letter was written, forty-four years after the events happened. As a result, some events spoken of in the letter are out of chronological order. The "Bull Battery" incident is confirmed by T. R. Bonner, "Sketches of the Campaign of 1864," *Land We Love,* Oct. 1868, 460, and Blessington, *Campaigns of Walker's Texas Division,* 174. Blessington obviously plagiarized from Bonner's account, but he has each gun pulled by "a dozen oxen" as opposed to Bonner's "dozen yokes of oxen." One source (Quensell diary) says that on March 21 the oxen gave out and the guns were buried, but if that is true, they were later recovered and the oxen replaced. Some two months after the battery left Fort DeRussy, a soldier from the 83rd Ohio complained that "our line of march was paralleled by a rebel line some mile or two to our right. They had a large gun hauled by oxen and we were often treated to a shell from it." This was on May 16, 1864, somewhere in the Marksville-Mansura area. Marshall, *History of the Eighty-Third Ohio,* 143.

Angelica Lucille Barbin was born at Barbin's Landing just three days before the fort was captured in 1864 and her home was burned down. She is the author's great-grandmother. (Photograph courtesy of Theresa Thevenote.)

landing on the river as little Angelica Lucille Barbin made her debut in the world. Angelica was the daughter of Ludger and Virginie Goudeau Barbin, the owners of the property on which Fort DeRussy stood and the operators of Barbin's Landing. With word of the movement against the fort, the birthday celebration was no doubt short-lived. Little Angelica was bundled up against the cool March air; Virginie, her heart as heavy as the Bull Battery's guns, took a long look at her home, hoping against hope that she would soon be able to return to it; and with anxious neighbors and family assisting, mother and child were taken from the landing to safer environs.[11]

On Sunday night, March 13, the men in the fort slept at their guns, after singing their camp songs. Perhaps they sang to hide their nervousness, or perhaps they sang to hide the growling of their stomachs— there had been no meals at the fort since Saturday morning. But more likely the former, for as John Murray ominously informed his diary, "It may be the last we'll sing together."[12]

---

11. Personal records of Lucille Coco Bordelon (daughter of Angelica Lucille Barbin).
12. Murray diary, Mar. 13, 1864.

The bulk of Walker's Division, on the bluffs at the head of the Long Bridge, also slept with their guns by their sides that night. Felix Pierre Poché, as gung-ho a staff officer as ever mounted a horse, arrived on Monday morning, March 14, to find preparations ongoing for the upcoming battle:

> Walker formed his line of battle on the Mansura prairie with his left wing placed on Mansura and his right in the woods at Grand Pont [Long Bridge]. Being anxious to see the fight, I offered my services as aide-de-camp to General Scurry who accepted immediately, and I fell in line with his general staff, helping to transmit his orders. The army was making preparations to fight, the regiments lined up one behind the other, the commands were given and promptly obeyed by the various commanders, the Batteries came at a gallop dispersing here and there among the regiments, the aides-de-camp of the various generals on their beautiful horses, galloped between the lines, and transmitted the orders of their superiors, the male nurses of the hospitals with their identification marks consisting of a white cloth attached to their arms, carrying their boyards, formed a spectacle at the same time interesting, sublime and sad to observe by those who know that soon the cannon will begin to rumble and belch forth their deadly missiles on that band of men and in a few minutes the ground will be covered with bloody corpses.[13]

While Poché awaited the battle and pondered his mortality, the advance elements of the approaching Union army, commanded by Col. William T. Shaw, arrived at Lemoine's Ferry. There Shaw found the Confederate advance lines, "a force of about 600 or 800 men," busy tearing up the low-water bridge across Bayou des Glaises. Sensing that the Rebels intended to make a stand here, Shaw called forward the 3rd Indiana Battery and a regiment of infantry and ordered them to clear the far bank of enemy. The battery "moved quickly up, unlimbered and sent her shells into the enemy's ranks with great rapidity. Under the protection

13. Edwin C. Bearss, ed., *A Louisiana Confederate: Diary of Felix Pierre Poché* (Natchitoches: Louisiana Studies Institute, Northwestern State Univ., 1972), 94.

14. Scott, *Story of the Thirty Second Iowa*, 131; Shaw to Sample, Mar. 17, 1864, ORA 34, pt. 1, 352. In A. J. Smith's official report of the campaign, he tells of crossing the bayou at Mansura. The crossing was actually made much closer to Moreauville, quite a few miles from Mansura. This error has been repeated in more recent accounts of the campaign. Smith to Sherman, ORA 34, pt. 1, 305; Winters, *Civil War in Louisiana*, 328.

of the battery we were ferried over in some rickety old flat boats." With the Rebels gone, Shaw called forward his engineers to replace the destroyed bridge.[14]

Lemoine's Ferry consisted of a crude bridge for crossing the bayou at low water along with a ferry boat for crossing during high-water periods. The bridge had been burnt by the Confederates, but in their haste to say goodbye to the guns of the 3rd Indiana, they had neglected to destroy the boat. While one small boat was not capable of ferrying across the entire army, it did allow the Yankees to establish a bridgehead on the far side. A cotton gin on the south bank of the bayou was quickly torn down, and the wood from the gin used to rebuild the bridge.

Wars are of necessity unpleasant affairs, but somehow soldiers will find time to laugh. And nothing, it seems, is more amusing for the troops than watching their senior officers take a dunking:

> A delay of some two hours was caused in crossing the Bayou
> DeGlaze & a very funny accident happened while crossing. Our
> brigade was crossing on a flat ferry while a bridge was building.
> The 178th [New York] & 49th [Illinois] had crossed over & the
> first load of our regiment [117th Illinois] was starting when the boat
> tipped water & began going down. The balance of our regiment
> was collected along the bank. The water was not deep so we knew
> there was no great danger. Col. Merriam was on and several other
> mounted men & a part of our company. Some of the horses fell off
> & the flurry & excitement was very laughable. Mr. Drum Major
> was scared & made many amusing gestures, bobbing up & down in
> the water trying to climb the bank—he would get just about out of
> the water & then slip back again.[15]

Gen. John Walker, CSA, was not laughing. His preparations for battle were complete, but the battle would never be. Walker explained his decision to sacrifice Fort DeRussy at length in his official report:

---

15. Hieronymus diary, Mar. 14, 1864. It is regrettable that this incident did not happen a short while earlier, while the 178th New York was crossing, for surely it would have been even funnier then. The 178th was a Zouave unit, and the men were dressed as follows: "scarlet wool fez with blue tassel, dark blue wool serge short jacket, vest and full trousers. Their sashes were turquoise blue. They had black leather cartridge box sliding on waist belt, oval U.S. brass belt plate and white canvas gaiters. The blue jacket and trousers had elaborate crimson or magenta lace and piping. The officers wore similar dress with scarlet French style caps." Margie Bearss, *Sherman's Forgotten Campaign: The Meridian Expedition* (Baltimore: Gateway Press, 1987), 327, second note 11.

In taking position at Bout de Bayou it had been my intention to give the enemy battle and hold him in check, at least until Mouton's brigade, which I supposed would reach me that night, could come up; but I soon found that the force of enemy was so overwhelming that my small division, numbering but 3,828 muskets present and twelve light guns, was entirely unequal to the task of checking more than momentarily the advance of the enemy. The position I had chosen offered some advantages against an enemy not so unequal in numbers, and if the swamps had been covered with water, as they usually are at this season of the year, even against a largely superior force; but the unusual dryness of the season had rendered the swampy grounds above and below Bout De Bayou bridge passable for artillery and trains, and rendered my position extremely hazardous, inasmuch as I was on [an] island formed by Red River, Bayous De Glaize, Du Lac, and Choctaw, the only outlet to which was Bayou Du Lac bridge, 8 miles to the south. In the event of the enemy turning my right, which he could easily have done, my march to Bayou Du Lac would have been intercepted and the destruction of my command inevitable. To have fallen back toward Marksville in order to cover Fort De Russy would equally have insured the disaster. By falling back, however, toward Bayou Du Lac and watching the movements of the enemy I was in hopes of finding an opportunity of attacking him should he march upon Fort De Russy with less than his entire strength. The prairie country through which the enemy would pass would give me an excellent opportunity for observing his movements and estimating his strength. All these considerations induced me to adopt the only course not dictated by folly or madness; and however mortifying it might be to abandon our brave companions in arms at Fort De Russy to their fate, it became my imperative duty to do so rather than attempt assistance, which at best could delay this danger but a few hours, and without a miracle from Heaven would insure the certain destruction of my entire command. I have never had a doubt about the propriety of my course, but do not expect to escape malignant criticisms. If they come from responsible sources I know how to meet them, and only ask that they be made in an open manner.[16]

With the Yankee army now moving across Bayou des Glaises, Walker began his retreat toward the Bayou du Lac bridge. The Grand Skedaddle was now back on in earnest, and it would not end for another three and half weeks.

16. Walker to Surget, Mar. 19, 1864, *ORA* 34, pt. 1, 599.

It took the Yankees only two hours to rebuild the bridge at Lemoine's Ferry, and by 11:00 A.M. they were back on the road to Marksville and Fort DeRussy. With no Rebel army in their way, they made good time, and the knowledge that a considerable Rebel force was in the near vicinity discouraged the men from straggling.

Two miles after leaving the Bayou des Glaises bridge, the Union soldiers came up onto the Avoyelles Prairie, and by all accounts they were rather impressed. Charles Lewis of the 27th Iowa declared the area as "the prettiest country we had seen in the South." He described "an open prairie country, settled wholly by French people. The plantations were large, the houses were neat and commodious. Large herds of cattle, horses, and sheep roamed over the most exquisitely beautiful prairies, dotted here and there with miniature lakes of clear water." Brig. Gen. Thomas Kilby Smith concurred: "We suddenly emerged in one of the most beautiful prairies imaginable, high table-land, gently undulating, watered by little lakes, with occasional groves, the landscape dotted with tasteful houses, gardens and shrubberies. This prairie, called Avoyelles, is settled exclusively by French emigrants, many of whom, as our army passed, sought shelter under the tricolor of France."[17]

The French ethnicity of the region seemed to be somewhat aggravating to many of the Union soldiers. The reasons behind the soldiers' exasperation were varied. Capt. William Burns of the 24th Missouri, well informed as to current events, stated, "Nearly all the citizens were French, and at almost every house the French flag was flying to protect them, which annoyed many of us, considering the French performances then being enacted in Mexico."[18] A correspondent was irritated that the locals would claim neutrality "although they have been living here, receiving the privileges of citizenship, for more than twenty years."[19] And some of the less sophisticated of the men seemed to find the fact that the area civilians did not speak English some sort of devilish plot: "We asked for food, but they did not understand us. We made signs, which helped some, for now they brought us a little food. We asked where the rebels were, but heard only the same refrain, 'nich forstay.'

17. Lewis to Friend Rich, Mar. 17, 1864; Smith to Maj. Gen. J. B. McPherson, *ORA* 34, pt. 1, 377.

18. Newspaper clippings, William S. Burns scrapbook, Schoff Civil War Collection, Clements Library, Univ. of Michigan, Ann Arbor (hereafter cited as Burns scrapbook).

19. Moore, *Rebellion Record* 8:430. Actually, most of the residents of the area were descended from Frenchmen who had settled the area over a hundred years earlier. Only a very small percentage were actually French citizens.

But we suspected that they knew better than they would let on." Later that day, after finding a fort full of hostile Rebels, the soldiers announced their suspicions confirmed: "We were thoroughly hungry and disgusted, not to say mad, and had we but gotten our claws into those wily Frenchmen, it would not have gone well with them."[20]

As the Union army continued through Mansura, they left Walker's Division to their rear. A cavalry detachment followed the retreating division, harassing the Southern rear guard and ensuring that the retreat had not been a ruse to lure the Yankees into a trap. But there was no trap. Walker's Division was gone, and the road to DeRussy was now open.

As the Yankees moved through Cocoville, the convent school proved to be as much of a temptation to the passing Yankees as it had been to the Confederate soldiers who had earlier found it such a pleasant diversion. At least two of the soldiers managed to slip in and take a peek at the girls, who "seemed to be terribly frightened at the sacrilege, but guess they were not so bad off as they pretended."[21] The nuns at the convent, Daughters of the Cross, implored to "the general" for assistance, and he assigned his aide-de-camp, a Frenchman, to guard the school while the army passed. "I assure you," wrote one of the nuns to her family, "he had plenty to do."[22]

While Brig. Gen. A. J. Smith's army marched boldly through Cocoville and Marksville and up the road to Fort DeRussy, a second Union force was also moving against the fort. David Porter's gunboat fleet was coming up Red River to join in a combined attack against the fort, followed by the transport fleet with all of Smith's soldiers who had been deemed unfit to make the overland march. At 9:00 A.M., about the same time as the troops were bridging Bayou des Glaises at Moreauville, *Fort Hindman,* followed by the gunboats *Eastport, Lafayette, Choctaw, Neosho, Osage,* and *Ozark* and the tug *Thistle,* "came in sight of a raft constructed partially across the river and earthworks thrown up on the bank." *Fort Hindman* opened fire on the earthworks, firing ten rounds of shrapnel before determining that the rifle pits were unmanned and the obstruction unprotected. With no covering fire to worry about, *Fort Hindman* commenced removing the obstacle. The thousands of

20. John Ritland, "John Ritland Civil War History," *Story City (Iowa) Herald,* Mar. 9–Apr. 6, 1922.

21. Stewart diary, Mar. 15 [14], 1864.

22. Mother Hyacinth to her parents, June 12, 1864, in Sister Dorothea Olga McCants, ed., *They Came to Louisiana: Letters of a Catholic Mission, 1854–1882* (Baton Rouge: Louisiana State Univ. Press, 1970), 171.

man-hours put in by hundreds of hard-laboring slaves and soldiers were
no match for the steam power available to the U.S. Navy. Within two
hours *Fort Hindman* had removed a portion of the raft, and the resulting rush of water helped enlarge the opening. The much heavier ironclad *Eastport* was then brought up, and her extreme weight was put
to good use. *Eastport* drove into the pilings at the weakened point, a
nine-inch hawser was fastened around the piles, and the boat backed
at full power. Again and again, the piles were rammed and pulled, the
hole in the barrier widening with each attack. By 4:30 P.M. a hole had
been torn through the raft of sufficient size to allow *Eastport* to pass
through. *Eastport, Osage, Fort Hindman,* and *Cricket* slipped through
the obstructions and moved upriver toward Fort DeRussy.[23]

Once again, Admiral Porter's version of the event varies widely from
everyone else's. According to Porter's memoirs, "When I first saw these
lower obstructions I began to think that the enemy had blocked the
game on us, and how astonished General Smith would be when he arrived in front of the forts and found no gun-boats to help him! It would
be mortifying to me, and might be disastrous to him." Porter went on
at length as to his thoughts on the issue, and then: "When I had made
up my mind about these obstructions which *looked* so formidable, I
simply gave the order, 'Clear that away!'" He then "in two hours undid
the works of many months." There is a problem with this account of
the incident, the least of which is that the clearing took seven and a
half hours, not two. But the main problem is that *Porter was not there.*
Admiral Porter was aboard *Blackhawk* at the time, some miles farther
down Red River. Lt. Cmdr. Seth Ledyard Phelps, captain of *Eastport,*
was the commanding officer on the scene at the removal of the raft.
Porter then goes on to tell us that the remnants of the raft then floated
down to New Orleans, "where they would furnish fuel enough for the
poor population of that city for a whole winter."[24]

While the Union pincers closed around Fort DeRussy, the men still
at the fort waited. Sgt. John Murray, Hutton's Artillery, sat down after
the war and wrote an account of what those final hours before the
attack were like:

---

23. Deck logs, USS *Fort Hindman* and USS *Eastport,* RG 24, NA.
24. Porter, *Incidents and Anecdotes,* 214–15. If we are to believe Porter, this is the
second year in a row that he has provided firewood for the winter for the poor of New
Orleans.

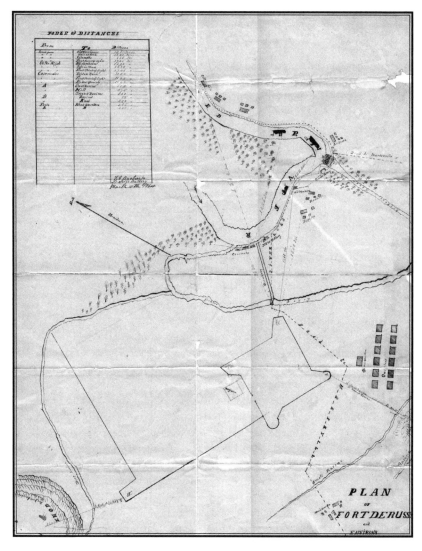

In early February 1864, Lt. J. F. Fuller, the fort's ordnance officer, was ordered to "get everything ready by measuring distance and making other preparations for practicing the Artillery at the Fort." This range map was prepared on March 4, just ten days before the fall of the fort. It is not drawn to scale, but the distances marked are accurate. (Courtesy of Special Collections, Tulane University Libraries.)

The morning of the 14th dawned clear and beautiful and found us at our guns, weary from watching and hunger, not having had a meal for 48 hours. All that strange uncertain feeling that pervades a soldier's bosom on the eve of battle thrilled through our veins and caused many an eye to dim and cheek to blanch as thoughts of loved ones far away would come swell to our hearts. Oh, the suspense, the terrible ongoing of mind that such an event occasions. None but the soldier knows or feels it. As I walked wearily to and fro before my piece, a 9-inch Dahlgren, singing or rather humming snatches of some stray ballad striving to drive away the mournful thoughts of the coming battle, our army surgeon with his corps of white badged "*body-snatchers*" with their stretchers made their appearance on the field. His coming was the cause of still stranger feelings, and while some gazed in awe and prayed that they might be spared the cruel knife and scalpel, others, and particularly one, jocularly remarked that they wished him to deal with them kindly when they came up for "dissection." Poor C. [John Clabby], who made the remark, had little use for either knife or saw. The second hour of the battle found him lying dead by my side, pierced by an unerring Minie through the brain.

As the enemy approached nearer and nearer, so also did our hopes and fears rise and fall. Presently, a courier was seen advancing at breakneck speed, his steed covered with foam and himself unable to articulate a word for several minutes after he had halted. It finally came, that dreadful news, the downfall of all our hopes. Walker had retreated, and was falling back on Alexandria, and we were left to bear the brunt of battle against 12,000 well-armed veteran troops fresh from victory across the Mississippi. As this dreadful news flashed upon us, we felt like the wrecked mariner who sees the ship which could save him receding from his view, leaving him but one hope—that, his God.

All day long, the enemies gunboats below had been forcing a passage through the raft with which we had dammed the river, and the long black line of smoke rising above the treetops told us but too plainly that they were coming. An occasional boom of heavy ordnance could be heard as they advanced, which to us was like the crack of Doom.[25]

---

25. Murray diary.

Chapter 11

And the Walls Came
Tumbling Down

Brig. Gen. A. J. Smith assigned the task of taking Fort DeRussy to Brig. Gen. Joseph Anthony Mower and his 1st and 3rd Divisions of the 16th Corps. Mower chose his 3rd Division, six thousand strong, as his assault division and held his 1st Division, with its twenty-four hundred men, in reserve. Backing them up, as a rear guard and deep reserve, were Brig. Gen. Thomas Kilby Smith's Provisional Division of the 17th Corps, numbering some two thousand soldiers.[1]

By most Confederate accounts, the first Union troops to arrive in front of Fort DeRussy showed up sometime shortly after 2:00 P.M. One Union account acknowledges their presence "near" the fort "about three o'clock," but most of the Yankees claim to have shown up around 4:00 P.M.[2]

One of the first Union men on the scene was Capt. William Burns, who was riding ahead of the approaching column with six other horsemen. On spotting several Confederates on horseback, Burns and his comrades set out in pursuit. The race passed through woods for three-quarters of a mile when the group rounded a bend in the road and saw the fort in the distance. They continued the chase, firing several shots at the Confederate cavalrymen as they disappeared into the fort. About five hundred yards from the fort, the group found the barracks ablaze, and here they captured a prisoner who told them that the fort was fully manned, although the Yankees had yet to see anyone there. Burns was pondering this information when "all at once the whole front was lined with heads and shoulders." Burns put his breech-loading rifle to his shoulder and

1. Abstract from returns, Mar. 31, 1864, *ORA* 34, pt. 1, 168. Perhaps the use of the word "men" is inappropriate. At least one of the divisions had a masquerading woman as a member. Gerhard Clausius, "The Little Soldier of the 95th: Albert D. J. Cashier," *Journal of the Illinois State Historical Society* 51, no. 4 (Winter 1958): 380–87.

2. Moore, *Rebellion Record* 8:420. The commanding general at Port Hudson reported "heavy firing heard . . . from 3 p.m. until dark." This firing was probably heard by his staff officer at the mouth of Black River and indicates that the fort was under attack well before the generally given Union time of 4:00 P.M. Andrews to Stone, Mar. 16, 1864, *ORA* 34, pt. 2, 629.

172   And the Walls Came Tumbling Down

fired three rounds into the fort, after which the little group decided that they would need reinforcements. They spun around, "put spurs to our horses," and rejoined the approaching Union column.[3]

While Captain Burns and company were entertaining themselves outside the fort, Captain King of the fort's siege battery was working desperately to finish emplacing his two 24-pounders inside the fort. After getting his guns into the fort, King found that there was no place to mount them. Using "square timbers and planks," he jury-rigged "platforms high enough to fire my guns over the parapet. By the time this was done, the Federals had begun their assault."[4]

Those Confederate soldiers who had earlier been placed in rifle pits downriver were also returning to the fort at this time. As they withdrew from the rifle pits, they paused just long enough to set fire to the Barbin house—"a nice frame building, consisting of four rooms, hall and piazza, neatly painted"—to deny its cover to the enemy. Little three-day-old Angelica was now homeless, perhaps the first casualty of the third Battle of Fort DeRussy.

As the men made their way back into the fort, there was some confusion as to whether they should remain with Captain Mabry, who had been in charge of them down the river, or return to their own units. Sgt. John Porter approached Capt. G. T. Marold "and asked where to go, at which time, the first shot . . . fired. Capt. Marold (being a Dutchman, and apparently not fond of such racket) tumbled down against the breastworks, as suddenly as if he had been hit by a bullet, and with a very forcible gesture, cried out 'Go to your Company, go to your Company!'" Porter went to his company.[5]

At 3:30 P.M., Capt. James Cockefair's 3rd Indiana Battery was called up on the "double-quick" and positioned astraddle the road leading to the fort, some eight hundred yards from the outer works. Supported by the 14th Iowa Infantry on the right and the 24th Missouri on the left, the battery opened fire at 4:15. Companies D and I of the 14th Iowa were sent forward as skirmishers to take possession of a line of rifle pits 350 yards from the fort. The fire by this time was becoming "exceedingly brisk from both artillery and musketry" as more Union regiments came up and formed a semicircle around the western and southern walls of the fort. Company K, 14th Iowa, moved up to join their comrades "in

3. Newspaper article, Burns scrapbook.
4. King letter, 14–15.
5. John Porter memoir, 27–28.

the swamp on the left of the other skirmishers." The 32nd Iowa filed off to the right, supporting the 14th Iowa's skirmishers in the rifle pits and taking the water batteries under fire but also receiving fire from the one gun in the Water Battery that could be brought to bear on them.[6]

Col. John Scott and his 32nd Iowa, in their position on the Union far right, were making things hot for the men in the Water Battery and those on the south wall of the fort, but they were getting as good as they gave. Sgt. J. Mitchell Boyd recalled the movements and maneuvering as that regiment closed on the fort:

> Starting on double quick, forward, and filing through a piece of heavy timber, we were exposed to a full raking fire from the heavy guns of the fort, when *"forward"* yelled Colonel Scott, and we sprung quickly into battle line to a slight hollow, among some scrubby thorn bushes, where Colonel Scott ordered: *"Down! Down! Every man, down flat!"* As down we dropped to mother earth, torrents of shot, shell and minnie balls passed over us, some vines over our heads were cut clean as if mown with a scythe. Again came the voice of Colonel Scott: *"Up, quick; by the right flank, double quick."* Just as the regiment started forward by the flank, a large shell from the fort came whizzing by, a little to our right and a little higher than our heads, and sweeping parallel with the regimental line; a little lower and a little farther to our left, a little delay on the part of the commanding Colonel, and the Thirty-second Iowa would doubtless have been swept out of existence. But the clear ringing voice of Colonel Scott was heard amidst the din and roar of musketery and artillery. *"Left half wheel, double quick,* forward: and shelter yourselves behind the old logs and stumps, and pick the gunners." This brought the regiment within close musket range under the heavy guns of the fort. The old stumps and logs on the field made a fair shelter.[7]

Just as the Union lines were extending to the right of the Marksville Road, so also were they extending to the left. The 58th Illinois, 119th Illinois, and 89th Indiana Regiments were called forward and sent to the left of the road, their lines extending for most of a mile. When these units were in position, three companies of skirmishers advanced and "opened a brisk fire" on the fort, which was responded to in kind.[8]

6. Cockefair to Shaw, Mar. 20, 1864, *ORA* 34, pt. 1, 370–71; Shaw to Sample, Mar. 17, 1864, *ORA* 34, pt. 1, 353; Lt. Col. Joseph H. Newbold to Shaw, Mar. 15, 1864, *ORA* 34, pt. 1, 359–60.

7. Scott, *Story of the Thirty Second Iowa*, 131–32.

8. Col. William F. Lynch to Mower, Mar. 18, 1864, *ORA* 34, pt. 1, 338–39.

While the noose was tightening around the outside of the fort, a most amazing situation was occurring inside the walls. Amazing, not so much because of what was happening, as because of who was involved in it. With artillery and small-arms fire pouring into the fort, and a seemingly endless procession of Northern troops continuing to arrive, Lieutenant Colonel Byrd, the fort's commanding officer, called a council of officers "to determine if it was worth while for us to make any further defense and to make the best terms of surrender he could." Byrd was a naturalized Texan, and most of the officers inside the fort were also Texans. They had no doubt been raised and had grown to manhood listening to stories of the Alamo, of a small group of poorly armed men fighting to the death against insurmountable odds. Unquestionably, they admired Travis, Crockett, Bowie, and the others who had fought to the last man, and they believed in their hearts that such conduct was honorable and should be emulated. But on that afternoon at Fort DeRussy, the majority of the officers were in favor of surrendering. It was the wild-eyed ravings of Capt. Edward T. King, a Louisianian and as crusty a curmudgeon as ever served any Lost Cause, that caused the Texans to remember who they were:

> I opposed them with all the zeal I could telling them our orders were to hold the Fort to the last extremity, that we were behind solid intrenchments with a deep moat in front of them, and that we could inflict great loss on them in spite of them and that our orders were to hold the Fort to the last extremity and it would be pusilanimous in us to surrender without making a fight or the loss of a single man and besides Gen. Taylor expected us to hold the enemy in check to give him time to retreat from Alexandria. One of the officers . . . said the Fort was not defensible and we would not be justifiable in defending it. I replied to him that might be the case if they had of demanded our surrender but they had rushed pell mell on us, and [we] were justifiable in making the best fight we could and that the more trouble we gave them the more of them we killed and wounded before they got us the more they would think of us after they captured us.[9]

King and several other officers carried the argument, and the battle continued. But in spite of his fervor, it seems even King realized that the situation was hopeless.

9. King letter, 15–16.

Nor was the hopelessness of the situation lost on the men in the Water Battery. Their guns faced the river, and with the attack coming from the land side, their rear was unprotected. They had been able to train one of their guns, the 32-pounder rifled Seacoast Gun, in the direction of the attacking Yankees and were able to fire one round from it before the hail of Minié balls from the 32nd Iowa and a "heavy artillery fire into the rear of the water battery" drove them out of the casemates and "into the excavations in front of the parapet." Family legends tell that Capt. Eloi Joffrion and some of the local militia men defending the fort slipped off at this time. Some rejoined the army; others simply went home. Capt. A. L. Adams of the 28th Texas Dismounted Cavalry and Lt. Elbert E. Jennings of the 13th Texas Dismounted Cavalry huddled with their men on the back side of the parapet "until it became apparent that they could do nothing and that in a few minutes they would be surrounded and captured."[10]

Captain Hutton, commander of the Water Battery, was a bit quicker in making up his mind. He disappeared early in the fighting. Hutton had been a prisoner earlier in the war, captured with his company in 1862 at the fall of New Orleans, and obviously had no desire to repeat the experience. His early disappearance from the fighting would result in charges of cowardice being brought against him and his men by Captain Adams and General Walker. Adams reported to the general that when he left the battery, Hutton was already gone. Hutton's company left with Adams, "but they threw away their arms and one by one disappeared, and, as Captain Adams supposes, returned to their homes."[11] Adams's charges may not stand up to scrutiny. While Adams says that Hutton's company left the fort with him, twenty-five of the seventy men in the company were in the fort when it fell. As to the charges that they threw away their arms, muster rolls from just two weeks before the attack show that more than half of the company was without arms, and concerning accoutrements, the company was "very deficient." Hutton was court-martialed in September 1864, but as the good captain was already under arrest prior to the fall of the fort, it is impossible to say what the September trial concerned.[12]

10. Walker to Surget, Mar. 19, 1864, *ORA* 34, pt. 1, 601.

11. Ibid.

12. Muster Roll, Company A, Crescent Artillery, Feb. 29, 1864, Jackson Barracks Military Library, New Orleans; "List of Prisoners Captured at Fort DeRussy," RG 109, NA; Murray diary, Sept. 19, 1864.

The charges against Hutton would certainly have been difficult to sustain. Hutton was chief of artillery aboard *Queen of the West* during the capture of *Indianola*—hardly a character reference for a coward. And while he left the fort before Adams did, he left well after General Walker. And in defense of the officers who suggested surrendering without a fight, perhaps they would have been more in the spirit of the Alamo had not some thirty-eight hundred of their comrades marched off for points elsewhere the day before.

In further defense of the Texans, at least one of the officers in the fort did seem to be imbued with the spirit of the Alamo. General Walker reported to headquarters:

> In striking contrast to this disgraceful conduct of Captain Hutton and his company, it is with great pleasure I record the gallant and noble conduct of a detachment of 9 men belonging to Captain King's company. Captain King, with the principal part of his company, was in the upper work, and this detachment, under Lieutenant Brooke, was sent to man one of the guns in the water battery. When it was proposed by the men here to make their escape, as they could do nothing, these 9 men declared their purpose of going into the upper fort to assist their comrades and share their fate, and amid a heavy fire of artillery and musketry set out with Lieutenant Brooke to carry out their design. Their fate is unknown, but such honorable and noble conduct deserves to be recorded.

Although King's men were Louisianians, the only "Lt. Brooke" captured at the fort was First Lt. J. R. K. Brooks of the 19th Texas.

As the sun slowly settled, the encircling Union troops drew closer and closer to the fort, continually pressing toward the walls and being forced back by the heavy fire from inside. And still the Union reserve stretched out into the distance. At 5:00 P.M. the 95th Illinois, rear guard for the army, was just arriving in Marksville, more than three miles from the fort. A party atmosphere seemed to pervade the reserve units, and the 95th "marched through town in open order and at rest arms. That is, four ranks, four feet apart, with guns across the shoulders back of the neck, bayonet to the left, and both hands resting on the gun. Two or three companies were singing the 'Battle Cry of Freedom' through the streets, the cannon still booming in front; the musketry could be distinctly heard, and we knew that the battle was near."[13]

---

13. Newsome, *Experience in the War*, 113–14.

Col. James Gilbert, 27th Iowa, was seriously caught up in the excitement of the moment. His regiment, originally with the advance brigade, had been left in Marksville as provost guard until the entire column passed through the town. Now, with the last units having passed by, Gilbert was bringing up the rear. He could hear the gunfire in the distance and knew that his regiment was quickly losing their opportunity for glory. Gilbert sent Lt. John E. Peck, his acting adjutant, up the line to find the brigade commander, Col. William Shaw, and get permission for the 27th to come forward and rejoin the brigade. Lieutenant Peck returned with the news that he could not find Colonel Shaw. That not being the right answer, he was sent back, this time returning with orders to move forward. The 27th Iowa rushed for the front.[14]

The 27th Iowa was not the only reserve unit anxious to get involved. The 33rd Wisconsin was also inspired by "the crack of rifels." As they rushed toward the sound of gunfire, the regiment "came nearly up to the double quick and many sore fotted boys began to drop out as it was impossible to keep up." But the 33rd would remain in reserve, forming a line within supporting distance of the assault forces but facing to the rear to protect them from any unexpected return of Walker's Division.[15]

The six guns of the 3rd Indiana Battery had had a busy day. By 6:00 P.M. they had fired nearly four hundred rounds of shot and shell into the fort in support of the encircling infantry and had exhausted their ammunition supply. The 9th Indiana Battery was called up to replace them. As that battery came forward, one of the guns stuck in the mud "right in range." The artillery bombardment of Fort DeRussy continued.[16]

The men in the fort were now being attacked by a force that outnumbered them by roughly fourteen to one. Figuring in the reserve force, the disadvantage increased to thirty-three to one. The Southerners had managed to repel two assaults against the walls, but it was getting increasingly difficult for a Rebel to put his head over the parapet to shoot.[17] Nonetheless, the firing from the fort continued. "During

14. Gilbert to Granger, Mar. 17, 1864, *ORA* 34, pt. 1, 362.

15. Henry Traber to sister, July 2, 1864, Archives Division, Wisconsin Historical Society, Madison.

16. Cockefair to Shaw, Mar. 20, 1864, *ORA* 34, pt. 1, 371; Fyan to Granger, Mar. 17, 1864, *ORA* 34, pt. 1, 368; Albert Underwood diary, Mar. 14, 1864, Indiana Historical Society, Indianapolis (hereafter cited as Underwood diary).

17. The 317 men in the fort were being attacked by approximately 6,000 men, while the Yankees had 4,400 men in a reserve/rear guard capacity. This, or course, ignores the approaching gunboat fleet with its 210 cannons.

this time," explained Captain Burns, "the fire from the fort was very severe, but did not do much execution. For two hours, shell, solid shot, shrapnel, and bullets passed between the two parties. We expected every moment to hear the heavy guns from the gun-boats, but not a sound; it was well; as in all probability unless every shot could have been planted in the fort, our troops would have suffered more from them than the rebels themselves."[18]

USS *Eastport* had been rushing upriver ever since slipping through the dam at Saline Point. As she rounded the bend below the fort just at sundown, three guns were discharged in the Water Battery. On the hill, the artillery had fallen silent in preparation for the final assault on the fort. A Union officer on the bank signaled the gunboat, advising *Eastport* that the troops were surrounding the fort, "but with no advice as to time or plan of attack." Seeing that any artillery support from his boat would surely cause more casualties to his fellow Yankees than to the men in the fort, Comdr. Seth Phelps wisely resisted the temptation to join in the fray. But not content to be merely a spectator, Phelps "fired a short-fuzed shell at an elevation as a signal gun, and then ventured one 100-pounder rifle shell at the water battery, which shell burst over it, and the enemy ran from it."[19]

The 27th Iowa had been a little tardy in joining the assault, having had to push their way forward through the waiting reserve troops as they moved up from their guard duty in Marksville. But on reaching the front lines, they were sent in to reinforce the 14th Iowa, whose skirmishers had exhausted their ammunition supply. Confederate artillery fire forced them from the road and into the trees, and their position near the Union battery ensured that they would continue to receive attention from the Confederate guns.

The Union batteries acted as a magnet for incoming shellfire, and before the 3rd Indiana Battery retired, Pvt. Charles Berkau had received a serious head wound from a shell fragment and two horses had been disabled. In the 178th New York, posted just to the right of the battery,

18. Newspaper article, Burns scrapbook.
19. Phelps to Porter, Mar. 16, 1864, *ORN* 26:30–31. There can be no explanation, other than faulty memory, for John Scott's assertion in his *Story of the Thirty Second Iowa,* that Porter's "advance boats, the Eastport and Neosho began to throw their shells with fearful rapidity, and we were in more danger from the explosion of his shells than from the guns of the enemy." *Eastport* fired only the two rounds, and *Neosho* did not arrive at the fort until the following morning. Deck logs, USS *Neosho,* RG 24, NA, and USS *Eastport.*

In David Porter's *Incidents and Anecdotes,* the admiral says that *"Benton* poked her nose around the point and opened on the enemy with her famous bow battery." This sketch, from Porter's *Naval History of the Civil War,* shows *Benton* attacking the fort with three other gunboats. In fact, *Benton* did not arrive at Fort DeRussy until 1:15 P.M. on March 15, some eighteen hours after the fort's surrender.

an incoming shell killed Cpl. Charles Hock, and Pvt. William Homan had his face peppered with splinters caused by a shell.[20]

The 27th Iowa had to endure a constant shelling as the regiments made their final alignments. Charles Lewis, H Company, described the last minutes before the charge: "When we were within several hundred yards of the fort, in the woods, the shells from the enemy's guns flying thick and fast about us, we were ordered to lie down and wait orders. . . . Sharpshooters were ordered forward to pick off the enemy's gunners. Only a moment passed, it seemed to us, when we were ordered forward, and alongside of a fence, where we again lay down. Again we were ordered forward." Van Buren Sargent, also of the 27th Iowa, did not care for the artillery fire: "Several of their shells burst aright over our heads but none of our Co. was hurt. Guess I was the worst scarde of

20. Cockefair to Shaw, Mar. 20, 1864, *ORA* 34, pt. 1, 371; R. M. Moore, "List of Casualties in the 3rd Brigade, 3rd Division, 16th A. C. on the 14 March 1864 in Charge on Fort De Russy La.," RG 94, NA.

anny one thare. A limb of a tree droped & brushed me just as a big shell exploded over head. Guess my nerves was strung up to a high pitch for that little brush went through me like lightning & nearly knocked me down. Don't think anny of the boys notised me. Their thoughts were on what's coming."[21]

With daylight fast fading, Joe Mower, in the center of the line with the 24th Missouri, gave the order to "fix bayonets and advance in line of battle." The Missourians moved forward, halting momentarily at the edge of the woods on the west side of the fort to straighten their lines. This done, Mower gave the final command, "charge bayonets, an order that was obeyed not only with promptitude but with the utmost furor."[22]

Within moments, the entire Union line was rushing toward the walls of Fort DeRussy.

In November 1863, Maj. Gen. Jeremy Gilmer, chief engineer of the Confederate army, observed that "experience in this war has shown that Federal troops are not inclined to storm intrenchments."[23] Inclined or not, the Federal troops stormed the works.

As the order to charge spread from the center of the line to both flanks, the entire assault force moved out on the "doublequick" across the field. The Union right raced across a clearing covered with logs from cut trees and fence rails that had been thrown down. The pace was too rapid to sustain, and the charge slowed, but it continued steadily toward the earthworks. On the left, the 58th and 119th Illinois and the 89th Indiana had crowded to within a hundred yards of the fort before the charge began, and those units quickly arrived in the moat. The musketry rang out in a continuous thunder, along with the roar of six thousand cheering voices. As the hail of lead flew over their heads, the men inside the fort huddled below the walls, firing back as best they could.

The deep moat and steep walls of the fort quickly packed with Union soldiers. While the men not yet into the moat provided covering fire, those in the pits beneath the walls were finding just how difficult it was to climb the twenty-foot vertical clay face while carrying their weapons. Pvt. John Ritland of the 32nd Iowa described the experience:

    21. Lewis to Friend Rich, Mar. 17, 1864; Van Buren Whipple Sargent, "The Civil War Memories of a Union Soldier," manuscript in private hands, transcribed by Tom Busby (hereafter cited as Sargent memoir).
    22. Fyan to Granger, Mar. 17, 1864, *ORA* 34, pt. 1, 368.
    23. Gilmer to Von Sheliha, Nov. 21, 1863, *ORA* 26, pt. 2, 432.

This sketch of the charge on Fort DeRussy, by *Frank Leslie's Illustrated Weekly* artist C. E. H. Bonwill, may be the ultimate "charge" drawing. Latter-day historians treat the attack on Fort DeRussy as nothing more than a glorified skirmish, but Bonwill and the participants obviously had a different opinion.

"I was nearly on the top once, but became so short of breath, that I hadn't the power to hold on, and slid back a considerable distance. I grabbed hold of an exposed root and pulled myself up again. In the meantime, the bullets flew thick and fast[.] Tom Lein said it was so steep where he happened to be that the men had to climb on each other's backs to be able to make headway."[24]

The inexorable blue tide was not to be stopped, and as the waves of Union soldiers mounted the walls, the defenders dropped their weapons in surrender. Fort DeRussy had fallen.

While it takes but moments to describe, the actual charge lasted for some ten to fifteen minutes. The attempts by the defenders to stop the wave of blue uniforms were futile, but when the shooting was over, some forty to fifty dead and wounded Union soldiers were scattered over the battleground. Lt. James Carey of the 58th Illinois, "a brave and gallant young officer," was severely wounded while leading his men against the fort's west wall. Pvt. Tom Ball of the 32nd Iowa took a Minié ball through the calf of his right leg just fifty yards from the south wall, and Pvt. William Leger, a twenty-five-year-old member of the 119th Illinois, lay dying with a gunshot wound in his stomach. A Union color-bearer lay dead on the parapet of the fort, killed as he planted the colors on the wall; he lay there through the night, covered by the flag he had so valiantly carried. Less gloriously, twenty-year-old Pvt. Jacob Beck, of the 27th Iowa, lay with a serious wound to his left breast, accidentally shot by a member of his own company; he would linger for six days before dying. Pvt. James Kent of the 32nd Iowa, on the other hand, would lie unconscious for ten days from a shot through the lungs before recovering.[25]

The charge against the fort was as impressive from the inside as it had been to the men making it. Captain King, himself suffering from a left eye destroyed by a bullet fragment glancing off a cannon barrel, said that the Yankees "poured in like bees." John Porter thought them more like a flock of birds: they "came over the works, as fast as black birds, and deeper than a man could climb out. I supposed they filled the

24. Ritland, "John Ritland Civil War History."
25. Lynch to Mower, Mar. 18, 1864, *ORA* 34, pt. 1, 339; David B. Danbom, ed., "'Dear Companion': Civil War Letters of a Story County Farmer," *Annals of Iowa* 47 (Fall 1984): 539; William Leger service record, family legend; John Porter memoir, 28; Gilbert to Granger, Mar. 17, 1864, *ORA* 34, pt. 1, 362. Jacob Beck is misidentified as Robert Beck (his brother, who served in the same company and was later wounded at Pleasant Hill) in one report. His date of death is variously given as March 20, 22, and 24. See Alexandria National Cemetery records, Lewis to Friend Rich, Mar. 17, 1864, and Sargent to Dear folks at home, Apr. 14, 1864, Sargent memoir, Scott, *Story of the Thirty Second Iowa,* 133.

ditch, and the others went over on their shoulders." Whether birds or bees, they definitely came over too fast for one young Rebel. Eighteen-year-old Andrew Green had just joined Walker's Texans two weeks earlier and was "young and thoughtless." He did not throw his gun down when the Yankees came over the wall, and "some said he advanced toward the Federals with his gun in his hand." Perhaps he was a little *too* imbued with the spirit of the Alamo. He was shot and killed.[26] Poor John Clabby, "the bravest of the brave," was already stiffening in the chill evening air. He had died early in the fighting, killed instantly by a shot through the head.[27]

There is some question as to which regiment was the first into the fort. Of the seven regiments in the charge, the commanders of four—the 58th and 119th Illinois, the 89th Indiana, and the 24th Missouri—claimed to be either the first into the fort or the first to plant their colors on the parapet; and the 32nd Iowa commander, while not claiming to be first into the fort, said that the Confederates acknowledged that his men "took the fort." Only the 14th and 27th Iowa seem to have stayed out of the argument. General Mower, as commander, had to remain unbiased; in his official report, he declared a four-way tie between the four regiments arguing their "first-in" status and explained that the terrain was responsible for the tardiness of the other three. Interestingly enough, Mower was overheard telling Gen. A. J. Smith that he personally was the first man on the wall.[28] Another staff officer, Capt. Menomen O'Donnell, a twenty-nine-year-old native of Ireland and apparently the only man to charge the fort on horseback, was also acknowledged by Mower as being "one of the first in the enemy's works." O'Donnell was the only man storming the fort that day to receive a Medal of Honor.[29]

26. King letter, 19, 17; John Porter memoir, 28; John C. Porter, roster of Company H, Eighteenth Texas Infantry, from Bible of William Henry Harrison Cope, original in possession of William Cope, Dallas, Tex.; Burmeister journal.

27. Murray diary.

28. Official reports of General Mower, Colonel Lynch, Colonel Kinney, Lt. Colonel Newbold, Colonel Gilbert, Colonel Scott, and Major Fyan, *ORA* 34, pt. 1, 316–17, 339, 344–45, 359–60, 362, 365, 368; Burns scrapbook.

29. O'Donnell's actions nine months earlier at Vicksburg also were mentioned in his Medal of Honor citation. In reports of the action at Fort DeRussy, O'Donnell is mentioned twice (by Mower and Lynch), but mainly in regard to his performance of staff duties. While undoubtedly an excellent staff officer, and apparently as brave a man as any other who charged the walls that day, O'Donnell does not seem to have done anything that six thousand other men did not do, albeit he did it on horseback. It is usually a good idea to exercise a certain amount of skepticism whenever a staff officer receives an award of this nature.

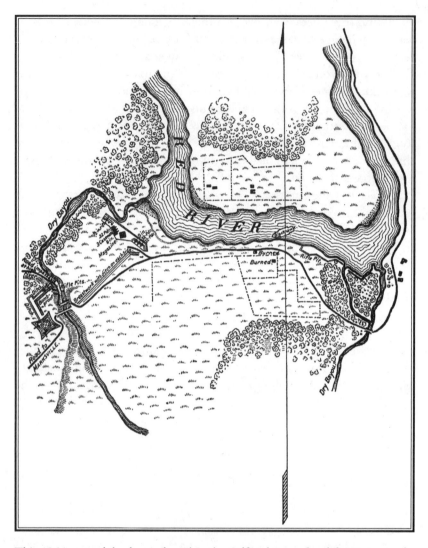

This 1864 map of the fort is found in the *Official Records of the Union and Confederate Navies* (vol. 26). Note that the buildings at Barbin's Landing are now marked "burned."

An unbiased observer reading the accounts of the capture of the fort would have to come to the conclusion that there was only a minimal amount of time, less than a minute, between the first regiment mounting the walls and the last. As the bluecoats came over the walls, Lieutenant Colonel Byrd mounted the rampart and waved a white kerchief on the end of a bayonet, surrendering the fort. A now-vanquished Sgt. John Porter was not at all happy: "My feelings at the time of the surrender, I can scarcely describe—my first impulse was a feeling of relief, for I knew that if we had not surrendered that soon, all would have been killed. I then thought of home and loved ones, and the little probability of ever returning."[30]

But the Yankees on the wall were anything but gloomy. For all but fifty of them, they were alive and well and now out of danger. It was the glorious start of a glorious expedition, and the glorious end to a glorious day. The euphoria swept over them, and they celebrated! "The soldiers of the brigade broke into one wild, ringing, vociferous yell of joy. The rattle of musketry, expressive of joy, for a time was incessant," wrote one soldier of the 27th Iowa.[31]

The long lines of reserve troops back toward Marksville could hear the loud hurrahs from the fort and suspected their significance. But "soon orderlies came riding down and cheer after cheer burst from the colum as they came. We were prepared to cheer lustily and throw our hat as he rode up to us and told us Fort DeRussy was ours with slight loss," wrote Henry Traber of the 33rd Wisconsin to his brother and sister. The men of the 117th Illinois "for at least five minutes . . . did nothing but cheer and wave our hats & caps & jump around and holler for our cause." Farther down the line, the 95th Illinois could hear the volleys, but not the hurrahs, from the fort. They "waited in breathless anxiety to hear the news, for we felt confident of a successful termination of the siege. Very soon, we heard a shout, at first faint and distinct, away to the right; it increased as it came nearer to the left, as a swift horse-man riding along the line, announced, '*The Fort is Ours*! THE FORT IS OURS!' Then such a burst of shouting and throwing up of hats in the air, that it seemed as if every one had gone wild with joy." The hats and caps of the Union reserve saw serious service that evening.[32]

With the passing of the euphoria, the conquerors of Fort DeRussy got down to business. The captured Confederates were herded to the center of the fort. The breastworks were lined with "thousands" of Union soldiers, some as guards but the vast majority there as curious

30. John Porter memoir, 28.
31. Lewis to Friend Rich, Mar. 17, 1864.
32. Henry Traber to Dear Bro & Sister, June 14, 1864, Archives Division, Wisconsin Historical Society, Madison; Hieronymus diary, Mar. 14, 1864; Newsome, *Experience in the War*, 114.

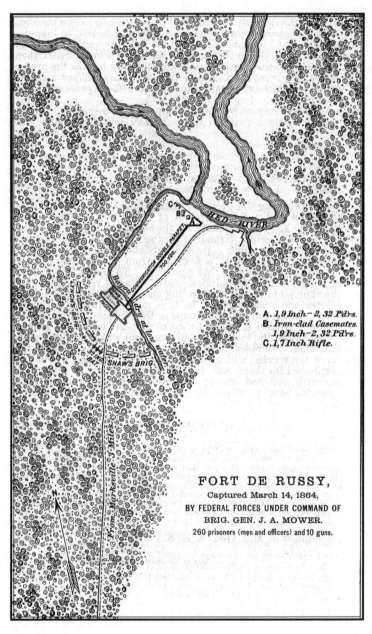

An 1864 map of Fort DeRussy from the *Official Records of the Union and Confederate Armies* (vol. 34, pt. 1).

onlookers, "asking questions and passing jokes" with their prisoners. As the night wore on, a cold, raw wind picked up, and the Rebels, curled up in their blankets and trying to sleep, "passed a cold unpleasant night." In that regard, they were no different from their captors, such as the soldier from the 33rd Wisconsin who found that the night "was so cold we did not get much sleep."[33] The sentinels remained on the walls, while most of the Union troops drew off, set up camps, and settled in for the night. The 27th Iowa "returned to the prairie near the hospital building" to camp.[34] The 9th Indiana Battery camped one mile south of the fort.[35] The other regiments moved to their respective bivouac areas, built fires, ate, then picketed or slept. "The leaves made good beds," noted one soldier.[36] After having marched over thirty miles and assaulted and captured the legendary Fort DeRussy, a bed of leaves was no doubt sufficient.

33. John Porter memoir, 28; Harvey Alexander Wallace diary, Southwest Arkansas Regional Archives, Washington, Ark. (hereafter cited as Wallace diary); William Parr diary, Wisconsin Historical Society, Madison. The Union troops attacking the fort were traveling light, having left their knapsacks, spare clothes, and other nonessential items on the boats. They had weapons, ammunition, food, and blankets, but nothing more in the way of shelter.

34. Lewis to Friend Rich, Mar. 17, 1864.

35. Underwood diary, Mar. 14, 1864.

36. Hieronymus diary, Mar. 14, 1864. Hieronymus, to judge by some of his other diary entries, was something of a connoisseur of bedding materials. On this particular night, he "slept well" on his bed of leaves.

Chapter 12

"Thus Much for Our Red River Gibraltar"

The capture of Fort DeRussy was a serious blow to Richard Taylor and the defenders of central and northwestern Louisiana. The Red River was now, for all practical purposes, open to Shreveport. A significant portion of Louisiana's heavy artillery had just been lost, along with large amounts of ammunition and supplies. While the advantage of twenty-twenty hindsight makes it evident now that Gen. A. J. Smith's concentration on the fort allowed for the escape of Gen. John G. Walker's Division and thereby doomed the Red River Campaign to failure at Mansfield, that redeeming fact would not become known for another month. At the time, the fall of Fort DeRussy was a Confederate tragedy.

Did Fort DeRussy have to fall? By all accounts, yes. Perhaps Gen. John Walker summed it up best in his report of March 19, 1864: "In accounting for the disaster at Fort De Russy it is unnecessary to look to other causes than the overwhelming superiority of the enemy's force; but even with this disadvantage, Fort De Russy might have been held for some days, perhaps, without relief from the outside, but for the vicious system of engineering adopted and the wretched judgment displayed in the selection of the position."[1] Hardly a glowing endorsement of Lewis DeRussy's engineering abilities. But to the credit of DeRussy, Boyd, Devoe, and the other engineers involved, Walker seems to be alone in his belittlement of the fort's defensive capabilities.

The Union soldiers attacking the fort were unanimously of the opinion that they were fortunate to have taken the fort as easily as they did. "If the fort had ben full maned & well defended we would have paid dear in men as the works were about the strongest that I saw during the war," said one. "Long might the rebels have held out if they had had a large force," wrote another. Echoing these sentiments, an Illinois soldier wrote his brother that "Fort DeRusy was not a Large fort but one of the

---

1. Walker to Surget, Mar. 19, 1864, *ORA* 34, pt. 1, 601.

strongest I have ever seen."[2] Col. Thomas Humphrey, 95th Illinois, the man assigned the task of destroying the fort, agreed with that assessment: "The works were very formidable, being by far the most scientifically and permanent constructed works of the enemy I have seen."[3] Capt. George Burmeister, 35th Iowa, "took a good look at the rebel works" and felt that they were "certainly planned by and executed under the guidance of a military genius."[4] Even David Porter, hardly an admirer of things Confederate, was complimentary to the fort's engineering: "The works . . . are of the most extensive and formidable kind. Colonel De Russy, from appearances, is a most excellent engineer to build forts . . ." —after which Porter returned to his more recognizable style—"but does not seem to know what to do with them after they are constructed. The same remark may apply to his obstructions, which look well on paper but don't stop our advance."[5]

Porter was not the only naval officer impressed by the fort. Capt. Thomas Selfridge, commander of USS *Osage,* declared Fort DeRussy "a formidable work, probably one of the strongest constructed by the Confederates during the war." But Porter, in his inimitable style, was definitely the most glowing in his praises. "This is one of the strongest works ever built of earth and iron," he declared six days after the capture.[6] Twenty years later, in his memoirs, Porter reached new heights in his praise of the Red River Gibraltar:

> General Smith remained behind to destroy Fort DeRussy. He said he was determined to show these Confederates that, notwithstanding their ingenuity in building the strongest forts in the world, he wouldn't leave one stone on another. He got enough of it in three days, and though at the end of that time he had somewhat changed the aspect of the works, their defensive power was as strong as ever; he left the defaced works as a monument of the industry and energy of the Confederates. . . . When we come to consider the herculean labors performed by the Southern people to maintain the cause which they considered so sacred, we can not withhold our admiration of their ability as soldiers.

2. Sargent memoir; Lewis to Friend Rich, Mar. 17, 1864; Robinson to Dear Bro Will, Mar. 22, 1864, Sidney Z. Robinson Letters (SC 1284), Illinois State Historical Library, Springfield.
3. Humphrey to Read, Mar. 17, 1864, *ORA* 34, pt. 1, 387.
4. Burmeister journal, Mar. 15, 1864.
5. Porter to Welles, Mar. 16, 1864, *ORN* 26:29.

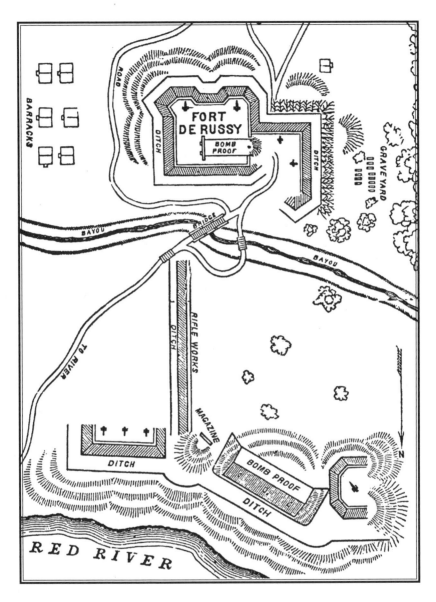

This is perhaps the best known sketch of Fort DeRussy. It appeared in *Harper's Weekly* shortly after the fort fell in 1864. The graveyard shown is still in use (2006).

> Without doubt, they established a new era in military engineer-
> ing which none have ever excelled, and on a scale only equaled by
> the works of the Titans of old.[7]

Fort DeRussy was built primarily for the purpose of stopping
Union gunboats from ascending Red River. It will never be known how
effective the fort would have been at this task, but it certainly cannot
be said that the fort's merits in this regard were never argued.

Admiral Porter was disappointed that the fort fell to the land
attack, as he had hoped to have "an old-fashioned gun-boat and fort
fight," and he opined that had DeRussy been fully manned, "it would
have been worthy of our guns." Porter felt confident that the battle
would have been totally one-sided and that the fort would have been
easy prey for his gunboat fleet: "Ten 100-pounder rifles, ten XI-inch
guns, twenty IX-inch, six 30-pounder rifles, and eight VIII-inch guns
would have been brought to bear on this work at one time, to say nothing of 50 guns firing shrapnel—the result can be easily imagined."[8] This
result can only be "easily imagined" if one's imagination is as active as
was Porter's. While the Union fleet did have the aforementioned guns,
the narrow and winding channel of the river would have made the posi-
tioning of all those guns bearing on the fort "at one time" a physical
impossibility. That being said, unless the Water Battery sank or disabled the first gunboat in the attacking column, the battery quickly
would become untenable. On the other hand, if the Water Battery sank
the first attacking boat, the river would be effectively blocked, making
the Union navy's vastly superior firepower worthless.

The Union soldiers had differing opinions on the navy's ability to
handle the Water Battery. One journalist with the expedition felt that
the works were of such a substantial nature that "the gunboats alone
might have vainly assailed for a month." General Smith declared in his
official report that "the gunboats would not have been able to pass"
the Water Battery. He was joined in this opinion by the adjutant of the
81st Illinois, who, after watching a test of naval gunfire on the battery,
declared the fort "impervious to gun-boats." Another officer, viewing

6. Thomas O. Selfridge Jr., *What Finer Tradition: The Memoirs of Thomas O.
Selfridge, Jr., Rear Admiral, U.S.N.* (Columbia: Univ. of South Carolina Press, 1987),
95; Porter to Welles, Mar. 20, 1864, *ORN* 26:33.
    7. Porter, *Incidents and Anecdotes*, 216–17.
    8. Ibid., 216; Porter to Welles, Mar. 20, 1864, *ORN* 26:33.

the same test, felt that, to the contrary, they "proved that two or three hours bombardment would have destroyed it."[9]

Which of these theories would have proved out will never be known. Even Admiral Porter admitted that the "victory, of course, belonged to the soldiers."[10] While the navy would be actively involved in affairs at Fort DeRussy in the following weeks, the ironclads *Eastport* and *Osage*, along with the tinclads *Fort Hindman* and *Cricket*, would provide the sole naval involvement in the 1864 capture of Fort DeRussy. And with the exception of the one round fired over the Water Battery by *Eastport*, that involvement would be strictly as spectators. Heavily armed spectators who would undoubtedly have participated had the need arisen, but spectators nonetheless.

There is a certain dichotomy in the accounts of the capture of the fort that is perhaps not as difficult to explain as would first appear. There are only a few Confederate firsthand accounts of the battle, and although the length of the fighting in these accounts varies between two and four hours, there is one consistent theme that is lacking in most Union accounts. The Confederates usually claim that there were two assaults against the fort that were repulsed, and it was not until the third assault that the fort was carried. This "three assault" interpretation is repeated by at least two New Orleans newspapers. The Union accounts (with the exception of the aforementioned Union-controlled New Orleans newspapers), on the other hand, mention only one assault, and although a two-hour length of battle was not uncommon, it was also not unusual for Yankee soldiers to limit the length of a battle to the time of the final assault. That is, it is frequently claimed in Union accounts that Fort DeRussy was taken in twenty minutes.

Did the Confederates repel two assaults or not? This question will never be definitively answered, but a good guess would be that some of the Union maneuvering had the appearance of an assault to the troops inside the fort, and the Southerners responded to these perceived assaults in an appropriate manner. And it is at this point where one's personal bias has to determine whether or not this constitutes a repulse or not. Obviously, had the men in the fort not responded to the "perceived" assault, the assailants would have continued their advance, and

9. Moore, *Rebellion Record* 8:421; Smith to Sherman, Sept. 26, 1865, *ORA* 34, pt. 1, 312; Newsome, *Experience in the War*, 116; Burns scrapbook.

10. Porter, *Incidents and Anecdotes*, 216.

the "perceived" assault would have become an "actual" assault. But because the movements toward the fort were responded to, the movements
halted short of the fort. Hence, the Rebels in the fort felt that they had
repulsed an assault, while the men assailing the fort interpreted their
advance as merely "getting into position" for the actual assault. In any
case, everyone seems to be in agreement that the Yankees only mounted
the walls once, in the final (or possibly only) assault.

What is not generally agreed upon is the severity of the fighting at
Fort DeRussy. David Porter—deprived of his "old-fashioned gun-boat
and fort fight"— belittled the action. "It is not the intention of these rebels to fight," he reported to Secretary of the Navy Gideon Welles. "The
efforts of these people to keep up this war remind one very much of the
antics of Chinamen, who build canvas forts, paint hideous dragons on
their shields, turn somersets, and yell in the faces of their enemies to
frighten them, and then run away at the first sign of an engagement."[11]
Later historians have been equally unimpressed with the capture of the
fort. Ludwell Johnson, author of the definitive work on the Red River
Campaign, felt that the fact that there were so few casualties gave "the
whole episode the character of a skirmish rather than a battle."[12] In a
war in which battle casualties were often counted in the hundreds, and
sometimes thousands, it is easy to mock a fight in which the killed and
wounded numbered less than sixty. Nonetheless, every known account
of the battle indicates that the fighting at Fort DeRussy was intense for
a battle of its limited scope.

While the fighting at the fort may or may not have impressed historians, the effect of the short defense was immense. Fort DeRussy was a
serious blockage to the Red River, but it was well known that the fort was
poorly defended from the land side—hence the decision to have Smith's
army attack the fort, as opposed to letting the navy go up the river and
allow the gunboats to reduce the fort. The departure of Walker's Division
of Texans from the fort meant that there would be no epic battle at Fort
DeRussy. In all probability, while it would probably have made for the
serious sort of bloodletting which would have appealed to modern-day
historians, a confrontation between Walker and A. J. Smith in the first
days of the campaign would also probably have resulted in the defeat or
serious weakening of Walker's Division and their possible removal from

11. Porter to Welles, Mar. 16, 1864, *ORN* 26:29.
12. Ludwell H. Johnson, *Red River Campaign: Politics and Cotton in the Civil War*
(Baltimore: Johns Hopkins Univ. Press, 1958), 93.

any later actions in the campaign. But Walker's Division played a pivotal role three weeks later at the Battle of Mansfield, where along with other Texas and Louisiana units, they whipped the Union army and reversed the Grand Skedaddle. It can be well argued that without Walker's Division, Richard Taylor's Confederates would not have been able to defeat Nathaniel Banks's army, Shreveport and Texas would have been taken, and the Red River Campaign would *not* have gone into the history books as the last great Confederate victory of the Civil War. But because of the handful of defenders left at Fort DeRussy, Smith's army was unable to chase and pin down Walker's Division. The fort had to be reduced first, and by the time the fort was captured, it was nightfall; Smith's army slept through the night as Walker's men marched, and Smith's troops stayed at the fort the entire next morning, waiting for their steamboat transportation to arrive. Walker's Division had the necessary head start to evade Smith's army, until they met them on the battleground of the Southerners' choosing. While the reduction of Fort DeRussy may have only lasted four hours, it gave Walker's Greyhounds a twenty-hour head start—and that was all they needed.

Even an "insignificant" action like the capture of Fort DeRussy generates its little mysteries. The missing men of the 178th New York Infantry are one of these riddles. These gaudily dressed Zouaves were in the second wave for the attack on the fort, sandwiched between the assault wave and the rear guard. Yet they still had two men missing when the battle ended. How would two men go missing on a battlefield of such limited size, fought over such a short period of time? And is there any connection between these two missing men and the two New Yorkers found pillaging homes and insulting ladies twenty miles upriver from the fort just twelve days later? When one of these men was caught by seamen from the gunboat *Benton*, he claimed to be a member of the 2nd New York Cavalry. He had gotten drunk in Alexandria and ran off with his friend, he said. But a search of the records turns up no one by the name he gave. Was he lying about his regiment and his name? Was he one of the 178th's "missing men"?

Another enigma in the Fort DeRussy story concerns the lack of weapons found in the fort after its capture. In the postcapture inventory, the Yankees found thirty thousand cartridges, but the number of shoulder-fired weapons was surprisingly small. There were only 117 smoothbore muskets and 56 rifles in the fort. The 317 men captured in the fort had been fighting with only 4 cannons and 173 small arms. Even allowing for a crew of 10 men per gun, this still left over 100

men—approximately one-third of the men in the fort—without weapons. Perhaps the real mystery of Fort DeRussy is how the defenders
managed to hold out as long as they did.

And then there is the incredible story of eighteen-year-old Adolphe
Rebouché, a Marksville native who joined Hutton's Artillery at Fort
DeRussy just five weeks before the capture. Years later, he would tell
his son a most remarkable tale. When Fort DeRussy was besieged by
the Yankees,

> the Federals were shooting from the gunboats, heavy balls tied
> together with chain so that they came roaring across, tearing up the
> ground, smashing trees and wrecking the fort. [Mind you, now, that
> by the Navy's own admission, only two shells were fired from the
> gunboats, neither hitting anything.]
>
> Our men saw that they had to retreat, so they loaded all the
> cannon and drew straws to see who would stay behind and fire them
> while the rest fell back toward Alexandria.
>
> The lot fell to my father and as the rest left with everything they
> could carry, he touched off the cannon.
>
> When the Federals charged, there was nothing to stop them, so
> they came in and captured my father and asked him, "Where the
> devil are all the others?" But he just said, "I'm the only one."[13]

Then, according to the story, Rebouché was given two weeks leave to
visit his family, then sent to jail in Louisville, Kentucky, for three years.

On its face, this seems to be an egregious lie told by an old man to
impress the kids. But if we take into consideration that this version of
the story was told by the son who was himself a very old man at the
time of the telling, and the natural tendency of stories to change small
details over the years, then maybe this story is not a total fabrication
after all. Let's examine this a little further.

There were several local men at Fort DeRussy the day of the attack.
Almost every one of them was able to slip out of the fort and make their
way to safety without being captured—except for Adolphe Rebouché.
He, and possibly two other men, were the only Avoyelles Parish natives
captured. Over on the Union side, the ironclad *Eastport* reported that
there were three shots fired from the Water Battery when the gunboat
appeared—but there is nothing in the report to indicate that the shots

---

13. "Louisiana Historical Review Featuring Avoyelles and Rapides Parishes," *Historical Review of the South* (Montgomery, Ala.) (n.d., probably mid-1980s).

were fired at the boat, or any sort of concern that the boat was in any danger from those shots.

Is it possible, then, that Rebouché's story is actually true, just horribly mangled from retelling over the years? Was Adolphe Rebouché the only man left in the Water Battery when the Yankees arrived, as opposed to the only man in the fort? He was a member of Hutton's Artillery, and they were stationed in the battery. The cannons there would, of course, have been loaded. Leaving one man behind to fire them would not be unreasonable. But that one man would not have been able to aim those guns, which weighed several tons apiece. Did Rebouché lose the lottery? He may well have. As for the three years in prison in Louisville, the captured men, including Rebouché, were sent to prison in New Orleans for four months (not three years) until they were exchanged. And while in New Orleans, the prisoners who fell ill—and many did—were sent to the St. Louis Hospital. St. Louis? Louisville? It's not that big a jump of logic to suppose that the Rebouché story may be one man's honestly told, but very mutilated, story of the capture of Fort DeRussy. And then again, it may simply have been an egregious lie told by an old man to impress the kids.

Chapter 13

"As Thoroughly Destroyed as Possible"

With Fort DeRussy now firmly in Union hands, A. J. Smith's next move was to take the city of Alexandria. To do this, he planned to send most of his army up Red River by steamboat, arriving at Alexandria before the retreating Confederates could get there. But the rising of the sun on March 15 found Red River in front of the fort empty of the transportation that Smith hoped to use. His troops worn from their exhaustive efforts of the day before, Smith could only wait for the steamboats to arrive.

When the fort surrendered at nightfall the previous evening, there were four gunboats in the river—*Eastport, Osage, Cricket,* and *Fort Hindman*. Seth Phelps, commander of *Eastport* and senior naval officer present, sent the tinclads *Cricket* and *Fort Hindman* upriver toward Alexandria shortly after 9:00 P.M. Some two hours later, the tug *Dahlia* arrived at the fort with orders from Admiral Porter for all of the gunboats to advance on Alexandria, but it was not until after 9:00 A.M. the following morning that *Eastport* and *Osage* got underway upriver.

It was a busy night back downriver below the obstructions. Porter, excited by the news of the fall of Fort DeRussy, roused his gunboat fleet and by 2:00 A.M. had started them all toward Alexandria. *Ozark* ran aground, blocking the river and causing a short delay, but the most serious delay came at the obstructions. The passageway through the Confederate dam was still narrow, and the ungainly ironclads had to be towed through the passage by the more maneuverable *General Price*. At 6:45 A.M., orders arrived from the admiral for the gunboats to tie up to the banks and let the transports pass. By 9:00 A.M. the last of the transports were through the obstructions, and the first boats through were already at the fort, but Smith's plan to move rapidly on Alexandria had been seriously hampered.[1]

---

1. Abstracts of deck logs of USS *Carondelet* and USS *Fort Hindman, ORN* 26:773–74, 784; deck logs, USS *Essex,* RG 24, NA, USS *Benton,* and USS *Eastport;* Jay Slagle, *Ironclad Captain: Seth Ledyard Phelps and the U.S. Navy, 1841–1864* (Kent, Ohio: Kent State Univ. Press, 1996), 357.

Tuesday, March 15, was a day of regrouping for the Union army at Fort DeRussy. While waiting for the steamers to arrive, the troops toured the fort and surrounding area and chatted with the prisoners. "You will catch hell when you get to Alexandria," the Yankees were told. At 9:00 A.M. the Rebel officers were separated from their men and sent aboard the steamer *Clarabell,* General Smith's flagship. At 2:00 P.M. they were finally given something to eat. "A good dinner," Capt. Harvey Wallace said, but one gets the impression he would have liked to have seen it sooner. Capt. Edward T. King was proud to note that "just as I predicted there was never a lot of prisoners treated with more consideration and respect than we were. Gen. Smith himself complimented us on the gallant defense we made."[2]

The Union navy lost no time in gathering souvenirs. Porter's flagship, *Black Hawk,* took on board the two 24-pounder siege guns from the fort on the hill shortly before 6:00 P.M. The guns may not have been meant strictly as souvenirs, though. At 7:15, the tug *Dahlia* made an additional delivery from the DeRussy magazines: 112 11-pound powder charges, 37 stands of canister, 40 rounds of grape, 61 solid shot, and 48 shells—all for the 24-pounders. *Black Hawk* also got 700 rounds of Rebel buck and ball for the boat's muskets. Confederate forces in Louisiana had a long history of getting their supplies from the Yankees. Now the tables were being turned.

By early afternoon most of the Union troops at Fort DeRussy were embarked back aboard their transports, but the fleet did not leave the fort until nearly sundown, and some of the boats did not leave until well after dark. When the army departed, they left behind Gen. Thomas Kilby Smith's detachment of the 17th Army Corps to destroy the fort. This was the second time the fort had been captured by Union forces—A. J. Smith had decided to make it the last time the job had to be done. Strangely enough, A. J. Smith, the commander of the expedition, remained behind at the fort with T. K. Smith's division. Joseph Mower, who had proven himself a quite capable field commander the day before, was in charge of the Union army now moving on Alexandria.

The soldiers aboard the transports need not have worried about the "hell" they would catch at Alexandria. By the time the transports departed from Fort DeRussy, Alexandria was already securely in the hands of the U.S. Navy. At 5:35 P.M., while the troops from Fort DeRussy

2. Hieronymus diary, Mar. 16, 1864; Wallace diary; King letter.

Black Hawk was Admiral Porter's flagship in the early days of the Red River Campaign. After the fort was captured, it took aboard the two 24-pounders that Capt. E. T. King's men had served in the Hill Fort. (Courtesy of Naval Historical Center.)

were just getting underway, *Lexington, Ouachita, Cricket,* and *Fort Hindman* anchored at Alexandria, just in time to see the last of the Confederate steamers heading upstream over the rapids. The Alexandria-Pineville ferry was left grounded and burning in the river, where it was misidentified as the Confederate steamer *Countess,* which had recently helped evacuate stores from the fort.[3] The Union navy's only opposition was a smattering of musket fire from the town. A few rifle shots and one howitzer shell from *Lexington* brought the town under control of the U.S. government. The soldiers arriving from the fort the following day found "the relicts of the most stupendous skedaddle Known in the

3. Lt. Cmdr. S. L. Phelps reported that *Countess* was burned by Confederate forces on Mar. 15, 1864, after grounding on the falls at Alexandria while trying to escape U.S. naval forces. This story is repeated by virtually all steamboat reference books. But on March 17, *Countess* was at Grand Ecore along with the Confederate steamers *Louis D'Or, Beauregard, Indian No. 2, Pauline, Anna Perret, T. D. Hine, Dixie, Colonel Terry,* and *Frolic.* Phelps to Porter, Mar. 16, 1864, *ORN* 26:31; May to Anderson, Mar. 17, 1864, *ORA* 34, pt. 2, 1051; May to Anderson, Mar. 18, 1864, *ORA* 34, pt. 2, 1054. *Countess* continued to operate late into the war. She was used as a flag-of-truce boat in January 1865 and was last recorded moving troops across the river at Shreveport in mid-April 1865. Szymanski to Dwight, Jan. 12, 1865, *ORA* 8 (ser. 2), 59; report of C. S. Bell, Scout, *ORA* 48, pt. 2, 402.

Latter day. 1,000's of Bu of corn lay scattered in the streets Govt wagons mules &c."[4]

Walker's Texans' twenty-hour head start had been lengthened by an additional ten hours, and they were making good use of the time. The Confederate forces in central Louisiana had retreated westward into the pine woods before heading north, heading for safety as fast as they possibly could and leaving Red River to the Yankees. They finally stopped to rest on March 17. "The men are weary and foot sore, broke down and jaded. Even the horses have fagged under it," Captain Petty wrote to his wife on that day. Theophilus Perry also wrote home that day, telling of his sore feet and their "great blisters as large as guinea eggs." But both men maintained their sense of humor. The pine camp-fires in the hills burnt with a black smoke, turning all the men "as black as a pot," and Petty joked that "the Yanks would have thought that we were fighting negroes against them if a battle had come off."[5]

While the Union 16th Corps soldiers were loading on to the transports the morning after the battle, the men of the 17th Corps were preparing to tear the fort down. T. K. Smith's Provisional Division consisted of two infantry brigades, each containing three regiments and one artillery battery. The whole division numbered about two thousand men. Their job was to level Fort DeRussy so that they would not "leave one stone on another."[6]

The men of the 17th Corps had a tedious job ahead of them. No work had been done toward the destruction of the fort on the fifteenth, but at 8:00 A.M. on March 16, work began in earnest to level the earthworks. It was a daunting job, as the works covered some 17,500 square yards. Col. Thomas Humphrey was put in charge of the destruction. Capt. Edmund Newsome of the 81st Illinois, along with three other officers, was assigned to make a survey and plat of the works. Newsome found

> two large water batteries near the river, one of which was a case-mate of rail-road iron, with port-holes for three guns, two being already mounted. There were positions for six other guns, but only four of them were mounted. The magazine was built of timbers

4. Robinson to Dear Bro Will, Mar. 22, 1864.

5. Brown, *Journey to Pleasant Hill,* 379, 382; Johansson, *Widows by the Thousand,* 230, 233.

6. Porter, *Incidents and Anecdotes,* 216.

The artist of this sketch in *Frank Leslie's Illustrated* took vast liberties with perspective. He compressed the half-mile between the Water Battery and the Hill Fort into just a few yards. The mountains in the background lead one to wonder if the artist had ever been to Louisiana.

nine inches square, and covered with an embankment of earth. The fort was of the same construction. The fort proper was very well arranged and located some distance from the battery on the river, but connected with it by a line of earth-works and a bridge over a bayou. This fort was made of nine inch square timbers and embankments with a ditch outside, which was protected by brush and tree-tops staked to the ground. It contained magazines and commissary rooms that were bomb-proof.[7]

Newsome also measured the inside of the magazines, a job he did not particularly enjoy. "They were nearly full of powder, shot and percussion shells. It was a dangerous place, for if I had hit my foot against one of the caps, the whole would have instantly exploded."[8]

While Newsome measured, the troops were hard at work dismantling: "The interior slope of the main redoubt, covering an area of 2,500 square yards, was wholly revetted with heavy 14-inch square timbers, firmly pinned upon each other, mortised and tenoned at the angles. These, with great labor, were one by one wedged off, pulled down with

7. Newsome, *Experience in the War*, 114–15.
8. Ibid., 115.

ropes, and piled for burning." While some men dislodged and piled timbers, others were busy with spades, "tearing down the revetments on the inside of the parapet and digging ditches across the parapet, so that, from the nature of the soil of which it was constructed, the first rain-storm would nearly level it." Others were hauling cannons to the river bank. And still others were demolishing the "extensive covered ways for commissary stores."[9] Those soldiers not at work tearing up the fort were scouting the area around the fort. A party from the 81st Illinois found and destroyed "two large camps of Rebel barracks."[10] On the night of the 16th, a sailor aboard *Essex* reported that "all the rebel camps hereabouts are in a blaze."[11]

The ironclads *Benton* and *Essex* remained at the fort during this period to provide protection to the soldiers working ashore, but working parties from the boats also assisted in the dismantling. The starboard watch from *Benton* spent the morning hauling shells from the fort's magazines, and the starboard watch from *Essex* spent the afternoon dismantling guns. Moving large guns down the riverbank was no easy task, but the men of *Essex* learned through experience that "a gun weighing over 9,000 pounds can be slung (dragging) to the axles of an army wagon and drawn by 18 mules."[12]

The tinclad *Fort Hindman* returned to the fort from Alexandria shortly before noon but did not tarry long. The 317 Confederate prisoners, along with a 55-man guard detail, were marched aboard the gunboat and at 3:30 P.M. *Fort Hindman* cast off and steamed downriver.

By 5:00 P.M., Colonel Humphrey felt that his job had been accomplished. He marched his men back to their brigade camp in the open field between the fort and the Water Battery, some 150 yards from the fort.

All work and no play makes Jack Tar a dull boy, so with the day's labors over the commander of *Essex* decided to liven things up. The sailors had been inspecting the water batteries for the past day and a half, and they all had to be wondering how their boats would have

9. Humphrey to Read, Mar. 17, 1864, *ORA* 34, pt. 1, 387; A. J. Smith to Sherman, Sept. 26, 1865, *ORA* 34, pt. 1, 306.

10. Newsome, *Experience in the War,* 116.

11. James E. Henneberry journal, kept while aboard the USS *Essex,* 1864, edited by Tom Baskett Jr., photostat in Chicago Historical Society (hereafter cited as Henneberry journal).

12. This would have been in reference to the 9-inch Dahlgrens, the barrels of which weighed ninety-two hundred pounds. None of the other guns were that heavy. Townsend to Porter, Mar. 17, 1864, *ORN* 26:32.

fared in a face-to-face confrontation with the notorious Fort DeRussy. They had also had to put up with the boasting of the Rebel prisoners concerning the "invulnerability" of the fort, along with gibes by both Southern and Northern soldiers of how lucky the sailors were that the army had reduced the fort before the gunboats arrived. Comdr. Robert Townsend consulted with A. J. Smith and "concluded to test . . . the powers of endurance of this paragon of rebel defensive works."[13]

Essex got underway at 5:20 P.M. and moved into position across the river from the water batteries. She tied up to the bank, 550 yards from, and directly in front of, the iron-plated casemate. Townsend was aware that there were soldiers beyond the casemate, so he had his best gunner, Acting Master John Parker, align the gun that would test the casemate. A 100-pounder Parrott was chosen for the task. The first round fired was an explosive shell. The glare from the setting sun made for a difficult shot, but Parker was up to the job. The shell hit the casemate just a little off center, squarely between two of the gun ports, and tore out about one square foot of iron plating. Four solid shot followed, and these were considerably more effective. These rounds would bury themselves up to two feet deep in the solid oak backing behind the railroad iron plating, making holes eighteen to thirty inches long and eight to eleven inches wide. While none of the shot penetrated the three- to four-foot oak backing into the interior of the casemate, they did manage to split timbers and start splinters on the inside. Charles Drew, a sailor aboard *Essex,* proudly stated that the test showed that "our fleet could batter down what the Rebels had supposed to be a shot proof battery in half an hour." Generals A. J. and T. K. Smith were in agreement, declaring that fifty such shots would "use up this seemingly invulnerable work."[14] It must be considered, however, that the Generals Smith may just have been being nice. Their comments were made to Commander Townsend, but when A. J. Smith's official report was sent in, he reported that "the gunboats would not have been able to pass" the "strong casemated battery."[15]

13. Ibid.
14. Ibid.; deck log, USS *Essex,* Mar. 16, 1864; Charles J. Drew diary, edited by Tom Baskett Jr. (hereafter cited as Drew diary), transcript in possession of author; U.S. Congress, Joint Committee on the Conduct of the War, *Red River Expedition: Report of the Joint Committee on the Conduct of the War* (Washington, D.C.: GPO, 1865; reprint, Millwood, N.Y.: Kraus Reprint, 1977), 234. Newsome, *Experience in the War,* 116, incorrectly identifies the boat involved as *Benton. Benton* was nearby at the time but did not fire on the casemate.
15. Smith to Sherman, Sept. 26, 1865, *ORA* 34, pt. 1, 312.

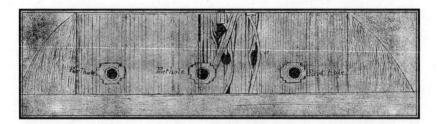

This sketch shows details of the damage inflicted on the Water Battery by the test shots fired by *Essex* on March 16, 1864. A view of the inside of the casemate would have been more informative relative to the survivability of the gun crews. (Congress, Joint Committee on the Conduct of the War, *Red River Expedition.*)

The soldiers watching the demonstration were not in total agreement with their generals, whatever their true opinions might have been. While some of them thought the demonstration proved that the navy could have taken the fort, many others felt it proved just the opposite. But all of the soldiers were probably in agreement on the fact that the demonstration showed a tremendous disregard for the well-being of the troops encamped behind the casemates. One of the four solid shots had glanced off the top edge of the works, and sent twisted iron bars flying through the air like boomerangs, one short piece landing in the woods over two hundred yards from the casemate, not far from the army camp. But no one seemed to recognize this incident for the harbinger it was.[16]

The day had been clear, cool, and pleasant, a perfect day for doing hard manual labor, and the men had taken advantage of the situation. They had worked hard and were now ready for a good night's sleep. But at 7:00 P.M., as so frequently happens in the army, the orders were changed. The three magazines in the fort, one of which contained fifty kegs and barrels of gunpowder, were to be blown up at 8:00 P.M. The brigade's horses and wheeled vehicles were to be immediately put

---

16. One account of this incident demonstrates the difficulty of obtaining accurate information on historical events such as this, even when firsthand accounts exist. William Burns watched the demonstration and wrote years later that the "prisoners had the utmost confidence that the gun-boats could not make any impression upon this work, and were surprised at the result, which proved that two or three hours bombardment would have destroyed it." But according to the deck logs of both the USS *Benton* and *Fort Hindman,* the prisoners had steamed away from the fort more than two hours before the test took place.

aboard the steamboats at the landing, and after the explosion the men were to return to the fort and burn the timbers that had earlier been stacked for that purpose. They were then to prepare to embark on the boats "at an early hour."

Although there were no orders from headquarters concerning moving campsites, the company commanders took it upon themselves to have their men move back some one to two hundred yards farther from the fort and take such shelter as they could find. But an hour passed beyond the designated time for the explosion, and then two hours. The night had turned cold—it would be twenty-nine degrees with a hard frost at daybreak—and the men were tired from their hard day's work. By 10:00 P.M. they had returned to their warm fires and cozy blankets. It seemed that the plans had been changed, but nobody had bothered to tell the men. The soldiers went to bed.

At 10:30 the men were roused by an explosion such as they had never before witnessed.[17] The earth sank beneath them, and the air was filled "for hundreds of yards with timbers, huge lumps of hard red clay, and other dangerous missiles." Captain Newsome watched in amazement. "I could see shells bursting high in the air, the whole heavens seemed to be on fire, pieces of timber and hard lumps of earth were falling in camp and even beyond," he recalled. "Men were running for life to the woods. . . . There was scarcely time to think before another magazine blew up, followed by a shower of fragments." Another member of the 81st Illinois described the scene as "indescribable. Dirt, stones, timbers and shells were thrown high in the air, coming down with terrific force. . . . The shells bursting and the fragments falling at a late hour, really made night hideous."[18]

Out in the river, a half mile away, the men on the steamers were equally awestruck. The explosion "brought me out of my hammock head first," reported James Henneberry aboard *Essex*. "No pen of mine can convey an idea of the terrific explosion," William Burns remembered. "Three thousand pounds of powder were used. . . . We stood on the upper deck of our steamer. . . . 1st came the bright triple flash, and we saw the timbers, earth, &c., &c., flying through the air. Then

17. Different witnesses give the time of the explosion as early as 9:00 P.M. and as late as 11:00 P.M. Colonel Humphrey and the deck logs of *Benton* and *Essex* agree on 10:30.
18. Col. Thomas Humphrey to Lt. John M. Read, Mar. 17, 1864, *ORA* 34, pt. 1, 387; Newsome, *Experience in the War*, 116–17.

1st Lt. Jerome Bishop, Company D, 81st Illinois Infantry, was decapitated by shrapnel from one of the 6-pounders burst on March 16. This photograph was taken by an army photographer in Vicksburg less than a year before Bishop's grisly death. He was thirty years old when the image was made. (Carte de visite, courtesy of Fort DeRussy State Historic Site library.)

followed the report, and the quivering of the steamer, and the roll of reverberations, and the ruin was complete, leaving only three immense excavations, broken timbers, scraps of iron, blocks of clay, &c., &c., where stood one of the strongest forts in the 'Southern Confederacy.'"[19]

The men in the camp were in varying states of shock and excitement. Some stood watching the spectacle. Edmund Newsome was still huddled in his blanket when "some one said, 'They are going to burst a cannon.' In a moment we heard a sharp explosion. I could hear one of the fragments coming towards us; it seemed to be a long time buzzing in the air—Some one said, 'let's run.' I said, 'lie still.' (for we were in bed.) It struck ten feet from our 'shebang.' I arose to see who was hurt, for I had heard a groan. I found two men down, side by side." William Stewart, a captain from the 95th Illinois, had a piece of the cannon pass "over my head not more than two feet."[20]

Throughout the camp, the men were dazed by the destruction this "friendly fire" had wrought. The magazine explosion alone was dev-

19. Henneberry journal; Burns scrapbook.
20. Newsome, *Experience in the War,* 116–17; Stewart diary, Mar. 17 [16], 1864.

astating. While several men of the 33rd Wisconsin had been pelted by falling debris, it was the Illinois troops who caught the brunt of the damage. In the camp of the 95th Illinois, Samuel Snyder of Company A was lying with his left leg broken so severely by "a lump of hard red clay" that it would require amputation above the knee. Cpl. Allen Giles of Company F had his right arm broken, also by a falling clod. Lt. John Abbe was slightly wounded in the face. But it was the fragments of the burst iron 6-pounder cannons that had wreaked the most havoc within the encampment. When Captain Newsome emerged from his "she-bang" into the moonlight, he found Sgt. Pembroke King, Company D, 81st Illinois, wounded and groaning. 1st Lt. Jerome Bishop, Company D, 81st Illinois, and Pvt. Samuel H. Jackson, Company C, 95th Illinois, were also down, but they were beyond groaning. Arthur McCullough recorded in his diary that both of their heads had been "carried away." It was, he wrote, "the most awful sight I ever witnessed." Newsome was more graphic: "The upper half of their heads were taken off. . . . I handled the piece of cannon soon afterwards with the brains still on it." Capt. David Young, Bishop's company commander, "was spattered with the brains, and in that condition went to Gen. A. J. Smith, to show that commander his work."[21]

The troops were infuriated by this wanton and needless loss of life, and they were a long time in forgiving A. J. Smith. He had become, as the adjutant of the 81st Illinois described it, "very unpopular with the boys." Two weeks later, as Smith was reviewing his troops, "as usual, the troops cheered him until he came to the 95th Ill. and 81st Ill. They groaned and hissed at him, and told him to blow up another fort and kill more of his own men. The General was mad, and swore that he would put those two regiments on boats and then they might go to H——a warm place if they wished."[22]

Colonel Humphrey moved his men back into the fort at midnight and proceeded to burn the timbers that had been piled earlier. No one slept much that night. On the morning of Thursday, March 17, the

21. Humphrey to Read, Mar. 17, 1864, *ORA* 34, pt. 1, 387; McCullough diary; Newsome, *Experience in the War,* 117. Snyder was not expected to survive the amputation, and did not; Giles did not return to his regiment until January; King would not return to duty until September; but Lieutenant Abbe's facial wound was so minor as not to be mentioned in his service record. Individual compiled service records.

22. Newsome, *Experience in the War,* 117, 122. The two regiments would continue to harass Smith until after the Battle of Pleasant Hill on April 9. They would not cheer him until the last day of the Red River Campaign.

brigade boarded the steamers waiting for them in the river. The wounded from the previous night's fiasco were put aboard the hospital boat *Woodford,* and the dead were buried. The transports lay at the wharf until the morning of March 18, when they departed for Alexandria.

The destruction of Fort DeRussy was declared accomplished. T. K. Smith's division "left the fortifications in ruins, and as thoroughly destroyed as possible within such a limited time."[23] But in fact, the fort was far from destroyed. Union military and naval forces would continue to tear at the fort for weeks to come.

23. Humphrey to Read, Mar. 17, 1864, *ORA* 34, pt. 1, 387.

Chapter 14

Gunboat Station and Contraband Camp

A. J. Smith may have told his superiors that Fort DeRussy was destroyed, but it was not, and he knew it. The fort was still a threat to river traffic, should the Confederates reoccupy it, and for that reason a continued Union presence at the fort was necessary. The U.S. Navy would maintain a gunboat station in the river at the fort to prevent any possibility of reoccupation, and the U.S. Army established several "contraband camps" near the fort for the recruitment of soldiers and laborers. By March 26, 257 newly freed slaves had been enlisted into the U.S. Army.[1] George Burmeister told of meeting one such potential soldier, a "young, able-bodied darkey," on the night of the fort's capture:

> He was almost entirely naked, without shoes and clad in rags, so
> that half of his skin was visible. He complained very bitterly of the
> ill treatment he had received at the hands of his masters. He told us
> the darkies were treated like brutes, forced to work hard and when
> they were unable to work any more, they were not taken care of
> by their owners. I gave him some crackers [hardtack], those which
> our men esteem so lightly. He liked them well and devoured several
> dozen with great avidity. He appeared to be nearly starved. And
> listen what he said: "O Lor massa, dis is de fust wheat cakes I've
> had since las Christmas a year ago." I took him to camp and told
> him he was free. It did me good to tell him so. He was very glad and
> expressed his joy by shouting, "O, tank de Lor, tank de Lor for it.
> I'se been waiting for you a long time and you all has come at las."[2]

Men in this condition were easily recruited into the Union army.

In addition to the newly recruited soldiers, the camps at Fort DeRussy also held seven to eight hundred other former slaves, mostly women and children. The army commander at the post was one Captain Lee, who,

1. Townsend to Porter, Mar. 25, 1864, *ORN* 26:35–36.
2. Burmeister journal, Monday, Mar. 14, 1864.

though mentioned frequently in gunboat log books, was never more completely identified.[3] In addition to his duties as a recruiting officer, he was also a one-man Freedmen's Bureau and was in charge of all activities relating to contrabands in the area. On the Saturday night following the capture of the fort, two ladies came aboard *Benton* "and reported that the negroes in the surrounding country were armed and becoming violent."[4] *Benton*'s captain and Captain Lee conferred about the matter, and whatever method they chose to handle the problem seems to have worked. The incidents of "outrages" decreased and afterward were confined mostly to threats and acts of insolence.

The contraband camps were never models of prosperity, and they soon became squalid. In mid-April, James Henneberry went ashore from *Essex* to tour the camps and returned with an extremely negative report: "I visited the different Negro camps today in company with 3 of our officers and found nothing but what would disgust me with the whole race of blacks, unless it was one beautiful octoroon girl who was among them but considered herself no better than the rest." Henneberry vowed to take no more such shore tours unless "I know where I was going before I started."[5]

With the departure of Smith's troops, the seamen aboard *Essex* and *Benton* continued the work of leveling the fort. After the disastrous affair of the magazine explosion on the night of March 16, the detonation of the magazine at the Water Battery was delayed until after the soldiers left. But the soldiers had barely steamed out of sight on the morning of March 18 when the sailors began preparations for another grand explosion. After removing forty-nine barrels of gunpowder to *Essex*, that boat dropped down a quarter of a mile below the fort. *Benton* was one mile upstream, having moved there the night before. The sailors had learned well from the army's mistakes. At 9:45 A.M., the Water Battery magazine was blown into oblivion. But the casemated battery was still standing, as strong as ever.[6]

Comdr. Robert Townsend was still interested in seeing just how well his guns would perform against the battery. He had seen what

3. The most likely candidate for this Captain Lee was Capt. Abner N. Lee of the 71st U.S. Colored Troops.
4. Deck log, USS *Benton*, Mar. 19, 1864.
5. Henneberry journal, Apr. 11, 1864.
6. One soldier, 1st Lt. Orrin R. Potter of the 14th Wisconsin, did stay behind to either assist with or supervise the blowing up of the magazine. He was put on a tug afterward and caught up with the departing fleet by noon. Stewart diary, Mar. 19 [18], 1864.

his 100-pounder Parrott could do, but his armament was varied. To appease his curiosity, he set up another test, this time at a range of only three hundred yards. He softened the casemate up with six rounds from his 100-pounder Parrott and then fired thirteen rounds of solid shot from his 9-inch Dahlgrens. He finished the cannonade with three five-second shells from his 100-pounder Parrott. Though none of the shot penetrated through—a testimony to the strength of the armor—large splinters of oak were torn off on the inside, one of the splinters being seven feet long, a foot wide, and six inches thick. This back-spalling effect would have made the inside of the casemate a veritable slaughterhouse during any sustained attack, given similar shot placement. On the other hand, the test was hardly a realistic analysis of combat shot placement and proximity.[7]

As the departing soldiers steamed up the river, they had time to make observations of the area. They were not impressed. The river seemed to turn "every few yards," making the trip to Alexandria a slow one. "I always called the Mississippi a crooked river," wrote one, "but the Red is all crooks, it is one continued succession of S, so much so that we frequently run ashore in turning." And the riverbank was "almost unbroken forest." When the occasional clearing would come in sight, they would see "a dilapidated building, apparently engaged in a perpetual conflict with the laws of gravitation; a few cattle and long-nosed hogs, and a great many lank dogs, roam about the apology for a garden; while groups of flaxen-haired children pour out of the doorways. It is the country of the poor whites, where labor is considered degrading, where education is unknown, and where Northern enterprise has never penetrated." But while they may have looked down their noses at the "poor whites," they did find them to be friendly. "Most of them cheer us by waving handkerchiefs or bonnets. One house we passed flaunted the stars and stripes to the breeze and we cheered them lustily." The black population was particularly jubilant—at two o'clock, the fleet passed a plantation where the soldiers saw "a great crowd of Negroes on shore swinging aprons hats & bonnets." All in all, the campaign seemed to be going splendidly.[8]

7. Deck logs, USS *Benton* and *Essex;* Townsend to Porter, Mar. 25, 1864, *ORN* 26:36.
8. George W. Powers, *The Story of the Thirty Eighth Regiment of Massachusetts Volunteers* (Cambridge Press, 1866), 127–28; Stewart diary, Mar. 19 [18], 1864. Powers actually passed up the Red on March 24, a few days after the first boats, but his observations enhanced those of Stewart.

The defense and protection of U.S. personnel and property at Fort DeRussy was unquestionably the number one priority of the gunboats stationed at the fort, but the continued acquisition of cotton was number two. In the days following the capture of the fort, *Benton* sent numerous scouting parties up and down the river. They would board the tugboat *Fern*, *Benton*'s tender, and set out in search of the valuable white fiber. The last cotton crop in the area had been grown in 1862, but that harvest was still lying under cotton sheds and gins all along the river. *Benton*'s crew made three trips to Eugene Brochard's gin, a mile and a half upstream and across the river from the fort, to gather nearly fifty bales. As that gin was close to the bank, the sailors rolled the bales down to the river and loaded them aboard the tug.

It was not always that easy. A few more miles upriver, at W. W. Johnson's place, the sailors found tiers of cotton bales piled beneath a shed, with more loose cotton inside the gin's lint room. But this gin was nearly a mile from the river, and it was necessary to round up mules and harness them to sleds to drag the cotton to the river. Two bales would fit on a sled, and on the first trip to the Johnson place, some eight to ten sled loads were carried down to *Fern*. On subsequent trips, another twenty-five or so bales were dragged to the river and loaded aboard. This left only the loose cotton, but the sailors were not put off. They brought canvas and bagging from the boat and operated the gin themselves for several days with the help of "negroes and several white men" from the neighborhood who were drafted for that purpose.[9]

Anyone familiar with cotton gins and cotton ginning can tell you that gins are prone to breakdowns, even with the most experienced crews.[10] Not unexpectedly, this was much more the case with a gin run by unwilling conscripts and enthusiastic but untrained sailors. The sailors were engaged in a very simple operation. The loose cotton had already been ginned—that is, the seed had already been removed from the lint—and the gin crews were merely feeding the lint into the press and compacting it into bales. And as long as Job Starr, *Benton*'s chief engineer, was up in the loft supervising the men feeding the press, there was no problem. But when Starr came down to take a break, the boat's carpenter took his place and tried to put too much cotton into one bale. The results were a broken screw and a disabled press.

9. Amos T. Bissell testimony, *Oden Deucatte v. United States*.
10. The author was manager of the cotton gin in Armistead, Red River Parish, Louisiana, for two growing seasons.

But even a breakdown of the cotton press did not stop the determined freebooters in their quest for easy money. They brought the broken parts back to *Benton,* where the boat's engineers were able to fabricate several nuts, bolts, and straps necessary to put the press back in working order. They returned the next morning and made the repairs. The ginning continued, and some twenty-one full bales, and a piece, were packed in this manner.[11]

The numerous contrabands swarming to the fort were full of tales of stockpiles of cotton in the surrounding countryside. One runaway slave had a particularly interesting story. He was crippled and partially paralyzed from having been hunted and caught by hounds, and he made a point to tell the Union sailors of all the hidden cotton that he knew of in the area around Marksville. The bait was just too tempting, and on March 30, Lt. Comdr. James A. Greer (*Benton*) sent out the largest "scouting party" ever, numbering nearly two hundred men. They headed inland several miles, going beyond Marksville to the farm of Constant Guillebert. Guillebert had not been unmindful of the threat of marauding Yankees and had taken pains to hide his cotton as well as his wagons. Unfortunately for him, the intelligence provided to the Yankees by the contrabands had been specific. The cotton was quickly found, and a search of his barn loft turned up the wagons and harness, all disassembled and hidden beneath hay. Wheels, axles, tongues, and beds were all hauled down piece by piece and reassembled in the barnyard, while mules and oxen were rounded up, harnessed,, and hitched to the wagons. Guillebert's strenuous objections resulted in his arrest, and he was hauled back toward the boats along with his cotton.

It was a motley crew making its way back to Fort DeRussy that afternoon. Wagons of all shapes and sizes were carrying varying amounts of cotton, pulled by any sort of animal that could pull and escorted by sailors and slaves. One large wagon had twelve bales of cotton aboard and was pulled by sixteen oxen. There were wagons with four-mule teams and six-mule teams, wagons with twelve-ox teams, and two-wheeled carts with four-ox teams, all loaded down with cotton and headed for the fort. The parade halted for a while in Marksville, between the courthouse and a brick store belonging to Auguste Voinché. A hearing was held for Guillebert, and he was released.

11. Job Starr, Hector Fairfowl, and Oliver Bray testimony, *Oden Deucatte v. United States.*

The halt at that particular location was not coincidental. The sailors had been advised beforehand that Voinché's store contained a large amount of cotton in its basement. While Guillebert's trial progressed, several sailors went around the building, smashed a large padlock off the door, and entered the store. On going down the stairs, they found a sight that no doubt made their hearts pound. The brick-floored basement, roughly forty-two by sixty-six feet, was packed to the rafters—"piled plum full to the top"—with bales of cotton. Narrow aisles between the bales gave access to the back of the basement. Their informants had told them there were "between eight hundred and a thousand bales" in the building. Acting Master E. C. Brennan, in charge of the expedition, and Master's Mate Amos Bissell estimated that there must have been "some five or six thousand bales in there." Actually, there were only 391 bales of cotton in the basement, but that was still an awful lot of cotton.[12]

Surprisingly, only fourteen bales were removed from the basement at that time. There were only two empty wagons available, and that was all they could carry. The "scouting party" headed back for the boats with plans to return in the morning. On the way back, they managed to pick up a few more wagons and teams and a few more bales of cotton. When they arrived back at the boat, the cotton was unloaded on the bank, and the wagons and teams were turned over to Captain Lee and his contrabands.[13]

With their booty disposed of, the men went back aboard the boats. They did not have long to wait before Auguste Voinché himself showed up at the boat. Voinché was indignant and demanded that his cotton be returned. He was a French citizen, he explained, and as a neutral, his cotton was not subject to seizure. He spoke no English, only French, so was forced to present his case to Acting Master Henry O'Grady, a salty old seadog who was fluent in French, Spanish, and German as well as his native English. When O'Grady told his shipmates that the man had come to get his cotton back, the sailors howled with laughter. O'Grady refused to let Voinché aboard the boat and sent him on his

12. William Kisner and Bissell testimony, *Oden Deucatte v. United States*. The store and basement still exist, and I stepped off the dimensions given.

13. Lee maintained the "corrals" at the fort, which contained all of the horses, mules, cattle, and sheep that were being brought in from the surrounding countryside, as well as large amounts of forage and grain, foodstuffs, and all of the firearms confiscated from local citizens. Starr testimony, *Oden Deucatte v. United States*.

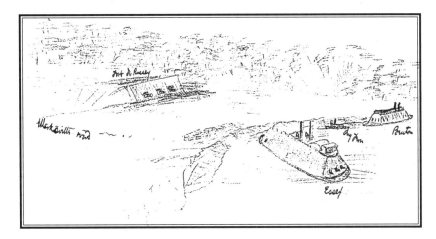

This sketch was made by Charles Fuller in 1888 for a French-American Claims Commission trial. Fuller had been an officer aboard *Essex* and testified at the trial concerning his role in the disappearance of cotton from August Voinché's basement. (Courtesy of National Archives.)

way with assurances that he would be paid for his cotton "later." It was a refrain that many Louisiana residents heard in 1863 and 1864. Most of them—Voinché included—were never compensated.[14]

The best laid plans of mice and men often go awry, and such was the case in this instance. The men of *Benton* would not be able to return for the rest of the cotton stored in Voinché's basement. Orders came during the night, and at 5:30 A.M., *Benton* got underway and headed upriver. But *Benton*'s departure did not mean the end of Union naval presence at the fort. The *Essex* remained, and Voinché's cotton-filled cellar was soon emptied.

Though not nearly as lucrative, the sailors at Fort DeRussy did have other work to do beyond just hauling cotton. They were members of the U.S. Navy, defending a significant strong point on the Red River.

---

14. Bissell and Oden Deucatte (Auguste Voinché) testimony, *Oden Deucatte v. United States*. There is an unexplainable discrepancy in the testimony of the two men. Both acknowledge the O'Grady-Voinché confrontation and describe it similarly. But Voinché (Deucatte) said that he was in Opelousas when the fourteen bales were taken and the confrontation occurred after he returned, when the cellar had been completely emptied. That is not possible, as O'Grady was aboard *Benton*, and *Benton* left the area within twelve hours of the return of the expedition. The testimony was given eighteen years after the event. Voinché was, by that time, in his late seventies. Perhaps a hazy recollection can be forgiven.

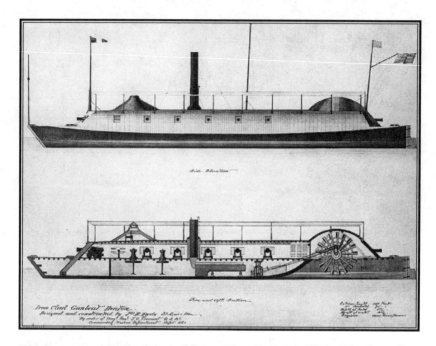

USS *Benton* spent a good deal of time at Fort DeRussy. The sailors from this boat have to share the responsibility for the Red River Campaign's reputation as a "cotton-stealing expedition." (Courtesy of Naval Historical Center.)

The policing of the river was a primary job of the gunboats on station at the fort. Throughout the Red River Campaign there was a nearly constant stream of steamer traffic up and down the river. Troop transports, supply boats, dispatch boats, tugs and barges, and gunboats of every type continually passed up and downstream. The gunboats at the fort naturally kept a close eye on who passed by. Many of the gunboats and transports would stop at the fort for one reason or another. The arrival of the steamer *Illinois* on March 28 seems to have been a more festive occasion than was typical. The steamer, on her way upriver carrying reinforcements to the army in Alexandria, came to the landing in high style. As a band aboard played, "crowds of happy blacks on each side of the river" gathered and watched. The captain of *Illinois* had a present for *Benton*. Seamen Samuel Roberts and Alvin Eldridge had deserted from *Benton* three nights earlier, taking with them two ship's pistols. When *Illinois* found them several miles downriver, they had already tired of their newfound freedom. They hailed the boat and, when taken aboard, seemed glad to get back to hardtack and salt pork.

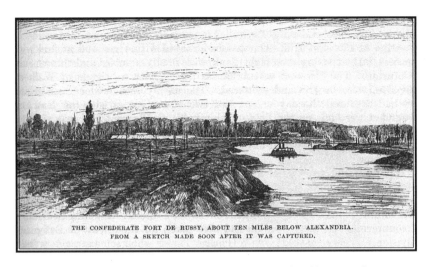

THE CONFEDERATE FORT DE RUSSY, ABOUT TEN MILES BELOW ALEXANDRIA.
FROM A SKETCH MADE SOON AFTER IT WAS CAPTURED.

Contrary to this map's legend, Fort DeRussy is considerably more than ten miles below Alexandria. (Underwood and Buel, *Battles and Leaders of the Civil War.*)

Roberts and Eldridge were returned to *Benton,* placed in double irons, and the pistols were returned to the armory. *Illinois* continued upriver to Alexandria. The band, an enthusiastic group that would break into serenade at the shooting of an alligator, celebrated their arrival there, too.[15]

In addition to keeping an eye on the river, the sailors continued their work of destruction on the fort's defensive capabilities. It had not taken long for the sailors to get all of the big guns down to the riverbank. Six of Fort DeRussy's eight big guns were in the water batteries, just a few yards from the river. The other two, 24-pounder siege guns, were in the fort on the hill. The 24-pounders were hauled the half mile to the river and loaded aboard USS *Black Hawk* within twenty-four hours of their capture. But the other six guns lay on the bank, under the watchful eyes of the sailors, for nearly a month before the two 9-inch

15. Alligators were plentiful in the Red during the campaign, and the soldiers on the transport frequently amused themselves by shooting at them. One soldier commented that the deserters turned themselves in because "they could get nothing to eat along that river but alligators," making the "hard tack and salt junk" they would get aboard the boat a welcome respite. George G. Smith, *Leaves from a Soldier's Diary* (Putnam, Conn.: G. G. Smith, 1906), 91–92; Robert A. Tyson diary, Mar. 28, 1864, MS 693, Louisiana and Lower Mississippi Valley Collection, Hill Memorial Library, Louisiana State Univ., Baton Rouge (hereafter cited as Tyson diary); deck log, USS *Benton.*

Dahlgrens were sent off on *New National* and the other four guns, on
April 8, were put aboard the transport *General Lyon*.[16]

The ammunition for the big guns was also removed. Some of the
ammunition and powder was taken by the gunboats; the remainder
was blown up with the magazines. Like the magazines, the casemates
on the river were soon destroyed. Sailors and contrabands worked until
March 20 removing railroad iron from the fort and hauling it to the
river bank. Shortly after noon on March 21, the crew of *Essex* set fire
to the now armorless casemate, burning it to the ground. Much of the
iron was still lying on the bank a month later when orders were given
to the commander of USS *Argosy* to have the iron loaded on barges for
transport to the U.S. boat yards in Cairo, Illinois. It was suggested at
the same time that contrabands from the fort be used to recover coal
from a sunken coal barge a few miles below the fort.[17]

Another job of the sailors at the Fort DeRussy gunboat station was
the pacification of the rebellious population. It was not unusual for residents of the surrounding area to be brought aboard the gunboats and
questioned. On the other hand, local citizens desiring to take the Oath
of Allegiance to the U.S. government went aboard *Essex* to handle the
formalities of that procedure. The *Essex*'s deck log records that some
fifty-four citizens swore their loyalty between March 19 and 25, but
sailors aboard the boat recorded in their diaries that the number of
citizens taking the oath was in the hundreds.[18] Perhaps because of this
small loyal pool, the fort also served as a gathering point for firearms
from the local citizenry. One outbuilding at the fort was piled high with
shotguns gathered from the area.[19]

The property owners of the area around Fort DeRussy had good
reason to be resentful of the naval presence in the river. It was not only
their cotton that was in jeopardy. One of *Benton*'s officers recalled
years after the war, "We seized a great deal of corn around the country
there, and mules, horses, cattle and everything we could get hold of.

16. The two 24-pounders taken aboard *Black Hawk* were turned over to *New
National* on April 19. Deck logs, USS *Black Hawk*, RG 24, NA, and USS *Essex*;
Townsend to Porter, Apr. 7, 1864, *ORN* 26:27.

17. Breese to Morong, Apr. 20, 1864, *ORN* 26:66.

18. Henneberry counted "no less than 125 standing out on the beach waiting for
their turn and the Capt swearing them as fast as he could" on March 24 alone and had
noted "large numbers" taking the oath in the days before that. Drew noted the planters
coming in "by the scores" to take the oath. Henneberry journal.

19. Starr and Martin Rabalais testimony, *Oden Deucatte v. United States*.

While we were there we lived on fresh beef altogether. . . . Wherever we heard of corn or anything of that kind which was available, we would go out and seize it." Probably some of the oaths of allegiance were taken in the mistaken belief that they would protect the oath takers from property loss. There is no indication that the oaths helped. The poorer class of the area fared better with the Yankees than the property owners did. Many of the contrabands, and some whites, were pressed into service on the seizure raids, but they were generally paid for their help. Occasionally money exchanged hands—one man who drove a team for the Yankees was paid a dollar a day for his services—but generally the pay was in supplies: flour, coffee, hardtack, bacon, and occasionally salt meat, shoes, or linen.[20]

The destruction of the fort was not the only security measure provided by the gunboats. Confederate deserters and prisoners were handled by the gunboat personnel, and the gunboats provided physical security for the contraband camps ashore. But by late March, Southern soldiers were starting to reappear in the neighborhood. On April 1, Captain Lee's contraband pickets spotted Confederate soldiers prowling the area shortly after dark. *Essex* was called to quarters, and one 9-inch shell was fired toward the suspected Rebels. The Rebels got the message and left; with the exception of a couple of musket shots around midnight from nervous sentries, the rest of the night was quiet. But the atmosphere around Fort DeRussy was changing, In the days to come, more and more Confederate soldiers would be seen in the area. With the departure of *Benton* on March 31, the crew of the *Essex* were the only naval personnel now permanently stationed at the fort. They managed to finish removing the cotton from Voinché's cellar, but after that they stayed closer to their boat. The policing of the area around the fort fell on the shoulders of Captain Lee's contraband Home Guard Company, under the command of one Captain Morters. Armed with muskets procured from *Essex*, the Home Guard began to actively search the area for Confederate "guerrillas" on April 10. They hit pay dirt on April 15, returning to the fort with ten horses and five prisoners, some of whom were suspected of being involved "with the murder of two of

---

20. Bissell testimony, ibid. The condition of the locals elicited sympathy from some of the sailors. Henneberry records that the "sufferings of the poor, as well as those whom we would consider rich could they get their products to market around here is fearful many of them not having a bite of food and no means of getting any[.] the boys show their Sailor Generosity [to] them as far as they can." Henneberry journal.

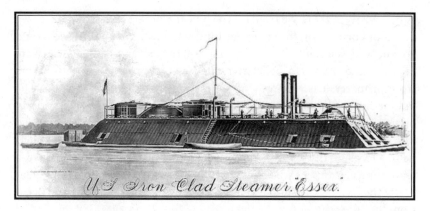

USS *Essex* spent more time at Fort DeRussy than any other U.S. gunboat. It was plagued with leaks and an underpowered engine but nonetheless had an illustrious career. (Courtesy of Naval Historical Center.)

Capt [Lee's] negroes while at church last Sunday at Marksville." The prisoners were put in confinement aboard *Essex,* and twenty-three borrowed muskets were returned to the boat.[21]

Mid-April 1864 was not a happy time for the Union army along the Mississippi and its tributaries. On April 8, Good Friday, the Grand Skedaddle that had started nearly a month earlier back at Fort Humbug and Fort DeRussy came to a screeching halt. Or, more appropriately, a screaming halt. For when the dust had settled on the battlefield at Mansfield, hundreds of soldiers lay dead and dying, but the Union juggernaut had been stopped. And not only had the Confederate skedaddle stopped, but the Red River Campaign had suddenly turned into a Union skedaddle. Nathaniel Banks gave up his plans for the conquest of Texas and moved his army back to Grand Ecore, preparatory to moving them down Red River. For all Union intents and purposes, the Red River Expedition was over. All that was left now was an ignominious retreat back the way they had come.

And on the Mississippi a few days later, on April 12, the Union army suffered another serious defeat which would also affect activities at Fort DeRussy. Fort Pillow, Tennessee, a river stronghold north of Memphis, fell to Confederate general Nathan Bedford Forrest's cavalry. Although Forrest held the fort for less than a day, the fear that the

21. Deck log, USS *Essex;* Drew diary.

Confederates would once again blockade the Mississippi gripped the navy. Admiral Porter examined his priorities and made a decision: the ironclads *Essex, Benton, Lafayette,* and *Choctaw* were essential to the free flow of river traffic on the Mississippi.

In the early morning hours of April 16, *Essex* received orders to leave Fort DeRussy. By 7:30 A.M. gangs of contrabands were carrying aboard the last of the captured materials from the fort. Shot and shell for the guns and two sling carts were loaded onto the boat. Sailors "went out and burned the Rebel quarters around the fort." Thirty-three muskets with ammunition were sent ashore to Captain Lee's contrabands, as they would shortly be without naval support. At 7:15 P.M., *Benton* arrived from above, departing downriver at 5:30 the next morning. At daylight, contrabands were once again brought from the camps. They were put to work throwing all of the remaining lumber from the fort into the river. At 11:00 A.M., *Essex* got underway and headed downstream.[22]

For the first time in nearly a month, Fort DeRussy had no Union gunboat on station. Captain Lee's contrabands were now the sole U.S. presence at the fort, but even they were not nearly at the strength they had been just a short while before. Ever since the fort's capture, contrabands had been actively encouraged to leave their masters and come to the several camps near the fort. On April 12, the steamer *Ike Davis* left the camps carrying a large number of the contrabands to government plantations near Vicksburg. When *Essex* left on April 17, most of the contrabands were already gone.[23]

While *Essex* may have left Fort DeRussy behind that pleasant spring morning, there was one thing that she did not leave behind. Shot, shell, and sling carts were not the only materials being loaded aboard *Essex* as she prepared to depart. *Essex* also took some "Small Pox darkies on board," much to the disgruntlement of the sailors. As one sailor commented, it was "an arrangement I don't like much but must put up with it." The mariner's displeasure was well founded, as a sailor came down with smallpox two days later.[24]

What else may have been aboard *Essex* as she departed that day is another one of Fort DeRussy's mysteries. The deck log does not mention it, nor do James Henneberry or Charles Drew in their journals, so in all

22. Deck log, USS *Essex;* Henneberry journal.
23. Deck log, USS *Essex;* Henneberry journal; Elsey Fox and Scott Normand testimony, *Oden Deucatte v. United States.*
24. Henneberry journal.

likelihood it never happened. But according to Charles Fuller, in sworn testimony some twenty-three years later, as *Essex* moved down the river "we had all the cotton we could pile on our deck, forward-deck, after-guard, gun-deck, and hurricane-deck. . . . There was a row about two bales thick extending on both sides and across the forward part of the upper deck; on the forward deck it was piled up so as not to prevent the use of the guns of the forward battery; the same way on the after-guard, or 'fan-tail,' as they called it there; also rows of cotton extending both sides of the boilers and engines on the gun-deck." If Fuller is to be believed, *Essex* steamed down Red River to the rescue of Fort Pillow carrying about 150 bales of cotton on her decks, with another 100 bales on a barge she was towing—with a cash value of about one hundred thousand dollars.[25]

25. Deck log, USS *Essex*; Charles Fuller testimony, *Oden Deucatte v. United States*. Further evidence that Fuller's testimony is in error is the fact that the engines on *Essex* were underpowered for the boat, and it frequently received assistance from other steamers when moving upstream. For *Essex* to have towed a barge, even going downstream, would have been out of character.

Chapter 15

Prison Life in New Orleans

A few days before *Essex* departed Fort DeRussy, the Officer of the Deck logged in the passage of another paddlewheeler heading downstream: "4:50 P.M. [April 15] Steamer *Polar Star* with 450 Rebel prisoners passed down." At this time of the Red River Campaign, shortly after the Battle of Mansfield, downward-passing boatloads of prisoners and wounded were commonplace, so this probably did not excite the attention of the officer. He might have been amused to know that most of the prisoners aboard *Polar Star* that afternoon had been captured at Fort DeRussy a month earlier.

When Fort DeRussy fell, not all of the men in the fort fell prey to the Yankees. Most of the soldiers in the Water Battery were able to slip away. Some of these made it back to Confederate lines, and others seem to have simply gone home. Aristide Dauzat of Hutton's Artillery, a self-professed Jayhawker, took to the woods and did not return to his company until a month after the Yankees left the area. He did manage to make a little spending money—a dollar a day for three days—hauling Auguste Voinché's cotton from Marksville to Fort DeRussy for the U.S. Navy during his "sabbatical." Dauzat unabashedly admitted after the war that all of his service to the Confederacy took place while the Yankees were well out of gunshot range. On the other hand, Capt. A. L. Adams and Lt. Elbert E. Jennings, of the 28th and 13th Texas Dismounted Cavalries, respectively, along with twenty-one of their men, rejoined their units at Carroll Jones's plantation just a few days after the fort fell.[1]

Pvt. John Singleton of the St. Martin Rangers was another escapee from Fort DeRussy. Carefully making his way westward, he arrived at Bayou Boeuf near Cheneyville four days later, where he was finally able to find something to eat. He crossed the bayou at two o'clock in the morning,

---

1. Dauzat testimony, *Oden Deucatte v. United States;* Walker to Surget, Mar. 19, 1864, *ORA* 34, pt. 1, 600.

just behind a Union cavalry patrol and just ahead of most of the U.S. Army advancing on Alexandria from south Louisiana. Singleton was able to evade the Yankees, but he was not as lucky with his own people. He was "shanghaied" by Capt. Charles Tertrou and forced into the 4th Louisiana Cavalry. He was still trying to make his way back to the St. Martin Rangers in July.[2]

Other escapees had equally harrowing tales to tell after the war. Family legend has it that Evariste Barré's life was saved by a spider on his escape from the fort. Barré found himself in the midst of a Union search party the morning after the fall of the fort. Desperately looking for a place to hide, he found a large hollow cypress tree. A spider had built a web across the hollow, so Barré crawled under the silken mesh and stood up inside the tree. The Yankees kept moving closer, bayoneting bushes and other hollow trees as they advanced. "Check out that one," he heard a sergeant call to one of the men. A voice responded from just outside his tree, "Ain't nothin' been in here lately, it's all webbed over." The Yankees moved on, and Barré escaped. And that is why, his great-great-grandchildren say, Grandpa Barré would never kill a spider for the rest of his life.[3]

But most of the men who manned the walls of Fort DeRussy were captured and sent down Red River on the afternoon of March 16 aboard the USS *Fort Hindman*. They were crowded on the lower deck under a strict guard and spent a "cold disagreeable night." It was also something of a dangerous night. The boat made her way uneventfully down the Red, but on entering the Mississippi, failed to notice the gunboat *General Bragg* on patrol nearby. *General Bragg*, not receiving the proper signals from *Fort Hindman*, took off after the unidentified boat. Nearly to Port Hudson, the *Bragg* finally overhauled the *Hindman* and fired a signal shot for the boat to "haul in." When that shot was ignored, *General Bragg* fired again, this time with a solid shot that fell short. A third shot went over, and a fourth shot clipped one of the posts that supported the hurricane deck, narrowly missing some of the prisoners. Sensing by now that the pursuing gunboat meant business, *Fort Hindman* came about. After some "sharp words" between the commanders of the two vessels, *Fort Hindman* continued on, arriving at Baton Rouge at 9:00 A.M. on Thursday, March 17. There the

2. Singleton to Brent, July 15, 1864, J. L. Brent Papers–Jackson Barracks.
3. Family story told to author by Gerard Dupuy, Moncla, La.

USS *Fort Hindman* carried the prisoners from Fort DeRussy down to Baton Rouge. They continued on down to New Orleans aboard the transport steamer *John Warner,* and *Fort Hindman* returned to Red River. (Courtesy of Naval Historical Center.)

DeRussy officers were brought to the jail, and the enlisted men were marched six blocks to the state penitentiary.[4]

Fortunately, the penitentiary was not to be a permanent home for the men, and on Friday night everyone was back on the river, this time aboard the steamer *John Warner.* The boat arrived at New Orleans on Saturday morning. Many of the Texas men were rural farm boys and were impressed by their first view of a real city. The river appeared to be "five or six feet" higher than the streets of the city, and the masts of the numerous ships in the port looked to one soldier like "an old cedar brake." The *Warner* tied up to the dock and put off the captured officers but then had to back out and anchor in midstream when the press of New Orleanians welcoming their POW heroes became a concern. The local citizens were not to be denied, however, and small boats soon crowded around the steamer, the occupants tossing "apples, oranges, and other such treats" to the prisoners. As word spread through New

4. Wallace diary; John Porter memoir; deck log, USS *Fort Hindman,* Mar. 16–17, 1864.

Orleans of the arrival of the Fort DeRussy men, the Crescent Artillery members among the prisoners began to recognize faces on the wharf as brothers, sisters, and neighbors arrived to welcome them. John Murray "heard the sad news that my mother had died since I left here." At dusk, with the crowds diminished, the steamer returned to the wharf and disembarked her passengers. The officers had earlier been sent to a prison at 21 Rampart Street, and the men were dispersed to various cotton presses—warehouse-like structures in which cotton bales are tightly compacted (pressed) before being loaded into the holds of ships—around the city. The Picayune Cotton Press No. 4 was described as "a square, containing two acres, enclosed by a brick wall, fourteen feet high, with a large gate on the east and west sides. The other two sides were shedded, about thirty feet deep, draining the water inside, which was carried off by gutters."[5] As an added touch, there were "broken bottles and the like fastened all over the top of the walls with cement to keep anyone from climbing over."[6] The officers' Rampart Street prison was a large 3-story building shared with twenty-seven other officers. It had a kitchen and two rooms on the lower floor and twelve rooms in the upper stories, along with a cistern and outhouse in a small yard. The officers fared on pickled beef, salt pork, bread, and coffee, as well as rice, potatoes, or dry beans, which were "prepared miserably by dirty Negroes." Of course, officers could not be expected to live under such conditions, so after ten days they "hired a Cook out side of the Prison."[7] The enlisted men had "coffee for breakfast with a small piece of beef, and a loaf of bread a day." No mention was made of the personal hygiene of their cooks.[8]

If one were going to be a prisoner of war during the American Civil War, one could ask no greater boon than to be a prisoner in New Orleans. The prisoners were housed in permanent quarters, fed tolerably well, and treated with some respect. Although the men were not happy to be in prison, their situation was for the most part pleasant when compared to the experiences of men in almost any other prison situation, North or South. Still, not everyone can (or wants to) adapt to prison life, so escape attempts did occur. Less than a week after arriving at the cotton press, two of the men dressed in blue approximations

---

5. John Porter memoir, 28–29; Wallace diary; Murray diary.

6. Terrence J. Winschel, ed., *The Civil War Diary of a Common Soldier: William Wiley of the 77th Illinois Infantry* (Baton Rouge: Louisiana State Univ. Press, 2001), 134.

7. Wallace diary.

8. Murray diary.

of Union uniforms and walked out of the gate, and "had gained a good distance in the street when they were recognized by an officer returning to the prison and brought back to the home they had left."[9]

Just two weeks after their arrival in New Orleans, rumors began to circulate among the prisoners that they would soon be exchanged, and on April 3 the officers were notified that they should be ready to leave in two days. The next day, Monday, was a day of high excitement at the Rampart Street prison. The ladies of New Orleans crowded the gates, wishing the men well and handing out last-minute farewell gifts. On Tuesday, everyone was packed and ready to go, and that night they signed paroles, agreeing not to attempt to escape until exchanged, nor to take up arms until exchanged; in return, they "were to be allowed all of the privilege of Passengers." On Wednesday, the day of departure, the atmosphere was even more carnival-like. At 7:00 A.M., with the citizens of New Orleans following along, the prisoners were marched to the foot of Canal Street, where the officers boarded the waiting *Polar Star*. As the boat steamed away from the dock, the ladies of New Orleans waved their handkerchiefs and cheered, and the men on the boat returned the favor, cheering the ladies of New Orleans and the Confederacy. The boat went two miles downstream and docked again to pick up the enlisted prisoners. And once again, crowds of ladies were waiting at the wharf. The ladies cheered the men, and the men cheered the ladies. At 11:00 A.M. the boat backed into midstream and the earlier scene was repeated, on an even grander scale. "Hurrah for Jeff Davis" and "Hurrah for the Confederacy" cheered the men, as the ladies of New Orleans gaily waved their kerchiefs and cheered their heroes on to further victories. Ironically, due to a major Confederate victory up Red River, the *Polar Star* would be back at New Orleans in just eleven days, complete with her contingent of very disappointed prisoners. But no one knew that as the boat moved up the river, and on this fifth of April 1864, everyone involved was very happy.[10]

The prisoners aboard *Polar Star* included more men than just those captured at Fort DeRussy. Among the officers now aboard the boat was Maj. David Boyd, former chief engineer at the fort who had been captured back in February. Boyd was a close friend of Union general William T. Sherman, as both had been on the faculty of the Louisiana

9. Ibid., Friday, [Mar.] 25.
10. Wallace and Murray diaries and John Porter memoir.

Seminary of Learning in Pineville before the war. Boyd had been taking advantage of this friendship with a senior Union officer over the past few months, and by his frequent demands had become a thorn in the side of Col. Curtis W. Killborn, the Union prison commandant in New Orleans. Killborn was probably as glad to see Boyd leaving New Orleans as Boyd was to be leaving.

Polar Star passed Fort DeRussy midmorning of Thursday, April 7, and the men aboard were disappointed to see that the Water Battery had been "leveled with the ground." They also noted the large number of contrabands nestled safely under the protection of *Essex*'s guns. The fort was soon out of sight, and by Friday night the prisoners had reached Grand Ecore. They continued upriver, being shot at once near Coushatta, and by Sunday night their thoughts—particularly those of the Texans—were not so much about being released and getting furloughs to visit their families as about getting exchanged and returning to the front lines to fight Yankees. The devastation they saw along the river made them sick with fear for the safety of their homes. It was one thing to level Fort DeRussy, a military installation, but as they moved up the river, they saw "Ginhouses Burnt, houses Burnt, the Enemy Anchoring at Every farm killing all the Stock not fit for use, carrying off all provision, Fowls and Every thing of value." When *Polar Star* met a downward-bound gunboat that night and received the message "Look out for yourselves, the Rebs are a comeing," the prisoners were not disappointed.[11]

They soon would be, though. With the boat now heading downstream, the prisoners were assured by Major Bradley, the Union officer in command, that the exchange would take place at a location farther downriver. Somewhere near the town of Coushatta, *Polar Star* grounded with her bow on one bank and stern on the other. Two Confederate officers approached the boat under a flag of truce and conversed with Major Bradley. Much to the dismay of the prisoners, the Confederates chose to honor the neutral status of the exchange boat. The crew lightened the boat, and *Polar Star* proceeded downstream some distance, where she was stopped again, this time by a Confederate battery posted on the bank. This time the prisoners were sure they would be released. Confederate officers boarded the boat and were again shown documentation that the boat was operating under a flag of truce for an exchange in progress, and once again the boat was allowed to proceed with the

11. Wallace diary.

prisoners still aboard. The opinion of the prisoners was that the boat had been captured fair and square, and since there had been U.S. soldiers put aboard the boat at Grand Ecore for transportation upriver, the boat's claim to neutrality was thus negated. Capt. Edward T. King, who had argued so vehemently for making the stand at Fort DeRussy, was infuriated: "There was never a greater mistake made for we were fairly recaptured and if given our liberty could have not only saved the large quantity of provisions she had in her hull which I saw her discharge at Natchitoches but we could have sunk her on some of the shallow places in the river and prevented the escape of the immense fleet above."[12]

While the Confederate officers involved in the capture of *Polar Star* were bending over backward to behave in an honorable manner, the same could not be said for the Union participants. Once the boat arrived back in Union-held territory near Alexandria, the prisoners were told that the exchange had been cancelled and they were bound back for New Orleans. Outraged at the treachery, some of the men attempted to escape by jumping in the river. Four succeeded in escaping the boat, but the fourth man "leaped from the top of the banister, which made a tremendous splash when he struck the water, and the guard upon the hurricane deck shot at him, with what effect none of us ever knew. But he had given away the plan, and the officers doubled the guard."[13]

One Confederate officer aboard *Polar Star* was not as concerned about the niceties of neutrality as his comrades on the bank at Coushatta had been. Maj. David Boyd was determined to do whatever he could to help the Southern cause, and though his prisoner status did cripple his abilities in that regard, he was not completely without means to contribute. His trip up the river and his conversations with Union soldiers aboard the boat had given him a knowledge of Union forces along the river that Boyd felt would be valuable to General Taylor. He made detailed notes concerning the Union positions, and when the boat stopped at Alexandria, he put his plan into action.

An agreement had been made in July 1863 between the U.S. and Confederate forces that doctors captured on the battlefields of western Louisiana would be allowed a somewhat neutral status and would not be taken prisoner. This was a gesture of humanity designed to allow surgeons to remain behind to treat their wounded without fear of ending

12. Ibid.; King letter.
13. John Porter memoir.

up in a prisoner-of-war camp. The Yankees were not particularly scrupulous in their adherence to this convention, and as a result there were four Confederate surgeons held as prisoners aboard *Polar Star.* Three of these men were released at Alexandria after one of them made a personal appeal to General Banks. They were blindfolded and carried six miles from town to the Rebel lines. The blindfolds were a good idea, but they were a little too late. Surgeon R. T. Gibbs was carrying a copy of the *New York Herald,* and penciled in the margins were notes from David Boyd to Gen. Richard Taylor detailing the location, strength, and positions of Union troops up and down the river, along with particulars on the river stages and a brief pep talk ("I hope you will soon give our enemies another good thrashing. They acknowledge themselves badly whipped.")

Gibbs had promised to deliver the paper to Taylor in person, and Boyd was frustrated after the war to learn that the paper had been given to a courier. The significance of the paper was apparently not explained, and the notes were not found until six days later, when an officer perusing the newspaper in Taylor's headquarters noticed them. While Boyd was very proud of his foray into espionage, it is doubtful that the information he sent would have made a difference, even had it been handled in a more timely manner. The Yankees in Alexandria had few secrets from the surrounding Confederates.[14]

The hapless prisoners aboard *Polar Star* arrived back in New Orleans after dark on Saturday, April 16, and lay at anchor in the river until the next morning, when they were marched back to the various prisons (the officers back to 21 Rampart Street, and the enlisted men back to the cotton presses).

The men settled down to the monotony of prison life. John Porter found it tedious:

> From this time up to July 21st, we never saw a green leaf, or anything cheerful, nothing but the walls, poor prisoners, and the guard.
> The men, as a general thing, made the best of it they could—most everyone had some occupation that he followed with as much energy as men follow their avocations at home. Some made rings, some fans, other traded, while still other gambled, in short, it was

14. Levy to Dwight, May 7, 1864, and Gibbs to Taylor, Apr. 16, 1864, *ORA,* ser. 2, vol. 7, 127–29; "Col. D. F. Boyd's letter while prisoner on US Gunboat on Red River . . . ," David F. Boyd Papers, Louisiana and Lower Mississippi Valley Collection, Hill Memorial Library, Louisiana State Univ., Baton Rouge.

just like a city, you could see every avocation followed that could possibly be inside the wall—every sort of game that is run in any city. Any sort of man from the lunatic and the dude, to the gentleman; also almost every nationality—the American, the Frenchman, the Dutchman, the Irishman, the Mexican and perhaps others. We too had here a natural artist, who could draw the picture of a man from sight, every feature. He drew the prison perfectly, completely, everything, and sold them for twenty-five cents apiece. Have ever regretted that I did not buy one.[15]

John Murray, on the other hand, found that the security had been relaxed, and being a native of New Orleans, he was pleased to be able to receive visits from his relatives. The ladies of New Orleans also continued to "send the prisoners all the delicacies imaginable, together with shoes, clothes, etc."[16] But the ladies of the city could not protect the men from the disease that spread among them.

Typhoid, pneumonia, diarrhea, and, most dreaded of all, smallpox began their spread through the men in the compounds. Some men recovered. John Murray first noticed symptoms of smallpox on May 4. He entered the "smallpox hospital" on Sunday, May 8. The hospital was "full of Confederate prisoners. 3 and 4 die every day," but Murray was not to be one of them. He was well enough on May 20 to receive a furlough to visit his home, and he made several trips there over the following ten days, visiting his mother's grave on one of his trips. He was discharged from the hospital on May 31. Not all of the prisoners were as fortunate. The 19th Texas Infantry had two men wounded during the fight at the fort, and thirty-two men captured. Of these thirty-two, six (over 18 percent) died of disease in New Orleans. At least three others contracted smallpox, but recovered. Captain King's St. Martin Rangers fared even worse, losing fourteen of forty-five men to disease. The 18th Texas, on the other hand, lost no men to disease.[17]

Given the monotony and the disease, it is no wonder that many of the men wished to escape. The men "tried to make their escape in various ways," John Porter explained, "some by bribery, some by picking through the wall, one by blacking himself, hoping to pass as one of the Negro cooks." The most ambitious plan was a variation of one of first escape methods, joining the outgoing guards. It worked well,

15. John Porter memoir.
16. Murray diary, Friday, [Apr.] 22, [1864].
17. Murray diary; Wallace diary; King letter; John Porter memoir.

for a while. A prisoner "started by making for himself a good wooden musket and cartridge box, ditto, etc., and everything being in readiness when the 8 o'clock relief came on, he traveled with the old guard and made good his escape. Next night two others might have been seen slowly winding their way past the guard and into the street. Next night four more got away, and the secret was discovered by the officer of the prison. Four more tried on the next relief, and of course were captured. Their fate was the Parish Prison."[18]

On July 21, 1864, the long-awaited exchange—a real one, this time—finally took shape. Nearly one thousand Confederate prisoners, most of whom were captured during the various battles and skirmishes of the Red River Campaign, were marched down to the steamer *Nebraska* and crowded aboard. The mood was upbeat, and when the failed "escapees" arrived from the Parish Prison, they were teased with whoops of "How many times have you been on guard since you left us?" The loading complete, the boat shoved off and arrived around 2:00 P.M. on July 22 at Red River Landing, where the men "raised a shout of joy." "Once more in our own country," exulted John Murray. "Viva La Confederacy!" The men went ashore and one by one signed their exchange papers. "I felt strange to have no guard around me," explained John Porter. "We went up to the mouth of Red River, where we overtook the ones who had preceded us. Here we spread down our blankets and spent the night—no one can imagine how free we felt."[19]

18. John Porter memoir; Wallace diary, Sunday, [June] 5, [1864].
19. John Porter memoir; Wallace diary; Murray diary.

Chapter 16

Gunboats Round the Bend

Fort DeRussy was deserted by the Union navy at 11:00 A.M. on April 17, 1864, but it did not stay deserted long. By 3:45 P.M. the next day, the large tinclad *Ouachita* was back at the fort. Or nearly back. *Ouachita* was grounded on a sandbar a short distance below the fort, where she remained until 6:00 P.M., when Admiral Porter's flagship *Black Hawk* arrived from upstream and pulled her off.[1] Both boats then moved up to the fort, where an armed party went ashore from *Ouachita* to bury a sailor, one William Winsell (contraband). Both boats remained tied to the bank overnight.[2]

The departure of *Essex* on the 17th seems to have also signaled the departure of Captain Lee and his contraband camps. No mention of any U.S. Army unit stationed at the fort appears after that time, and the fact that the burial party went ashore armed would indicate a certain amount of concern for security. The concern may have been well founded. Around midnight, a musket shot was fired from the north bank.

Ouachita and *Black Hawk* both departed the fort at daybreak, headed downstream, and once again there was no Union presence at Fort DeRussy. It was not until 10:30 the following night that USS *Argosy* arrived on station. She was tasked with preventing the Rebels from reoccupying the fort, providing protection to Union-sympathizing inhabitants of the area, and keeping an eye on the railroad iron remaining at the fort.

Argosy lost no time in making sure that the local population knew that the U.S. Navy was still in control. On the evening of April 21, less than twenty-four hours after the boat's arrival, two men in the fort who appeared a little too curious received a shot from one of the boat's guns.

---

1. Porter was not aboard his flagship at this time, having transferred to USS *Cricket* earlier in the month. *Cricket*'s shallow draft allowed her to go above Alexandria, but the larger *Black Hawk* remained below.
2. Deck logs, USS *Ouachita,* Apr. 18, 1864, RG 24, NA, and USS *Black Hawk,* Apr. 18, 1864.

The large tinclad *Ouachita,* like the ram *Queen of the West,* spent time at Fort DeRussy as both a Union and Confederate vessel. In the early days of the war, before her capture, she was the Confederate steamer *Louisville.* As USS *Ouachita,* she came by the fort during the Red River Campaign and at the end of the war in 1865. (Courtesy of Naval Historical Center.)

The point seems to have been made, and over the next few days *Argosy* settled into rather routine duty, watching the area around the fort and occasionally patrolling up or down river. On Monday, April 25, she made a run down to the sunken coal barge that *Queen of the West* had lost over a year before and took on 204 bushels of coal. On Tuesday night, *Argosy* again made it clear to the neighborhood that trespassing at the fort would not be tolerated, firing on a light that appeared near the fort just after dark. Things remained calm for the next few days, but *Argosy* had no intention of letting the Rebels forget who was in charge. On Saturday afternoon, April 30, she held target practice for her 12- and 24-pounder howitzers, firing seven rounds into the fort's upper works. Should the Rebels appear, *Argosy* had their range.

Troop transports were still routinely running up and down the river, and most of those were not nearly as conservative as *Argosy* with their cannon fire. Confederate snipers along the lower Red had become a nuisance in late April. Three men had been killed and seventeen wounded on the steamer *Superior* near the mouth of Red River, so when *Kate Dale* passed Fort DeRussy with members of the Chicago

Mercantile Battery aboard on April 24, the soldiers "worked the two guns on board, shelling the woods all the way down."[3]

Argosy, too, would soon find that a few shells every four or five days was no longer all that was necessary to keep the peace. On May 2, *Argosy* weighed anchor before daybreak and proceeded upriver, escorting the transports *Laurel Hill* and *Rob Roy.* The sailors aboard *Argosy* were unaware that the steamer *Emma* had been captured and burned along this reach of river the day before.[4] But shortly before 9:00 A.M. a woman on the bank hailed the boat and warned of "300 Rebels a short distance above." Minutes later, a flame of musketry and cannon fire opened on the boats from the right bank. *Laurel Hill* responded with her cannon, *Rob Roy* answered with muskets, and *Argosy* opened up with both bow and broadside guns. The shooting lasted over half an hour. *Argosy* was struck repeatedly with musket balls, and on *Rob Roy* one man was killed and one wounded.[5]

The action that day was inconsequential in itself, but it signaled a reversal. Prior to this, actions against Union gunboats below Alexandria had been hit and run. An occasional sniper, or maybe a handful of snipers, would fire at a boat and then disappear into the brush. But on this day, the Confederates had stood and fought, and their muskets were backed up by artillery. The war on the lower Red had changed.

Argosy returned to the fort at nightfall, where she anchored with three other gunboats, *St. Clair, Covington,* and *Signal,* which had come down the river that afternoon. Acting Vol. Lt. Thomas Gregory, *St. Clair*'s captain, was a cautious man. Upon arrival at the fort, he shelled the works for half an hour before coming to anchor. From 8:00 P.M. to midnight, *St. Clair* fired into the fort every thirty minutes, and then at least once an hour throughout the rest of the night. Perhaps "cautious" is not strong enough a word to describe Lieutenant Gregory. Nonetheless, there was no firing from the banks that night.

In all fairness to Gregory, he may have come by his cautious nature honestly. *St. Clair* had arrived in the Red River toward the end of the campaign and had been fired into sporadically by Rebels on the banks ever since her first night in the river. The results were always frightening, but on at least one occasion provided some humor for the boat's

3. "The Civil War Diary of Florison D. Pitts," *Mid-America* 40 (1958): 22–63, entry for Apr. 24, 1864.

4. W. Randolph Howell diary, Barker Texas History Center, Univ. of Texas, Austin.

5. Deck log, USS *Argosy,* May 2, 1864.

officers. On that particular night, while *St. Clair* was anchored at what was assumed to be a "safe" spot in the river, the boat was aroused by a fusillade from the bank. As Ens. Cort Williams rushed through the wardroom on his way to the gun deck, he was shocked to see

> by the dim light of the battle lantern, one of our officers, partly dressed, spinning around, by the help of table and chair, on one leg apparently, while the other flopped helplessly about. Thinking him seriously wounded, with an exclamation of horror and sympathy, I went to his assistance, and then discovered that, in fancied security, on turning in for the night he had, against all precedent in that river, undressed to sleep, as he afterward explained, as a Christian should. On turning out as the drum beat to quarters, in his hurry in the dim light, dressing in "one time and two motions," he had rammed both of his legs into one leg of his trousers with such force that he was unable to extricate himself. . . . It is easier to imagine than to describe it, as, with the bullets whistling about him, he kicked and struggled in the effort to clear himself. With my assistance he was soon relieved without either of us stopping long enough to fully enjoy the joke at the time.

But for many days afterward, the wardroom of *St. Clair* would rock with laughter at the story of how their chief engineer "lost his leg."[6]

The Union navy still controlled Fort DeRussy, but they no longer controlled Red River. *Argosy* and the other gunboats left Fort DeRussy on various errands on the morning of May 3, and later that day another unescorted U.S. transport, *City Belle,* ran afoul of the same Rebel battery that had confronted the gunboats the day before. The boat was sunk as she attempted to pass upriver to Alexandria with the 120th Ohio Infantry, seven hundred men strong, aboard. Between a third and a half of the men of that unit were reported captured, the others escaping to the north bank of the river, some heading upriver and some down. Their commander, Col. Marcus Spiegel, died of wounds received.[7]

6. E. Cort Williams, "Recollections of the Red River Expedition," in *Sketches of War History, 1861–1865: Papers Read before the Ohio Commandery of the Military Order of the Loyal Legion of the United States, 1886–1888* (Cincinnati: Robert Clark, 1888), 2:114–15.

7. Colonel Spiegel's brother, Joseph, was also wounded in the ambush. Joseph survived the war and started a dry goods store that would grow to become the Spiegel Catalog Company. Ullman to Crosby, May 6, 1864, *ORN* 26:123; Frank L. Byrne and Jean Powers Soman, *Your True Marcus: The Civil War Letters of a Jewish Colonel* (Kent, Ohio: Kent State Univ. Press, 1985), 336–39.

Tinclad No. 19, the USS *St. Clair,* shelled the fort throughout the night of May 2–3, 1864. (Courtesy of Naval Historical Center.)

Argosy returned to the fort on the evening of May 4, firing one shell "in the direction of the fort," apparently just as a matter of principle. At 10:30 that night she was hailed from the bank by one of the survivors from *City Belle.* At daybreak, *Argosy* weighed anchor and headed upstream. As an increasing number of soldiers from *City Belle* were brought aboard, the sound of firing from upriver became more and more intense. *Argosy* continued to pick up men from *City Belle* and at 10:00 A.M. began shelling the woods.

Just upriver, the gunboats *Signal* and *Covington* were finding themselves in a bad situation. Since the Confederate battery had located in Egg Bend, some twenty miles above Fort DeRussy, the two tinclads were escorting the transport *John Warner* through that reach of river. But two tinclads were not going to be enough to save *John Warner* on this day. The three boats were under fire from two Rebel batteries and several hundred cavalrymen.[8] The *Warner* was disabled first, then *Signal.* The fighting was fierce, lasting some five hours and ending with *John Warner* and *Signal* grounded and captured and *Covington* burned. In spite of the fact that *Signal* surrendered and her guns were taken by the

8. Captain Lord, of *Covington,* gives this number as "4,000 to 5,000 infantry." Lord to Porter, May 8, 1864, *ORN* 26:113.

Confederates, six men from that boat received Medals of Honor for their actions during the battle. *Covington,* on the other hand, fought on until all of her ammunition was expended. Her guns were spiked and the boat burned, and of a crew of fourteen officers and sixty-two men, nine officers and twenty-three men escaped. None of these sailors received medals.[9]

Argosy, meanwhile, proceeded up the river and continued picking up men from the ill-fated *City Belle.* She arrived at Egg Bend after the surrender of *Signal* and *Covington* and was rewarded with the full attention of the Southern batteries. She immediately took two direct hits, damaging her escape pipe and starboard tiller, but managed to turn downstream and get out of range while returning fire against a section of guns that had limbered up and followed her down. *Argosy* expended ninety-six rounds of artillery ammunition in the running battle.[10]

A short way downriver, *Argosy* found the gunboat *Forest Rose* coming up. While *Argosy* made repairs, *Forest Rose* moved up to take a crack at the batteries. One shell through the hull and another through the casemate quickly waned the enthusiasm of *Forest Rose*'s skipper, and the two boats, along with the transport *Shreveport,* which *Forest Rose* had been escorting, fell back to Fort DeRussy. As they passed downstream, the boats picked up some three hundred escaped soldiers, sailors, and civilians (including "one wounded white woman") from the captured boats.[11] The boats arrived at Fort DeRussy at 3:45 P.M. to find USS *Nymph* laying along the far bank, shelling the fort on the hill where Rebel soldiers had been seen. After an hour of shelling, the "enemy retreated to the woods," and at 5:00 P.M. both *Argosy* and *Nymph* headed downriver. *Forest Rose* stayed on station at the fort through the night.

The loss of *Covington, Signal,* and *John Warner,* and the troops aboard them, stands as one of the most stunning defeats of the Union

---

9. Apparently Lieutenant Morgan, captain of *Signal,* was a better hand at the paperwork necessary for obtaining Medals of Honor than was Lieutenant Lord of *Covington.* The men of *Signal* receiving medals were Quarter Gunner Charles Asten, Gunner's Mate George Butts, Seaman John Hyland, Boatswain's Mate Michael McCormick, Seaman Timothy O'Donoghue, and Pilot Perry Wilkes. Interestingly, of the eight men mentioned for particularly courageous conduct in Morgan's official report of the battle, only Hyland and Wilkes received medals. Medal of Honor citations; Morgan to Lee, Feb. 27, 1865, *ORN* 26:117–19.

10. Deck log, USS *Argosy,* May 5, 1864.

11. Deck log, USS *Forest Rose,* RG 24, NA, and deck logs, USS *Argosy* and USS *Nymph; Milligan, From the Fresh-Water Navy,* 273–74.

forces in a campaign that stands out for its Union defeats. Perhaps the most embarrassing facet of the loss is that it never should have happened. On May 3, Nathaniel Banks ordered a brigade (two regiments of infantry and a four-gun battery, numbering about one thousand men) under Brig. Gen. Frank S. Nickerson to leave Alexandria aboard transports and clean out the Confederate batteries on the river between there and Fort DeRussy. As the Confederate forces on the river were between four and five hundred men, Nickerson's force should have been sufficient to open the river again. But on May 4, the day before the loss of the three Union boats, Nickerson's brigade was stopped below Alexandria by USS *St. Clair,* acting under orders to stop any transports from moving downriver without an escort. Nickerson's brigade returned to Alexandria and was never sent back out. Had they been allowed to proceed (or had they been sent out again the next day, after appropriate orders had been issued to *St. Clair* to escort Nickerson's expedition), it is likely that the river would have been reopened to transport traffic. As it was, even the two-gunboat escort on May 5 was not enough to save *John Warner* or her escorts. It is perhaps most ironic that Admiral Porter, who at every possible opportunity ridiculed Banks as a blundering fool, caused the loss of his own gunboats by his no-escort, no-passage policy, which overrode one of Banks's few sound decisions of the campaign.[12]

With the cancellation of Nickerson's raid, the U.S. Army and Navy forces at Alexandria were effectively cut off from communications with the outside. Tinclads were ordered not to attempt passage of the Confederate batteries at Egg Bend, and naval forces were concentrated at Fort DeRussy. But on Friday, May 6, the only gunboat at the fort was *Forest Rose.* Throughout the day, men trickled in from above. Seventeen sailors from *Covington* and eight from *Signal* arrived, including Seaman George McClurg.

McClurg had been responsible for the escape of many of the sailors from *Signal* the day before, when he and three other men had volunteered to carry a line ashore to tie the gunboat to the north bank of the river. Scrambling up a twenty-foot, nearly perpendicular bank under a

---

12. Dwight to Nickerson, May 3, 1864, *ORA* 34, pt. 3, 412; Dwight to Nickerson, May 4, 1864, *ORA* 34, pt. 3, 430; Dwight to Porter, May 5, 1864, *ORN* 26:111; Metcalf to *St. Clair,* May 5, 1864, *ORN* 26:111. The gunboat stopping the transports is identified in *ORN* as "No. 10" but was actually No. 19, USS *St. Clair.* Deck log, USS *St. Clair,* May 4, 1864, RG 24, NA. There was no gunboat No. 10 at this time, the first one, USS *Linden,* having sunk in February 1864 and the second No. 10, USS *Ibex,* not being acquired until December. Silverstone, *Warships,* 167, 173.

hail of musket balls, everyone but McClurg had fallen back to the boat. McClurg alone reached the top and tied off the boat.[13]

Also arriving at the fort that day were numerous members of the 56th Ohio Infantry. These men were headed home on a veterans' furlough and had the misfortune of taking *John Warner* for passage down the river. Pvt. J. O. Bingham's experience was probably typical of the soldiers who made it down to the fort. After getting off the boat on the north bank, he and several comrades made their way downriver. "You had better believe it was bitter work, going as we did without food or rest, and half the time carrying a man," he recalled. "We suffered very much for water, as we did not dare to go to the bank of the river, for the reb troops were all along the other side." Bingham considered surrendering, but after creeping to the edge of the river and viewing his potential captors, he decided that "they looked so revengeful, that . . . I couldn't muster up courage to surrender." That night, with the help of a sympathetic Frenchman, they stole a canoe and paddled down to the fort. "Thus we proceeded during the long, weary, toilsome night, and at daybreak we caught sight of the Union flag floating over Ft. DeRusse. Never in my life did I see such a glorious sight, and never was my heart so light as I paddled that canoe under the fort; and never was my body so heavy. Tired was no name for it. I dragged myself to the fort; laid down under a cannon and went to sleep, and didn't wake til the middle of the afternoon, though the boys declared that cannon was fired off four times while I was sleeping under it."[14] Bingham's memory seems to have been a bit faded, as there was no cannon on the bank at that time. The USS *Avenger* did throw nine shells into the fort that evening, though, from 4:45 to 6:20 P.M., to discourage the Confederate soldiers who peered at them from the parapets of the fort.

With their supply lines cut, the situation for the Union troops in Alexandria was looking bleak. The army could not leave the ironclads trapped above the falls, the town was surrounded by hostile natives, and no supplies were coming up the river. A Union soldier walking the streets of Alexandria could not help but hear the despair in comments like "Things look pretty dark," "We are getting in a tight place," and "If we get out with what we have on, we will be lucky now." But the op-

13. Nonetheless, when medals were passed out, McClurg was overlooked. Morgan to Lee, Feb. 27, 1865, *ORN* 26:118.

14. *Ironton (Ohio) Register,* Jan. 19, 1888. Courtesy of Sharon M. Kouns and Martha J. Kounse.

timists were also spreading their rumors, as "General Sherman is at Fort DeRussy with 12,000 men" and "Commodore Farragut is coming up the Red with a fleet of ironclads" were also making the rumor circuit.[15]

There was a small element of truth to the optimists' hopes. On May 7, there was one ironclad at Fort DeRussy. The mighty *Choctaw* had arrived that Saturday, and the Confederate batteries at Egg Bend did not have enough firepower to even dent the armor plating on that monstrous gunboat. But armor has tradeoffs, and the added draft that it gave *Choctaw* meant that the ironclad could not get up the shallow river to the batteries. But *Choctaw* was not alone at the fort. She arrived that morning accompanied by the tinclad *Tallahatchie* and the transports *Colonel Cowles*, *Black Hawk,* and *Madison,* loaded with the 23rd Iowa Infantry and a portion of the 22nd Iowa, approximately one thousand soldiers. In addition, the tinclads *Forest Rose* and *Avenger* were already at the fort. The tinclad *Meteor* arrived that afternoon. It was not "a fleet of ironclads" and "12,000 men," but it was a start.[16]

Supposedly, the troops aboard the transports had been sent to Fort DeRussy "for the purpose of dislodging the enemy from their position above here on the river," but they did no such thing.[17] The troops stayed at the fort for three days, then left without accomplishing much one way or the other. On the first day, the 23rd Iowa reconnoitered the area and found "a few Confederates scattered through the timber," but no action ensued. On the second day at the fort, one company of the 23rd Iowa "came pretty nigh geting our Skelps taken." In spite of their knowledge of Rebel troops in the area, they had gone out about a half mile from the boats to get some beef. As they were preparing the beef for transport back to the river, a runner arrived from the boat with a message from the colonel to return at once. Confederate soldiers were quietly surrounding the Yankees as they worked, and while this could be seen from the upper decks of the boats, the "cattle rustlers" ashore were unaware of their impending doom. With the tinclad *Meteor* shelling the woods to cover their retreat, the Iowans made it back to the river, without their fresh meat but with their "skelps" still intact. The

15. Tyson diary, May 7, 8, 1864.

16. Warren to McClernand, May 9, 1864, *ORA* 34, pt. 2, 520. Brigadier General Warren was expecting an additional sixteen hundred men at the fort by that night, but they apparently never arrived.

17. Milligan, *From the Fresh-Water Navy,* 275.

tinclad *Nymph* arrived at the fort just in time to join in the shelling, throwing an additional seventeen shells into the woods.[18]

Choctaw and most of her tinclad escorts were unavailable to protect the men ashore that Sunday morning because they had gone upriver hunting the now infamous Confederate battery. *Avenger* and *Choctaw* fired on some Rebels in the woods at 8:40 A.M. but disengaged after only ten minutes. The water on Snaggy Point was too shallow for *Choctaw* to proceed, so *Forest Rose* and *Avenger* went ahead to locate a channel, but nowhere was there enough water to safely get the ironclad through. The expedition returned downriver to the fort, never having found the "impudent rascals" or their cannons.[19]

The Union army killed several of their own people at the fort on the night of March 16. On the night of May 8, the navy nearly duplicated the act.

Three cavalrymen from Alexandria had made it through with dispatches to the fleet at the fort on May 6 and departed the following day. Whether or not they made it back to Alexandria is not reported, but on May 8, Capt. David Bunker of the 3rd Massachusetts Cavalry was called to General Banks's headquarters in Alexandria and told that it was essential that communications be established with Fort DeRussy and that to that effect, Bunker would be leading a detail of four hundred men down to the fort. Bunker countered with an offer to sneak down to the fort with a dozen men, explaining, "If I take four hundred men I will have to fight there; but when I carry dispatches, I go to run, and not to fight." They compromised on twenty men and four scouts.

The scouts who guided them that night were members of the Louisiana Scouts Battalion, "a body of gray-coated scouts, natives of this portion of the country, acquainted with all the by-ways and the hiding-places of the rebels, who went out and in at their pleasure, and who were looked upon rather uneasily at times by the troops."[20] These Jayhawkers were subject to summary execution if caught by Confederate troops, and as a result they tended not to play by the established rules of war. The chief guide on this particular mission was known only as "Joe."

18. S[amuel] C[alvin] Jones, *Reminiscences of the 22nd Iowa Infantry* (1907; reprint, Iowa City, Iowa: Press of the Camp Pope Bookshop, 1993), 67; Harold Brinkman, ed., *Dear Companion: The Civil War Letters of Silas I. Shearer* (Ames, Iowa: Sigler, 1995), 78–79; deck logs, USS *Meteor*, RG 24, NA, and USS *Nymph*.

19. Deck logs, USS *Avenger, Choctaw,* and *Tallahatchie*, May 8, 1864, RG 24, NA, and USS *Forest Rose*, May 8, 1864; Milligan, *From the Fresh-Water Navy*, 276.

20. Powers, *Story of the Thirty Eighth Regiment*, 129–30.

This is the only known photograph of Joseph Laprairie, a resident of the Brouillette community who served with the Louisiana Scouts Battalion. Joe died in 1937 at the age of ninety-four and is buried in the Fort DeRussy Cemetery, the only Yankee soldier still known to be interred there. (Courtesy of Randy Decuir.)

There has been speculation that he may have been Joseph Laprairie, a member of that unit who lived in the Brouillette Community downriver from Fort DeRussy for many years after the war and is buried in the Fort DeRussy Cemetery.[21]

Captain Bunker went immediately to his regiment and asked for volunteers for a secret and dangerous mission. All but three stepped forward. The chosen men then selected horses and packed three days' rations. The messages were hidden in the collar of the captain's coat, and at 3:00 P.M. they crossed the pontoon bridge into Pineville and set off down the river.

The first Confederates were encountered at 8:00 P.M. The Rebel pickets halted the column but were not really expecting to find any Yankees on that road at that time of night. Bunker was ordered to advance and be recognized, at which time he and Joe each fired at a picket and galloped the command through the post before the surprised Rebels

21. Joe Laprairie has the distinction of being the only Yankee soldier still buried in the fort's cemetery. All of the Northerners buried there during the war were moved in 1868. Laprairie was buried there after his death in 1937. Many of his descendants still live in the Fort DeRussy/Brouillette area.

could react. At eleven o'clock, they were again halted and again bluffed and charged their way through the sentry post. Just before midnight, with the night as black as pitch, the men were halted and challenged for a third time. Joe was no longer with the column, but Captain Bunker responded as he had before, that they were "Colonel Harrison's men." This time the challengers fired first. There were more of them this time, some fifty men, but Bunker's men returned their fire briskly and charged past the post, making their way through trees felled across the road. Suddenly, "the heavens were illuminated" as a gunboat in the river opened fire. Bunker immediately realized that "the picket we had just passed was United States troops, and, turning in the saddle, I shouted, 'In God's name, who are you?' And back came the welcome response, 'We are the Twenty-Second Iowa.' Said I, 'We are the 3rd Massachusetts Cavalry—Go and stop that gunboat!'"

The Iowans "cheered us heartily, and stopped the gunboat just as the gunner had stepped aside to discharge a broadside of grape and canister at us." Bunker's arrival aboard *Choctaw* caused quite a stir. Lieutenant Commander Ramsey "nearly fainted" when he realized how close he came to wiping out the cavalrymen, although Bunker assured him he would have not harmed them. On the first shot from *Choctaw,* Bunker had dismounted his men and had them lie on their backs, holding the bridles. He assured Ramsey that "you might have fired away all night, and not hit a man of us." Bunker did not say what would have become of the horses.

Bunker reported to Brig. Gen. FitzHenry Warren, the senior army man on site, and presented him with the dispatches from Banks. Warren studied him intently and demanded, "Are you the little devil who has been firing at my men?" Bunker assured him that he was, upon which Warren hugged him and said, "You are the first cavalryman I ever saw, that would fight."

Captain Bunker was treated like royalty by the officers aboard the boats, and while dining the next day he met Ensign Burns, the naval dispatch carrier who had been trying to get messages up the river to Admiral Porter for several days. Upon learning that Bunker planned to return to Alexandria the next day, Burns turned over the admiral's dispatches to the cavalryman. Shortly thereafter, the inevitable discussion came up at the table over the respective merits of the army and navy. When Bunker pointed out that they had "just made me the custodian of dispatches to your Admiral, and I intend he shall have them before tomorrow night," Burns flushed and insisted, "If I had a horse, I would

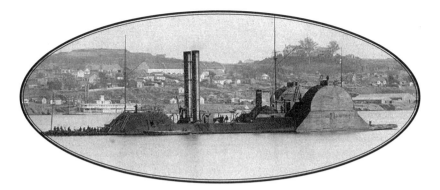

The ironclad USS *Choctaw,* restricted by the shallow water in Red River, was unable to go much beyond Fort DeRussy in the spring of 1864. It was the last Union vessel to leave the fort at the end of the Red River Campaign. (Courtesy of Naval Historical Center.)

go with you." Burns, of course, did not have a horse. The conversation turned to other matters, and Bunker excused himself and had a short conversation with one of his sergeants, after which he returned to the wardroom and the other officers.

Half an hour later, Bunker was called from the wardroom. Going up on deck, he looked to the bank and saw his grinning sergeant holding the halter of a "fine roan horse" that had only recently changed its allegiance to the Union side. Bunker returned below and called for Ensign Burns to come out, and "as he reached the door, I stepped aside for him to precede me; turning, I motioned in fun for all the others to follow. When we got on deck, I took the officer's arm, and, facing him toward the bank of the river, pointed with my hand, 'There is your horse!'" Burns was surprised, but he immediately declared his willingness to accompany the cavalry to Alexandria. Admiral Porter was even more surprised the next day when his dispatch bearer arrived from below on horseback.[22]

After the excitement at midnight on May 9, the situation at the fort was relatively quiet for a while. *Argosy* had pulled a dead sailor from the river the evening before about three hours steaming time downstream, and a squad went ashore to bury the body after they arrived

22. David T. Bunker, "Carrying Dispatches for Banks at Alexandria," in *The Third Massachusetts Cavalry in the War for the Union,* by James K. Ewer (Boston: Historical Committee of the Regimental Association, 1903), 351–56; Jones, *Reminiscences of the 22nd Iowa,* 67; deck log, USS *Choctaw.*

at the fort. *Forest Rose* went upriver in the afternoon for what had become something of a ritual shelling of the Rebels, then returned. An expected attack on the gunboats kept the watches especially alert that night, but it never materialized. Tuesday, May 10, dawned windy with a misty rain falling. Captain Bunker and his contingent of Massachusetts cavalrymen, along with Ensign Burns and his new horse, set off for Alexandria. Just after noon, General Warren's infantry brigade, aboard the transports *Col. Cowles, Madison, Black Hawk,* and *Curlew,* left the fort headed downstream, escorted by *Forest Rose.*[23]

Perhaps the departure of the transports emboldened the nearby Confederates, or maybe they were encouraged by the gunboats' obvious inability to defeat the battery upstream. Whatever the reason, on May 11 the Rebels around the fort began a prolonged attack against the gunboats in the river. By 2:30 P.M. Confederate snipers has infiltrated the rifle pits along the river bank below the fort and began firing at the gunboats with their muskets. Both *Choctaw* and *Forest Rose* responded with their big guns, and the sniping ceased after only fifteen minutes, only to start again an hour later, this time continuing for an hour and a half. Ens. Symmes Browne, aboard USS *Forest Rose,* described the situation in a letter to his wife: "The sharpshooters of the enemy came down in the rifle pits below the fort, almost abreast of us, and endeavored to pick off our officers and men whenever they appeared on deck. They did not always wait for the men to show themselves, for several bullets were fired through the cabin and wardroom, one passing within six inches of the Captain's head. We fired 1" shrapnel at them and drove them out for a time, but it was not long before they returned, so in order to save our heavy ammunition, we got some rifles up in the pilothouse and fired down into their pits with very good effect, for they soon left there and kept at a more respectful distance."[24]

The snipers quit for the day at 5:30 P.M., but they were back again bright and early at six o'clock the next morning. They may have "kept

23. This *Black Hawk* was a transport, not to be confused with Admiral Porter's flagship; and this *Curlew* was also a transport, not the USS *Curlew,* tinclad No. 12. *Madison* had smallpox cases aboard when it left the fort. This trip downriver was particularly morbid. In addition to the presence of smallpox amongst them, the men could stand on the deck and see "a great many bodies floating down stream and some lodged near the river bank and buzzards picking at them. It is horrible!" As the boats neared the mouth of Red River, the bodies became fewer, and only two were seen on the second day of the trip. The men did, however, see quite a few large alligators that day. Jones, *Reminiscences of the 22nd Iowa,* 68.

24. Milligan, *From the Fresh-Water Navy,* 278.

USS *Forest Rose,* tinclad No. 9, was sniped at unmercifully by Confederate soldiers at Fort DeRussy during the latter days of the Red River Campaign. (Courtesy of Naval Historical Center.)

a more respectful distance," but they did not go away. *Forest Rose* exchanged fire with the snipers until 7:45 A.M., when she and *Choctaw* steamed upriver for the obligatory daily artillery duel with the Confederate battery above Snaggy Point. USS *Naiad* remained at the fort, exchanging rounds with the snipers throughout the day, with neither side doing any apparent damage. *Argosy* arrived at the fort at 2:30 P.M., at which time she also joined in the shooting, taking musket fire and returning it with shrapnel and shells from her 24- and 12-pounders. *Naiad, Forest Rose,* and *Argosy* steamed downriver that evening, leaving *Choctaw* to host the shooting match alone the next morning. On Friday, May 13, Rebel sharpshooters began on schedule at 6:10 A.M. and continued throughout the day. When two sailors were wounded that afternoon, the shooting began to get personal.[25] Shooting continued until 6:30 P.M., during which time *Choctaw* fired eleven rounds from her big guns and more than three hundred rounds of Spencer and Enfield rifle ammunition.

25. The wounded men were Adna (?) Legg and Ordinary Seaman James Moselman. Both men's wounds were slight.

Friday the 13th was anything but unlucky for the U.S. Navy fleet at Alexandria. On that morning, the last of the gunboats trapped above the rapids made their way through Bailey's Dam and set off downriver with the rest of the fleet and Nathaniel Banks's army. The city of Alexandria was left in flames.

A few diehard Confederate snipers tried to continue their feud with *Choctaw* on May 14, but their time was running out. The Union army was advancing from Alexandria, and the fleet was moving downriver. The shooting began at 8:30 A.M. but was over by 10:30. *Choctaw* never bothered to respond. The last shots to be fired in anger at Fort DeRussy had been fired.[26]

The rest of that Saturday passed uneventfully, but shortly after noon on Sunday, May 15, USS *Neosho* appeared in tow of the steamer *Hamilton,* followed by the gunboats *Carondelet, Cricket, Pittsburg, Mound City,* and *Ozark.* The river in front of the fort soon filled with dozens of gunboats and transports headed for Simmesport. By 6:20 P.M., the river was empty again, save for *Choctaw* and *Lexington,* standing sentinel at Fort DeRussy.

The river was empty, but after dark the fields around the fort were once again full of soldiers—Union soldiers, many of them the same men who had captured the fort two months earlier—and this time they were the ones who were suffering the humiliation of defeat. The resulting short temper of one Union officer was the reason for the presence of two brigades of Yankees at the fort that night. The area between Marksville and the fort was crowded with Union soldiers, and they were all hot, hungry, and thirsty after a long day's march. Col. William Shaw, a brigade commander under Gen. A. J. Smith, had been teasing the general about the need to "go to water." This double-entendre referred not only to the brigade's need for drinking water but was also a play on the reference to the desire of a pursued animal or person to run into a body of water to hide one's scent and lose a pursuing pack of dogs. A. J. Smith was not known for his sense of humor, and he was in a particularly foul mood now, as he retreated before a numerically inferior foe. After one too many comments about "going to water," Smith told Shaw "to take his Brigade & go to *Hell* with it." Shaw, who probably figured there was

26. Deck log, USS *Choctaw,* May 14, 1864. Confederate troops camped near Marksville reported "cannonading" heard in the direction of Fort DeRussy on May 12 and 13 and reported "fighting" in that direction on May 14. Record Book, Capt. Buck's Company (Company F, Twenty-second Texas Cavalry, Dismounted), May 12–14, 1864.

no water in Hell but knew there was plenty of water at the fort, decided to go there instead. For the past two days, the entire army had been moving almost constantly, stopping and starting, stopping and starting. So as Shaw's 2nd Brigade moved out, Col. Risdon Moore's 3rd Brigade automatically followed, and they finally camped to the south and east of the fort, within a few hundred yards of the river. The men hoped to find the fleet there and embark aboard boats for the rest of their trip, but they found only the two gunboats standing guard. At 3:00 A.M., the two brigades were back on the road and rejoined their command near Marksville.[27] The U.S. Army had left Fort DeRussy for the last time.

At 4:45 A.M. on May 16, 1864, *Choctaw* and *Lexington* weighed anchor and steamed down the river. Then, for some unexplained reason, they "rounded to and returned." At 9:15 A.M., they left again.[28] And this time, they left for good.

27. Heironymus diary, May 15–16, 1864. Edwin G. Gerling, *The One Hundred Seventeenth Illinois Infantry Volunteers (The McKendree Regiment) 1862–1865* (Highland, Ill.: published by author, 1992), 74–75. After the incident at Fort DeRussy on March 16, A. J. Smith had given permission for two regiments to go to Hell—but this is the first recorded instance of his *ordering* an entire brigade there. The residents of central Louisiana had no doubt but that the whole division would end up there eventually.

28. Deck logs, USS *Lexington*, May 16, 1864, RG 24, NA, and USS *Choctaw*, May 16, 1864.

Chapter 17

Aftermath and Renaissance

When the Confederates returned to Fort DeRussy in late May 1864, they found the empty ruins of the place they had left on March 14. The Water Battery was gone, both casemates and guns, the powder magazines had been blown up, and the revetments and bombproofs of the fort on the hill had been destroyed, but more to the point, there was nothing left in the lower Red River valley to defend. All of the cotton was gone, stolen or destroyed, along with the tools, horsepower, and manpower necessary to make any more. From Natchitoches to Simmesport, the area was now known as "The Burnt District."

While Union troops stayed in Pointe Coupee Parish along the Mississippi River around their fort at Morganza and made occasional patrols up toward Simmesport, they never evinced any interest in trying to move west of the Atchafalaya. The Confederate intelligence service, as reliable as ever, indicated that the Yankees had no desire to return to the Red River Valley. With the cotton gone and the war going well in the East, there was really no reason for them to return. The defense of the lower Red was moved to Alexandria, and two forts, Randolph and Buhlow, were built on the Pineville side of the river in the fall of 1864. Fort DeRussy would never be rebuilt.

The fort, however, was not totally abandoned. Within three weeks of the departure of *Choctaw* and *Lexington*, the fort was back in operation as a Confederate post. By June 11, Texas troops recuperating from the Red River Campaign were camping at some of General Walker's old camp sites near the fort.[1] On June 16, the steamer *New Champion*, now a Confederate boat as a result of her recent capture up the Red River, arrived at the fort in company of another transport. Both boats were loaded with wounded Yankee prisoners. The boats stopped at the fort

---

1. James Allen Hamilton diary, 1862–1864, June 11, 1864, Barker History Center, Univ. of Texas, Austin. The 15th Texas Infantry stayed in the camps near the fort until July 4.

long enough for the prisoners to sign their parole papers, then headed down to Red River Landing, where the wounded men were turned over to their own army for transportation down to New Orleans.[2]

The fort remained in use as a picket station and was the site of a prisoner exchange in January 1865.[3] In late May 1865, the Confederate forces west of the Mississippi joined their defeated brethren east of the river and surrendered. When the Union navy passed up the river in early June, the fort was no more than a landmark.[4] The mighty Fort DeRussy had outlived its usefulness.

There is no documentation concerning the history of the fort in the years after the war. It seems that as life returned to normal, the walls of the fort were cut and the old public road was reinstated, severing the L-shaped earthworks from the main redoubt. Barbin's Landing reestablished its prominence as a steamboat landing. Other nearby landings were established and competed for the Marksville trade, and by the turn of the century there was a railroad track, with a mule-powered train, leading from Marksville to Ware's Landing, just downstream from Barbin's. The coming of railroads to central Louisiana in the 1890s spelled the death knell of the glory days of steamboating, and by the 1920s the steamboat landings on Red River were only a memory. Barbin's Landing, like Fort DeRussy, had become a part of history.

Fort DeRussy remained in the memory of local inhabitants for years after the war. The Marksville camp of the United Confederate Veterans was known as "Camp DeRussy," and for many years into the twentieth century, the fort site was well known as a picnic ground. In the 1930s, Marksville attorney Marc Dupuy Sr. attempted to start a movement to preserve the fort, but the necessary groundswell of support seems to have been overcome by the Great Depression. Over the years, a house was built just outside of the main redoubt's south wall by the Oliver family, and an oil well was drilled just east of the fort in

2. The repatriated Yankees were far from thrilled at their return to friendly lines. They found life in New Orleans much more confining than had been the case in the Southern hospital at Pleasant Hill, where "the 'Confeds' kept no guard round our hospital. While at Pleasant Hill, many of us would wander out a mile or more from the hospital for exercise or in search of blackberries. In short, while I have been a prisoner I have had more privileges, or rather more liberty, than at any other time since being in the army, for our own army most always kept up either a Camp guard, picket or patrol, to catch stragglers." Solon Benson to Dear Mother, June 20, 1864, in Solon Benson, *Civil War Battle of Pleasant Hill, Louisiana* (Tangipahoa, La.: Camp Moore Reproductions, n.d.).

3. Jackson to Hurlbut, Apr. 14, 1865, *ORN* 27:142; Dwight to Ullman, Jan. 29, 1865, *ORA*, ser. 2, vol. 8, 146.

4. Deck logs, USS *Little Rebel*, June 1865, RG 24, NA, and USS *Ouachita*, USS *Benton*, and USS *Fort Hindman*, June 1865.

1949 by the Hunt Oil Company. Fortunately for the fort, it was a dry hole, and the damage done to the fort itself was minimal.

In 1940, the fort came under the control of the Belton Bordelon family. The Bordelons actively protected the fort from relic hunters. The picnicking was stopped, and visitation to the fort was strictly controlled. Cows from their dairy kept down the grass and underbrush on the earthworks, but when the dairy closed, the grazing also ceased, and by the late 1980s the earthworks had become so overgrown that the fort was no longer visible from the road. Even within the fort, there were areas where the view was limited to a matter of yards. Visitors who came looking for the fort often cruised up and down Fort DeRussy Road and left with the impression that the fort no longer existed.

A few weeks after the capture of the fort in 1864, Union troops occupying the town of Natchitoches took over the newspaper office there and printed their own newspapers. One of the first editions of the *Natchitoches Union* made the boast that "Fort de Russy has fallen, like Lucifer, never to rise again."[5] For a while, it looked like that boast might be true—at least in regard to Fort DeRussy. But never is a long, long time.

The Renaissance and Other Things

In February 1994, several members of La Commission des Avoyelles (the Avoyelles Parish historical society) met in Marksville to discuss the possibility of purchasing the Fort DeRussy property and establishing some sort of park there.[6] The idea met with the approval of all present, and work began on bringing the dream to fruition. On March 4, 1996, the five acres containing the Main Redoubt of the fort were bought from Mrs. Mary Ann Frey Wilt of Tennessee, who had inherited the property from her husband. Work began immediately by the newly formed Friends of Fort DeRussy on preparing the property for eventual turnover to the Louisiana Office of State Parks, with the eventual goal of the site becoming a part of the state parks system.[7]

---

5. Germaine Portré-Bobinski and Clara Mildred Smith, *Natchitoches: The Up-to-Date Oldest Town in Louisiana* (New Orleans: Dameron-Pierson, 1936), 82.

6. The meeting was called by Carlos Mayeux Jr., president of La Commission. Attending were Eleanor Gremillion, Marc Dupuy Jr., Randy Decuir, David Floyd, and Steve Mayeux.

7. Friends of Fort DeRussy was originally a committee of La Commission des Avoyelles. The group quickly became larger than its parent organization and finally "seceded" from La Commission and incorporated as an independent nonprofit organization in January 2003. The secession was amicable, with many Friends members maintaining membership in both groups.

Minor setbacks occurred. A month after the property was acquired, the group was told by the State Division of Historic Preservation that the site did not qualify for inclusion on the National Register of Historic Places as it was "nothing but an overgrown mound," and that the preservation office should be recontacted when there was something to show them. The Friends of Fort DeRussy set to work. Over the next several years, the fort took on a new life. The nearby state prison at Cottonport lent prisoners to fence the property and clear underbrush, the parish prison provided workers to keep the grass mowed, and volunteers showed up for annual clean-up days. Whenever anything happened at the fort, the local news media were contacted. Newspaper coverage by the local paper was intense, and stories also appeared in the regional papers. The Alexandria television stations also became involved, covering the cleanups and visits by an Australian tourist and tour groups from the *Delta Queen* steamboat. In October 1994, before the purchase of the fort, a tour bus headed for the fort was stopped by a well-meaning native who tried to turn the driver around because he was going the wrong way. "The casino is back that way," the driver was told. By 1997, such incidents were no longer happening. The fort that had for years been lost in the woods became one of the best known places in Avoyelles Parish.

While all of this physical activity was going on at the fort, administrative steps were also being taken. The fort property was donated to the city of Marksville to allow for the acquisition of state grant money. The grant money was spent on maintenance, publicity, and improve-

When the state of Louisiana made money available to the Friends of Fort DeRussy to develop the fort site, one of the first items bought was this sign. The author broke a posthole digger handle putting in the sign and gained a healthy respect for the men who built the fort. (Photograph by author.)

After 140 years of erosion, the west wall of the fort is still nearly perpendicular. This wall received the brunt of the attack in 1864. (Photograph by author.)

This bridge is a reconstruction of the one that crossed Barbin's Bayou here during the war. It leads to the east wall of the fort. (Photograph by author.)

ments at the site. In 1999, the Red River Waterway Commission gave an additional $150,000 for the purchase of additional adjoining property, increasing the site holdings to seventy acres. That same year, the legislature passed a bill making Fort DeRussy Louisiana's newest state historic site. In October 1999, the city of Marksville donated the property to the Louisiana Office of State Parks. Work on the site's master plan began in 2003 and was completed in early 2005.

The Cemetery

> There is a haunted wood near Marksville on the Red River. Near-by
> residents will not enter the dim interior after sundown or at night.
> Many witnesses swear to have seen headless men marching among
> the trees. It is said that these are soldiers who once fought a battle in
> this wood. After the battle a long trench was dug and the killed were
> buried without religious service. Now the ghosts of these soldiers
> cannot rest and must march all night.
>
> *Gumbo Ya-Ya: A Collection of Louisiana Folk Tales*

The graveyard at Fort DeRussy has long been rumored to be haunted by the ghosts of soldiers who died in battle. Local high school students still enjoy scaring themselves with trips to the isolated cemetery on dark nights, especially on Friday the 13th and Halloween. The author, who spent a long Halloween night in the graveyard while working on this book, can attest to the fact that, unfortunately, the cemetery is not haunted. No headless soldiers, no runaway slaves, no shrieking apparitions of any sort. Lots of hooting owls, the occasional carload of school kids through the parking apron, a few rooting armadillos, and one large pack of howling coyotes made for an interesting night, but no ghosts of any kind made an appearance. Perhaps they were afraid that the large number of questions they would have been asked would have kept them up past sunrise.

In defense of the youngsters who have fled in terror from the graveyard in the middle of the night, it must be admitted that when the wind blows, the large branches of some of the larger trees do make a creaking, groaning sort of noise that can be a bit unnerving. And if one of the local tomcats starts yowling about that time, anyone with an active imagination will be hard pressed to hold their ground.

The origin of the cemetery at Fort DeRussy is shrouded in mystery. Some local residents claim that it predates the fort, but this belief is based solely on the fact that burials in the low-lying flood plains below the fort were impractical and the residents of that area have always brought their dead to be buried on the high ground. As Fort DeRussy occupies the nearest high ground to the river, it is reasonable to expect that the early settlers of the river bottom did bury their dead somewhere near the fort. For them to have chosen that exact spot would have been coincidental.

The earliest documentation for the cemetery is provided by a *Harper's Weekly* map of the fort made shortly after her capture in 1864. This shows the fort's graveyard in the same location as the current cemetery. It is reasonable to assume the cemetery was started shortly after work began on the fort in late 1862. Certainly, when the smallpox epidemic hit the fort in January 1863, there was a need for a cemetery.

The number of burials in the graveyard has long been an item of speculation. If burial records were ever kept, they are no longer extant. No Civil War–era graves are currently marked, the wooden markers having long since rotted away.[8] No one knows whether or not the slaves were buried in the cemetery, and the number of Confederate soldiers buried there is also unknown. In 1868, eighteen Union soldiers were disinterred at Fort DeRussy and moved to the Alexandria National Cemetery at Pineville. Of these, only seven were identified, and of these seven, two were identified only by initials. One of the seven, James Rood of the 32nd Iowa, is listed in the National Cemetery records as having come from the Yellow Bayou battlefield (seventy-six bodies were disinterred from that area). Another set of remains supposedly removed from the cemetery was recorded as belonging to one T. Hartley of the 32nd Iowa, but further research has identified this man as Thomas J. Hartley of the 2nd Illinois Cavalry, killed at Yellow Bayou. Apparently, the exhumed bodies from Yellow Bayou and Fort DeRussy were brought to the National Cemetery at the same time, and the paperwork—if not the bodies themselves—became intermingled in the process. One can perhaps sympathize with the soldiers assigned the task of hauling wagonloads of four-year-old human remains over fifty miles of dirt roads and attempting to maintain accurate records of who came from where.

The cemetery is sited on a narrow finger of land, with the fort's northernmost moat on one side and a ravine on the other. It has been in continuous use since its inception, but the earliest marked grave is dated 1898. The cemetery has no real governing board, and no plots are sold.

---

8. There are Civil War veterans buried in marked sites in the cemetery, but all of those interments took place in the 1900s, long after the war.

Interments are made by individuals going out to the cemetery, finding a likely looking site, and having a grave dug. Given the small area covered by the cemetery and the large number of burials (many unmarked) over the years, it is not surprising that many, if not most, of the recent burials are on top of older graves. The oldest graves are in a highly decomposed state, and unless the soil is closely examined, the remains are not apparent. As a general rule, the soil is not closely examined. When obvious skeletal remains are found, the new grave will sometimes be moved; at other times, if the grave is already at a legal depth, the gravediggers will simply stop where they are and bury there. By the year 2003, some gravediggers had begun a policy of digging down less than two feet and enclosing the coffin in a concrete vault, effectively ceasing the problem of digging into the deeper unmarked graves.

As of this writing, the cemetery is not a part of the Fort DeRussy State Historic Site.

The Cannon

Of all the artillery pieces that saw service at Fort DeRussy, only one is still known to exist. The surviving Fort DeRussy cannon is a banded and rifled Model of 1829 32-pounder Seacoast Gun, cast at the Columbia Foundry in Georgetown (Washington, D.C.) in 1834. It was marked with the foundry number 289 and was proofed by William Jenkins Worth, whose proof mark *WJW* was stamped on the muzzle face. Originally a smoothbore, the gun was rifled and banded by Confederate ordnance workers early in the war. The gun's history between its origin and January 1864 cannot be determined.

On January 17, 1864, Gen. John Walker strongly recommended that the "most effective guns" of the fort should be in the Water Battery, and therefore, the 9-inch Dahlgren and the rifled 32-pounder that were in the Hill Fort should be moved down to the river. Those guns were still in the Hill Fort on March 4, but by March 10 they had been moved to the Water Battery. The 32-pounder was placed *en barbette* in the northernmost of the three batteries—that is, it was mounted on a barbette carriage and placed so as to fire over an earthen embankment. When the fort was attacked on March 14, it was the only gun in the Water Battery that fired at the attacking infantry. Regrettably, after only one round, the gun crew was driven away by return fire and the gun was abandoned. On April 8, the 32-pounder rifle was loaded aboard the U.S. transport *General Lyon* and taken away.

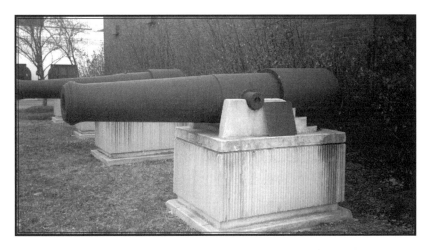

This rifled and banded Model 1829 32-pounder Seacoast Gun, currently on display at the Washington Navy Yard, is the only surviving Fort DeRussy cannon. It was the only gun in the Water Battery to fire a round at the attacking Yankees when the fort was captured in 1864. (Photograph by Baird Webel.)

Over the years, all of the other guns that served at Fort DeRussy have disappeared. Some were destroyed during the war, others were sold for scrap afterward. When the Fort DeRussy "renaissance" began in the 1990s, only one gun could be found. That gun, the Model of 1829 Seacoast Gun, was located at the Navy Museum at the Washington Navy Yard in Washington, D.C. One can only imagine the consternation of the Fort DeRussy historical researchers when they found on the gun evidence of one more of David Porter's hoaxes.

The gun was captured by the U.S. Army at Fort DeRussy on March 14, 1864. This fact is well documented, without any room for question or doubt. But stamped into the iron on the left side of the breech band is the notation:

> ARMY 32 PDR
> BANDED AND RIFLED BY THE REBELS
> CAPTURED FROM THEM BY
> R. ADMIRAL D. PORTER
> AT FORT DERUSSY
> MAY 4, 1863

There was a naval battle at Fort DeRussy on May 4, 1863. The navy did capture a damaged 32-pounder cannon when they took the fort on May 5, 1863, but that gun was destroyed by bursting on May 10, 1863, by the crew of USS *Benton*. The gun captured by Porter's fleet in May 1863 is *not* the gun on display at the Washington Navy Yard. The gun on display at the Washington Navy Yard is a souvenir, not a war trophy, presented to the navy by the army.

No one will ever know whether David Porter was personally involved in the subterfuge involved in mislabeling this cannon. The inscription does specifically mention Porter, and given his past actions, it certainly would not have been out of character for him to have participated in the deception. Navy historians say that the records of this particular cannon have been "lost in the mists of time," and they either can not or will not give any input into the origins of the notation on the gun.[9]

With the development of Fort DeRussy as a state historic site, it will be most appropriate for the gun to be returned to the fort for permanent display at the site where it once saw action. Given the long history of acrimony between the U.S. Navy and Fort DeRussy, it is not expected that the return of the cannon will be accomplished easily. But there are still iron men who will fight for those earthen walls, and for the iron gun that belongs in them.

Whatever Happened to ... ?

Most of the men who served at Fort DeRussy slipped back into anonymity rather quickly after the war. Here is a small taste of what happened to a few of them.

It would normally be assumed that losing *Indianola* under the circumstances that Lt. Cmdr. George Brown did would be a real career destroyer for a naval officer. Surprisingly, such was not the case. Brown retired from the navy in 1897 with the rank of rear admiral. He died in 1913, just ten days after his seventy-eighth birthday, and is buried in Crown Hill Cemetery in Indianapolis, Indiana.

Charles Rivers Ellet was another Yankee gunboat captain who did not fare too well in his match-up with the crew from Fort DeRussy. After the fall of Vicksburg, he returned to Illinois on sick leave, suffering severely from neuralgia in the face. On the night of October 16, 1863, he died of an overdose of morphine, which he took for the pain.

9. Ed Ballam, "The Navy Won't Give Up Captured Gun," *Civil War News* 25, no. 3 (Apr. 1999): 1, 23.

Little Angelica Lucille Barbin, the baby born at the fort just three days before its capture, grew up to be a beautiful young lady and an accomplished pianist. She accompanied her father to the New Orleans World Exposition in 1885 and died in childbirth in January 1900, leaving a six-year-old daughter to mourn her. Fifty years later, that daughter would become the grandmother of the author of this book. Angelica is buried in St. Mary's Catholic Cemetery, Cottonport, Louisiana.

Dr. Batey, the "Little Steamboat that Could," survived her meeting with *Indianola* but did not survive the war. A sailor aboard USS *Lafayette* reported seeing her sunken hulk in the Ouachita River between Columbia and Monroe, Louisiana, on April 9, 1864.

Grand Era, the tender for the *Indianola* expedition and the boat that helped pull *Dr. Batey* up to the fight, also did not survive the war. She was dismantled at Shreveport in 1864, and her machinery went into the ironclad CSS *Missouri.* The *Missouri* did survive the war, primarily because she drew too much water to get down the shallow Red River to where the action was. She was seized by the U.S. Navy after the war, taken up the Mississippi to Mound City, Illinois, and sold.

After the capture of the fort, the rumor made the rounds of Walker's Division that Lt. Col. William Byrd had been killed in the fighting. The rumor was not true. Byrd, a Virginia native, returned to Virginia after the war and did not die for another thirty-four years. Byrd had three grandsons whose fame exceeded his own: Virginia governor and U.S. senator Harry Byrd, World War I hero Tom Byrd, and Rear Adm. Richard E. Byrd, USN, a renowned Arctic and Antarctic explorer who was the recipient of a Medal of Honor.

Lt. John Abbe, 95th Illinois, received such a minor wound when the magazine blew up that it was not even mentioned on his service record. But he suffered a serious sunstroke at the Battle of Brice's Cross Roads several months later, which disabled him to the extent that he had to resign his commission in September 1864. Capt. David Young, 81st Illinois, the company commander who had presented his brain-spattered self to Gen. A. J. Smith to show the general "his work," was captured at Brice's Cross Roads and spent most of the rest of the war in prison.

Col. Thomas Humphrey, commanding officer of the 95th Illinois, the man in charge of demolishing Fort DeRussy, was not as fortunate as either Abbe or Young. He was killed at Brice's Cross Roads.

In the early 1880s, Auguste Voinché filed a claim for reimbursement for his "stolen" cotton with the French-American Claims Commission.

Government lawyers were able to find several witnesses from the town of Marksville who swore that Voinché never had a cellar full of cotton. Surprisingly, Voinché's most convincing witnesses were former *Benton* crewmen, who testified in detail as to the room full of cotton that they found beneath the store. In spite of this compelling testimony, Voinché never collected from the government. Eugene Brochard's widow did manage to collect for the cotton that was taken from the Brochard gin, although she was paid only one-tenth of what she asked. Spencer Thorpe, a Marksville attorney (and former Confederate officer) who served as chief counsel for the U.S. government in fighting the claims arising after the war, was particularly adept at assassinating the character of anyone who dared to testify for a claimant, and he made so many enemies among his neighbors, friends, and family that he had to leave the area after the trials ended. He resettled in California. Voinché filed his claim under the name Oden Deucatte, his birth name but a name he had never used while living in Louisiana. No explanation for this peculiarity was given; Thorpe felt it indicated a criminal background.

The CSS *Queen of the West* had a noble, but very short, career. After her participation in the capture of *Indianola,* she returned to Fort DeRussy and dropped off her volunteer soldiers and stokers then ran up to Alexandria for repairs. She then returned to the fort and proceeded down the Red River into the Atchafalaya, along with the detachment from the 3rd Maryland Artillery. On April 14, 1863, in an engagement in Grand Lake with the U.S. gunboats *Calhoun, Clifton,* and *Arizona, Queen of the West* was burned and blown up. Sgt. Edward H. Langley, who served so valiantly in the engagement with *Indianola,* was either killed in action or drowned in an attempt to escape the burning boat, as were his fellow Marylanders, Corporals Joseph Edgar and Michael H. O'Connell, and Privates Thomas Bowler, S. Chafin, Edward Kenn, and H. L. McKisick. Only four members of the 3rd Maryland detachment survived.

William H. Webb, the other Confederate ram that pummeled *Indianola* into submission, almost survived the war, but not quite. In April 1865, under the command of Lt. Charles Read, the *Webb* made a legendary run from Shreveport down the Red and into the Mississippi, then through the gauntlet of the entire U.S. Mississippi River Squadron, headed for the Gulf of Mexico and Cuba. The plucky little vessel was finally trapped just below New Orleans, and Read was forced to run her aground and burn her.

John Clabby, "the bravest of the brave" of the Crescent Artillery, died from a Minié ball to the head when the fort was captured in 1864. His epitaph, which was written by Sgt. John Murray years after the war—"No storied urn or sculptured marble bear / the hero's name who fought so well. / Upon his grave we could not drop a tear / and had to leave him where he fell"—remains true to this day. Clabby's remains lie somewhere near the fort in an unmarked grave.

David French Boyd, chief engineer at Fort DeRussy after the departure of Lewis DeRussy, went on to much greater fame as an educator. He was the second superintendent of the Louisiana State Seminary of Learning (which became Louisiana State University in 1870), and it was his heroic efforts that held the school together through Reconstruction and afterward. David Boyd justly claims the title of "Father of Louisiana State University." He died and was buried in Baton Rouge in 1899.

Brig. Gen. Joseph Anthony Mower, a Mexican War veteran, commanded the assault on Fort DeRussy in March 1864. After the Red River Campaign, he served under Gen. William T. Sherman (the first superintendent of the Louisiana State Seminary of Learning) on the infamous March to the Sea through Georgia. After the war, Mower served in the military Reconstruction government and became commander of the Department of Louisiana in January 1869. He died in New Orleans of pneumonia in January 1870.

Acting Ens. Cassilly Adams, of the USS *Ouachita*, spent some time in the river in front of the fort during the latter part of the Red River Campaign. He went on to become a fairly well-known artist after the war. His most famous painting was a nine-by-sixteen-foot mural of *Custer's Last Stand*. The rights to the painting were bought by Anheuser-Busch (the Budweiser people) and it was made into a lithograph that was distributed to bars all over the country. In the first half of the 1900s, almost every saloon in the country had one of these pictures hanging on the wall.

Capt. Theophilus Perry, of the 28th Texas Dismounted Cavalry, spent the winter of 1863–64 near Fort DeRussy and wrote many letters home to his wife. In a poignant letter dated February 21, 1864, shortly after his birthday, he wrote his wife, "I am thirty one years old. My Mother died at thirty three. I may be in the downward road already. I feel sad very often, and nothing makes me more so than the idea of growing old." Theophilus need not have worried about growing old. He was wounded at the Battle of Pleasant Hill on April 9. His leg was amputated, and he died on April 17 in the hospital at Mansfield.

Charles Brooks was one of the slaves who survived building Fort DeRussy. But not for long. On March 19, 1864, he enlisted in Company E of the 71st U.S. Colored Infantry. With the onset of warm weather, he relapsed with the chronic diarrhea that he had contracted while working at the fort the previous winter and died on May 20. The company Descriptive List says that Charles was born in Evergreen, Louisiana, was twenty-two years old, was six feet two inches tall, had black hair and black eyes, and that his body bore the marks of dog bites received when he was chased down after escaping from a work party at the fort.

Col. John Scott of the 32nd Iowa Infantry was elected lieutenant governor of Iowa in 1867.

Capt. J. M. White was the captain of CSS *Grand Duke* during the Gunboat Fight at Fort DeRussy in May 1863. He had a long and illustrious career as a steamboat captain both before and after the war. Perhaps no name has come to symbolize the glory days of steamboating in the late 1800s nearly as much as has his. The side-wheeler *J. M. White,* named for the captain, was built in 1878 and was considered "the supreme triumph in cotton boat architecture." The boat could carry ten thousand bales of cotton and was the ultimate "floating palace" on the Mississippi River. When one thinks of the grandeur of steamboating, one thinks of the *J. M. White.* Captain White died and was buried in Cloverport, Kentucky, in 1880.

The gunboat *Grand Duke* did not fare as well as her captain. She burned at Shreveport a few months after the Gunboat Fight.

In 1863, Charles Chalfant shot Master's Mate Thompson while *Queen of the West* was passing in front of his home, an incident that led to the capture of the *Queen* at Fort DeRussy and her later use in the capture of the ironclad *Indianola*. While this would seem to be quite an accomplishment for one man, Charles paid a heavy price for his actions. His mother, Caroline Burrows Chalfant, was very sick at the time of the incident, and when the Yankees returned and burned down the Chalfant home and outbuildings, Caroline was left without any sort of shelter. She died a short time later as a result of exposure. To add insult to injury, Union soldiers later broke into her tomb looking for hidden valuables. And to add even further insult, some of the family silver that had been stolen from the plantation was seen on display at the World's Columbian Exposition in Chicago in 1893. To this day, some of the Chalfant descendants wish that "the one [Charles] had been a dozen."

Thomas Handy, the young lieutenant who helped capture *Queen of the West,* was made prize master of USS *Indianola* after her capture, and insisted on fighting in the Gunboat Fight "as long as there was a man to pull a lanyard," was thrown from his horse in August 1863 and broke his thigh. He underwent several operations and ended up with one leg three inches shorter than the other. After the war, he was elected civil sheriff in New Orleans, where he played a prominent role in Reconstruction politics. He died in 1893.

Not everyone involved at Fort DeRussy went on to become a sheriff, or a lieutenant governor, or the superintendent of a university, or had grandchildren who became senators and famous Antarctic explorers. Some just went back to lives of quiet desperation. And some did worse than that.

Levi "Doc" Miles may have been an alcoholic before he enlisted. It was rather strange for a man of his age—forty-four years old, married with children—to join the army in 1864. One would get the impression that he was not doing too well in civilian life and was looking for the military to give him another chance. After all, there was an enlistment bonus to consider. But Miles did not come out of the service a better man.

A bullet through the upper neck, received in the charge on Fort DeRussy just two months after he joined the army, left Doc hard of hearing and with frequent seizures. Formerly a healthy man, he could no longer hold down a job and sometimes forgot where he was or what he was doing. "Old Uncle Dockey," as the kids called him, became a fixture in Rising Sun, Indiana, after the war. He ably held the position of town drunk and could often be found passed out in the street. One particularly cold afternoon in December 1872, he headed into town to pick up some pills and was seen lying in the road a little before dark that night. As the night grew colder, two men who had seen him returned to pick him up, but by that time he was gone.

Old Uncle Dockey never made it home that night. Dazed and disoriented, either from whiskey or a seizure, he took the wrong fork in the road on his way home and wandered over a bluff along the Ohio River. Three days later, his wife began to make inquiries as to his whereabouts, leading one to believe that he may not have been too sorely missed. When the river thawed in May, Doc's body was found about four miles downstream in a good state of preservation. His widow's claim for a pension, based on her belief that his death was the result of his head wound, was denied.

For the most part, the people who made history at Fort DeRussy just went back to their lives. Some of those lives were glorious and heroic, some were wretched and pathetic, but mostly they were just your standard, everyday American lives with the standard mixture of glory and pathos. Their children and grandchildren went on to fight other wars and raise more kids and make this country what it is today. Some of them were good, some were bad. But they were who they were, and because of them, we are who we are.

Appendix A

Lewis Gustave DeRussy

Some children are said to be born with silver spoons in their mouths. Lewis Gustave DeRussy seems to have been born with a steel bayonet in his. He was the son of Thomas Benoit DeRussy, a native of St. Malo, a city on the northwest coast of France in the province of Brittany. Up until the nineteenth century, St. Malo was known as a city of pirates and corsairs, and Thomas DeRussy appears to have followed in those footsteps, at least to the extent of seeking adventure on the high seas. Thomas was born about 1761, the oldest of two sons of Jacques Jules Gilles de Russy and Marie Françoise Servanne Rivere. By 1778, Thomas had become an officer in the French navy. While in Paris, he was influenced by Benjamin Franklin, the American commissioner to France who was attempting to persuade French officers to assist the colonies in their fight for independence from the British Crown. Swayed by Franklin's arguments, Thomas went to Nantes in the spring of 1779, where he was assigned as second officer on the frigate *Pallas* under Capt. Dennis Cottineau. *Pallas* was a merchantman fitted out as a thirty-two-gun frigate and was owned, at least in part, by Thomas's father. *Pallas* soon sailed to L'Orient and joined a squadron of four French ships that were being loaned to the American navy. The fleet was under the command of Commodore John Paul Jones. By early summer, Thomas had resigned his commission in the French navy and taken a commission as a midshipman in the American Navy.

In September 1779 the American ships found a forty-one-ship British convoy in the North Sea, off Flamborough Head, England. The convoy was escorted by two British warships, HMS *Serapis* and HMS *Countess of Scarborough*. The ensuing battle has gone down in the annals of U.S. naval history. With nightfall coming on, *Bonhomme Richard* engaged *Serapis*, and *Pallas*, with Thomas DeRussy as second officer, took on *Countess of Scarborough*. After almost an hour,[1] the

---

1. About fifty minutes by Thomas DeRussy's reckoning.

captain of the *Countess* said, "I was so unfortunate as to have all my braces, great part of the running rigging, main and mizzen top-sail sheets shot away, seven of the guns dismounted, four men killed and twenty wounded."[2] *Countess of Scarborough* surrendered to *Pallas*. Meanwhile, after a particularly brutal fight, *Serapis* surrendered to *Bonhomme Richard,* but only after John Paul Jones had gained immortality with his "We have not yet begun to fight" comment.

With the *Richard* in sinking condition, Jones sent Lieutenant DeRussy from *Pallas* with a crew of men to work the pumps that had been placed on the *Richard*. Boats stood by to get the crew off should the ship go under. Despite the untiring efforts of DeRussy and his men, the pumps could not keep up with the water pouring in from the rising seas, and the pumping crew was forced to abandon ship just before *Bonhomme Richard* went down.

Thomas DeRussy was breveted by Benjamin Franklin for his role in the Flamborough Head affair, but his naval career soon ended. In spite of this, he seemed doomed to a life of excitement. With the French Revolution brewing, he left France for family holdings on Santo Domingo in the French West Indies, in what is now Haiti. On August 15, 1787, he married Madeleine Baissiere, a native of Cap Français.[3] Their first son, René Emile, was born at Cap Français in 1788. Their next son, René Edward, was born on June 19, 1792, also at Cap Français. But the life of a wealthy sugarcane planter was not to be Thomas DeRussy's fate. Slave uprisings on the island were becoming more and more frequent, and some time after René Edward's birth, a particularly violent rebellion caused the DeRussys to flee for their lives. The elder DeRussy, aware of the situation that was brewing, had made preparations to board an American warship that was in the harbor. Family tradition has it that the ship had been sent by John Paul Jones to rescue his former shipmate. The DeRussy family was forced to abandon all of their possessions, including Thomas's brevet papers, which had been signed by Benjamin Franklin, and race through the town to the safety of the ship. The infant René was carried through the burning town in the arms of a nurse, and Thomas DeRussy himself barely escaped capture on his way to the harbor. The family arrived safely in New York City, and Lewis

---

2. Gardner W. Allen, *A Naval History of the American Revolution* (New York: Russell & Russell, 1962), 2:475.

3. Madeleine Baissiere, or possibly de Bessiere, or some variation thereof, was born at Cap Français about 1767. DeRussy family legend has it that she was of royal blood.

Gustave was born there on September 17, 1795.[4] René Emile, Lewis's oldest brother, died in June of 1796, but three other boys were born to the family in New York City. René Amedee was born on November 19, 1797,[5] Jean Baptiste Adolphe was born on December 31, 1802,[6] and Charles Gaston was born at the family home at 3 Read Street at 9:00 A.M. on August 12, 1806.[7]

Thomas DeRussy became a naturalized U.S. citizen on May 28, 1805. He supported his family as a merchant in New York City from 1800 to 1813, trading with the islands of Cuba, Tenerife, Martinique, and Guadaloupe. Toward the end of that time he did business with merchants in Nantes and Bordeaux, France, but this must not have been too profitable, as his business failed. Fortunately, Thomas had begun teaching French classes in 1809, and he continued in this occupation until 1820. On Christmas Eve 1820, he had an erisypelas inflammation of the right leg and thigh, which left him bedridden and unable to move. By early February 1821 he was forced to sell his collection of several hundred volumes of French books, but the amount they brought him was so small that he was forced to request that he be reestablished on the pension rolls.[8] He died soon after that, on February 21, 1821. His wife, Madeleine, relocated from New York City to Old Point Comfort, Elizabeth City County, Virginia, and died there sometime after 1842.

Thomas DeRussy's veteran status had served him well during the insurrection in Santo Domingo, and he used it again when his two

---

4. There is some debate over whether Lewis's middle name is actually Gustave or Gustavus. Records show the name spelled both ways. No signature with his middle name spelled out is known to exist. He definitely spelled his first name *Lewis,* which is peculiar considering that his parents were French and would be expected to spell the name *Louis.*

5. René Amedee DeRussy, called Amedee by his father, stayed in the New York City area and died in New Brunswick, New Jersey, in 1870.

6. Jean (John) Baptiste Adolphe DeRussy, called Adolphus by his father, married Caroline Fearing in Philadelphia, Pennsylvania, in 1838. They settled in Louisiana and raised seven children. He was Sheriff of Natchitoches Parish in 1839 and provisional mayor of Baton Rouge in 1862. He died on October 28, 1867, in Baton Rouge.

7. Charles Gaston DeRussy apparently died young. A sworn statement by Thomas DeRussy, dated September 1820, states that the DeRussy family consisted of Thomas, his wife, and two sons, Amedee and Adolphus. René Edward and Lewis were both in the army by that time, which would explain their exclusion from the list.

8. Thomas DeRussy had first applied for a pension in 1818 and received it for a while. His possessions were inventoried at the time of his initial application, and his library was valued at $250, which was the original cost of the books. Thomas objected to this appraisal but was assured that it would not count against his pension, as the books were tools of the trade for his profession as a teacher. He later lost his pension due to the high value of the books. When the books were sold, he was only able to get $42.65 for them.

oldest sons came of age. René Edward DeRussy was appointed to the United States Military Academy at West Point, a result of his father's intervention on his behalf. He entered on March 20, 1807, and received his commission as a second lieutenant five years later, on June 10, 1812. Lewis entered West Point on April 14, 1813, and graduated with the rank of third lieutenant, in just eleven months, on March 11, 1814, the speed of his passage through the academy possibly due to the fact that the War of 1812 was in full swing.[9] Or possibly, the speed of his passage through West Point was an indication of his aptitude for the military life. Lewis was assigned to the 1st Artillery, and his first duty station on leaving West Point was back in his home town of New York City, where he served as acting assistant engineer in erecting temporary defenses for the city and environs. The war soon ended, but Lewis DeRussy's military career was just beginning. He began making his way up the military ladder, promotions coming slowly but surely. On January 7, 1816, while still on garrison duty at New York, Lewis married Elizabeth Claire Boerum.[10] From 1819 to 1821 he served as a surveyor and topographer under Brig. Gen. P. B. Porter, putting in the boundary line between the United States and Canada as prescribed under the terms of the Treaty of Ghent. Lewis was a popular man with his colleagues on that assignment, if for no other reason than that he was the only man in the party whose wife sent him packages of cakes and preserves. How these items made the journey, via steamboat and Indian messengers to a land of "savages, rocks, and sterility," would no doubt make a good story in itself.[11] Lewis finally returned to his thoughtful wife, and the next few years were spent alternating between garrison duties as the commanding officer of Archer's Company of Artillery and topographical duties under Col. John J. Abert, an engineering officer whom he greatly admired. In September 1826, he was promoted to major and appointed to serve as paymaster of the Red River posts, those being

9. Though fast, this was not a record for students passing through the U.S. Military Academy in that era. It was not unheard of for students to enter and graduate from the academy in seven months, even without a war in progress.

10. Elizabeth Claire Boerum was born on Long Island, New York, on March 19, 1792. She was the granddaughter of Simon Boerum, a New York delegate to the Continental Congress in 1774–75. The Boerums were an old New York family, Willim Jacobse Van Boerum having arrived there around 1646.

11. Joseph Delafield, *The Unfortified Boundary: A Diary of the First Survey of the Canadian Boundary Line from St. Regis to the Lake of the Woods* (New York: privately printed, 1943), 316.

Lewis Gustave DeRussy. (Courtesy
of Edith DeRussy.)

Fort Jesup, Louisiana, and Fort Towson, Arkansas.[12] Major DeRussy
served at this office from 1826 until 1842.

While the job of paymaster would seem to indicate a somewhat easy
life of administrative tasks and office work, this was not the case on the
western edge of the country in the early nineteenth century. DeRussy
had to deliver a cash payroll to the soldiers at Forts Jesup and Towson,
and in that day that was no easy task. In 1828, for instance, the post
at Fort Jesup was warned just prior to DeRussy's trip up to Canton-
ment Towson that "a Band of Robbers have been organized, and intend
to rob him in the Wilderness." DeRussy requisitioned six extra horses
for this particular trip. The last sentence of a letter to Gen. Thomas
Jesup in Washington is indicative of his commanding officer's faith in
DeRussy's ability to make the trip unscathed: "On his return, how shall
the horses be disposed of?" Apparently, the thought that the "Band of
Robbers" might dispose of the horses was not even considered.[13]

12. George W. Cullum, *Biographical Register of the Officers and Graduates of the
U.S. Military Academy at West Point, N.Y. from Its Establishment, in 1802, to 1890,*
3rd ed. (Boston: Houghton, Mifflin, 1891), 114–15.

13. Francis Lee to Thomas Jesup, Mar. 1, 1828, Fort Jesup State Historic Site
Archives, Many, La.

DeRussy and his growing family lived off base in a house on the road between Fort Jesup and Natchitoches. There were ultimately seven children in the family. Lewis Jr. was born in New York in 1818.[14] Marie Emilie was the only daughter and may have been the oldest child. She was the first married. Thomas Edward's birth date in not known. He married in 1842. William was born in New York in 1824, and Gustavias was also born in New York in 1827, indicating that Elizabeth did not come immediately to Louisiana with Lewis in 1826. When she did come, she must have brought her little sister Ann with her. And as seventeen-year-old New York girls were a rarity at Fort Jesup in 1828, it did not take long for her to find a beau. Ann Boerum was soon married to Maj. George Birch, one of DeRussy's fellow officers. Unfortunately, Ann died in October, 1829, a few months after her eighteenth birthday.[15] Lewis's fifth son, George Birch DeRussy, was born several months later.[16]

Lewis's sixth, and last, son was also named for a neighbor and friend. John Cortez DeRussy, born 1832, was named for John François Cortes, a wild young man from Natchitoches who would marry Marie Emilie DeRussy in 1834. By all accounts, John Cortes was an arrogant, violent, hateful man who could be absolutely charming when he wanted to be. But he was a mean drunk and a poor choice for a husband. Or son-in-law.[17]

On August 30, 1836, Elizabeth Boerum DeRussy died. Family tradition has it that she died in childbirth. She was buried in the Fort Jesup cemetery under a large marble slab.[18] Her grave remained at Fort Jesup

---

14. Like his father, Lewis Jr. would also attend the U.S. Military Academy at West Point, but Lewis Jr. did not graduate. He was dismissed from the academy in 1839 for throwing a lump of coal at an officer on Christmas Eve 1838. Letter to author, Sept. 30, 2005, from Alicia Mauldin-Ware, Special Collections and Archives, U.S. Military Academy Library, West Point, N.Y.

15. In J. Fair Hardin's book, Ann was said to be forty-eight years old at the time of her death. The Boerum family Bible shows that she was born in 1811. For her to have been forty-eight, she would have had to have been born when her mother was only twelve. And she was Jane Fox Boerum's thirteenth child. Hardin, *Northwestern Louisiana*, 192; Boerum-Yarrington family Bible records.

16. U.S. Census, Natchitoches Parish census records, 1850; Elizabeth Mills, *Natchitoches Parish Church Marriages, 1818–1850*, (Tuscaloosa, Ala.: Mills Historical Press, 1985), Boerum-Yarrington family Bible records.

17. Marie Windell, "A Double Standard of Justice: Is Adultery by a Wife Worse than Murder by her Husband?" in *Historic U. S. Court Cases: An Encyclopedia*, 2nd ed., ed. John W. Johnson (New York: Routledge, 2001), pt. 1, *Crime and Criminal Law*, 1:39–45 (New York: Routledge, 2001); and my personal opinion.

18. The Louisiana climate has been kind to Elizabeth in the years since her death. Her grave marker lies parallel to the ground and is inscribed "In memory of Elizabeth

until 1913, when her body was disinterred along with all of the others in that graveyard; she was reinterred in the Alexandria National Cemetery in Pineville, Louisiana.[19]

With his wife's passing, DeRussy seems to have thrown himself into local politics. Although still serving as an active duty officer, DeRussy was nominated by the Whig Party for the Louisiana state senate in April 1838. He was defeated by Pierre Bossier.[20] This would not be DeRussy's only loss to Bossier.

François Gaiennie, adjutant general of the Louisiana Militia, was a prominent Whig in Natchitoches Parish and a friend of Lewis DeRussy. While at the residence of a neighbor, General Gaiennie had somehow insulted Pierre Bossier, who was also a general in the state militia, and, since his victory over DeRussy, a serving member of the Louisiana senate. General Bossier was a Democrat, and a serious rift developed over this incident along political lines. On September 14, 1839, Bossier challenged Gaiennie to a duel. Bossier did not want to fight, but Gaiennie had denounced him as a coward, and Bossier felt that he had no choice. Sylvester Bossier, Victor Sompayrac, and Peabody A. Morse, acting as seconds for Bossier, delivered the challenge to Major DeRussy, Felix B. Sherburne, and Judge James G. Campbell, Gaiennie's seconds.[21] The challenge was accepted, and as the challenged party, it was up to Gaiennie to choose the weapons to be used. He chose rifles. From this choice, one of two possibilities can be surmised. A rifle is a weapon that is more easily mastered than a pistol. A man could be a terrible pistol shot and still be able to hit a target reasonably well with a rifle. A rifle is also a deadlier weapon than a pistol, given the larger charge of powder, the larger bullet fired, and the greater inherent accuracy of the weapon. Possibly Gaiennie's friends did not think that he was Bossier's equal as a pistol shot, and they may have

---

Clair, consort of Major L. G. De Russy, USA, who departed this life on the 30th Aug. 1836, aged 44 years." The angled portion of the 4s were not inscribed as deep as the upright legs, and years of wind and rain have eroded the surrounding stone enough to make the second 4, at first glance, look like a 1, in effect subtracting three years from Elizabeth's age.

19. Although several marker inscriptions from the fort were quoted by Hardin in *Northwestern Louisiana*, Elizabeth's is the only one presently at the National Cemetery. The other remains moved there are under a single stone inscribed "25 Unknown Soldiers." This presumably includes Elizabeth's sister, Ann. Personal observation and conversation with cemetery caretaker, Feb. 2002.

20. Gen. Pierre Evariste Jean Baptiste Bossier, born in Natchitoches on Mar. 22, 1797, was the eponym of Bossier Parish.

21. Judge Campbell was later a member of the Louisiana Supreme Court, and Sherburne, a native of France, was a local attorney.

figured that with a rifle, he had at least a chance of hitting Bossier. The other possibility is that there was so much bad blood between the two parties that the duel was intended to be to the death, with Gaiennie not intending for Bossier to survive the possibly minor wound that might be inflicted by an errant pistol shot.

General Gaiennie lived in the southern part of Natchitoches Parish, about a mile above Chopin. General Bossier lived three miles away, at Live Oak Plantation on Cane River. In order to avoid publicity, the duel was held several miles from their homes, behind the plantation of Emile Sompayrac. Gaiennie made one final preparation for the duel that indicates that he may have been less than confident of the outcome. Before leaving his home, he told his wife that if he survived the contest, the messenger bringing the news would be mounted on a white horse; if he did not survive, the courier would be on a black horse. That way, she would know the outcome long before the rider could make his way across the level stretch of Cane River country in front of their home.

The duel took place on September 18, 1839. In addition to the contestants and their seconds, the duel was attended by two doctors, Dingles and Johnson, and by T. E. Tauzin, Phanor Prudhomme, and John F. Cortes, DeRussy's son-in-law. Gaiennie fired first, at a distance of forty yards, and missed, lending credence to the theory that he may not have been a particularly accomplished duelist. Bossier's shot hit Gaiennie in the heart, killing him instantly, and the messenger of death rode off on his black steed. Eleven men died as the result of the animosities generated by this duel.[22] General Bossier lived to be elected to Congress in 1843 but committed suicide on April 24, 1844, before finishing his first term.

DeRussy was involved not only in temporal politics but also in politics of a spiritual nature. In March 1839, Leonidas Polk, Episcopal bishop of the Southwest Diocese, visited the town of Natchitoches and held the first Protestant services in that town at the courthouse. When the church was formally established after a second visit to the town by

22. These casualties included, but were not limited to, the following: George Williams killed W. L. McWilliams in a duel; M. Busy killed Sylvester Rachal in a duel; Irasteal Rachal, Sylvester's brother, killed M. Busy in a duel the following week; Jack McNaulte (General Gaiennie's overseer) and Breville Perot killed each other in a pistol duel; Hypolite Bordelon killed Jack McNaulte's brother, after McNaulte said that Bordelon could have prevented the McNaulte-Perot duel "had he not cast slanderous remarks concerning the previous duels"; and Sylvester Bossier (one of General Bossier's seconds) killed Alexis Adlee in a sword duel following an argument over the outcome of the Bossier-Gaiennie duel. Louis Raphael Nardini Jr., *My Historic Natchitoches, Louisiana and its Environment* (Natchitoches, La.: Nardini Publishing, 1963), 167.

Bishop Polk in 1841, DeRussy was elected as one of the vestrymen of the church. Although Polk was much younger than DeRussy, he was also a West Point graduate, and no doubt the two men found much in common to discuss during Polk's visits. The two men would meet again in 1862, under much less pleasant circumstances.

DeRussy seems to have been as much involved with his family as with politics during this period of his life. His brother Jean, his name now anglicized to John, had joined him in Natchitoches and was sheriff of Natchitoches Parish in 1839. Another of his wife's sisters had also come down from New York, and in 1840 Louisa Boerum married Thomas P. Jones, the deputy clerk of court.[23] And just seven months after the Gaiennie-Bossier duel, on April 28, 1840, Lewis DeRussy married Eliza Teresa Davenport Russell, the daughter of Samuel Davenport and Marie Louise Gagnon and the widow of Dr. Samuel P. Russell.[24] Eliza was a woman of means, the Davenports having been the founding fathers of the river port of Grand Ecore.[25] DeRussy moved into the Russell home at Grand Ecore, which stood at what is now the southern approach to the Grand Ecore bridge. Although the house never belonged to DeRussy, it came in later years to be called the DeRussy house, causing varying degrees of aggravation to the descendants of the Russell family.[26]

But that aggravation was nothing compared to what DeRussy suffered in 1842. Emilie DeRussy had married the tempestuous John Cortes in 1834, and the marriage had not been a happy one. Cortes was a jealous man, prone to fits of violent temper. He abused Emilie both physically and mentally, and frequently humiliated her in public. Lewis often acted as peacemaker after particularly embarrassing events, pressing his daughter to live with her husband's increasingly outrageous behavior rather than endure the dishonor of divorce. The situation came to a head when, after accusing his wife of adulterous

23. Hardin, *Northwestern Louisiana*, 493; Boerum-Yarrington family Bible records.

24. Russell died on Dec. 21, 1838, at the age of forty-one. Hardin, *Northwestern Louisiana*, 291–92; Natchitoches Parish Marriage Records, Book 27-90, No. 2526, Natchitoches Parish Clerk of Courts Office.

25. Legend suggests that the elder Davenport may not have made all of the family fortune by scrupulous adherence to the law. Some stories even connect the family to the notorious outlaw John Murrel and link the Davenport property, most notably the old Russell graveyard, with legends of Murrel's buried gold.

26. Note from Scharlie Russell in scrapbook, Northwestern State Univ. Archives, Natchitoches, La. The old Russell/DeRussy house burned in 1888.

The DeRussy home, at Grand Ecore, can be seen on the hill in the center of this engraving from *Frank Leslie's Illustrated*. The tin-clad *Cricket* threw a shell at the house from near this point during the Red River Campaign.

behavior, Cortes accosted and killed the man—who was apparently completely innocent of any wrongdoing, as was poor Emilie—that he suspected of showing inappropriate attentions to his wife. Cortes fled the country and received a commission as a captain in the Mexican army, which was then at war with the Republic of Texas. Amazingly, Cortes sued Emilie for divorce after the murder and was granted both the divorce and custody of the couple's child.[27]

They say that when it rains, it pours, and that was certainly true for Lewis DeRussy in 1842. DeRussy had served on active duty in the U.S. Army since 1813, and while he obviously had other irons in the fire, he had apparently served the past twenty-nine years as a faithful and obedient servant of his government. But in 1842, while carrying a payroll up the Red River to the post at Fort Towson, the steamboat on which DeRussy was riding exploded and sank, and the money was lost in the river. DeRussy was responsible for the payroll, and was unable to repay it. As such, he was found in default, and was dropped from the service. He immediately appealed his release, and the appeal went all the way to President John Tyler, who in 1844 determined that DeRussy had been "too rigidly dealt by" and ordered that he be "restored to his original Rank and position upon the happening of the first vacancy." But no opening appeared in that department until President James Polk took office, and that opening went to another officer. DeRussy was philosophical: "Whether President Polk had been induced to overlook my claim, or whether he was purposely kept in ignorance of it, I have never learned, but as I was aware that the PayMaster general was opposed to my return to the Department of which he was the chief, I am justified in the assurance that one or the other means suggested must have been resorted to, to my great prejudice and injury." For whatever reason, he never received orders returning him to active duty in the regular army.[28]

DeRussy's return to civilian life had to have been a shock, but his familial, military, and political activities continued. In 1844 DeRussy took in Emily DeRussy Brandt, the thirteen-year-old daughter of Jane Clementina Boerum Brandt, one of his first wife's youngest sisters. Emily

27. Emilie won the suit in court but lost on appeal. It was her misfortune to have the appeal heard by a judge who, three years earlier, had gone through a nasty divorce after being caught cheating on his wife. The judge apparently used this case to exorcise some of his own demons. Windell, "Double Standard of Justice." Cortes died in Mexico in 1846. The fate of his child, Edward, is unknown.

28. DeRussy to Cullum, Nov. 28, 1855, in Lewis DeRussy Alumni Files, Special Collections and Archives, U.S. Military Academy Library, West Point, N.Y.

came down to Louisiana from New Jersey when her mother died, and
perhaps DeRussy thought that he could do a better job of raising his
young niece than he had with his own Emilie. Little Emily thrived at
her new home in Grand Ecore and eventually married her stepbrother
Samuel.

In 1846, the Mexican War broke out and the old warhorse left
the plantation and went back into harness. DeRussy had been serving
as a major in the Louisiana militia, and in December he was elected
colonel of the 1st Louisiana Regiment of Volunteers. The New Orleans
newspapers were high in their praise of the selection. DeRussy was "a
gentleman of exemplary character, great worth, undoubted valor, and
high military attainments. A more judicious selection could not have
been made. He is well known to many of the U.S. Army officers now in
the city, some of whom we have heard express their high gratification
at the result." Gen. Winfield Scott himself "expressed himself strongly
in favor" of the choice of DeRussy as regimental commander.[29]

DeRussy's Regiment shipped out for Mexico from New Orleans on
January 16, 1847. Although many of the men no doubt thought they
were embarking on a great adventure and all planned on returning
as heroes, the realities of the expedition were anything but glorious.
Bad weather wrecked the steamer *Ondiaka,* with DeRussy and several
companies of his regiment, on the Mexican coast in early February.
The men soon found themselves ashore in a destitute condition, having
lost most of their supplies and weapons. They were soon confronted
by a force of Mexicans under General Cos, who demanded DeRussy's
immediate and unconditional surrender. As evening was drawing near,
DeRussy requested that Cos give him until the following morning to
make his decision, and Cos, who apparently did not have nearly the
number of men with him that he was represented as having, agreed
to the delay. At nightfall, the Louisianians built their campfires and
made a show of bedding down, after which they shed their knapsacks
and any other "burdensome materials which could in the least impede"
and set off up the beach for Tampico. They covered thirty-five miles in
the first twenty-four hours of their march and arrived at the city, sixty
miles from the wreck site, after three days of marching. General Cos's

29. *Daily Tropic,* Dec. 24, 1846, and *New Orleans Commercial Bulletin,* Dec. 24,
1846, in *Historical Military Data on Louisiana Militia, 1846* (hereafter cited as *HMDLM*),
WPA Project, Jackson Barracks, New Orleans, 1941. Scott, the commander of the American
forces during the Mexican War, was one of the handful of men who, like DeRussy, would
serve on active duty during the War of 1812, the Mexican War, and the Civil War.

troops did not follow. The schooner *Pioneer* went down the coast and burned *Ondiaka* to the waterline, and the incident ended. It was an inauspicious start to a long, tedious, and inglorious campaign.[30]

The regiment, having lost most of its equipment, was considered unfit for active service, and though they remained hopeful, the regiment's dreams of combat were not forthcoming. Instead, they were left as a garrison unit in Tampico, where they were soon wracked by boredom, dysentery, and malaria. The morale sank to the point that on March 6, Colonel DeRussy and Capt. Copeland Hunt engaged in a duel. An account from Tampico stated, "All rank was waived and the parties appeared on the ground as private citizens. Under the circumstances, there was no way to avoid the hostile meeting." The circumstances were not explained. The duel resulted in a flesh wound to Copeland's breast, which was "very slight, hardly taking him from his duty."[31] A bill in the Louisiana legislature to send six thousand dollars to the regiment for "clothing and other necessary supplies" failed to receive the necessary votes for passage. A New Orleans newspaper complained, "What has Louisiana done for them? Has she compensated the officers and men shipwrecked on board the *Ondiaka*? Where is the $7000 talked about? Why cannot this State uniform the whole regiment? Those who enjoy themselves comfortably at home appear to have forgotten that a regiment from Louisiana exists at all."[32] The 1st Louisiana Regiment, holed up in Tampico, was undoubtedly asking the same questions.

In July 1847, Colonel DeRussy and his regiment finally got their opportunity to experience combat at the Battle of Tantayuka.[33] On July 7, DeRussy was ordered on an expedition to recover some U.S. prisoners of war then in the hands of General Garay of the Mexican army. DeRussy departed Tampico with a detachment of 126 men, which included infantry, cavalry, and one piece of artillery. The mission was supposed to be a peaceful one, with the prisoners being released through negotiations. The report does not explain why this would require a unit of the size and make-up sent, but events would prove the wisdom of taking it.

30. *New Orleans Daily Picayune*, Feb. 21, 1847, and *Le Courrier de la Louisiane*, Mar. 26, 1847, in *HMDLM, 1847, January–July;* DeRussy to Cullum, Nov. 28, 1855.

31. *New Orleans Daily Picayune*, Mar. 22 and 23, 1847, *HMDLM, 1847.*

32. *Le Courrier de la Louisiane*, Mar. 23, 1847, and *New Orleans Daily Picayune*, June 19, 1847, both in *HMDLM, 1847.*

33. This engagement is also known as "the affair at Calabosa River." It would be hard to find a lesser known battle in this or any other American war, but one must work with what one has.

DeRussy's men moved toward General Garay's headquarters at Waughutla, asking for directions and food from the villages along their way. The villagers were friendly enough, but on July 11, at the town of Tantayuka, DeRussy "perceived indications of uneasiness." The next morning, about eight miles from the town, the advance element of the column was ambushed by General Garay's troops, losing one captain (Boyd) and six enlisted men in the initial volleys. DeRussy pushed forward with his main body of troops and was able to break up the ambush, due mostly to the work of his one field piece under the direction of Capt. Francis Wyse.[34] But by the time the Mexicans broke off contact, six of the artillerymen had been wounded and the gun was down to its last three cartridges.

DeRussy realized at once that his mission to negotiate a prisoner release was negated and began to fall back toward Tantayuka. As the retrograde movement began, the American column was fired at on their flanks and rear by seemingly large numbers of Mexicans, who fortunately were keeping some distance away. The situation was precarious, however, and as the town of Tantayuka was approached, DeRussy found the Mexicans in force at the summit of a hill to his front. Captain Wyse, in the advance, sent his men forward to clear the road. With the gun now at the top of the hill, Wyse turned his gun rearward and, once all of the Americans has passed his position, fired two rounds of canister at the closely following Mexicans, effectively demoralizing the pursuers and stopping their pursuit.

On approaching the town, it was found that Mexican forces were already in possession. DeRussy's advance prepared to charge the town. Wyse's artillerymen moved their piece to a favorable position and fired their last round of canister into the Mexicans. This was followed immediately by a charge by the infantry, and the Mexicans dispersed.

DeRussy now held Tantayuka, and he posted his men on a high mound overlooking the town. While the Mexicans were gone, the men moved through the town looking for gunpowder, balls, and anything else that could be of use. As the expedition's ninety-mule pack train, along with all their provisions, had been stolen early in the fight, ammunition was in short supply. Makeshift canister shells were made for the field piece by filling champagne bottles with balls and dirt, and by dark the gun had ten new rounds ready, while each soldier had an average of nine rounds per musket. The men had also looted many of the homes in

---

34. Francis Octavus Wyse was a West Point graduate, class of 1833.

the town, justifying their actions by noting that the Mexicans had not warned them earlier of the fact that they were about to be ambushed.

While DeRussy's detachment regrouped in Tantayuka, they noted that large numbers of Mexicans could be seen moving to cut them off from Tampico. The Americans had noticed a very nice site for an ambush on the road before coming into Tantayuka and determined to retreat as soon as it was dark but to use a road other than the one that they had earlier used to come into the town. The plans to retreat were spoiled when Mexicans carrying a flag of truce entered the town at around 9:00 P.M. to ask for the surrender of the Americans to the forces of General Garay. This was followed by a very polite exchange between the two parties. DeRussy explained that he had no intention of surrendering, as he felt quite in control of the situation; he also was shocked that the Mexicans would attack his party considering the "friendly character" of his expedition. The Mexicans were equally diplomatic, regretting the incident and blaming it all on a misunderstanding of DeRussy's intentions, and arranged for General Garay himself to meet with DeRussy at 10:00 that night. Midnight came and went, but Garay never appeared. At 2:00 A.M. on July 13, with a rain falling, DeRussy broke camp, and it was not until 9:00 that morning that the Mexicans were again on his flanks and rear. The Mexicans pursued for some fifty miles but never seriously threatened the column. DeRussy had lost twelve men killed, four severely or mortally wounded, and two missing.[35] Captain Wyse was breveted for his gallantry in the fight at Calaboso River.[36]

The Louisianians would remain in Mexico for another year, but this would be their only combat of the war. The rest of their time was spent involved in public works around Tampico. DeRussy's engineering expertise was put to use in making a feasibility report on cutting a two-mile-long channel across a marsh that allowed steamers to go some hundred

35. These figures are from DeRussy's official report, which included the names of the casualties. Another newspaper article reported 20 killed, 10 wounded, and 2 missing. DeRussy estimated the Mexican losses at around 200, while the newspaper article called for 150 Mexican dead and 120 wounded. The author's experience with Civil War reports of enemy "estimated losses" would lead him to believe that the actual Mexican losses was probably very much lower than that. DeRussy report in *Le Courrier de la Louisiane*, Aug. 2, 1847, and "Colonel DeRussy's Battle," *Le Courrier de la Louisiane*, July 22, 1847, both in *HMDLM, 1847*.

36. In his 1855 letter to Cullum, DeRussy seemed a bit peeved that while his subordinate in the battle received a promotion, he never got so much as a "complimentary order, or any other notice."

miles up the Tampico River, opening the port to inland trade. The report being completed, DeRussy then modified a boat into a channel cutter and over a one month period dug out the channel using the boat's submerged propeller. The collector of customs in Tampico reported that the new channel increased the port's revenues by $120,000. During his tenure at Tampico, DeRussy also served as chief of police, justice of the peace, storekeeper at the custom house, and various other assorted titles.

In July 1848, DeRussy's Regiment returned to New Orleans. Disease and hardship had been unkind to the unit, as Governor Isaac Johnson addressed his welcoming remarks to "the remnant of that brave band who went to Mexico." DeRussy's veterans probably chafed at their presence at the governor's speech—one newspaper reported that "Col. De Russy's Regiment did not present as fine an appearance as we might have expected; but this was owing to the fact that some of the companies had been discharged, and were necessarily collected together indiscriminately for the occasion."[37]

DeRussy returned to civilian life and his occupation as a civil engineer. He was promoted to major general in the state militia, and in 1851 he was elected to the Louisiana House of Representatives. His term there ended in 1853, at which time he was elected to the state senate. Not content with serving only at the state level, DeRussy also served as the Natchitoches Parish assessor in 1854. But engineering seemed to be his true love, and his primary work was in that field. He made surveys of different sections of the Red and Ouachita Rivers, including an 1853 survey of the Red River rapids at Alexandria that would be used by Union officers during the Civil War.[38] Had his plans for a channel through the rapids at Alexandria been completed before the war, the Red River Campaign might have had a drastically different outcome.

DeRussy's reputation as an engineer took him to jobs throughout the state, and in 1858 he presented the legislature with a *Special Report Relative to the Cost of Draining the Swamp Lands Bordering on Lake Pontchartrain*. DeRussy's "imaginative" work detailed a long-term plan

37. *Weekly Picayune,* July 10, 1848, in *HMDLM 1847–48 Supplement.* One can imagine in what section of New Orleans the recently discharged men were found. One hesitates to think of their reaction to being told they were needed for an appearance in a ceremony, and of their condition upon their arrival at said ceremony. And one can only hope, for the reporter's sake, that none of them later came upon the reporter who disparaged their appearance.

38. One copy of DeRussy's 1853 survey is in the Library of Congress, where it is incorrectly identified as an 1864 map.

for the recovery of silt from Mississippi River floodwaters and its use to build up adjacent swamplands though a series of levees and holding basins or, alternately, through a series of pumping plants with leveed enclosures and internal drainage systems. A 1947 article concerning DeRussy's plan explained that its implementation was prevented by the outbreak of the Civil War, "but later the drainage plans of the city of New Orleans were extended to this area and basically similar plans were devised and carried out. . . . His designs for levees and drains, while by no means original, stimulated much thinking and later served as an example for marshland reclamation efforts. His plan for using the silt load of the Mississippi River in a land development program was doubtless impractical in detail but had much to recommend it in essence." But while DeRussy's plan may have been impractical in 1947, a similar system of silt recovery was used successfully during the Red River Waterway projects of the 1980s.[39]

In addition to his engineering and political activities, DeRussy was also something of a riverman. In 1858, he was "granted the privilege of operating a steam ferry for a period of ten years" at Grand Ecore, with an allowance for the substitution of a flat boat for the steamboat during low water periods.[40]

Being the political creature that he was, there can be no question that Lewis DeRussy was involved in the debate over secession that swelled over the land as the 1860s arrived. But there is no recording of DeRussy's opinion on the subject. Given his diplomatic nature, and the fact that he still had family ties in the North, it is hard to imagine that he did not push for Louisiana to maintain her ties with the United States. But when secession occurred, DeRussy had to make the choice. Would he stay with the land of his birth, a land to which he had given over twenty-nine years of active military service, or would he emulate his father and throw his lot with a new nation seeking to throw off the yoke of an oppressive mother country? We will never know what deliberations went into DeRussy's decision or whether his choice was easy or hard. Surely there were good arguments for both sides. But in the end, DeRussy chose to serve his adopted state. In May 1861, he left his

39. Robert W. Harrison and Walter M. Kollmorgen, "Drainage Reclamation in the Coastal Marshlands of the Mississippi River Delta," *Louisiana Historical Quarterly* 30, no. 2 (Apr. 1947): 667–69.
40. Hardin, *Northwestern Louisiana*, 488. No record could be found of whether the ferry ever operated.

position as commanding general of the Fourth Division of the Louisiana Militia and was elected colonel of the 2nd Louisiana Infantry Regiment. The unit left New Orleans for Virginia on May 11 and arrived in Richmond on May 16. Shortly thereafter, the regiment moved to Yorktown, where Colonel DeRussy got a surprise that he no doubt received with mixed emotions.

When the war broke out, U.S. forces had maintained control of Fort Monroe, Virginia, at the tip of a narrow peninsula. They could be supplied from the sea but were cut off from the rest of Virginia by Confederate troops at Yorktown, astride that peninsula only a few miles up from the fort. When the 2nd Louisiana became a part of that blocking force, Colonel DeRussy found that he was stationed only a short distance away from his older brother, René. There was one problem, though. René was a lieutenant colonel in the U.S. Army, stationed inside Fort Monroe.

René Edward DeRussy had a military career every bit as illustrious as that of his younger brother. He had entered West Point in 1807 and graduated in 1812. He participated in several battles in the War of 1812 and was breveted to the rank of captain for "gallant conduct" at the Battle of Plattsburgh, New York. When that war ended, he began a lengthy term as a military engineer. He was involved in the building and improvements to many of the early coastal defenses of the budding young nation, in New York, Virginia, and on the Gulf and Pacific Coasts. He served as superintendent of West Point from 1833 to 1838, and by 1861, with an astounding fifty-four years of active duty under his belt, René DeRussy was second in seniority only to Brig. Gen. Joseph Totten in the U.S. Army Corps of Engineers. May 1861 found René at Fortress Monroe, in charge of the defenses there.

Family legend, buttressed by contemporary accounts, suggest that somehow the two brothers met. Supposedly, the meeting ended with the two men doing the only honorable thing that they could. While the Civil War may have been a war of "brother against brother" to some, the DeRussy boys would have none of that. But at the same time, they were both professional soldiers whose honor demanded that they serve their respective countries. There was only one solution, of course—both men would continue to serve as their consciences demanded, but they would put as much distance as they could between the two of them so that they would not have to face each other in combat. Lewis resigned his colonelcy of the 2nd Louisiana on July 19, 1861, and by July 30 he was serving as chief engineer on the staff of Maj. Gen. Leonidas Polk at

Fort Pillow, Tennessee.[41] René next shows up on the record in San Francisco, California, in November 1861 as engineering officer in charge of the West Coast defenses. The brothers' paths would never again cross, but their sons would not be so lucky. Capt. George Birch DeRussy (Lewis's son), of Louisiana's Washington Artillery, was seriously wounded at the Battle of Malvern Hill in 1862. His cousin, Gustavus Adolphus DeRussy (René's son), also fought in that battle as a Union artillery officer.[42]

While serving with General Polk in Tennessee, DeRussy was "demoted" a notch and served on the general's staff as his chief engineer with the rank and pay of major. This demotion did not seem to affect the regard which was felt for DeRussy, for it was while serving with General Polk that Lewis first had a fort named for him.

In September 1861, Brig. Gen. Gideon Pillow seized Columbus, Kentucky, a very touchy move from a political standpoint because Kentucky was a neutral state. After the seizure, Polk fortified the high bluffs at Columbus that overlooked the Mississippi River. The river was blocked by a huge chain, supposed to have been more than a mile in length, and earthworks were built at the top of the bluffs. The largest of these works was christened Fort DeRussy. When the Confederate camp just across the river from the fort at Belmont, Missouri, was attacked by Brig. Gen. Ulysses S. Grant's troops on November 7, 1861, the guns of Fort DeRussy engaged the Union troops there.

DeRussy's seniority in age, if not in rank, required him at times to serve as a mediator as well as an engineer. Generals Polk and Pillow were both strong-willed men, with Polk being the senior of the two officers. Shortly after Pillow seized Columbus, Polk directed Pillow to

41. Polk to Walker, July 30, 1861, *ORA* 4:376; St. John R. Liddell, *Liddell's Record,* edited by Nathaniel Hughes (Dayton, Ohio: Morningside House, 1985), original typescript in Louisiana Historical Association Collection, Howard-Tilton Memorial Library, Tulane Univ., New Orleans, 1866; *Mobile Daily News* article, undated but probably 1865, quoted in Steven Sheppard Papers (private collection). On July 15, 1861, just prior to DeRussy's resignation as regimental commander, U.S. general Benjamin Butler reported that DeRussy was killed in a skirmish between 150 men of the 2nd Louisiana and 25 men of the 9th New York Infantry. The report was in error. Butler to Scott, July 15, 1861, *ORA* 2:741.

42. One descendant told me that differences in allegiances led to bad blood between the two branches of the family that continued on into the early 1900s. At last accounting, everyone is getting along fine. Gustavus would leave the war with the rank of brigadier general of volunteers. René was promoted to brigadier general on his deathbed in 1865, in appreciation for fifty-nine years of service to his country.

issue an order putting the town under martial law. Pillow objected to the order on the grounds that it was unnecessary, as the people of the town were friendly to the Confederates and the issuance of such an edict would anger the citizens while doing nothing to enhance Pillow's control over them. He then continued his argument on philosophical grounds, telling Polk that "martial law was the organization adopted and enforced by the Lincoln Government and Army; that it was the expedient of tyrants and usurpers, and that the South had nowhere adopted it; that it was a violation of the constitutional rights of the citizen, and could only be justified by extreme necessity." Needless to say, Polk bristled at being called a Yankee tyrant by a subordinate officer and insisted that Pillow issue the order. Pillow continued to refuse, in such a manner as to further provoke Polk. As Pillow explained, "My opposition to the measure and my refusal to issue the order exasperated him beyond control; his rage exceeded anything I had ever seen in a *sane man*. He said he would show me whether his *subalterns* should dictate to him his orders." Finally, before the two men could come to blows, DeRussy stepped in and calmed them down, convincing Polk that the order might be ill advised.[43]

DeRussy's whereabouts are unrecorded after December 1861 until he reappears back home in Louisiana in October 1862. But Lewis's younger brother John does appear on the public record during that blank period. Sometime after serving as sheriff of Natchitoches Parish in 1839, John DeRussy had moved with his family to Baton Rouge, and he was living there with his family in August 1862. Baton Rouge was the scene of a major battle early in that month, which was accompanied by a severe shelling of the town by Union gunboats. Many of the citizens, including the duly elected city officials, left for less hostile environments at that time. When the U.S. troops stationed in the town were attacked again on August 20, the Union gunboats *Essex* and *Itasca* shelled the area for about two hours, driving back the Confederates. Nonetheless, the Union troops occupying the town evacuated the city on August 21, leaving the place to the few remaining inhabitants. On the morning of the twenty-second, a public meeting was held in the town, with John DeRussy serving as chairman. His first duty was to appoint a committee of three men to go out to *Itasca* and find out the commander's intentions in regard to the now open city. The three returned with assurances that the town

43. Pillow to Benjamin, Jan. 16, 1862, *ORA* 3:314.

would not be shelled if the Rebel army would not enter the city or make any "demonstrations of a hostile nature" against the Union naval forces in the river. Another meeting was held that afternoon, at which time John DeRussy was elected provisional mayor of Baton Rouge.[44] The younger DeRussy brother's reign was short-lived, however, as no record of his tenure exists in the Baton Rouge mayor's office.[45]

Apparently, early 1862 passed uneventfully for Lewis, but by November his talents were once again in demand by his government. In late October, DeRussy accompanied Gen. Richard Taylor on an excursion down Red River to "examine and select a site for the construction of a work for the defense of that river." By the end of November, work had begun under DeRussy's supervision on the fortifications at Barbin's Landing near Marksville. With the abandonment of the fort in May 1863, DeRussy's work there ended.[46]

With the loss of Fort DeRussy and the occupation of Alexandria by U.S. forces in May, the defense of the Red River automatically moved upstream. Although perhaps not actually a fort—it was debated years later in the local newspapers whether there had ever been a Confederate fort at Grand Ecore, and the general consensus was that there had not—the Confederates did construct some earthworks at Grand Ecore. Exactly what part DeRussy played in the construction of these works is unrecorded, but they were within shouting distance of his home.[47]

44. Reports on "Skirmish at and evacuation of Baton Rouge, La.," *ORA* 15:129–31. *Itasca* is identified only as gunboat No. 7 in these reports, with the boat being properly identified for the author by Tom Baskett.

45. John may not have stayed in Baton Rouge much longer. By early September, his daughters Estelle and Harriet were at their Uncle Lewis's house in Grand Ecore. It is unknown whether their father was with them.

46. DeRussy's niece, Emily, was incensed when she learned that the fort had been abandoned. On May 1, 1863, she confided to her diary, "We have been forced by panic and cowardice of our militia troops to evacuate 'Fort DeRussy.'"

47. These earthworks still exist as of this writing, and the U.S. Corps of Engineers has recently built a Visitors Center at the site. Maj. Thomas O. Benton, of Benton's Bell Battery, claims to have surrendered Fort DeRussy to the Federals on June 4, 1865. At that time, Benton and his men were stationed at Grand Ecore, so at least some people considered this site to be another of the many Forts DeRussy. R. W. Oglesby, "More Grand Ecore History is Recited by Phanor Breazeale," scrapbook clipping from Natchitoches, La., newspaper, Oct. [1929], Cammie G. Henry Collection, Northwestern State Univ. Archives, Natchitoches, La.; Thm. O. Benton to Joseph Anderson, June 14, 1904, Virginia Military Institute Archives, Lexington, Va.; Arthur W. Bergeron Jr., *Guide to Louisiana Confederate Military Units, 1861–1865* (Baton Rouge: Louisiana State Univ. Press, 1989), 22.

When work recommenced on the "real" Fort DeRussy in December 1863, Lewis DeRussy was no longer the chief engineer. That job was being capably handled by Maj. David Boyd. But DeRussy was not yet ready to be put out to pasture. He continued to serve as an engineering consultant on the fortifications and was present at the fort in December; he was found there again in January 1864, giving advice to Boyd on modifications to the earthworks. It was DeRussy's concurring opinion that encouraged David Boyd to use iron to cover the bombproofs in the fort, which led to Major Douglas's recall of slaves headed to work at the fort in January.[48]

Contrary to rumors, DeRussy was not killed at the fort when it was captured.[49] His whereabouts during the Red River Campaign are subject to speculation. When Union gunboats arrived at Grand Ecore on April 3, 1864, two Confederate officers were seen riding along the road. The men, one of whom may or may not have been Lewis DeRussy, were observed to dismount and enter the DeRussy home. By order of Admiral Porter, aboard USS *Cricket,* a percussion shell from a 100-pounder Parrott gun was fired at the house. As the men aboard the boat watched, the shell sailed just over the roof of the house and exploded a short distance beyond.[50]

In the period after the initial shelling of the house, the Union navy seems to have been much more considerate of the well-being of the DeRussy family. Capt. William Hoel of the gunboat *Pittsburgh,* along with Capt. Elias Owen of the gunboat *Louisville,* made a social call at the DeRussy home that same night.

With the Union defeat at Mansfield and the retreat of that army to Grand Ecore, the area around the DeRussy house was soon an immense armed camp. Over a mile of earthworks were built around the village—these with no assistance from DeRussy. But by the end of April, the Federals had abandoned their plans of conquest and were back in Alexandria, eagerly awaiting a rise in the river so that they could leave that part of the state. Although the army burned and looted

---

48. Liddell, *Liddell's Record;* Boyd to Taylor, Jan. 17, 1864, *ORA* 34, pt. 2, 893.

49. A 1991 letter from Betty (Mrs. Hugh) Walmsley to the Confederate Resource Center in Hillsboro, Texas, indicates that the story of DeRussy's death at the fort comes from a WPA Writer's Project report.

50. Deck log, USS *Cricket,* Apr. 3, 1864, RG 24, NA; Church diary, 42. The log and the Church diary disagree on the time of the incident. The log has the shot being fired at 1:00 P.M., while Church maintains that *Cricket* arrived at Grand Ecore at 1:30 and fired on the house at 4:00 P.M. Log entries from other boats concur with *Cricket*'s time frame.

all the way back, the towns of Grand Ecore and Natchitoches were for the most part unharmed. The DeRussy house still stood.[51]

Lewis DeRussy's military duties ended with the departure of the Yankee army from Grand Ecore. But his retirement would be short-lived. On Friday evening, December 16, 1864, while at his home on the bluff overlooking the river, DeRussy had a meal of spiced beef. He retired to bed and awoke feeling ill around 10:00 P.M.. He died at midnight. On the seventeenth, Emily DeRussy Brandt Russell noted in her diary: "What a void in our family circle! Uncle dead. How sudden—in perfect health a few hours since and now in Eternity! before the great Jehovah. this to be hoped He can say unto him 'Come, thou faithful servant unto the Joy of the Lord.' Surely, 'in the midst of Life we are in Death.' May we take this bereavement as a solemn warning, and be ready when our call comes." Emily blamed the death on indigestion.[52] Modern doctors would be more prone to blame a heart attack.

On Sunday morning, December 17, 1864, Lewis Gustave DeRussy was laid to rest in the Russell family cemetery on the hill above the family home at Grand Ecore. His cypress coffin was lined with fabric and trimmed in lace, and he was wearing a red and white cotton waistcoat with elaborate porcelain and gold button studs down the front, as befit a man of his stature.[53]

When Lewis DeRussy was born, George Washington was president of the United States, a country then in its infancy. At the time of his death, Abraham Lincoln was president of the United States and the Confederate States was in its death throes. In so many ways, an era had ended.

Lewis DeRussy: The Second Going

An era had ended, but the story of Lewis DeRussy had not. There is an interesting, and totally unplanned, tradition of sorts with Lewis DeRussy and some of his closest relatives. Lewis's first wife, Elizabeth Claire Boerum, was buried in the Fort Jesup cemetery in 1836. In 1907, her remains, along with those of her sister and twenty-five unknown

51. The Russell house (it never actually belonged to DeRussy but was his second wife's property) burned in 1888.
52. Emily DeRussy Russell diary, Hunter Collection, Henry Research Center.
53. Jenna Tedrick Kuttruff, "Col. DeRussy's Coffin Lining and Burial Waistcoat" (paper presented at Louisiana Archaeological Society Annual Meeting, Baton Rouge, La., Feb. 2000).

soldiers from that cemetery, were removed to the Alexandria National Cemetery in Pineville. Lewis's older brother, René Edward DeRussy, was buried in San Francisco, California, when he died in 1865. In 1907, his body was disinterred and moved to the cemetery of the U.S. Military Academy at West Point, New York, where he had served as superintendent. The astute reader might now see a pattern forming.[54]

One of the first steps taken in the rehabilitation of Fort DeRussy was some serious research into the history of the fort. In the process of doing this research, it was found that very little was known about the man for whom the fort was named.[55] Most accounts only stated that DeRussy was "a planter from Natchitoches." With that information as a starting point, the author made a trip to the archives at Northwestern State University at Natchitoches, where he found a helpful librarian who told him of the location of the Russell-DeRussy Cemetery at Grand Ecore and provided a detailed plat of the graveyard.[56] A visit to the graveyard that same afternoon revealed that all but one of the gravestones in the cemetery had been destroyed, but the plat showed clearly which of the graves was that of DeRussy. The cemetery itself was in shambles—headstones and a wrought-iron fence broken and missing and most of the graves showing signs of having been dug into over the years. The graveyard's isolated location, along with rumors of large amounts of buried gold, had obviously proven too tempting to some of the less morally encumbered individuals of the area. Fortunately, DeRussy's grave was protected by a brick vault, and the excavations at that grave extended only slightly below ground level. The grave seemed basically intact. But the dishevelment in that lonesome little graveyard on that gray January afternoon in 1996 planted the germ of an idea.

By late 1998, the idea had grown from a germ into a plan. The fort was now looking really good, and the cemetery at Grand Ecore was, if

54. The removal of remains from Fort Jesup occurred between 1907 and 1913. Hardin, *Northwestern Louisiana,* 192; Alexandria National Cemetery records. René DeRussy's removal came about as a result of his widow's desire to be buried next to her husband, which could not be done in the Laurel Hill Cemetery in San Francisco. DeRussy died in 1865 at age seventy-three. For his widow to have still been alive in 1907, forty-two years after his death, is noteworthy. Post Cemetery Records, 1816–1908, Special Collections and Archives, U.S. Military Academy Library, West Point, N.Y.

55. It was later found that some descendants knew a great deal about Lewis DeRussy, but their information was not found in any writings about the fort.

56. The author was accompanied on this trip by Randy Decuir, editor of the Avoyelles Parish newspapers. The helpful librarian was Mary Linn Wernet.

anything, looking worse than it had two years earlier. With the blessings and permission of several of DeRussy's descendants and the owners of the cemetery, a court order was obtained by the Friends of Fort DeRussy to have DeRussy's remains disinterred and moved to the grounds of the fort that bore his name. On a hot August day in 1999, the disinterment began.

The original plans had called for the remains to be removed by members of the Sons of Confederate Veterans, but a few weeks prior to the event, Dr. Tommy Ike Hailey and his team of archaeologists from the Cultural Resource Office at Northwestern State University (NSU) in Natchitoches volunteered for the job. Their offer was gratefully accepted, and it proved a godsend. The archaeologists arrived at the site before sunrise on August 7, 1999. They began carefully measuring and digging around the brick coping of the grave, and as the day wore on, a crowd of onlookers gathered. The pace of the archaeologists was painstakingly slow and frustrating to all of those watching. The job was to have been finished in one day, but by noon the diggers were only a few inches below ground level. Every piece of brick, every inconsistency in the ground, was closely examined. All dirt removed from the grave was screened for artifacts. When Hailey finally sent one of his workers down to the truck for a pick, the bystanders heaved a sigh of relief. At last, they thought, they are going to start digging. When the worker returned with a dental pick, the visitors knew it was going to be a long day. And a hot one. With the temperature approaching one hundred degrees by the end of the day, the conditions in the hole—after it finally became a hole—were brutal. A tarp was stretched over the work site, but the heat was debilitating. A little after 8:00 P.M., with darkness descending, the archaeologists called it a day. The grave was half dug; the crew agreed to return and finish the job the following day.

Digging began again at sunrise on Sunday, with one digger missing, the result of heat exhaustion the day before. By 2:00 P.M., Hailey and his crew were convinced that they had been bamboozled. The bottom of the grave was only inches away, and a core had been taken down to virgin earth, with no sign of a body or coffin. An old letter in the archives at NSU said that DeRussy's body had been moved to the National Cemetery with his wife, but that letter had always been discounted, as all other evidence pointed to DeRussy still being in his original grave. Now Hailey was wondering if there was something to the letter. Still, all indications were that the grave had never been disturbed much below ground level. Though disheartened, the archaeologists continued to dig.

The temperature once again hovered around the one-hundred-degree mark, and there was no hint of a breeze at the bottom of the grave, four feet below ground level. Around 3:00 P.M., a buzz of excitement filled the area. The diggers' trowels had reached bottom, finding a discolored spot. Closer examination revealed minute bone fragments embedded near the area.

"Ashes to ashes, dust to dust" had never been more true than in this case. The highly acidic soil of Grand Ecore had returned Lewis DeRussy to the earth. Several small bone fragments were recovered, along with a few buttons, coffin fragments and nails, and cloth remnants. Dr. Mark J. Hartmann of the University of Arkansas at Little Rock, serving as a consultant to the NSU archaeologists, commented that of the four hundred disinterments that he had observed, he had seen only one other instance in which remains had so totally disintegrated. With darkness nearing, the entire bottom inch of the grave was bagged and tagged as to location within the grave and brought to a van for transportation back to the lab at NSU.

It was now time to refill the grave. The diggers did not want anyone else to have to undergo the emotional roller coaster that they had been on for the past few hours, so they left a message for any future gravediggers. At the bottom of the grave, they left a plastic bag with a 1999 coin enclosed. They also placed several recovered graveyard bricks in the bottom of the hole—lined up neatly to spell out *NSU*.[57] The grave was then filled and returned to its predig condition. Dark settled as the crew left the site.

With the reburial scheduled for September 26, there was no time for dawdling. There was little over a month in which to obtain any information possible from the artifacts recovered from the grave, and the archaeologists immediately began a careful examination of their findings. Back in the lab, all of the grave dirt was carefully sifted for identifiable items—bone fragments, coffin fragments, cloth, buttons, and miscellaneous bits all had to be scrutinized. The coffin wood was sent to Louisiana Tech and identified as bald cypress. The Louisiana State University Textile Museum matched the clothing fragments to similar garments in their collection, and despite the small amount of material recovered, it was able to deliver a good description of the general's burial clothes.

---

57. That was their only payment for two days of extreme labor. In addition to Dr. Hailey, the other members of the digging team were Dr. George Avery; graduate students Jason Lott, Brian Cable, and Brian Cockrell; and undergraduate Caleb Johnson.

Activity continued on other fronts as well. Alfred Cook of Kramer Funeral Home in Alexandria was also a member of the Sons of Confederate Veterans (SCV), and he had been intimately involved with the funeral preparations from the start. His father, a woodworker of some repute, immediately began construction of a beautiful handcrafted nineteenth-century style coffin for the general's remains. Alfred handled all of the administrative details of the funeral and coordinated with other members of the SCV who planned on participating in the funeral.

The situation down at Fort DeRussy was equally hectic. A grave site had to be chosen, an honor guard arranged, pallbearers named, family and dignitaries invited, a parking lot created, and numerous minor and major obstacles overcome.

The whole situation was nearly brought to a screeching halt when one elderly descendant of the general came forward and announced that the exhumed remains were not those of Lewis DeRussy. She claimed to have visited Lewis DeRussy's grave frequently as a child, in a cemetery just outside of New Orleans. But the evidence available proved overwhelmingly that the right remains had been recovered, so the preparations continued. (In 2001, I located the grave in question, in the DeRussy family plot in Greenwood Cemetery, Metairie, Louisiana. It was the grave of Lewis DeRussy's grandson and namesake, who died at age fifteen in 1886.)

That was not the only problem to arise. When Fort Polk was asked if they could provide an honor guard to fire a salute for this veteran who had served as a U.S. soldier for more than twenty-nine years, the personnel handling honor guards responded enthusiastically. The one-month notification they were given was about thirty days more than they usually got, and the organizers were told that the Fort Polk Honor Guard was excited at the prospect of attending the funeral. This news did not go over quite so well with an extremist element from one SCV chapter, whose commander told the funeral organizer that an honor guard of U.S. soldiers was unacceptable at a Confederate officer's funeral, and that his men would not attend if that honor guard was present. As problems went, this one was perhaps the most easily solved. The funeral organizer, a former Marine Corps officer, immediately told that group's commander that if he felt that this created a problem, then he and anyone else who felt that way should stay away from the funeral. The commander at once took a more conciliatory position. Ironically, a few days later the army honor guard backed out of their agreement, claiming their attendance was necessary at a suddenly announced change-of-command

Mallory Mayeux, portraying DeRussy's niece Emily, mourns his second passing at his 1999 wake at the Marksville Fire Station Annex. (Photograph by author.)

ceremony, but their claim had a hollow ring to it. Sadly, it seems that there were bigots on both sides of the fence.

Generally, however, cooperation was the rule. Louisiana State University's Pershing Rifles, an elite ROTC unit, quickly agreed to replace the Fort Polk honor guard. Pallbearers consisted of two reenactors from each of the wars in which DeRussy had served—the National Park Service's Chalmette Battlefield unit provided War of 1812 reenactors, State Parks' Fort Jesup State Historic Site provided Mexican War reenactors, and the Alexandria SCV unit provided Civil War reenactors. A farmer next door to the fort sold the fort two acres of soybeans, which were plowed under, and the field was then steamrolled by the Louisiana National Guard to make a parking lot. The city of Marksville, which was having its 190th birthday celebration the weekend of the funeral, invited funeral attendees to their Birthday Parade and volunteered their fire station annex as a makeshift funeral parlor—even though this required a slight schedule change, as one of the firemen on duty the night of the wake refused to "sleep in a building with a dead man."

The remains were brought from NSU to Kramer Funeral Home on September 23 by two NSU students.[58] All identifiable remains and

---

58. The students bringing the remains to Alexandria were Dustin Fuqua and Paul Decuir. Decuir was wearing his National Guard uniform at the time, so in effect, DeRussy had a military escort to the funeral home. In 2003, Paul Decuir participated in Operation Iraqi Freedom, the U.S. invasion of Iraq.

Over three hundred people turned out for Lewis DeRussy's September 1999 interment at Fort DeRussy. (Photograph by author.)

about eighty pounds of dirt were left there to be placed in the coffin for burial. The grave dirt in excess of that eighty pounds was placed in the bottom of the new grave at Fort DeRussy on September 24.

The remains of Lewis DeRussy lay in state at the Marksville Fire Station Annex and were visited by some three hundred "mourners" through the afternoon and night of September 25. Sunday morning, September 26, 1999, dawned cloudy with the threat of rain in the air. The funeral cortege left the fire station promptly at 10:15 A.M., escorted by every police car in Marksville and trailing back for a mile behind the hearse. The procession slowly made its way the three miles up to the head of Fort DeRussy Road, where the coffin was transferred from the funeral home's hearse to a horse drawn wagon. Escorted by descendants and reenactors, the wagon proceeded the final quarter mile to the fort.

It was a spectacle worthy of Lewis DeRussy. The fort grounds were carpeted by over three hundred spectators who had come to see the famed warrior, statesman, and family man buried in a fitting place of honor. The reenactors were interspersed with visitors in their normal Sunday clothes. Eight descendants of Lewis DeRussy were present at the service. An Episcopal priest conducted the religious rites, a brief recitation of DeRussy's accomplishments was given, and an excerpt from Emily DeRussy Brandt Russell's diary, mourning the loss of her uncle, was read. Artillery and rifle salutes were fired, and as "Taps" was played by a lone bugler and the coffin flag was presented to Deborah

DeRussy Caraway, DeRussy's
remains were lowered into a
vault near the northeast corner
of the Main Redoubt.[59]

The solemn affair was not
without its humorous moment.
An audible outburst erupted
from the crowd as the coffin began lowering into the ground.
The handcrafted coffin had
been admired by hundreds of
people for the past two days, and
apparently many in the audience thought it was too beautiful to bury and had believed
that the general's remains would
actually be put on display at
the fort's museum when it was
built.[60] A murmur of disbelief
swept through the crowd when
some people apparently realized
for the first time that this was a
real funeral and burial. Perhaps
the presence of so many reenactors confused them, but this
was no reenactment.

To conclude the ceremony,
onlookers were invited to pass
by the grave and throw in a
handful of dirt, fulfilling the

A rare sight. The fresh grave of a man
who was born when George Washington
was president. (Photograph by author.)

59. The descendants were Myles DeRussy Jr.; his daughter, Valerie Jenkins, and her
children, Laura and Steven Jenkins; Deborah DeRussy Caraway; Steven Sheppard; Husted
DeRussy; and Bill Hughes. The officiating priest was Rev. Joseph Bordelon. The eulogy
was given by Steve Mayeux, and the diary entry read by Mallory Mayeux. "Taps" was
played by Wanda Clark, the artillery salute was handled by the Cenla Historical Reenactors Society, and the rifle salute was fired by member of Louisiana State University's Pershing Rifles. The funeral director was Alfred Cook Jr.

60. The coffin was built by Alfred Cook Sr., a respected cabinetmaker in the Alexandria area and father of the funeral director.

biblical admonition to "bury the dead." Everyone participated, and as the crowd drifted off, a few hard core DeRussy enthusiasts stayed behind to finish filling the grave.

Lewis DeRussy's final remains now lie beneath a granite obelisk on the grounds of the fort that bears his name.[61] May he rest in peace.

And this *is* the end of this story.

61. The obelisk design chosen by Vickie Mayeux, my wife, was based on a marker over the grave of Isaac R. Adams in the Greenwood Cemetery in Pineville. After the marker had been chosen, it was discovered that Adams had served as a coal heaver aboard the Confederate gunboats *Webb, Missouri,* and *Cotton,* all of which were intimately involved with Fort DeRussy.

Appendix B

Lewis G. DeRussy's Military Career

Born September 17, 1795, New York City

Cadet at U.S. Military Academy, West Point, New York, April 14, 1813–
   March 11, 1814
   (Promoted to third lieutenant, 1st Artillery, March 22, 1814)
   (Promoted to second lieutenant, 1st Artillery, May 1, 1814)

Transferred to Corps of Artillery, May 12, 1814

Acting assistant engineer in erecting temporary defenses for New York City
   and environs during the War of 1812, 1814–15

In garrison, New York Harbor, 1815–16

Battalion adjutant of artillery, November 1, 1816–May 20, 1819
   (Promoted to first lieutenant, artillery corps, May 20, 1818)

Surveyor and topographer of commission to establish the northern boundary
   of the United States under the Treaty of Ghent, 1819–21

In garrison, commanding Samuel B. Archer's Company of Artillery, Fort
   Moultrie, South Carolina, 1821
   (1st lieutenant, 3rd Artillery, in reorganization of army, June 1, 1821)

Topographical duty under Col. John J. Abert, January 14, 1822–May 1824

In garrison, commanding Archer's Company of Artillery, Fort Monroe,
   Virginia (Artillery School for Practice), 1824

Topographical duty, under Colonel Abert, June 4, 1824–December 11, 1825
   (Promoted to captain, 3rd Artillery, December 11, 1825)

In garrison, commanding Archer's Company of Artillery, Fort Monroe,
   Virginia (Artillery School for Practice), 1825–26
   (Major, staff–paymaster, September 21, 1826)

Paymaster for Red River posts, 1826–42

Dropped from rolls, July 26, 1842

Planter, Grand Ecore, Natchitoches Parish, Louisiana, 1842–46

Served in Mexican War, 1846–48

Elected colonel, 1st Louisiana Volunteers, December 23, 1846
    Shipwrecked on Mexican coast
    Completed defenses of Tampico, Mexico
    Opened new channel to the Rio Tamesi
    Engaged in combat, Rio Calabaza, July 12, 1847
    Engaged in Skirmish of Tantoyuca, July 1847
    Disbanded, July 10, 1848

Major general, Louisiana Militia, 1848–61

Civil engineer, 1848–61

Colonel, 2nd Louisiana Infantry, May 11, 1861–July 19, 1861

Major, on staff of Gen. Leonidas Polk, 1861–62

Superintendent of defenses of Red River, November 1862–May 1863

Civilian consultant to defenses of Red River, 1864

Died December 17, 1864

Appendix C

Commanding Officers of Fort DeRussy

Capt. John Kelso, ?–February 18, 1863

Lt. Col. William S. Lovell, February 18–20, 1863

Maj. William Mallory Levy, February 20–mid-March 1863

Lieut. Col. Aristide Gérard, mid-March–late April 1863

Fort abandoned, May–November 1863

Lieut. Col. William Byrd, December–March 14, 1864

Appendix D

Fort DeRussy Combat Casualties

Capture of *Queen of the West,* February 14, 1863

Confederate Losses: None

No losses known. Given the circumstances of the battle, there probably were none.

Union Losses: 1 Killed, About 50 Captured or Missing

KILLED

George Davis, supposed drowned

CAPTURED

1st Master James Thompson, wounded on Atchafalaya
River; died in Alexandria, February 26, 1863.
2nd Mate Cyrus Addison
3rd Mate Henry Duncan
David Taylor, engineer, scalded by steam
David S. Booth, surgeon
George W. Bailey, adjutant
Name unknown, blacksmith
George Andrews, carpenter
James Foster, carpenter
Pvt. John A. Bates, Mississippi Marine Brigade (MMB)
Pvt. William Brown, MMB
Pvt. Charles Faulkner, MMB
Pvt. Edward Hazleton, MMB
Pvt. George W. Hill, MMB
Pvt. L. C. Jarbon, MMB
Pvt. Charles Launer, MMB
Pvt. David McCullom, MMB
Pvt. Norton F. Rice, MMB
Pvt. Carroll Smith, MMB
Pvt. Thomas Williams, MMB

Finley Anderson, war correspondent for the *New York Herald*
About thirty Negroes

This list was compiled by "Bod" Bodman, a correspondent for the *Chicago Tribune*. Colonel Ellet reported twenty-four men taken prisoner in his official report. The body of a drowned soldier, which may or may not have been George Davis, was found downriver from the scene some time after the event, carrying a pipe with the name "Adams Butler" carved into it.

Gunboat Battle, May 4, 1863

Confederate Losses: 2 Killed, About 20 Wounded or Missing

CREW OF GUNBOAT *COTTON NO. 2*
Emile Dugas, engineer, scalded on face and neck
Sam Horsley (?), engineer, scalded slightly on shoulder
Wm. Turner (?), pilot, scalded slightly on shoulder and arm
Two or three black men supposedly drowned by jumping overboard
St. Martin Rangers, serving aboard Cotton No. 2
Pvt. Thomas Burns, knocked overboard by exploding shell and drowned
Pvt. John O'Quinn, knocked overboard by exploding shell and drowned
Lt. F. G. Burbank, slightly wounded in face and breast
Cpl. Alex Mills, slightly wounded in body
Pvt. Neville Guillory, wounded in head
Pvt. G. G. Walker, wounded in left side
Pvt. E. S. Fleurot, wounded in breast and neck
Pvt. E. J. Savage, wounded in hand
Pvt. Edward. Bourgouin, wounded in head

HUTTON'S ARTILLERY (CRESCENT ARTILLERY, COMPANY A), SERVING ABOARD *GRAND DUKE*
Sgt. A. Morais, slightly wounded
Cpl. John Muller, "blown up and wounded for life"
Pvt. G. F. Buckingham, seriously but not dangerously wounded
Pvt. Victor Casreno, seriously but not dangerously wounded
Pvt. Charles W. Heno, seriously but not dangerously wounded
Pvt. J. B. Poole, seriously but not dangerously wounded
Pvt. James Wallace, badly burned, lost one eye

Union Losses: 2 Killed, 4 Wounded

ABOARD USS *ALBATROSS*

Pilot Isaac B. Hamilton, killed by cannon ball
Seaman John W. Brown, killed by cannon ball
Pilot Archibald D. Merritt, hands ripped by splinters
Ordinary Seaman James Dunn, slightly wounded
Seaman George Fife, seriously wounded in thigh by cannon shot
Landsman Frank Vincent, slightly wounded

Capture of the Fort, March 14, 1864

Confederate Losses: 2–5 Killed, 4–7 Wounded, 317 Captured

KILLED IN ACTION

Pvt. John Clabby, Hutton's Artillery, hit in head by Minié ball
Pvt. Andrew Green, Company H, 18th Texas Infantry, killed as U.S. soldiers came over wall

WOUNDED

Capt. E. T. King, King's Artillery, struck in eye by metal fragment
Pvt. James E. Bane, Company H, 19th Texas Infantry, severely wounded
Pvt. John M. Nall, Company H, 19th Texas Infantry, gunshot wound to right shoulder

LIST OF PRISONERS CAPTURED AT FORT DERUSSY, LOUISIANA

Staff Officers
Lt. Col. William Byrd, 14th Texas, commanding, Fort DeRussy
Capt. James G. White, quartermaster (paroled June 4)
1st Lt. James F. Fuller, 1st Artillery, chief of artillery
1st Lt. William. L. S. Bringhurst, 1st Artillery, ordnance officer (paroled June 4)
2nd Lt. L. A. Denson, 14th Texas, acting post adjutant
2nd Lt. A. Turnbull, engineer (paroled June 4)

11th Texas Infantry, Company A
1st Lt. John C. Fall
2nd Lt. Joseph W. Little
3rd Lt. John N. Spinks
Sgt. Thomas Mooney
Sgt. E. N. Pool
Sgt. James S. Skillern

Cpl. Benjamin Herrarer
Cpl. William C. Lambert
Pvt. William W. Alvis
Pvt. William Amerson
Pvt. S. W. Armstrong
Pvt. Matteas Bascus
Pvt. Joseph F. Cordiway
Pvt. Leander Cordiway
Pvt. J. K. T. Ellis
Pvt. William J. Farthing
Pvt. James P. Fewell
Pvt. Robert C. Hagy
Pvt. W. R. Haldeman
Pvt. J. R. Hobbs
Pvt. William D. King
Pvt. Thomas W. Kooce
Pvt. John J. Koonce
Pvt. Charles A. Laraby
Pvt. B. H. Little
Pvt. John M. Little
Pvt. Needham Lowery
Pvt. David C. Mast
Pvt. J. R. McAnally
Pvt. Henry F. Mincheus
Pvt. A. S. Moore
Pvt. Joseph Mora
Pvt. Robert Mora
Pvt. J. M. Morrison
Pvt. George Morton
Pvt. Abner Pipes
Pvt. H. L. Rector
Pvt. Theophilus Rector
Pvt. James H. Scott
Pvt. Joseph C. Spurgeon
Pvt. J. K. P. Weedin
Pvt. G. B. Wyatt
Pvt. John S. Yates
Pvt. John Ybarbo
Pvt. Richard Ybarbo

13th Texas Dismounted Cavalry, Company E
Pvt. Elisha Gosnell, age twenty-five, admitted to St. Louis Hospital,
New Orleans, in May and June for intermittent fever and chronic
pneumonia

Pvt. Thomas P. Mathews, age twenty-one

Pvt. Littleton B. McBride, age thirty-three, admitted to St. Louis Hospital June24–July 7 for typhoid fever

Pvt. John W. Mitchell, age twenty-four, died May 24, 1864, of "congestion of the brain"; buried in Monument Cemetery, New Orleans, Lot 17

Pvt. John W. Piearcy, age twenty-five, admitted to St. Louis Hospital July 5–7

14th Texas Infantry, Company G

Capt. D. C. Laird

1st Sgt. J. B. Reilly

Sgt. J. P. Gallman

Sgt. W. H. Hix

Sgt. John Pinson

Cpl. J. W. Gilliam

Cpl. Newton Gilliam

Cpl. C. L. Hamil

Cpl. E. B. S. Turner

Pvt. Mark Crosby

Pvt. Edward Gilliam

Pvt. J. P. Gilliam

Pvt. Jasper N. Gilliam

Pvt. Y. W. Gober

Pvt. Noah Hollowell

Pvt. A. S. Holt

Pvt. William A. Holt

Pvt. James J. McCain

Pvt. John Mitchell

Pvt. J. C. Powell

16th Texas Infantry, Company E

Capt. G. T. Marold

1st Lt. A. F. Jordan

2nd Lt. Christoper H. Hahnke

Sgt. H. Bock

Sgt. William Buerger

Sgt. John Graborv

Sgt. William Hahnke

Sgt Friedrich Knispel

Cpl. William Bock

Cpl. Ch. Grimm

Cpl. H. Streckert

Pvt. H. Bosse

Pvt. William Bosse
Pvt. J. Emner
Pvt. Ch. Emshoff
Pvt. H. Emshoff
Pvt. J. Frieske
Pvt. C. Holht
Pvt. H. Klanke
Pvt. G. Krueger
Pvt. William Kuehn
Pvt. F. Lehde
Pvt. W. Lehde
Pvt. W. Remmert
Pvt. H. Rene
Pvt. Ch. Richter
Pvt. William Schoeffer
Pvt. H. Wilkening
Pvt. W. Wilkening
Pvt. L. Zeiss
Pvt. Allen Attebery, Company B
Pvt. Robert L. Harris, Company I
Pvt. M. V. New, Company A

17th Texas, Company E
Capt. Seth Mabry
Sgt. J. B. Eaker
Sgt. F. P. Epperson
Sgt. P. R. Smith
Cpl. Clinton Breazeal
Cpl. William M. White
Miles Barler, drummer
Pvt. J. K. Arant
Pvt. Henry Butry
Pvt. William Clark
Pvt. J. H. Davis
Pvt. R. M. Davis
Pvt. William Jasper Eccles
Pvt. John N. Entwistle
Pvt. Jesse Faid
Pvt. J. B. Hanna
Pvt. H. W. Harris
Pvt. Rufus Hinyard
Pvt. J. W. Larrimore
Pvt. Martikya Y. Owins
Pvt. Granville Pierce

Pvt. James Raines
Pvt. C. W. Smith
Pvt. Moses Smith
Pvt. Ryanheart Smith
Pvt. Henry Waller
Pvt. D. K. Williams
Pvt. J. F. Williams
Pvt. Floury Yarny
Pvt. E. Pope, musician
Pvt. E. Lousel, musician
Pvt. E. Ermel, musician
Pvt. James M. Harris, Company A
Pvt. G. W. Fellows, Company B
Pvt. W. W. Jones, Company B
Pvt. Henry C. Perry, Company D
Pvt. Sgt. T. A. Casbeer, Company G
Pvt. B. B. Perry, Company G
Pvt. B. A. Brundige, Company I
Pvt. J. W. Josselyn, Company K

18th Texas, Company H
Capt. Thomas W. Stephens
Sgt. G. W. Tucker
Sgt. William Henry Harrison Cope
Sgt. John Samuel Corley Porter
Sgt. John L. Patterson
Cpl. N. A. Seals
Cpl. E. N. Davis
Cpl. J. B. Ray
Pvt. J. B. Bellgard
Pvt. Jeremiah C. Clinton
Pvt. Joseph L. Deen
Pvt. John H. Freeman
Pvt. E. T. Jones
Pvt. Ant. Johnson
Pvt. John A. Johnson
Pvt. W. L. Montgomery
Pvt. Joseph Augustus Newberry
Pvt. M. V. Newman
Pvt. L. Y. Smith
Pvt. Thomas N. Steed
Pvt. Thomas G. Vines
Pvt. A. J. Worley

19th Texas, Company H
Capt. Harvey Alexander Wallace
1st Lt. John R. Brooks
2nd Lt. William E. Barksdale
Sgt. John N. Conner, sick, died in St. Louis Hospital July 7, 1864
Sgt. John L. Hull, smallpox, recovered
Sgt. Asa J. Parker, sick, recovered
Sgt. Thomas J. Riley, pneumonia, died in St. Louis Hospital May 30, 1864
Sgt. Benjamin F. Hays, smallpox, recovered
Cpl. Rice R. Turner
Cpl. T. P. Billingsley, chronic diarhhea, died in St. Louis Hospital June 9, 1864; buried in Cypress Grove Cemetery, Grave 230
Cpl. Charles G. Burns
Cpl. Pleasonton G. Conner, typhoid fever, died in St. Louis Hospital July 2, 1864; buried in Cypress Grove Cemetery, Grave 246
Cpl. Simeon S. Duncan
Pvt. James E. Bane, wounded in foot
Pvt. James Bradford
Pvt. Joseph C. Deason
Pvt. John T. Ghentry
Pvt. Marion H. Grimes
Pvt. Thomas C. Guthrie
Pvt. John H. Harper
Pvt. Daniel Madison Hays
Pvt. Green W. Holleman
Pvt. Thomas J. Hull, smallpox, recovered
Pvt. James M. Jones, smallpox, died at Jackson Barracks, June 27, 1864
Pvt. G. M. Kuykendall
Pvt. W. W. Lee
Pvt. Joseph B. McCarter, died of disease soon after release, August 22, 1864
Pvt. John M. Nall, gunshot wound to right shoulder
Pvt. John C. Patrick
Pvt. James Foy Peterson
Pvt. Jerome D. Smith
Pvt. Peter Wynn Stovall Stone, pneumonia and smallpox, died in St. Louis Hospital May 29, 1864
Pvt. William A. Strickland
Pvt. John R. Thompson
Pvt. Houston West, escaped in New Orleans, returned to unit

Pvt. Leonard T. Wood
Pvt. Jordan Reeves, Company A

22nd Texas, Company E
1st Lt. B. P. Stout
2nd Lt. George J. Ball
Sgt. William P. Brown
Sgt. Cornelius Bullock
Sgt. E. R. Miller
Sgt. John B. Sparkman
Cpl. J. Gave
Cpl. E. L. Townsend
Cpl. Enoch West
Pvt. Thomas Benton Boyd
Pvt. William T. Baldwin
Pvt. F. M. Kroue
Pvt. William B. Crabb
Pvt. Thomas Cummings
Pvt. J. Q. Dennis
Pvt. B. H. Ellis
Pvt. J. J. Knight
Pvt. J. T. Knight
Pvt. J. W. Patrick
Pvt. J. E. Pinson
Pvt. Robt. Rounsavill

28th Texas Dismounted Cavalry, Company D
Sgt. James W. Ivey
Pvt. Augustus H. Bonner
Pvt. B. C. Chamness
Pvt. William Choate
Pvt. William Henry Lowery
Pvt. John R. Mooney
Pvt. Thomas W. Scott
Pvt. E. N. Stevenson
Pvt. Morris Ward
Pvt. Joseph Woodward
Pvt. William C. Aydelott, Company I

Crescent Artillery, Company A (Hutton's Artillery)
2nd Lt. William Hervey
2nd Lt. Alex Assenheimer Jr.
Sgt. J. G. Dalton, took oath of allegiance July 7
Sgt. Abin Morais

Cpl. Charles Tate, paroled from St. Louis Hospital May 13 to the home of a friend, where he died that day

Pvt. A. Albright

Pvt. H. Anchor

Pvt. William Aymond

Pvt. John J. Barry, escaped from barracks hospital July 1

Pvt. Joseph Bernious (Burnicus?)

Pvt. Victor Casreno

Pvt. J. Darmody

Pvt. William Edwards

Pvt. Joseph Gerard, not exchanged on July 22; sent to Ship Island, Mississippi, October 5; sent to Elmira, New York, November 5

Pvt. L. Hubble, escaped from barracks hospital June 20

Pvt. Charles Keller

Pvt. John Krease, escaped from exchange boat July 21/22

Pvt. P. Lugenbuhl, not exchanged July 22; sent to Ship Island, Mississippi, October 5; forwarded to Elmira, New York, in November

Pvt. T. McLaughlin

Pvt. S. M. Morgan

Pvt. John Muller

Pvt. John C. Murray

Pvt. François Raphin

Pvt. Adolphe Rebouché

Pvt. L. Schoedel, escaped from exchange boat *Polar Star* April 10

Pvt. James Wallace

St. Martin Rangers (King's Artillery)

Capt. Edward T. King, St. Louis Hospital, March 22–April 5

2nd Lt. F. G. Burbank

2nd Lt. Michael Fogarty

Sgt. James Bellin

Sgt. Arthur Cook

Sgt. William A. Phillips, exchanged July 22; recaptured soon afterward and sent to Elmira, New York, in November; exchanged again and captured again near mouth of Red River in April 1865

4th Sgt. E. Whigham, smallpox, died at barracks hospital June 3; buried in Monument Cemetery

Cpl. Robert Fish, St. Louis Hospital June 27; died July 11

Cpl. W. C. Hardegree, not sent to New Orleans until July 10

Cpl. T. J. Walker

Pvt. James Allen

Pvt. J. C. Ayers

Pvt. J. C. Bishop

Pvt. Joseph Brouillette

Pvt. A. H. Brown, St. Louis Hospital Mar 25–Mar 30

Pvt. Michael Burke

Pvt. S. M. Burnett (Barnett?), St. Louis Hospital Mar 20–Apr 10;
  escaped from Barracks Hospital April 20

Pvt. Onezime Carriere

Pvt. Octave Comau, smallpox, died May 31

Pvt. John S. Folkes, St. Louis Hospital May 3

Pvt. Gerau Fontenot

Pvt. Hylaire P. Fontenot, St. Louis Hospital May 4, typhoid, died
  May 8

Pvt. R. Gillett

Pvt. N. D. Guillory

Pvt. R. J. Hankins, St. Louis Hospital May 6, died May 7

Pvt. P. R. Hymell, died July 30

Pvt. Andrew J. Johns, escaped May 16

Pvt. J. F. Lawrence, exchanged July 22; recaptured August 8
  in Tensas Parish; sent to Elmira, New York, in November;
  exchanged again in February 1865

Pvt. W. T. Long

Pvt. Oscar Magnon

Pvt. E. McCarthy

Pvt. P. H. Norman, St. Louis Hospital May 13–June 13

Pvt. Zedekia Parker, St. Louis Hospital May 4; barracks hospital
  May 5; admitted again June 23; returned to duty July 8

Pvt. Claiborne Paulk, St. Louis Hospital May 4, smallpox, died
  May 20

Pvt. Victor Pennison

Pvt. B. F. Quinn, St. Louis Hospital, June 6–July 21

Pvt. H. S. Reynard

Pvt. W. Riser

Pvt. L. Sandez, St. Louis Hospital June 6–20

Pvt. E. J. Savage, St. Louis Hospital March 25–April 30, and again
  May 6–July 3

Pvt. Jean Baptiste Savoy

Pvt. Thomas S. Singleton

Pvt. William Spencer, St. Louis Hospital May 25–June 13

Pvt. William Sutherland, barracks hospital, died June 23; buried in
  Monument Cemetery

Pvt. J. J. Taylor

Pvt. A. D. Theriot

Pvt. J. B. Theriot

Pvt. Thomas J. Toler (Tober?), St. Louis Hospital March 28; still
    under treatment May 31; signed oath of allegiance May 5
Pvt. F. Turbitt, St. Louis Hospital July 19–21, age fifty
Pvt. John A. Worrel
Pvt. N. H. Young

Red River Sharpshooters, Company A (Cassidy's Cavalry)
Pvt. G. W. Price
Pvt. Edward Smith
Pvt. Lewis J. Timms

Miscellaneous Individuals
Pvt. I. T. Feurl, 11th Louisiana Infantry, Company A, died St. Louis
    Hospital July 22
Pvt. Abraham Mayeux, 18th Louisiana Infantry
Pvt. John Robertson, 3rd Louisiana Cavalry, Company H

Union Losses

In eight different recorded reports there are seven different casualty figures
listed, ranging from thirty-four to fifty-one U.S. casualties. The figure of seven
killed and forty-four wounded is perhaps the most accurate. The losses break
down as listed below. It will be noted that the numbers do not always add up
correctly. That is the nature of casualty reports. Civil War casualty lists are
particularly idiosyncratic documents. Creative spelling, creative handwriting,
and the later creative interpretations of those spellings and writings, along
with plain old errors in fact, have lead to some confusing situations. As an
example, one individual from the 24th Missouri Infantry wounded during the
capture of Fort DeRussy in 1864 is either John McDonald or J. McDaniel,
he is in either Company E or Company F, and he was wounded in either his
right side or right arm. And the possibility does exist that there might actually
be two men involved here, and one of them might be Benjamin McDaniel. It
would seem that an examination of service records would settle the confusion,
but if a man were only slightly wounded, it was frequently not mentioned in his
service record. And it should also be pointed out that at the time of the battle
in question, Company E of the 24th Missouri was composed of men from
the 21st Missouri who were only temporarily attached to the 24th, while the
actual Company E, 24th Missouri was serving in Tennessee, separated from
its parent regiment.

3RD INDIANA BATTERY: 0 KIA, 1 WIA, 2 HORSES DISABLED

Pvt. Charles T. Berkau, age nineteen, severely wounded in head by
    piece of shell, recovered and left the service in August 1864 at the
    expiration of his term.

14TH IOWA INFANTRY: 0 KIA, 6 WIA

Pvt. Peter D. Schmidt, Company A, age thirty-eight, mortally wounded in right lung, died May 2, 1864, on hospital steamer *R. C. Wood* at Vicksburg

Pvt. Jefferson W. Knapp, Company A, age twenty-eight, wounded in hand, put aboard hospital steamer *Woodford*, then recuperated in hospital in Memphis until his return to duty in September

Pvt. Samuel Vaughn, Company E., severely wounded, left hand and side, went home on furlough in late June, returned to duty in September

Pvt. Turner McClain, Company G

Pvt. Elihu Thomas, Company H

Pvt. Daniel Ream, Company H

24TH MISSOURI INFANTRY: 1 KIA, 12 WIA (1 MORTAL, 4 SEVERE, 7 SLIGHT)

Sgt David Simpson, Company C, age thirty-eight (possibly twenty-eight or forty-nine), killed. Discharged in May 1863 for recurring rheumatism that left him "broken down, unfit for service," reenlisted shortly thereafter, reinterred in Alexandria National Cemetery in 1868 from Fort DeRussy

Pvt. Lewis F. Banfield, Company A, wounded in left thigh

Pvt. Henry Clay Bradshaw, Company H, slightly wounded

Pvt. George W. Filbeck, Company C, wounded severely in left lung, back on duty in May

Pvt. Granville B. Stubblefield, Company D, severely wounded in face

Pvt. Hazelwood McKinzley, Company E, severely wounded in bowels, left side

Pvt. John McDonald (J. McDaniel?), Company E, severely wounded in right arm

Pvt. James Mc. White, Company I, slight wound in head from shell fragment

27TH IOWA INFANTRY: 0 KIA, 1 WIA

Pvt. Jacob Beck, Company G, age twenty, dangerously wounded in left breast by accidental discharge; died March 22 aboard hospital boat *Woodford* at Alexandria; buried in Alexandria National Cemetery; sometimes erroneously listed as Robert Beck, his brother

32ND IOWA INFANTRY: 1 KIA, 2 WIA

Pvt. James Rood, Company I, age twenty-five, wounded by shell, died in field hospital later that day; reinterred in Alexandria National Cemetery in 1868 from Fort DeRussy

Pvt. James Kent, Company A, age twenty-six, gunshot wound to chest, the ball entering above the right scapula, passing through the lung obliquely downward and forward and emerging at the ninth rib of the left side followed by partial consolidation of the lung; unconscious ten days, recovered; discharged with total disability October 5, 1864

Pvt. Thomas A. Ball, Company K, age twenty-seven, Minié ball in calf of right leg; back on duty in September

*Pvt. Oliver M. Hess, Co. A, is erroneously listed in Scott's *Story of the Thirty-Second Iowa* as having been severely wounded during the assault on Fort DeRussy. Hess's service record and his widow's pension application both agree that Hess was discharged from the unit over a year prior to the attack on the fort.

*Pvt. T. Hartley, Company I, is erroneously listed on the Alexandria National Cemetery rolls as having been killed at Fort DeRussy. The T. Hartley buried there is actually Pvt. Thomas J. Hartley of Company I, 2nd Illinois Cavalry. He was killed at Yellow Bayou on May 18, 1864, and reinterred at the National Cemetery in 1868 at the same time as the remains moved from the fort. Records indicate that there was some confusion with the paperwork (at least) on the remains from Fort DeRussy and Yellow Bayou.

52ND INDIANA INFANTRY (ATTACHED TO 89TH INDIANA)

Pvt. Levi L. Miles, Company C, severe head wound

Sgt. Thomas Hewston, Company D, slight head wound

58TH ILLINOIS INFANTRY

Pvt. Henry Yearin (also Yarin or Yeardon), mortally wounded, died

Lt. James Carey, Company H, age twenty-four, fell severely wounded by gunshot to left groin while urging his men forward; ball was not removed and remained in his thigh near the joint; returned to his unit in September, "still too lame for active service" put on recruiting duty

89TH INDIANA INFANTRY: 1 KIA, 9 WIA

Pvt. Benjamin Schooler Johnson, Company H, age twenty-eight, missile entered right eye, emerged at the occipital protuberance; died while being removed from field to hospital

Pvt. John Brown, Company A, severely wounded, right hip and thigh

Pvt. Jacob S. Bair, Company A, slight wound to face

Cpl. Joseph M. Freed, Company G, slight shoulder wound

Pvt. George Dunlop, Company G, severe foot wound

Pvt. William P. Mullikin, Company G, severe head wound

Pvt. Jacob Cook, Company I, slight wound to left forearm

Pvt. Joseph Shady, Company I, gun shot wound through right side

119TH ILLINOIS INFANTRY: 2 KIA, 8 WIA (1 SEVERE, 7 SLIGHT)

Pvt. William Leger, Company B, age twenty-five, shot in stomach; died March 15 in the hospital at fort

Pvt. William P. Phelps, Company B, age eighteen, died aboard hospital boat *Woodford* on March 16 of gunshot wound to chest

Pvt. Martin McCombs, Company B, slightly wounded

Pvt. John Gorsage, Company B, slightly wounded

Pvt. Stephen Myers, Company C, slightly wounded

Pvt. John W. Gentry, Company D, scalp and forehead

Pvt. Meredith Sherman, Company F, mortally wounded, left thigh

Pvt. Thomas Garrett, Company G, age thirty-four, severely wounded, gunshot to abdomen; recovered and returned to unit in July; died December 6 in Quincy, Illinois, of typhoid fever; death blamed on wound

Pvt. John Wright, Company G, slightly wounded

Sgt. J. H. Lemon, Company H, slightly wounded

Pvt. Reuben Richardson, Company K, slightly wounded; slightly wounded again just two months later, receiving a contusion to his right hand at Yellow Bayou

178TH NEW YORK INFANTRY: 1 KIA, 2 MIA

Cpl. Charles Hock, Company F, hit in head by shell, killed

Pvt. William Homan, Company F, lightly wounded in face by splinters from shell

Pvt. Hermann Trauernicht, missing

Pvt. Alfred Legart, missing

Destruction of the Fort, March 16, 1864

Confederate Losses: None

Union Losses: 2 Killed, 4 Wounded

33RD WISCONSIN INFANTRY: 9 SLIGHTLY WOUNDED

William Truman, E Company, hit on top of head by chunk of dirt, not hurt

81ST ILLINOIS INFANTRY: 1 KILLED, 1 WOUNDED

1st Lt. Jerome Bishop, D Company, age thirty-one, severe head injury from shrapnel from burst cannon, killed

Sgt. Pembroke N. King, D Company, age twenty-eight, wounded; never returned to unit

95TH ILLINOIS INFANTRY

Pvt. Samuel H. Jackson, Company C, age twenty-six, decapitated by shrapnel from burst cannon

Pvt. Samuel Snyder, Company A, age twenty-nine, enlisted January 4, 1864, left leg broken by lump of hard red clay, required amputation above the knee; died aboard hospital boat *Woodford*

Cpl. Allen Giles, Company F, right arm broken by falling debris; returned to unit in January 1865

Miscellaneous Confederate Casualties

Unknown number of smallpox casualties, January 1863

Pvt. Rufus Gleason, Company D, Burnett's Sharpshooters, died at hospital in Marksville, February 28, 1863

Sgt. Christopher Columbus Neal, Burnett's Sharpshooters, died of pneumonia at the hospital in Marksville, March 2 (7?), 1863

Pvt. William T. Pratt, Company A, Burnett's Sharpshooters, died at hospital at Marksville, March 3, 1863

Pvt. Wade H. Pratt, Company A, Burnett's Sharpshooters, died at hospital at Marksville, March 5, 1863

Pvt. Shugar Jones Mathews, Company A, 11th Battalion Louisiana Infantry, died at hospital at Marksville, March 23, 1863.

Pvt. William Y. Glover, Company A, 13th Texas Infantry, drowned January 22, 1864, while working on raft

Pvt. W. A. "Colonel" Tarleton, Company F, 28th Texas Dismounted Cavalry, died of typhoid February 23, 1864

John L. Page, of Natchitoches Parish, died at the fort in 1864 while working as an overseer

Appendix E

Slaves Who Died Building Fort DeRussy

Slave	Owner
Daniel	A. J. Ogilvie
Charlie	John A. Sigur
Nelson	Estate of D. F. Dickson
Levi	Michael Boyce
Tom	George W. Robinson
Charley	James N. Platt
Greene	A. L. Hillman
Edmond	William Stewart
Wisdom	Samuel E. Guyin
Henry Brown	Hodge Raburn
Horace	W. D. B. Edens
Unknown	E. Strickland
Hicks	Mrs. Eleanor Lake
Unknown	John H. Burns
Unknown	C. Z. Nottingham
Unknown	H. W. Springfield
Daniel Bogan*	Henry Marshall
Sam	R. F. Bruton
Harry	J. W. Bryan
Charles	George W. Morse
Cyrus	T. W. Bledsoe
Solomon	C. W. Martin
Isaac Gregg	Henry Marshall
Jim	T. F. Keith
Henry	David Bush
Mose	George Hays

Chance	A. J. Worthy
Bill Flemming	A. Flournoy Jr.
Charles Young	Estate of J. R. Mead
Jeff	Joseph E. Adger
Bose	J. C. McCary
Bob Scott	J. T. Belknap
Arch	W. W. Allen
Ted	Mumford Wells
Charlie	J. R. Andrews
Lewis	Thomas O'Neal
Robert	Estate of John Compton
Fred	Robert L. Tanner
Solomon	S. Duncan Linten
John	E. W. and J. Wells
Mike	J. A. Bynum
Cornelius	J. A. Bynum
Henry	Mrs. Elizabeth James
Sambo	A. J. Beatty
Primus	Thomas Hunter
Esau	Asa Rourke
Reuben	Madame Adolphe Sompayrac
Charles	John Prudhomme
Plutarch	A. Lacombe
Harrison	Henry Boyce
Henry	Henry Boyce
Frank	William P. Morrow
Sam	Joseph Janin
Moses	Phanor Prudhomme
Jeff	George W. Gilmer
Fielding	George W. Gilmer
Abraham	James Gibson
Nicholas	Victor Rachal
John	William Benoist
Johnson	T. W. Callihan
Joe	J. H. Cunningham

Daniel	John Adger
Charles	Lestan Prudhomme
Bob	Mrs. Abagail Dawkins
Allen	Mrs. Sarah Harris
Jim	James R. Pickett
Paul	Jean Francois Hertzog
Pinck	J. F. Manning
Lazarus	Samuel E. Guy

*Daniel Bogan died at Fort DeRussy, but he did not die from injury or disease incurred at the fort. He died while serving as a bugler with the St. Mary's Cannoneers, a Confederate artillery unit, from wounds received in an engagement with Union soldiers.

Source: "Appn. of $500,000 to Pay for Slaves etc. lost by Death or Otherwise," *Louisiana State Auditor's Records, 1862–1865,* Louisiana State Archives, Baton Rouge.

Appendix F

Jayhawkers Who Captured David F. Boyd

Five and a half miles from Alexandria on David's Ferry Road
About 4:00 P.M., February 3, 1864

1. George Doman[?] (captain)
2. Indian Sam (guide)
3. Dr. Brown
8. Ryland Brothers (five in number)
9. James Harland
10. Anderson Peevey
11. Wills
12. Wilson
13. Lewis Paul
14. Craig
15. Peter Hanes

All of these men resided in or near Holloway's Prairie, except for James Harland, who lived in Point Maigre [currently Vick], Avoyelles Parish. These men were joined at Natchez by Mike Paul and three other unarmed Jayhawkers.

Source: David F. Boyd Papers.

Appendix G

The Other Forts DeRussy

While this book has specifically centered on Fort DeRussy, Louisiana, there were at least five different Forts DeRussy scattered across the country from Virginia to Hawaii, all named for two brothers and a son/nephew. I would be remiss were I not to make some mention of the other forts (and one battery) of the same name.

1. Fort DeRussy, Columbus, Kentucky (CSA)

This was the first Fort DeRussy built. It was a Confederate fort, and like its counterpart in Louisiana, it was named for Lewis DeRussy, who was Leonidas Polk's chief engineer at the time of its construction. It was built on a high bluff overlooking the Mississippi River and was part of a group of fortifications meant to deny passage of the river to the Union navy. On November 7, 1861, the fort actively engaged in the Battle of Belmont, Missouri, by shelling the Union troops involved in the battle across the river. The fort was ultimately abandoned in March 1862 and was renamed Fort Halleck by the U.S. forces, in honor of Maj. Gen. Henry Halleck. Portions of the earthworks still exist and are now preserved as part of Kentucky's Columbus-Belmont State Park.

2. Fort DeRussy, Washington, D.C. (USA)

This Fort DeRussy is located in Rock Creek Park, Washington, D.C. It was one of the many earthen forts defending Washington from Confederate attack during the Civil War and provided interlocking fire with Fort Stevens on its east and Forts Kearny and Reno on its west. It remains in a well-preserved state and is now maintained by the National Park Service. The fort was most likely named for René Edward DeRussy, the oldest brother of Lewis DeRussy. When the fort was built, René was a senior engineer officer in the U.S. Army and had been serving on active duty for an incredible fifty-four years.

National Park Service brochures state that this Fort DeRussy was built by the Fourth New York Heavy Artillery and named after that unit's commander, Gustavus Adolphus DeRussy, but this is chronologically impossible. This fort was built, armed, and named by December 1861, several months before the Fourth New York Heavy Artillery arrived in Washington and over a year before Gustavus DeRussy became its commander. At the time the fort was named, Gustavus DeRussy was only a captain in a regular army artillery unit. The confusion over the naming probably arose from the fact that during the latter part of the war, Gustavus was a brigadier general of volunteers and in charge of the defenses of Washington south of the Potomac, resulting in the assumption by many people that the fort was named in his honor. Gustavus was the son of René and the nephew of Lewis.

3. Fort DeRussy, Grand Ecore, Louisiana (CSA)

This small earthwork might not have been an official Fort DeRussy. It is located at Grand Ecore, Natchitoches Parish, Louisiana, overlooking a bend in the Red River. The works were manned by Confederate artillery toward the end of the Civil War, although they may have been in existence as early as 1863.

During the early twentieth century, there was debate in the Natchitoches newspapers as to whether there had ever been a Confederate fort at Grand Ecore. Although the fact that there were Confederate earthworks there can not be denied, the consensus was that there had not been an actual fort there. However, in 1904 Col. Thomas Benton, former commanding officer of the 3rd Louisiana Artillery (the Bell Battery), stated that he "surrendered Fort DeRussy on Red River on June 4th, 1865." Benton's Battery was at Grand Ecore at that time, and the "real" Fort DeRussy was already in U.S. hands prior to that. Since the Grand Ecore works were located within a few hundred yards of Lewis DeRussy's home, it can be assumed that these works were the "Fort DeRussy" to which Benton was referring. This small fort, or at least a portion of it, can still be seen in front of the Corps of Engineers Visitor Center at Grand Ecore.

4. Fort DeRussy, Honolulu, Hawaii (USA)

Fort DeRussy on Waikiki Beach, Honolulu, Hawaii, was built in 1915 to protect Honolulu and Pearl Harbor. It may be the best known of all of the Forts DeRussy, but it has the least tangible claim to the name. The fort was named for René Edward DeRussy, who was in charge of West Coast defenses in California during the Civil War. California was as close as René ever got to Hawaii, and he died fifty years before the fort was built.

In 1950, the Coastal Artillery was disbanded, and Fort DeRussy is now used as an Armed Forces Recreation Area. It is also the home of the U.S. Army Museum of Hawaii.

Battery DeRussy, Fort Monroe, Virginia (USA)

Battery DeRussy was a concrete battery armed with three 12-inch guns mounted on disappearing carriages. It was built between 1898 and 1903 and manned by the Coastal Artillery in 1904. It was originally named for René DeRussy, but in 1909 the fort was officially named in honor of Gustavus Adolphus DeRussy. René was one of the early proponents of the disappearing carriage, and it seems ironic that a battery with guns mounted in this way should have René's name swapped out for that of his son.

On July 21, 1910, a premature discharge in one of the guns caused the breech to blow out, killing eleven artillerymen and injuring six others. The battery was decommissioned in 1944.

Bibliography

Primary Sources

Ambrose, Stephen E., ed. *A Wisconsin Boy in Dixie: Selected Letters of James K. Newton*. Madison: Univ. of Wisconsin Press, 1961.

Anderson, John Q. *A Texas Surgeon in the C.S.A.* Tuscaloosa, Ala.: Confederate Publishing, 1957. (Walker's Texas Division.)

Bartlett, Napier. *Military Record of Louisiana*. 1875. Reprint, Baton Rouge: Louisiana State Univ. Press, 1992.

Bearss, Edwin, ed. *A Louisiana Confederate: Diary of Felix Pierre Poché*. Natchitoches: Louisiana Studies Institute, Northwestern State Univ., 1972.

Beecher, Harris H. *Record of the 114th Regiment N.Y.S.V.: Where It Went, What It Saw, and What It Did*. Norwich, N.Y.: J. F. Hubbard Jr., 1866.

Benson, Solon F. *Civil War Battle of Pleasant Hill, Louisiana*. Tangipahoa, La.: Camp Moore Reproductions, n.d.

Biographical and Historical Memoirs of Louisiana. Vol. 1. Chicago: Goodspeed Publishing, 1892.

Biographical and Historical Memoirs of Northwest Louisiana Comprising a Large Fund of Biography of Actual Residents, and an Interesting Historical Sketch of Thirteen Counties. Nashville: Southern Publishing, 1890.

Blessington, Joseph P. *The Campaigns of Walker's Texas Division*. New York: Lange, Little, 1875. (16th Texas Infantry.)

Boggs, William R. *Military Reminiscences of Gen. Wm. R. Boggs, C.S.A.* Durham, N.C.: Seeman Printery, 1913.

Boynton, Charles B. *The History of the Navy during the Rebellion*. Vol. 2. New York: D. Appleton, 1869.

Brent, Joseph Lancaster. *The Lugo Case. Capture of the Ironclad "Indianola."* New Orleans: Searcy & Pfaff, 1926. (Two separate works in one edition. All citations in the notes are to the latter work.)

Brinkman, Harold D., ed. *Dear Companion: The Civil War Letters of Silas I. Shearer*. Ames, Iowa: Sigler, 1995. (23rd Iowa.)

Brown, Norman D. *Journey to Pleasant Hill: The Civil War Letters of Captain Elijah Petty, Walker's Texas Division, CSA*. San Antonio: Univ. of Texas Institute of Texan Cultures, 1982.

Bryner, Cloyd. *Bugle Echoes: The Story of Illinois 47th.* Springfield, Ill.:
    Phillips Bros., 1905.

Byers, S. H. M. *Iowa in War Times.* Des Moines: W. D. Condit, 1888.

Crandall, Warren D., and Isaac D. Newall. *History of the Ram Fleet and the
    Mississippi Marine Brigade in the War for the Union on the Mississippi
    and Its Tributaries.* St. Louis: Society of Survivors, 1907.

Cullum, George W. *Biographical Register of the Officers and Graduates of
    the U.S. Military Academy at West Point, N.Y. from Its Establishment,
    in 1802, to 1890.* 3rd ed. Boston: Houghton Mifflin, 1891.

Delafield, Joseph. *The Unfortified Boundary: A Diary of the First Survey of
    the Canadian Boundary Line from St. Regis to the Lake of the Woods.*
    New York: privately printed, 1943.

Ewer, James K. *The Third Massachusetts Cavalry in the War for the Union.*
    Boston: Historical Committee of the Regimental Association, 1903.

Frey, Jerry. *Grandpa's Gone: The Adventures of Daniel Buchwalter in the
    Western Army, 1862–1865.* Shippensburg, Pa.: Burd Street Press, 1998.

Hewett, Janet B., ed. *Supplement to the Official Records of the Union and
    Confederate Armies.* 100 vols. Wilmington, N.C.: Broadfoot, 1994–2001.

Irwin, Richard B. *History of the Nineteenth Army Corps.* 1892. Reprint,
    Baton Rouge, La.: Elliott's Book Shop Press, 1985.

Johannson, M. Jane. *Widows by the Thousand: The Civil War Letters of
    Theophilus and Harriet Perry, 1862–1864.* Fayetteville: Univ. of Arkan-
    sas Press, 2000.

Jones, James P., and Edward F. Keuchel, eds. *Civil War Marine: A Diary of
    the Red River Expedition, 1864.* Washington, D.C.: History and Muse-
    ums Division, HQUSMC, 1975.

Jones, S[amuel] C[alvin]. *Reminiscences of the 22nd Iowa Infantry.* 1907.
    Reprint, Iowa City, Iowa: Press of the Camp Pope Bookshop, 1993.

Knox, Thomas W. *Camp-Fire and Cotton-field: Southern Adventure in Time
    of War. Life with the Union Armies, and Residence on a Louisiana
    Plantation.* New York: Blelock, 1865.

Liddell, St. John R. *Liddell's Record.* Edited by Nathaniel Hughes. Dayton,
    Ohio: Morningside House, 1985. Original typescript (1866) in Louisiana
    Historical Association Collection, Howard-Tilton Memorial Library,
    Tulane Univ., New Orleans.

Marshall, T. B. *History of the Eighty-Third Ohio Volunteer Infantry: The
    Greyhound Regiment.* Cincinnati: The 83rd Ohio Volunteer Infantry
    Association, 1912.

Mason, Jane Fullilove. "Dear Lizzie: Letters of a Confederate Cavalryman."
    Unpublished manuscript, copy in possession of author.

McCants, Sister Dorothea Olga, ed. *They Came to Louisiana: Letters of
    a Catholic Mission, 1854–1882.* Baton Rouge: Louisiana State Univ.
    Press, 1970.

Milligan, John D., ed. *From the Fresh-Water Navy, 1861–1864: The Letters of Acting Master's Mate Henry R. Browne and Acting Ensign Symmes E. Browne.* Annapolis, Md.: U.S. Naval Institute, 1970.

Moore, Frank, ed. *The Rebellion Record: A Diary of American Events.* Vols. 6 and 8. New York: D. Van Nostrand, 1866, 1867.

Moore, Jonathan B. *Military History of the 33rd Regt. Wis. Infty Vols from Oct. 1, 1862, Its Organization to Oct. 1st, 1864, 1863–1864.* Copy in Wisconsin Historical Society Archives, Madison. (Letter of Maj. H. H. Virgin to A. H. Fitch, May 28, 1864.)

Newsome, Edmund. *Experience in the War of the Great Rebellion.* 1880. Reprint, Murphrysboro, Ill: Jackson County Printing, 1984. (81st Illinois.)

Parmenter, Almon W., ed. *Civil War Diaries of Pvt. Almon Wilson Parmenter.* By Sally K. Moore. San Jose, Calif., 1994. (Company C, 32nd Iowa Volunteer Infantry.)

Porter, Admiral. *Incidents and Anecdotes of the Civil War.* New York: D. Appleton, 1885.

Porter, David D. *The Naval History of the Civil War.* 1886. Reprint, Mineola, N.Y.: Dover, 1998.

Powers, George W. *The Story of the Thirty Eighth Regiment of Massachusetts Volunteers.* Cambridge Press, 1866.

Richards, A[mable] P. *The St. Helena Rifles.* Houston: privately published, 1968.

Roberts, Jobe M. *The Experience of a Private in the Civil War.* Sylvan Beach, N.Y.: published by author, 1904. (41st Illinois.)

Scott, John. *Story of the Thirty Second Regiment Iowa Volunteers.* Nevada, Iowa, 1896.

Selfridge, Thomas O., Jr. *What Finer Tradition: The Memoirs of Thomas O. Selfridge, Jr., Rear Admiral, U.S.N.* Columbia: Univ. of South Carolina Press, 1987.

Skelton, Stephen R., ed. *Through the Valley of the Shadow of Death: The Civil War Manuscript Collection of Captain Harvey Alexander Wallace.* Westminster, Md.: Willow Bend Books, 2004 (19th Texas Infantry).

Smith, George G. *Leaves from a Soldier's Diary.* Putnam, Conn.: G. G. Smith, 1906. (1st Louisiana Volunteer Infantry [White].)

Sprague, Homer B. *History of the 13th Infantry Regiment of Connecticut Volunteers during the Great Rebellion.* Hartford, Conn.: Case, Lockwood, 1867.

Taylor, Richard. *Destruction and Reconstruction: Personal Experiences of the Late War.* New York: D. Appleton, 1879.

Wight, Levi Lamoni. *The Reminiscences and Civil War Letters of Levi Lamoni Wight: Life in a Mormon Splinter Colony of the Texas Frontier.* Edited by Davis Bitton. Salt Lake City: Univ. of Utah Press, 1970.

Williams, E. Cort. "The Cruise of 'The Black Terror.' (Porter's Dummy at Vicksburg)." In *Sketches of War History, 1861–1865: Papers Prepared*

for the Ohio Commandery of the Military Order of the Loyal Legion of
the United States, 1888–1890, vol. 3, edited by Robert Hunter. Cincinnati: Robert Clarke, 1890.

Williams, John M. *"The Eagle Regiment," 8th Wis. Inf'ty Vols.* Belleville,
Wisc.: Recorder Print, 1890.

Winschel, Terrence J., ed. *The Civil War Diary of a Common Soldier: William
Wiley of the 77th Illinois Infantry.* Baton Rouge: Louisiana State Univ.
Press, 2001.

Wisconsin. Adjutant General's Office. *Annual Report of the Adjutant General of the State of Wisconsin.* Madison, 1864.

Yeary, Mamie, ed. *Reminiscences of the Boys in Gray, 1861–1865.* Dallas:
Smith & Lamar, 1912.

Secondary Sources

Alden, Henry Mills, and Alfred Hudson Guernsey. *Harper's Pictorial History of the Civil War.* Puritan Press, 1866.

Allardice, Bruce S. *More Generals in Gray.* Baton Rouge: Louisiana State
Univ. Press, 1995.

Allen, Gardner W. *A Naval History of the American Revolution.* Vol. 2.
New York: Russell & Russell, 1962.

Andreas, Alfred Theodore. *History of Chicago.* Vol. 2. New York: Arno
Press, 1975. (Articles on Fifty-eighth Illinois Infantry and Chicago Mercantile Battery.)

Bearss, Edwin C. *The Vicksburg Campaign.* 3 vols. Dayton, Ohio: Morningside Press, 1985–86.

Bearss, Margie Riddle. *Sherman's Forgotten Campaign: The Meridian Expedition.* Baltimore: Gateway Press, 1987.

Bergeron, Arthur W., Jr., and Lawrence L. Hewitt. *Boone's Louisiana Battery: A History and Roster.* Baton Rouge: Elliott's Bookshop Press,
1986.

Bergeron, Arthur W., Jr. *Guide to Louisiana Confederate Military Units,
1861–1865.* Baton Rouge: Louisiana State Univ. Press, 1989.

———. ed. *The Civil War in Louisiana,* Part B, *The Home Front.* Lafayette,
La.: Center for Louisiana Studies, 2004.

Bragg, Jefferson Davis. *Louisiana in the Confederacy.* Baton Rouge: Louisiana State Univ. Press, 1941.

Brockett, L. P. *Battle-Field and Hospital; or Lights and Shadows of the Great
Rebellion.* Edgewood Publishing, n.d. (Ballad, "The Vicksburg Scow.")

Brooksher, William Riley. *War Along the Bayous: The 1864 Red River Campaign in Louisiana.* Washington, D.C.: Brassey's, 1998.

Byrne, Frank L., and Jean Powers Soman. *Your True Marcus: The Civil War
Letters of a Jewish Colonel.* Kent, Ohio: Kent State Univ. Press, 1985.

Caren, Eric C., comp. *Civil War Extra: A Newspaper History of the Civil War from 1863 to 1865.* Vol. 2. Edison, N.J.: Castle Books, 1999.

Casey, Powell A. *Encyclopedia of Forts, Posts, Named Camps and other Military Installations in Louisiana, 1700–1981.* Baton Rouge: Claitor's Publishing, 1983.

Coco, Gregory. "The Canvas Fort." Unpublished manuscript, 1969, copy in possession of author.

Coombe, Jack D. *Thunder Along the Mississippi: The River Battles that Split the Confederacy.* New York: Sarpedon, 1996.

Cullum, George W. *Campaigns of the War of 1812 Against Great Britain, Sketched and Criticised; with Brief Biographies of the American Engineers.* New York: James Miller, 1879.

Davis, James Henry, ed. *Texans in Gray: A Regimental History of the Eighteenth Texas Cavalry, Walkers Texas Division in the Civil War.* Tulsa, Okla.: Heritage Oak Press, 1999.

Des Cognets, Anna Russell. *William Russell and His Descendants.* Lexington, Ky.: Samuel F. Wilson, 1884.

Dupuy, R. Ernest, and Trevor N. Dupuy. *The Compact History of the Revolutionary War.* New York: Hawthorn Books, 1963.

Dyer, Frederick. *A Compendium of the War of the Rebellion.* New York: Thomas Yoseloff, 1959.

Edmonds, David C., ed. *The Conduct of Federal Troops in Louisiana During the Invasions of 1863 and 1864.* Lafayette, La.: Acadiana Press, 1988.

Edmonds, David C. *The Guns of Port Hudson: The Investment, Siege, and Reduction.* Lafayette, La.: Acadiana Press, 1984.

Eliot, Ellsworth, Jr. *West Point in the Confederacy.* New York: G. A. Baker, 1941.

Garrison, Webb. *Creative Minds in Desperate Times.* Nashville: Rutledge Hill Press, 1997.

Gerling, Edwin G. *The One Hundred Seventeenth Illinois Infantry Volunteers (The McKendree Regiment), 1862–1865.* Highland, Ill.: published by author, 1992.

Gosnell, H. Allen. *Guns on the Western Waters: The Story of River Gunboats in the Civil War.* Baton Rouge: Louisiana State Univ. Press, 1949.

Hamersly, Lewis R. *Living Officers of the U.S. Navy and Marine Corps, 1861–1865.* 1870. Reprint, Mattituck, N.Y.: J. M. Carroll, n.d.

Hardin, J. Fair. *Northwestern Louisiana: A History of the Watershed of the Red River, 1714–1937.* 3 vols. Shreveport, La.: Historical Record Association, 1939.

Headley, J. T. *Farragut and our Naval Commanders.* New York: E. B. Treat, 1867.

Hearn, Chester G. *Admiral David Dixon Porter: The Civil War Years.* Annapolis, Md.: Naval Institute Press, 1996.

————. *Ellet's Brigade: The Strangest Outfit of All.* Baton Rouge: Louisiana State Univ. Press, 2000.

Herman, Marguerita Z. *Ramparts: Fortification from the Renaissance to West Point.* Garden City Park, N.Y.: Avery Publishing, 1992.

Hoehling, A. A. *Damn the Torpedoes: Naval Incidents of the Civil War.* New York: Gramercy Books, 1989.

Houp, J. Randall. *The 24th Missouri Volunteer Infantry "Lyon Legion."* Alma, Ark.: J. Randall Houp, 1997.

Huber, Leonard V. *Advertisements of Lower Mississippi River Steamboats, 1812–1920.* West Barrington, R.I.: Steamship Historical Society of America, 1959.

Ingersoll, Lurton Dunham. *Iowa and the Rebellion: A History of the Troops Furnished by the State of Iowa to the Volunteer Armies of the Union.* Philadelphia: J. B. Lippincott, 1866.

Ingram, Henry L., comp. *Civil War Letters of George W. and Martha F. Ingram, 1861–1865.* College Station: Texas A&M Press, 1973.

Johansson, M. Jane. *Peculiar Honor: A History of the 28th Texas Cavalry, 1862–1865.* Fayetteville: Univ. of Arkansas Press, 1998.

Johnson, Clint. *Civil War Blunders.* Winston-Salem, N.C.: John F. Blair, 1997.

Johnson, Ludwell H. *Red River Campaign: Politics and Cotton in the Civil War.* Baltimore: Johns Hopkins Univ. Press, 1958.

Johnson, Robert Underwood, and Clarence Clough Buel, eds. *Battles and Leaders of the Civil War.* Vol. 4, pt. 1. New York: Century, 1889.

Joiner, Gary Dillard. *One Damn Blunder from Beginning to End: The Red River Campaign of 1864.* Wilmington, Del.: Scholarly Resources, 2003.

Jones, Virgil C. *The Civil War at Sea: The Final Effort.* New York: Holt, Rinehart and Winston, 1962.

Korn, Jerry, and the Editors of Time-Life Books. *War on the Mississippi: Grant's Vicksburg Campaign.* Alexandria, Va.: Time-Life Books, 1985.

Lowe, Richard. *Walker's Texas Division, C.S.A.: Greyhounds of the Trans-Mississippi.* Baton Rouge: Louisiana State Univ. Press, 2004.

Lytle, William M., and Forrest R. Holdcamper, comp. *Merchant Steam Vessels of the United States, 1790–1868: "The Lytle-Holdcamper List."* Staten Island, N.Y.: Steamship Historical Society of America, 1975.

Mahan, A. T. *The Navy in the Civil War.* Vol. 3, *The Gulf and Inland Waters.* New York: Charles Scribner's Sons, 1883.

Mayeux, Steven M. "A Concise History of Fort DeRussy, Avoyelles Parish, Louisiana." Unpublished manuscript, 1994, copy in possession of author.

Meyer, Steve. *Iowa Valor.* Garrison, Iowa: Meyer Publishing, 1994.

Miles, Jim. *A River Unvexed: A History and Tour Guide to the Campaign for the Mississippi River.* Nashville: Rutledge Hill Press, 1994.

Milligan, John D. *Gunboats Down the Mississippi.* New York: Arno Press, 1980.

Mills, Elizabeth Shown, and Gary B. Mills. *Tales of Old Natchitoches.* Vol. 3, Cane River Creole Series. Natchitoches, La.: Association for the Preservation of Historic Natchitoches, 1978.

Minnesota Board of Commissioners. *Minnesota in the Civil and Indian Wars, 1861–1865.* St. Paul, Minn.: Pioneer Press, 1891.

Nardini, Louis Raphael, Sr. *My Historic Natchitoches, Louisiana and Its Environment.* Natchitoches, La.: Nardini Publishing, 1963.

Nash, Howard P., Jr. *A Naval History of the Civil War.* New York: A. S. Barnes, 1972.

Nichols, James L. *Confederate Engineers.* Confederate Centennial Studies No. 5. Tuscaloosa, Ala.: Confederate Publishing, 1957.

Olmstead, Edwin, Wayne E. Stark, and Spencer C. Tucker. *The Big Guns: Civil War Siege, Seacoast, and Naval Cannon.* Alexandria Bay, N.Y.: Museum Restoration Service, 1997.

Ordway, Frederick Ira, Jr., ed. *Register of the General Society of the War of 1812.* Washington, D.C.: General Society of the War of 1812, 1972.

Page, Dave. *Ships versus Shore: Civil War Engagements along Southern Shores and Rivers.* Nashville: Rutledge Hill Press, 1994.

Parrish, T. Michael. *Richard Taylor: Soldier Prince of Dixie.* Chapel Hill: Univ. of North Carolina Press, 1992.

Pearson, Charles E., George Castille, and M. Melanie Thigpen. *Archaeological Reconnaissance of the Below Red River Project Area, Avoyelles Parish, Louisiana.* Baton Rouge: Coastal Environments, 1983.

Petrie, Donald A. *The Prize Game: Lawful Looting on the High Seas in the Days of Fighting Sail.* Annapolis, Md.: Naval Institute Press, 1999.

Phisterer, Frederick, comp. *New York in the War of the Rebellion, 1861–1865.* Albany: J. B. Lyon, 1912.

Portré-Bobinski, Germaine, and Clara Mildred Smith. *Natchitoches: The Up-to-Date Oldest Town in Louisiana.* New Orleans: Dameron-Pierson, 1936.

Prud'homme, Lucile Keator, and Fern B. Christensen. *The Natchitoches Cemeteries.* New Orleans: Polyanthos, 1977.

Reed, Germaine M. *David French Boyd, Founder of Louisiana State University.* Baton Rouge: Louisiana State Univ. Press, 1977.

Reid, Thomas. *Spartan Band: Burnett's 13th Texas Cavalry in the Civil War.* Denton: Univ. of North Texas Press, 2005.

Reilly, John C., Jr. *The Iron Guns of Willard Park.* Washington, D.C.: Naval Historical Center, 1991.

Ripley, C. Peter. *Slaves and Freedmen in Civil War Louisiana.* Baton Rouge: Louisiana State Univ. Press, 1976.

Robinson, Michael C. *Gunboats, Low Water, and Yankee Ingenuity: A History of Bailey's Dam.* Baton Rouge: FPHC, 1991.

Saucier, Corinne L. *History of Avoyelles Parish, Louisiana*. 1943. Reprint, Gretna, La.: Pelican, 1998.

Saxon, Lyle, Edward Dreyer, and Robert Tallant. *Gumbo Ya-Ya*. New York: Bonanza Books, 1945.

Scharff, John Thomas. *History of the Confederate States Navy, from Its Organization to the Surrender of Its Last Vessel*. New York: Rogers & Sherwood, 1887.

Silverstone, Paul H. *Civil War Navies, 1855–1883*. Annapolis, Md.: Naval Institute Press, 2001.

———. *Warships of the Civil War Navies*. Annapolis, Md.: Naval Institute Press, 1989.

Slagle, Jay. *Ironclad Captain: Seth Ledyard Phelps and the U. S. Navy, 1841–1864*. Kent, Ohio: Kent State Univ. Press, 1996.

Smith, Walter George. *Life and Letters of Thomas Kilby Smith*. New York: G. P. Putnam's Sons, 1898.

Spencer, J. W. *Terrell's Texas Cavalry*. Burnet, Tex.: Eakin Press, 1982.

Stern, Philip Van Doren. *The Confederate Navy: A Pictorial History*. Garden City, N.Y.: Doubleday, 1962; New York: Da Capo Press, 1992.

Stuart, A. A. *Iowa Colonels and Regiments: Being a History of Iowa Regiments in the War of the Rebellion*. Des Moines, Iowa: Mills, 1865.

Tenney, W. J. *The Military and Naval History of the Rebellion in the United States with Biographical Sketches of Deceased Officers*. New York: D. Appleton, 1866.

Texas Historical Foundation. *Red River Campaign Centennial Commemoration, Center, Texas–Mansfield, Louisiana, April 4, 1964*. Austin: Texas Historical Foundation, 1964.

Thorpe, Maner L. *The Barbin and Goudeau Families of Louisiana: Ancestry and Descendants*. Santa Barbara, Calif.: published by author, 1999.

Twain, Mark. *Life on the Mississippi*. Hartford, Conn.: American Publishing, 1883.

The Union Army: A History of Military Affairs in the Loyal United States, 1861–65—Records of the Regiments in the Union Army—Cyclopedia of Battles—Memoirs of Commanders and Soldiers. Vol. 5. Madison, Wisc.: Federal Publishing, 1908.

Waite, Otis F. R. *New Hampshire in the Great Rebellion*. Claremont, N.H.: Tracy, Chase, 1870.

Warner, Ezra J. *Generals in Blue: Lives of the Union Commanders*. Baton Rouge: Louisiana State Univ. Press, 1964.

Way, Frederick, Jr., comp. *Way's Packet Directory, 1848–1983: Passenger Steamboats of the Mississippi River System Since the Advent of Photography in Mid-Continent America*. Athens: Ohio Univ. Press, 1983.

West, Richard S., Jr. *The Second Admiral: A Life of David Dixon Porter, 1813–1891*. New York: Coward-McCann, 1937.

Wilson, James Grant, and John Fiske, eds. *Appleton's Cyclopædia of American Biography*. New York: D. Appleton, 1888.

Winters, John D. *The Civil War in Louisiana*. Baton Rouge: Louisiana State Univ. Press, 1963.

Wooten, Dudley G., ed. *A Comprehensive History of Texas, 1685–1897*. Austin: Texas State Historical Association, 1986.

Zeitlin, Richard H. *Old Abe the War Eagle*. Madison: Wisconsin Historical Society, 1986. (Eighth Wisconsin Infantry.)

Government Documents

Avoyelles Parish Police Jury Records, 1861–1865. Avoyelles Parish Courthouse, Marksville, La.

Booth, Andrew B., comp. *Records of Louisiana Confederate Soldiers and Louisiana Commands*. New Orleans: Office of the Commisssioner, Louisiana Military Records, 1920.

Confederate Proofs and Land Warrants. Louisiana State Archives, Baton Rouge. Thomas Burns, Microfilm Reel 1, Claim 67, Act 116; William Fountain, Microfilm Reel 6, claim rejected, Act 55; Hugh McNeal, Microfilm Reel 6, claim rejected, Act 55; John Muller, Microfilm Reel 2, Claim 720, Act 116; John O'Quinn, Microfilm Reel 1, Claim 44, Act 116; James Wallace, Microfilm Reel 1, Claim 426, Act 96.

"Deaths of Confederate Prisoners of War in New Orleans, La." Manuscript. Louisiana State Archives, Baton Rouge.

Deck logs. RG 24, National Archives. USS *Albatross, Argosy, Avenger, Benton, Black Hawk, Carondelet, Chillicothe, Choctaw, Cricket, Eastport, Essex, Estrella, Forest Rose, Fort Hindman, Gazelle, General Sterling Price, Juliet, Kenwood, Lafayette, Lexington, Little Rebel, Louisville, Meteor, Mound City, Naiad, Neosho, Nymph, Osage, Ouachita, Pittsburgh, St. Clair,* and *Tallahatchie.*

"Descriptive Roll of Company E, 71st Regiment, U. S. Inf. (Colored)." RG 94, National Archives.

Engineer Department Letters Received Relating to the U. S. Military Academy, 1819–1866. National Archives Microfilm Publication 2047.

French-American Claims Commission Files. RG 76. National Archives. No. 101, *Oden Deucatte v. United States;* No. 110, *A. D. Brochard v. United States.*

General Court-Martial Transcripts. RG 125. National Archives. Lt. Cmdr. Augustus P. Cooke, GCM 3288, Microfilm Roll 110, Vol. 101; Daniel P. Upton, GCM 3289, Microfilm Roll 110, Vol. 101.

Heitman, Francis B. *Historical Register and Dictionary of the United States Army*. 2 vols. Washington, D.C.: GPO, 1903.

Indianola Vessel Papers. File I-14, RG 109, National Archives.

Letters and Telegrams Received, Department of Texas and the Trans-Mississippi Department. Records of Military Commands, Records of the Confederate War Department and Army, Box 52, RG 109, National Archives.

Letters Sent, District of West Louisiana. Records of the Department of Texas and the Trans-Mississippi Department, Records of Military Commands, Records of the Confederate War Department and Army, Vols. 75 and 76, RG 109, National Archives.

"List of Prisoners Captured at Fort De Russy La. March 14th 1864." Louisiana Station Rolls, Baton Rouge List 1, RG 109, National Archives.

Louisiana State Auditor's Records, 1862–1865. Louisiana State Archives, Baton Rouge.

Map of Avoyelles Parish, Louisiana, 1863. Collection of Captured Confederate Maps, RG Z-33, Nos. 73 and 74, National Archives.

Moore, R. M. "List of Casualties in the 3rd Brigade, 3rd Division, 16th A.C. on the 14 March 1864 in Charge on Fort De Russy La." RG 94, National Archives. (178th New York.)

Porter, David D. Sketch, "Dummy Taking a Shoot: Recapture and Blowing Up of the 'Indianola' by the U.S.Str *Wooden Dummy*." Photo NH 53235. Naval Historical Foundation, Washington, D.C.

Quartermaster General's Office. *Roll of Honor: Names of Soldiers Who Died in Defence of the American Union*. Vols. 9, 25, and 27. Washington, D.C.: GPO, 1866, 1870, 1871.

Register of Burials. Alexandria National Cemetery, Pineville, La.

Roster and Record of Iowa Soldiers in the War of the Rebellion Together with Historical Sketches of Volunteer Organizations, 1861–1866. 5 vols. Des Moines, Iowa: Emory H. English, State Printer, 1908–11.

Secretary of the Navy. *Official Records of the Union and Confederate Navies in the War of the Rebellion.* Washington, D.C.: GPO, 1894–1922.

Secretary of War. *The War of the Rebellion: A Compilation of the Official Records of the Union and Confederate Armies.* 128 vols. Washington, D.C.: GPO, 1880–1901.

United States Military Academy. Lewis G. DeRussy and René E. DeRussy, Alumni Files. Special Collections and Archives, U.S. Military Academy Library, West Point, N.Y.

U.S. Army Corps of Engineers. Vicksburg District. Red River Survey, 1891.

U.S. Congress. Joint Committee on the Conduct of the War. *Red River Expedition: Report of the Joint Committee on the Conduct of the War.* Washington, D.C.: GPO, 1865; Millwood, N.Y.: Kraus Reprint, 1977.

War Department. "Fort De Russy, May 4, 1863, Consolidated Report." Confederate States Army Casualties: Lists and Narrative Reports, 1862–1865. Microfilm 836, Reel 2, RG 109, National Archives.

Magazine and Newspaper Articles

"1863 drawing of Fort DeRussy Area a Rare Find." *Marksville Weekly News* 156, no. 24 (Feb. 15, 2001): 2.

"Admiral Porter's Report of the Capture of Fort De Russy." *New York Times*, Mar. 29, 1864, p. 1, col. 3.

Anderson, Finley. "A Year in the Confederacy: Account of the Special Correspondent of the Herald: Graphic Description of His Capture and Imprisonment." *New York Herald*, Mar. 6, 1864, p. 8.

"A. P. Richards." *Confederate Veteran* 22 (May 1914): 226.

"Avoyelles Parish Police Jury Proceedings." Mar. 14, 2000. *Marksville Weekly News* 157, no. 32 (Mar. 23, 2000): 13.

Ballam, Ed. "The Navy Won't Give Up Captured Gun." *Civil War News* 25, no. 3 (Apr. 1999): 1, 23.

Barnhart, Donald L., Jr. "Admiral Porter's Ironclad Hoax." *America's Civil War*, Sept. 2003: 30–36, 73.

"Battle Begins to Return Cannon to Fort DeRussy." *Town Talk* 115, no. 335 (Feb. 14, 1999): D-3.

Bearss, Edwin C. "The Story of Fort Beauregard." Pts. 1 and 2. *Louisiana Studies* 3, no. 4 (Winter 1964): 330–84; 4, no. 1 (Spring 1965): 3–40.

Bingham, J. O. "Interesting War Experiences." *Ironton (Ohio) Register,* Thursday, Jan. 19, 1888.

Bod [A. H. Bodman]. "The Expedition of the Ram Queen of the West." *New-York Daily Tribune,* Mar. 6, 1863, p. 8.

Bonner, T. R. "Sketches of the Campaign of 1864." *Land We Love,* Oct. 1868. (18th Texas Infantry, Walker's Division.)

Bonwill, C. E. H. Sketch of "Grand Ecore, The Base of Operations of General Banks." *Frank Leslie's Illustrated Newspaper,* May 21, 1864, 140.

Brasseaux, Carl A. "The Glory Days: E. T. King Recalls the Civil War Years." *Attakapas Gazette* 11 (Spring 1976): 2–33.

Braud, Stuart. "Avoyelles Civil War Action Recorded in N.O. Newspaper." *Marksville Weekly News* 151, no. 49 (July 28, 1994): 2.

Byrd, William. "The Capture of Fort De Russy, La." *Land We Love* 6, no. 3 (Jan. 1869).

Carson, John M. "Capture of the Indianola." *Confederate Veteran* 32 (1924): 380–83.

"City of Marksville Council Proceedings." *Marksville Weekly News* 155, no. 36 (Apr. 23, 1998): sec. 1, p. 7.

"Civil War Site to Be Preserved." *Avoyelles Journal* 18, no. 50 (Oct. 13, 1996): 1.

Clausius, Gerhard. "The Little Soldier of the 95th: Albert D. J. Cashier." *Journal of the Illinois State Historical Society* 51, no. 4 (Winter 1958): 380–87.

Coco, Gregory A. "When War Came to Avoyelles." *Marksville Weekly News*, Sept. 16, 1983, p. 2.

"Cruise of the Queen of the West; Detailed Account of her Capture; Perils and Incidents of the Escape." *New York Daily World,* Mar. 5, 1863, p. 1.

Cutrer, Thomas W., ed. "'An Experience in Soldier's Life': The Civil War Letters of Volney Ellis, Adjutant, Twelfth Texas Infantry, Walker's Texas Division, C.S.A." *Military History of the Southwest* 22 (Fall 1992): 109–72.

Danbom, David B., ed. "'Dear Companion': Civil War Letters of a Story County Farmer." *Annals of Iowa* 47 (Fall 1984): 537–43. (Thomas A. Ball, 32nd Iowa.)

DeCuir, Randy. "Undermanned Fort De Russy, Central Louisiana's Hope." *Avoyelles Post,* Feb. 2, 1977.

"DeRussy Sword a Welcome Gift." *Avoyelles Journal,* Apr. 6, 1997, sec. 2, p. 1.

Eakin, Sue. "Theresa Milburn's Journal during the Civil War." *Marksville Weekly News* 149, no. 17 (Jan. 9, 1992): 2.

"Effort to get Fort's Cannon Back Continue." *Marksville Weekly News* 156, no. 46 (July 1, 1999): 1.

"The Fate of the Invader." *Pelican* 23, no. 45 (Mar. 21, 1863): 1.

Flanders, Arlene. "Impressive Ceremony for DeRussy Interment." *Marksville Weekly News* 157, no. 8 (Oct. 7, 1999): sec. 2, p. 1.

"Fort DeRussy Being Readied for Public." *Avoyelles Journal* 18, no. 32 (June 9, 1996): 1.

"Fort De Russy, La." *Frank Leslie's Illustrated Newspaper,* Apr. 30, 1864, 87.

"Fort DeRussy: Location Helps Preserve Site." *Marksville Weekly News* 154, no. 18 (Dec. 19, 1996): 1.

"Fort DeRussy Master Plan Outlined." *Marksville Weekly News* 161, no. 36 (May 6, 2004): 1.

"Fort de Russey Memorial Cemetery." *Marksville Weekly News,* Apr. 19, 1990, 3.

"Fort DeRussy Sold to La Commission." *Marksville Weekly News* 153, no. 30 (Mar. 14, 1996): 1.

"Fort DeRussy Surveyed and Mapped by USL Workers." *Marksville Weekly News* 155, no. 27 (Feb. 19, 1998): 1.

"Fort DeRussy to be Part of Park Day '98." *Marksville Weekly News* 155, no. 36 (Apr. 23, 1998): 1.

"Ft. DeRussy Cemetery Gets Needed Face-Lift, Thanks to Volunteers." *Avoyelles Journal* 22, no. 14 (Jan. 30, 2000): sec. 2, p. 1.

"Funding Approved, Ft. DeRussy May Become State Park." *Marksville Weekly News* 156, no. 36 (Apr. 22, 1999): 1.

Furman, Francis Chandler. "A Confederate Artilleryman Remembered." In *Forgotten Confederates: An Anthology about Black Southerners,* vol.

14, edited by Charles Kelly Barrow, J. H. Segars, and R. B. Rosenburg, 137–41. Journal of Confederate History Series. Atlanta: Southern Heritage Press. 1995.

Furman, Greene Chandler. "A True Legree of the Red River Valley." Unpublished manuscript, 1970, copy in possession of author.

Gillespie, W. C. B. "War Reminiscences." *Macon (Mo.) Republic,* Mar. 14, 1903. Clipping in scrapbook, David Boyd Papers, Louisiana State Univ., Baton Rouge.

Griffin, Andrew. "Volunteers Seek to Preserve Cemetery: Fort DeRussy Grounds Resting Place for Civil War Veterans." *Alexandria Daily Town Talk,* Wednesday, Aug. 30, 2000, p. A-3.

Guice, E. T. "Heroes of the Confederate Navy." *Confederate Veteran* 4 (Sept. 1896): 313.

Harder, William. "Confederates Who Are Congressmen." *Confederate Veteran* 19 (Aug. 1911): 378–79.

Harrison, Jon, ed. "The Confederate Letters of John Simmons." *Chronicles of Smith County, Texas* 14, no. 1 (Summer 1975): 25–40.

Harrison, Robert W., and Walter M. Kollmorgen. "Drainage Reclamation in the Coastal Marshlands of the Mississippi River Delta." *Louisiana Historical Quarterly* 30, no. 2 (Apr. 1947): 654–709.

Hoel, William R. "The Red River Expedition of 1864." *S&D Reflector* 10, no. 3 (Sept. 1973): 11–16. (Excerpts of Capt. William Rion Hoel diary, Inland Rivers Library, Cincinnati.)

Howell, Thomas. "Forts Buhlow and Randolph in the Civil War." *Louisiana History* 36, no. 2 (Spring 1995): 197–204.

"An Interesting Incident about the Civil War." Morgantown, W.Va. newspaper, Aug. 1904. Clipping in scrapbook, David Boyd Papers, Louisiana State Univ., Baton Rouge.

Jacobs, Eloise Tyler. "Commodore Montgomery: A Confederate Naval Hero, and His Adventures." *Confederate Veteran* 25 (Jan. 1917): 26–27.

Jeffries, Clarence. "Running the Blockade on the Mississippi." *Confederate Veteran* 22 (Jan. 1914): 22–23.

"Joffrion Genealogy." *Marksville Weekly News* 148, no. 9 (Nov. 8, 1990): 2.

Kendall, John S. "Fourth Louisiana Volunteers." *Confederate Veteran* 9 (May 1901): 210–12.

Kuttruff, Jenna Tedrick. "Col. DeRussy's Coffin Lining and Burial Waistcoat." Paper presented at the Louisiana Archaeological Society Annual Meeting, Baton Rouge, La., Feb. 3–5, 2000.

Lackner, Edgar E. "Diaries of Edwin F. Stanton, USA, and William Quensell, CSA." *East Texas Historical Journal* 18 (2): 25–59. (114th New York and Haldemann's battery.)

Legan, Marshall Scott. "The Confederate Career of a Union Ram." *Louisiana History* 41, no. 3 (Summer 2000): 277–300.

"List of Burials of Union Soldiers Killed in Avoyelles." *Marksville Weekly News* 151, no. 25 (Feb. 10, 1994): 2.

Long, Owen G. Sketch of Fort DeRussy. *Frank Leslie's Illustrated Newspaper,* Apr. 30, 1864, 89.

Mayeux, Steven M. "Black Soldiers Played Important Role in Fort deRussy." *Marksville Weekly News* 152, no. 27 (Feb. 23, 1995): 2.

———. "Fort de Russy: 125 Years Ago." *Bunkie Record/Marksville Weekly News,* Apr. 20, 1989, sec. 2, p. 1.

———. "The Origin and Initial History of Fort Humbug." *Marksville Weekly News* 151, no. 34 (Apr. 14, 1994): 2.

Mayeux, Vickie. "Lewis DeRussy: Civil War Colonel's Body Disinterred: Will Be Re-buried Sept. 26 at Fort that Bears His Name." *Marksville Weekly News* 157, no. 4 (Sept. 9, 1999): 5.

[McCullagh, Joseph]. "Second Cruise of the Queen of the West Below Vicksburg." *New York Herald,* Mar. 6, 1863, p. 2.

McDowell, E. C. "Ships that Passed at Night: Account of Passing the Batteries at Port Hudson, 1862[3]." *Confederate Veteran* 6 (June 1898): 250–51.

Miller, Robin. "Civil War Era Becomes Northerner's Passion." *Alexandria Daily Town Talk,* Sunday, June 21, 1998, p. F-8.

———. "Queen of the Red." *Alexandria Daily Town Talk,* Sunday, June 21, 1998, p. F-1.

Odom, Van D. "The Political Career of Thomas Overton Moore, Secession Governor of Louisiana." *Louisiana Historical Quarterly* 26, no. 4 (Oct. 1943): 975–1054.

"Officials Tour Ft. DeRussy." *Marksville Weekly News* 154, no. 29 (Mar. 6, 1997): 1.

Oglesby, R. W. "More Grand Ecore History Is Recited by Phanor Breazeale." Scrapbook clipping from Natchitoches, La., newspaper, Thursday, Oct. [1929]. Cammie G. Henry Collection, Northwestern State Univ. Archives, Natchitoches, La.

"Our Mississippi Correspondence: The Loss of the Indianola; Destruction of the Indianola; Admiral Porter's Mock Monitor." *New York Times,* Mar. 16, 1863, p. 1.

"Park Day '99: Ft. DeRussy Gets Spruced Up." *Marksville Weekly News* 156, no. 42 (June 3, 1999): 5.

Pelham, A. J. Query Concerning. *Confederate Veteran* 21 (Mar. 1913): 98.

Pinnell, Gary. "Marksville Celebrates 190 Years." *Alexandria Town Talk,* Aug. 27, 1999, p. A-14.

Pitts, Florison D. "The Civil War Diary of Florison D. Pitts." *Mid-America* 40 (1958): 22–63. (Chicago Mercantile Battery.)

"Poem Tells of Love Story during Civil War in Avoyelles." *Marksville Weekly News* 153, no. 50 (Aug. 1, 1996): 2.

Powles, James M. "The Ironclad that Never Was." *Civil War Times Illustrated* 35, no. 6 (Dec. 1996): 66–70.

Prichard, Walter, ed. "A Tourist's Description of Louisiana." *Louisiana Historical Quarterly* 21 (1938): 1110–1214.

"The Red River Expedition: Successful Operations on the Atchafalaya: A Brilliant Piece of 'Yankee' Strategy: Gen. Dick Taylor Outmaneuvered by Gen. Smith: Remarkable Footrace in Which Two Large Armies Contend: The Rebels Outstripped in the Race: Fort De Russy, 11 Guns and 300 Prisoners the Prize." *New York Times,* Mar. 25, 1864, p. 1.

Ritland, John. "John Ritland Civil War History." *Story City (Iowa) Herald,* Mar. 9–Apr. 6, 1922. (32nd Iowa.)

Ritter, William L. "Reminiscences of the Confederate States Navy: Letter from Captain William L. Ritter." *Southern Historical Society Papers* 1 (May 1876): 362–63.

———. "Sketch of Third Battery of Maryland Artillery: Paper No. 2." *Southern Historical Society Papers* 10 (Aug.–Sept. 1882): 392–96.

———. "Sketch of Third Battery of Maryland Artillery: Paper No. 3." *Southern Historical Society Papers* 10 (Oct.–Nov. 1882): 464–71.

———. "Third Battery of Maryland Artillery, CSA: Its History in Brief, and Its Commanders." *Southern Historical Society Papers* 22 (Jan.–Dec. 1894): 19–20.

"Sketches of Veterans—Louisiana Division: Albert Estopinol." *Confederate Veteran* 6 (Dec. 1898): 574–75.

"Sous La Tente." *Pelican* 23, no. 45 (Mar. 21, 1863): 1.

Thorpe, Manor L. "Ludger Barbin: Prosperous Steamboat Landing Owner." *Marksville Weekly News* 149, no. 37 (May 28, 1992): 2.

Thurston, James. "Capture of the Indianola." *Confederate Veteran* 6 (Dec. 1898): 573.

Toumey, William S. "A Young Lawyer of Natchitoches of 1836: The Diary of William S. Toumey." *Louisiana Historical Quarterly* 17 (1934): 315–26.

"The War and Reconstruction." In *Louisiana Historical Review, Featuring Avoyelles and Rapides Parishes,* 18–21. Montgomery, Ala.: Historical Review of the South, n.d.

Williams, E. Cort. "The Cruise of the 'Black Terror.'" In *Sketches of War History, 1861–1865: Papers Read before the Ohio Commandery of the Military Order of the Loyal Legion of the United States, 1888–1890,* 3:144–65. Cincinnati: Robert Clark, 1890.

———. "Recollections of the Red River Expedition." In *Sketches of War History, 1861–1865: Papers Read before the Ohio Commandery of the Military Order of the Loyal Legion of the United States, 1886–1888,* 2:96–120. Cincinnati: Robert Clark, 1888.

Williams, John Calvin. "The Fires of Hatred." *Civil War Times Illustrated* 17, no. 9 (Jan. 1979): 20–31. (34th Texas Cavalry.)

Wilson, A. F. "Would Not Surrender the Flag: Reminiscences of the 'Queen of the West.'" *Confederate Veteran* 10 (Feb. 1902): 72–73.

Windell, Marie E. "A Double Standard of Justice: Is Adultery by a Wife Worse than Murder by Her Husband?" In *Historic U.S. Court Cases: An Encyclopedia,* 2nd ed., edited by John W. Johnson, pt. 1, *Crime and Criminal Law,* 1:39–45. New York: Routledge. 2001.

Wright, Elizabeth. "La. Man Disputes Navy Ownership of Artillery Piece." *Alexandria Town Talk,* Sunday, June 27, 1999, p. E-4.

Manuscripts and Maps

Avoyelles Parish. Map. 1863. Collection of Captured Confederate Maps. Nos. 73 and 74, RG Z-33, National Archives.

Becton, E. P. Papers. Barker History Center, Univ. of Texas, Austin.

Bellows, Amos W. Diary. Warren David Crandall Collection. Illinois State Historical Library, Springfield. (Mississippi Marine Brigade.)

Boyd, David F. Papers. Louisiana and Lower Mississippi Valley Collection. Hill Memorial Library, Louisiana State Univ., Baton Rouge.

Brent, Joseph L. Papers. Louisiana Historical Association Collection. Howard-Tilton Memorial Library, Tulane Univ., New Orleans.

Buck, John A. Record Book, J. A. Buck's Company [F], Stevens' [22nd Texas Cavalry] Regiment. Microfilm. Cammie G. Henry Research Center, Watson Memorial Library, Northwestern State Univ., Natchitoches, La.

Burbank, F. G. "Plan of Ft. DeRussy and Environs, with Table of Distances. March 4, 1864." Louisiana Historical Association Collection. Howard-Tilton Memorial Library, Tulane Univ., New Orleans.

Burke, Lemuel. Journal of the Red River Campaign. Illinois State Historical Library, Springfield. (Company K, 119th Illinois Infantry.)

Burmeister, George C. Journal. 1864. Transcript in possession of Ginny Torres, Tacoma, Wash. (35th Iowa.)

Burns, William S. Scrapbook. Schoff Civil War Collection. Clements Library, Univ. of Michigan, Ann Arbor.

C., A. B. "New Orleans Letter: Some Interesting Ante-War Reminiscences of Sherman." J. T. Walker Collection. Box 2-A-2, Folder 7, Cammie G. Henry Research Center, Watson Memorial Library, Northwestern State Univ., Natchitoches, La.

Corwin, Cornelius. Diary. Indiana Historical Society, Indianapolis. (89th Indiana.)

"Deaths in 1863." Marshall Ledger Book. Marshall-Furman Papers. Louisiana and Lower Mississippi Valley Collection, Hill Memorial Library, Louisiana State Univ. Press, Baton Rouge.

DeRussy, Lewis. Files. Jackson Barracks Military Library, New Orleans.

DeRussy, Lewis G. Photograph. Private collection, Edith DeRussy.

Drew, Charles J. Diary. Edited by Tom Baskett Jr. In manuscript. Transcript in possession of author. (USS *Essex*.)

Ewringmann, Charles. Diary. Transcript translated from original German by David Beck. Original in private hands. (27th Iowa.)

Farrow, S. W. Papers. Barker History Center, Univ. of Texas, Austin.

Flaugher, Nehemiah. Map of Fort DeRussy. Original in possession of Richard Burns, copy in possession of author.

Fullilove, Mrs. Thomas Pope [Elizabeth Jane Samford]. Journal, 1915. Typescript by Jane Fullilove Mason of original handwritten manuscript, 1982.

Gaines, Milton Pinkney. Diary, 1862–1864. Transcript in possession of Charles Ham, Montalba, Tex. (13th Texas Cavalry.)

Hamilton, James Allen. Diary, 1861–1864. Barker History Center, Univ. of Texas, Austin. (15th Texas Infantry.)

Handy, Thomas H. Scrapbook. Compiled by Thomas Hughes Handy (grandson) and Kim Douglas Handy. Copy in possession of author.

Hemenway, Herman C. Letters dated April 20 and May 20, 1864, to Messrs. Editors. In *History of Buchanan County, Iowa 1842 to 1881*. Edited by C. S. and Elizabeth Percival. Cleveland: Williams Brothers Publishers, 1881), 204–5. (27th Iowa Infantry.)

Henneberry, James E. Journal. Kept while aboard the USS *Essex*, 1864. Edited by Tom Baskett Jr. Photostat in Chicago Historical Society, Chicago, Ill.

Hervey, Horace Peyton. "A Tale of Some Plain Folks of Two Unique Cities of the South—New Orleans, La. and Galveston, Texas, 1800–1920." Unpublished manuscript, 1943. Copy in possession of author.

Hieronymus, Benjamin R. Diary (SC 694). Illinois State Historical Library, Springfield. (117th Illinois.)

Historical Military Data on Louisiana Militia. WPA Project. Jackson Barracks Military Library, New Orleans, 1941.

Howell, W. Randolph. Diary. Barker History Center, Univ. of Texas, Austin.

Hutchinson, Eli Merritt. Memoirs. Typescript in Mayeux Collection, Fort DeRussy State Historic Site, Marksville, La.

Jefferson, Col. John. "Military History of His Regiment from Oct. 1, 1863 to Aug. 1, 1864." Wisconsin Historical Society, Madison. (8th Wisconsin.)

Jefferson, Lt. Col. John H. Report on Red River Expedition to Governor of Wisconsin. May 22, 1864. Wisconsin Historical Society, Madison. (8th Wisconsin.)

Journal of US Steamer *Diana*. Clarke Historical Collection. Central Michigan Univ., Mount Pleasant, Mich.

Justice, Elihu P. G. Diary. Illinois State Historical Library, Springfield. (117th Illinois.)

Klinger, Timothy C., Robert Cande, Richard Kandare, and Roy Cochran Jr. "Below Red River: Cultural Resources Survey, Testing and Assessment in Eight Areas, Twelve Localities and at Eight Archaeological Sites in

Avoyelles Parish, Louisiana." Historic Preservation Associates Reports 84-4. Fayetteville, Ark.: Historic Preservation Associates, August 1984.

Knight, Jonathan T. Letters. Gary Canada Collection. Keller, Tex.

Letters from Adjutant General, La. Militia, 1862–1865. Jackson Barracks Military Library, New Orleans. (Jackson Barracks Military Library, a prime repository for information on early Louisiana military units, was severely damaged in the 2005 Hurricane Katrina catastrophe. The condition and disposition of its collection are unclear as of this writing.)

Levy, William. Funeral Card. Cammie G. Henry Research Center, Watson Memorial Library, Northwestern State Univ., Natchitoches, La.

Mason, Jane Fullilove. "Dear Lizzie: Letters of a Confederate Cavalryman." History report, Northwestern State College, n.d.

McCullough, Arthur D. Diary, 1862–65. Microcopy. Illinois State Historical Library, Springfield. (81st Illinois.)

Mooney, Edward. Diary. Transcript. Gray and Blue Naval Museum, Vicksburg, Miss. Original in private hands. Transcription provided by Alma Dudley and Lamar Roberts. (USS *Lafayette.*)

Murray, John C. Diary. Collection 524, No. 52. Howard-Tilton Memorial Library, Tulane Univ., New Orleans.

Muster Roll. Company A, Crescent Artillery. Feb. 29, 1864. Jackson Barracks Military Library, New Orleans.

Paisley, John M. Diary. Gregory A. Coco Collection. Copy in possession of author. (Company C, 117th Illinois.)

Parr, William. Diary. Wisconsin Historical Society, Madison. (Thirty-third Wisconsin.)

Pearce, Henry Davis. Diary. Manuscript in private hands.

Perry, Theophilus. Letters. Presley Carter Person Papers, Duke Univ. Library, Durham, N.C.

Porter, John C. "Life of John C. Porter and Sketch of His Experiences in the Civil War." Eighteenth Texas Infantry File. Confederate Research Center, Hill College, Hillsboro, Tex.

———. Roster of Company H, Eighteenth Texas Infantry. From Bible of William Henry Harrison Cope. Original in possession of William Cope, Dallas, Tex.

Ray, David M. Letters. Barker History Center, Univ. of Texas, Austin.

Robinson, Sidney Z. Letters (SC 1284). Illinois State Historical Library, Springfield. (117th Illinois.)

"Roll of Prisoners of War Paroled at New Orleans, La." Jackson Barracks Military Library, New Orleans.

Russell, Emily De Russy Brandt (Mrs. Samuel Davenport Russell). Diary. Misc. Box 11, Hunter Collection, Cammie G. Henry Research Center, Watson Memorial Library, Northwestern State Univ., Natchitoches, La.

Sargent, Van Buren Whipple. "The Civil War Memories of a Union Soldier."
Manuscript in private hands. Transcribed by Tom Busby. (27th Iowa.)

Sheppard, Steven. Papers. Collection of documents concerning DeRussy
family. Copies in possession of author.

Simmons, John. "The Confederate Letters of John Simmons." Edited by Jon
Harrison. *Chronicles of Smith County, Texas* 14, no. 1 (Summer 1975):
25–40.

Stewart, Captain William R. Diary. Manuscript Division, Univ. of North
Carolina Library, Chapel Hill. (95th Illinois.)

Tamplin, William H. Letters. Louisiana and Lower Mississippi Valley Collections. Hill Memorial Library, Louisiana State Univ., Baton Rouge.
(Company E, 11th Texas Infantry.)

Tanner, Linn. "The Capture of the Indianola." Oct. 6, 1902. Manuscript letter in private hands.

Tyson, Robert A. Diary. MS 1693. Louisiana and Lower Mississippi Valley
Collection. Hill Memorial Library, Louisiana State Univ., Baton Rouge.

Underwood, Albert. Diary. Indiana Historical Society, Indianapolis.

Venable, Richard M. "Fort DeRussy on the Red River, Louisiana." Jeremy
Francis Gilmer Papers 276, Southern Historical Collection. Wilson
Library, Univ. of North Carolina, Chapel Hill.

Waddill, John P. Diary. Copy in possession of Randy Decuir, Marksville, La.

Wallace, Harvey Alexander. Diary. Southwest Arkansas Regional Archives,
Washington, Ark. (19th Texas Infantry, Walker's Division.)

Wells, E. H. "Sketch of the Country between Atchafalaya and Mississippi
Occupied by Maj. Gen. Walker's Division during Part of November and
December 1863." Within a letter to Major General Walker, from Mount-
ville, La., Oct. 16, 1863. John G. Walker Papers, Southern Historical
Collection. Manuscripts Department, Wilson Library, Univ. of North
Carolina, Chapel Hill.

Williams, John M. Diaries. Wisconsin Historical Society, Madison. (8th
Wisconsin.)

Index

Fort Gum, 126n5
Fort Hindman, US tinclad, 150,
167–68, 193, 199, 201, 204,
206n16, 226, **227**, 254n4
Fort Humbug, 125–29, 136, 145,
151–52, 154, 160, 222
Fort Jesup, La., 273–74, 291,
292n54, 296
Fort Lafayette (Fort Humbug), 125
Fort Monroe, Va., 286
Fort Morgan (Fort Humbug), 125
Fort Pillow, Tenn., 6, 222, 287
Fort Polk, La., 295–96
Fort Scurry (Fort Humbug), 125,
154
Fort Taylor (Fort DeRussy), 9, 11,
13, 17, 20, 26–27, 31, 32n34,
35, 37, 40, 42, 51–53, 63, 76,
81, 87
Fort Taylor (Fort Humbug), 125,
154n19
Fort Towson, Okla., 273, 279
Foster, James, USMMB, 305
Franklin, Benjamin, 269–70
Frederic, Lt. H. A., CSA, 87
Freed, Cpl. Joseph M., USA, 318
Freeman, Pvt. John H., CSA, 311
French citizens, 166, 216, 263–64
Friends of Fort DeRussy, 255–56,
293
Frieske, Pvt. J., CSA, 310
Frolic, CS steamer, 161, 201n3
Fuller, Acting Ens. Charles M., USN,
217, 224
Fuller, Lt. James F., CSA, 119, 169,
307
Fullilove, Thomas, 107, 112, 132
Fuqua, Dustin, 296n58

Gagnon, Marie Louise, 277
Gaiennie, François, 275–76
Gallman, Sgt. J. P., CSA, 309

Garay, General, Mexican Army,
281–83
Garrett, Pvt. Thomas, USA, 319
Garvey, Thomas W., 20–21, 27,
31–32
Gave, Cpl. J., CSA, 313
Gazelle, US tinclad, 150
General Beauregard, CS steamer,
137, 201n3
General Bragg, US timberclad, 150,
226
General Lyon, US steamer, 220, 260
General Quitman, CS steamer, 38
General Sterling Price, US timber-
clad, 95, 97, 100, 150, 199
Gentry, Pvt. John W., USA, 319
Gérard, Col. Aristide, CSA, 81–85,
87, 97–99
Gerard, Pvt. Joseph, CSA, 314
Ghentry, Pvt. John T., CSA, 312
Gibbs, Surgeon R. T., CSA, 232
Gilbert, Col. James, USA, 177
Giles, Cpl. Allen, USA, 320
Gillett, Pvt. R., CSA, 315
Gilliam, Pvt. Edward, CSA, 309
Gilliam, Pvt. J. P., CSA, 309
Gilliam, Cpl. J. W., CSA, 309
Gilliam, Pvt. Jasper N., CSA, 309
Gilliam, Cpl. Newton, CSA, 309
Gilmer, Col. Jeremy F., CSA, 6, 6n9,
6n10, 180
Gleason, Pvt. Rufus, CSA, 320
Glover, Pvt. William Y., CSA, 320
Gober, Pvt. Y. W., CSA, 309
Gordon's Landing. *See* Gorton's
Landing
Gorgas, Col. Josiah, CSA, 6, 6n11
Gorgas, William C., 6n11
Gorsage, Pvt. John, USA, 319
Gorton, Lewis, 1
Gorton's Landing, 1, 30
Gosnell, Pvt. Elisha, CSA, 308
Gottheil, Capt. Edward, CSA, 111

Williams, Pvt. D. K., CSA, 311
Williams, Ens. E. Cort, USN, 79n66,
  238
Williams, Pvt. J. F., CSA, 311
Williams, Col. John, USA, 148
Williams, Pvt. Thomas, USMMB,
  305
Wilt, Mary Ann Frey, 255
Winsell, William, USN, 235
Wisconsin troops: 8th Wisc. Inf.,
  148; 14th Wisc. Inf., 212n6;
  33rd Wisc. Inf., 177, 185, 187,
  209, 319
Withenbury, Wellington W., 3, 5
Wood, Elias, 41
Wood, Pvt. Leonard T., CSA, 312
Wooden Dummy, USS. *See* dummy
  gunboat
Woodford, US hospital boat, 150,
  210, 317, 319, 320
Woods, George, 17
Woodward, Pvt. Joseph, CSA, 313
Worley, Pvt. A. J., CSA, 311
Worrel, Pvt. John A., CSA, 316

Wright, Pvt. John, USA, 319
Wyatt, Pvt. G. B., CSA, 308
Wyche, Maj. R. E., CSA, 140
Wyse, Capt. Francis, DeRussy's
  Regt., 282–83

Yarny, Pvt. Floury, CSA, 311
Yates, Pvt. John S., CSA, 308
Ybarbo, Pvt. John, CSA, 308
Ybarbo, Pvt. Richard, CSA, 308
Yearin (Yarin, Yeardon), Pvt. Henry,
  USA, 318
Yellow Bayou, La., 108, 125–29,
  259, 318, 319
Young, Capt. David, USA, 209, 263
Young, Pvt. N. H., CSA, 316

Zeiss, Pvt. L., CSA, 310
Zimmerman, Master's Mate William,
  USN, 98
zouaves, 164, 164n15, 195

Earthen Walls, Iron Men was designed and typeset on a Macintosh OS 10.4 computer system using InDesign software. The body text is set in 10/13 Sabon and display type is set in Viva. This book was designed and typeset by Stephanie Thompson and manufactured by Thomson-Shore, Inc.